Children's Encyclopedia of Nature

Compiled and edited by Kenneth Bailey

Collins

Glasgow and London

Designed by Peter Sullivan, Charles Gould, David Nash

Written by Alfred Leutscher, Joyce Pope, David Roberts, Kenneth Bailey

Illustrated by Fred Anderson, Norman Barber, Derek Bold, Catherine Bradbury, Patricia Caley, Patrick Cox, E. Crosby-Smith, Esme Eve, The Garden Studio, Charles Gould, John Grimwade, David Johnson, Anthony Joyce, Ivan Lapper, Peter McGinn, Gladys Mason, Duncan Mil, David Nash, Will Nickless, Kenneth Ody, Edward Osmond, David Pratt, John Rignell, Christopher Sinden, David Sizer, E. Smart, Prue Theobalds, George Thompson, Ann Thomson, Adrian Williams, Maurice Wilson, Janice Woods, Michael Woods

First published 1973 as Collins New World of Knowledge: NATURE
Sixth impression 1978
Published by William Collins Sons and Company Limited, Glasgow and London
©1973 William Collins Sons and Company Limited
Filmset by Typesetting Services Ltd, Glasgow
Printed in Great Britain
ISBN 0 00 106208-5

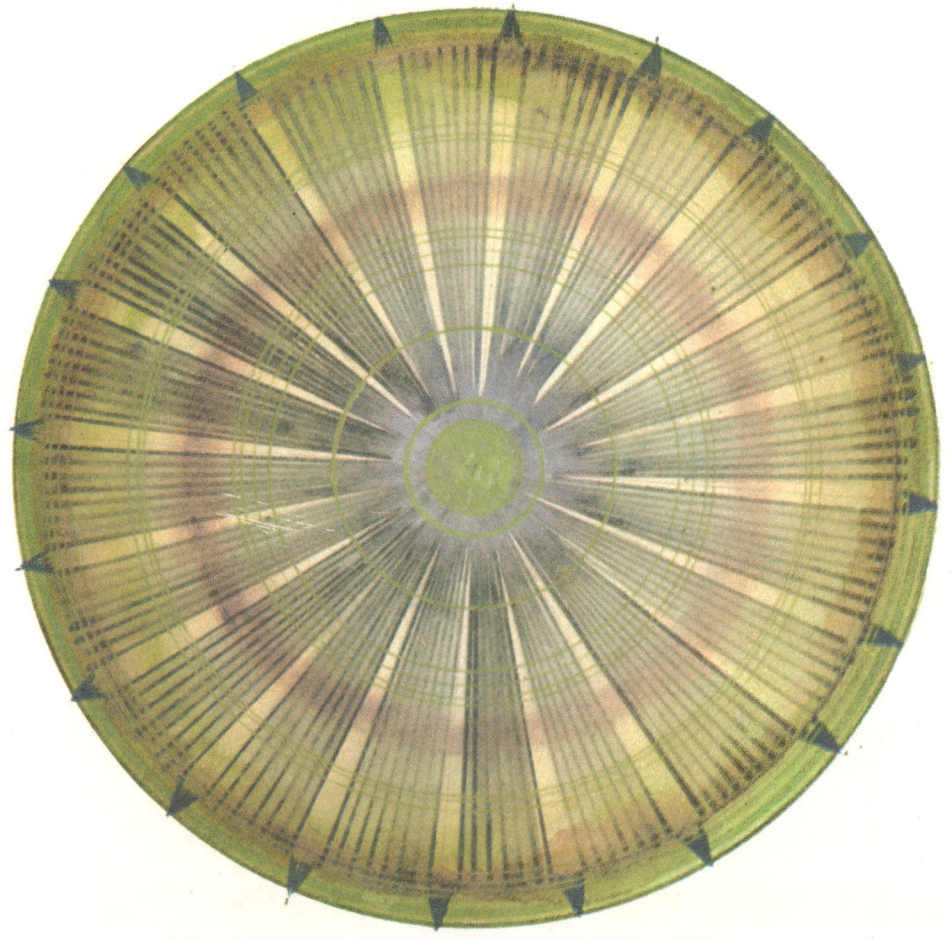

Contents

8 Plants and the Origin of Life
Evolution of Life—The Chain of Life

10 The Tree of Life
Simple Plant Cells—Two Main Branches—In the Beginning—The Age of Cycads—Plant Cells
Plant or Animal?
Zoospores—Differences in Growth

14 Giving Plants Names
Descriptive Names—Linnaeus Genus and Species—The Main Groups—A Common Language

17 Primitive Plants
Bacteria
Fungi and Lichens
The Mycelium—Useful Moulds Invasion of the Land
Seaweeds
The Sargasso Sea—Air-bladders

22 Early Land Plants
Mosses and Liverworts—Roots and Rhizomes
Cycads and Conifers
Reproduction by Seeds—Seed Plants—Fertilisation—The Embryo Plant

27 Flowering Plants
The Flower Head—The Ovule Box Flower Stems—Formation of Trees Flowering Heads—Variety of Seeds

33 Plant Behaviour
The Plant Cell—The Growing Root Plant Stems—Working Leaves How Plants Live—Chloroplasts Cell Activity—The Nucleus Cell Division—Dispersal by Animals—Colour and Shape Pollination

40 Plant Ecology
Land Masses—Water Supply Marram Grass—Influence of Animals—Erosion

43 Man and Plants
Wild Plants
Food Crops
The First Farmers—Harvesting Grain—Over Cultivation—Clean Seed—Agricultural Machinery
Gardens for Pleasure
Formal Gardens—Garden Plants Growing New Plants—Perennial Plants
Fruit and Vegetables
In Warmer Climates—The Soya Bean
Herbs, Flavours and Spices
Flavouring—The Spice Trade
Wine and Vineyards
The Colour of Wine—Champagne Fermentation
Oil Crops and Rubber
Linseed Oil—Invention of Rubber The Uses of Rubber
Timber and its Uses
New Forests—The Forester Paper-making—Hard and Soft Woods
Medicines and Drugs
Herb Gardens—Herbal Drugs
Fibres and Dyes
Harvesting Flax—Hemp and Jute Cotton Growing—Spinning Cotton

65 Science and Plants
Botanical Gardens—Using Hormones—Mendelism—Pests and Diseases

68 The Evolution of Animals
Population Explosion—Survival of the Fittest—The Peppered Moth

70 Prehistoric Animals
Dating the Past—The Land Invasion

Fossils and First Animals
Fossils in Water—Pre-Cambrian Rocks—Written on Stone Changes of Climate

Fishes and Amphibians
The 'Bony Skins'—Lobe-finned Fishes—The Coal Age—Giant Dragonflies

Reptiles and Birds
Land Invasion—Amphibious Life Jurassic Seas—Winged Lizards The Duckbills—Armoured Dinosaurs—The Dinosaurs' End Dinosaur Eggs

The Age of Mammals
A New World—Early Marsupials The Ice Ages—Neanderthal Man

88 Animals of Today
The Mighty Whale—The Tiny Amoeba—Animal Skeletons

Animal Classification
Grouping Animals—Linnaeus's System—Naming Species—Law of Priority

Animal Behaviour
Reflex Actions—Mating Instinct The Stickleback—Release of Tension—Pack Leaders Migration—Survival Instinct Mother and Child—Shape, Size and Touch—Change of Habit

Animals and Man
Farm Animals—Sheep and Goats The Domestic Cat—Hunting Animals—Animals in Combat—The Horse in Battle—Animals in Art

Zoos and Nature Reserves
Natural Habitats—The Study of Ecology

Science and Animals
Blood Transfusion—Fighting Illness—Exploration Designing Machinery

108 Animals without Backbones
Arachnids—Millipedes Crustaceans—Molluscs—Worms

Primitive Animals
Protozoans—Rotifers and Sponges—Coelenterates

Molluscs
Snails and Limpets—Cephalopods

Echinoderms

Arthropods
Leaf and Stick Insects Grasshoppers—Dragonflies Butterflies—Moths—Ants, Wasps and Bees—Social Groups Termites—Flies—Beetles Fleas—Lice—Bugs Crustaceans—Krill—Arachnids Spiders—Scorpions—Mites

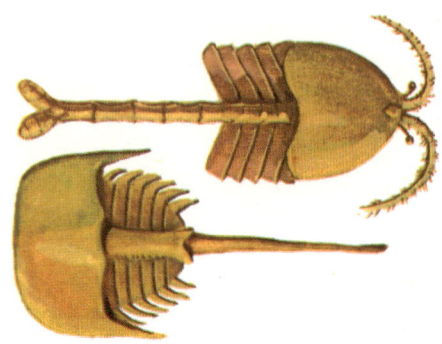

128 Animals with Backbones

Living in Water—The Vertebral Column—Primitive Chordates The Five Classes

130 Fishes
Freedom in Water

Sharks and Rays
Sharks—Rays and Skates

Bony Fishes
Herrings—Eels—The Salmon Family—Trout—Pike—Carp and Catfishes—Deep-sea Fishes The Angler Fish—The Cod Family The Stickleback—The Perch Tribe—Flatfishes

138 Amphibians
Tadpoles and Adults—Lines of Defence—Secretive Animals Frogs and Toads—Climbing Frogs

141 Reptiles
Egg-Laying—Eating and Movement

Tortoises and Turtles
Growth Rings—Slow Movement Return to the Sea

Lizards and Snakes
The Ways of Lizards—Poison Glands

Crocodiles
Water Animals—Breeding Habits

148 Birds
The Organs of Flight—Flying Machines

Flightless Birds
Ratites—Australasian Birds Penguins—Emperor Penguins

Water Birds
Tubenoses—Swans, Geese and Ducks—Types of Geese—Duck Species—Herons and Flamingos Cranes—The Waders—Gulls, Terns and Skuas

Birds of Prey
Types of Nest—Vultures

Game Birds
Primitive Species—The Prairie Chicken—Pheasants—Peafowl

Tropical Birds
Parrots—Swifts—Trogons Kingfishers—Pigeons—Cuckoos Woodpeckers

Perching Birds
Egg-laying—Bird Tables—The Robin

Bird Migration
Migration Routes—Tracing Bird Movement

167 Mammals
Varieties of Mammals—Well-developed Senses

Primitive Mammals
Marsupials

Insect-eaters
Shrews—The Hedgehog

Rodents
Enemies of Rodents—Three Main Groups

Toothless Mammals

Flying Mammals
How Bats Fly

Marine Mammals
Demands of the Sea—Baleen Whales—Seals

Hoofed Mammals
Wild Horses—Rhinoceroses Pigs and Hippos—Camels—Deer Giraffes—Sheep and Goats Antelopes

Elephants
Plant-eaters

Carnivores
The Cat Group—Hyenas—The Dog Family—Bears—The Giant Panda

Primates
Tree Shrews and Lemurs—The Aye-Aye—New World Monkeys Old World Monkeys—Apes Chimps and Gorillas

Plants and the Origins of Life

A spaceship journeys into outer space, sending back information about the universe of which our earth is just a tiny part. A modern microscope explores what might be termed 'inner space', examining the tiny particles, called cells, which make up all living matter. With powerful microscopes, we can see what goes on in the smallest living creature or plant.

The earth came into being about 6,000 million years ago. Perhaps it began as a whirling globe of hot gases which cooled to a liquid. Further cooling produced a hard, rocky crust surrounded by a steamy atmosphere. Steam condensed and fell as rain, creating rivers, lakes and seas.

Two great mysteries from the early years of our planet have yet to be explained. First, how did life begin on this hot, wet, steamy globe? Second, how did living things manage to leave the waters and survive on dry land? In the beginning, it seems that certain chemicals came together in the waters. Under the action of sunlight, they somehow formed themselves into protoplasm, which is the name given to the contents of a single living cell, the physical basis of all life.

Cells on Land

Once they were formed, the cells became capable of growing and reproducing themselves. Some of the cells joined and built themselves into the living creatures we call animals. Others became the living cells from which plants are built up.

In tidal waters, some of the cells settled on rocks. They lodged in minute crevices or developed a gummy substance with which to cling on. When the water receded or the rocks were raised above water level by earthquakes, some of the plant cells managed to adapt themselves to life in the rain-washed air. The first plants to do this, the intermediate stages between sea plants and land plants, have long disappeared, leaving no trace. Water plants and plants on the seashore have adapted themselves to life half in and half out of the water. They cannot spread either on to dry land or into deeper water.

Evolution of Life

One thing is certain: plants and animals have always been able to produce variations of themselves to adapt to new conditions. Had the first formation of protoplasm into a living cell been perfect in itself, things would have stayed as they were. But in its growth the cell broke down or suffered some accident which has led to variations. Over a very long period of time, countless numbers of these accidents have led to the development of the millions of species living on earth today. This is the gradual process we call evolution.

The microscope has one great advantage over the spaceship. It can travel in time. Perhaps one day a spaceship will land on a planet that has not yet reached our own stage in evolution. Perhaps there will be dinosaurs and other extinct animals and plants for the intrepid astronauts to study. At the moment, however, we can learn about the past history of our own planet only by studying fossil remains and the more primitive forms of life that still survive. Here, the microscope is our spaceship, carrying us back to the days when the earth was showing its first signs of life.

Many of the first kinds of plants still exist on earth. They are invisible to the naked eye. But the microscope can help us to examine them and get some idea of what life on this planet was like millions of years ago.

The Chain of Life

Plants in the sea get their food from the air, sun and water to which the whole of their surface is exposed. The smallest and most primitive sea animals, called plankton, can feed on the single plant cells by drawing the cells into themselves. Larger sea creatures eat the plankton and are themselves eaten by even bigger animals. Thus a chain is created where each form of life depends on another more numerous and smaller form. The beginning of the chain is the plant life on which even man depends for his existence.

Early man hunted animals, ate the fruit of trees and shrubs, and chewed the seeds of tall grasses. In time, he learned how the seeds grew. He saw that they needed water and sunlight to flourish. He cleared the ground, planted and watered the seeds. He helped certain plants to grow, and the plants helped him to live.

The farmers were followed by the first scientists who discovered the particular properties of different

plants. The earliest books to be written about plants were concerned with their healing properties when made into medicines and drugs. Later, man's curiosity led him to study the whole of plant life, to classify the plants into family groups and different species. The invention

During the Carboniferous Period plants grew profusely in the northern hemisphere. There were forests of tall, slender trees with giant horsetails and many evergreen, fern-like plants.

of the microscope helped these studies enormously. The farmer had already found ways to produce bigger heads of grain and better fruit. The scientist with his microscope discovered how plants work. He was able to produce new species and to make artificial fertilisers for a greater yield of foodstuff from every acre of land.

Man has conquered the natural world, cultivated and tidied the land, and built his cities upon it. He has been so successful that his numbers have increased alarmingly. It is possible that one day there will not be enough land available to grow the crops and graze the cattle necessary to man's survival.

The answer may be to try to solve those two great mysteries already mentioned. If man can find out how the various chemicals in the sea first came together to create the living cell, it will be but a step to producing living matter—and food—in the laboratory. If it is discovered how plants that began life in the sea managed to invade the land, perhaps the oceans themselves can be brought under cultivation.

Perhaps the spaceship will discover new planets for man to conquer and colonise. Or perhaps it will be the microscope, exploring inner space, that will find new uses to which the wealth of the earth can be put.

The Tree of Life

More than two thousand years ago, the Greek philosopher Aristotle began to formulate a theory of evolution. He spent two years of his life on the Mediterranean island of Lesbos, studying nature and particularly life in the sea. His ideas were taken up in the eighteenth and nineteenth centuries by such naturalists as Linnaeus, Buffon, Lamarck and Erasmus Darwin, grandfather of Charles Darwin who wrote *The Origin of Species* and *The Descent of Man*.

All these people began with the idea that man, because of his greater skills and brainpower, is the supreme being of creation. If all other animals are lesser beings then it follows that the greatest achievement of nature has been the creation of man.

Fossil remains show us that there have been plants and animals on this earth which disappeared long ago. For one reason or another, they did not adapt to changing conditions and died out. They were failures. Only the most adaptable living things survived. The adaptations that were made over millions of years led step by step to the creation of the most adaptable creature of all, man.

Simple Plant Cells

Yet the history of life on earth as we know it does not really support this theory. Simple plant cells and cells with some animal characteristics have floated in the oceans almost since life began, without finding the need to change. Nor has man yet proved himself the fittest to survive. The earliest remains of ape-like man go back barely three million years, whereas the extinct dinosaurs dominated the world for more than 100 million years.

Much more important than whether man is the highest achievement of nature is the fact that he is gaining control over the evolution of all living things. It is man who will decide in the future which plants and animals will continue to exist and which will be allowed to become extinct. Yet without knowledge of the way evolution ought to go in his own interests, man's efforts will be as unreasoning as those of the humblest plant struggling for survival in a tropical forest.

For nature has always been haphazard in its progress. There has not been one simple path from the single cell to the complicated structure of bone, muscle, nerve and brain that is man. Life has developed along many branches like those of a tree. Some branches have become stunted, others have flourished, dividing into further branches and twigs.

Two Main Branches

The trunk of the 'tree of life' divided early into two main branches, one representing plant life, the other animal life. How this came about is not yet known. Some minute organisms still have the characteristics of both plant and animal yet this seems to be a stunted branch of the tree with no possibility of further development. Nature will never produce a walking flower or an animal rooted in the soil.

The story of plants begins in the sea, with a free-floating, single cell. From this plant cell have developed the different kinds of cells which are the building bricks of all plants. Each plant cell keeps itself alive, grows and reproduces itself by activities common to all plants.

Using the sun's energy during daylight hours, the plant cell absorbs a gas called carbon dioxide to make sugar through photosynthesis and breathes out another gas, the excess oxygen. At night, when photosynthesis stops, oxygen is breathed in from the surrounding air to help burn up excess sugar made during the day, and carbon dioxide is expelled.

The sugar made inside the plant cell is combined with other chemicals dissolved in the sea water to build up large molecules called proteins. Thus the cell must take in water to provide materials for the proteins, which in their turn are built into the living material of the cell. In this way the cell can be said to feed itself.

All this activity takes place in single plant cells floating in the surface water of the ocean, the smallest of them measuring no more than a thousandth of a millimetre across, and the biggest perhaps as much as two millimetres.

In the Beginning

It took the first 4,000 million years of the earth's existence to create the plant cell. Something happened to join certain carbon compounds and form substances called amino-acids. These are essential in the creation of protein. Protein itself is not alive, but is the food without which no living thing can grow. Plants differ from animals in that, through photosynthesis, they can build protein from a combination of chemicals. So it can

Diatoms are primitive forms of plant life living in the sea. The geometric diatom above is many times enlarged.

be said that over a period of thousands of millions of years the action of sunlight on chemical salts dissolved in sea water created life.

During the next 160 million years, something else happened. Single plant cells joined together, end to end in hair-like chains or side by side in mat-like formations. Some of them settled on rocks, lodging in microscopic crevices, or developing a gummy substance on the cell wall which held them fast. Such simple seaweeds are called algae. Some of them secreted lime which built into a hard skeleton, helping to form reefs and limestone rock.

By the end of the next 40 million years plants had invaded the dry land. They developed sap tubes and breathing holes in spine-like leaves, and fungus was already growing in peaty deposits.

Forests grew in the swampy lowlands about 300 million years ago. All the plants were evergreens. Palm-like trees called lycopods grew as high as thirty metres (100 feet), above an undergrowth of fern-like plants and creepers. Lycopods had close-set leaf cushions on the trunks giving them a scaly look. They grew seed cones at the ends of leafy shoots. Horsetail trees with rings of leaves on hollow, jointed stems like bamboo, grew to twelve metres (forty feet) in height. Plants that looked like ferns, but with fronds bearing nut-like seeds, were common.

The stems, branches and leaves of these plants fell into the swamp as

The 'tree of life' diagram (right) is a device which has been used for many years as a method of illustrating the relationship between the different forms of animal and plant life.

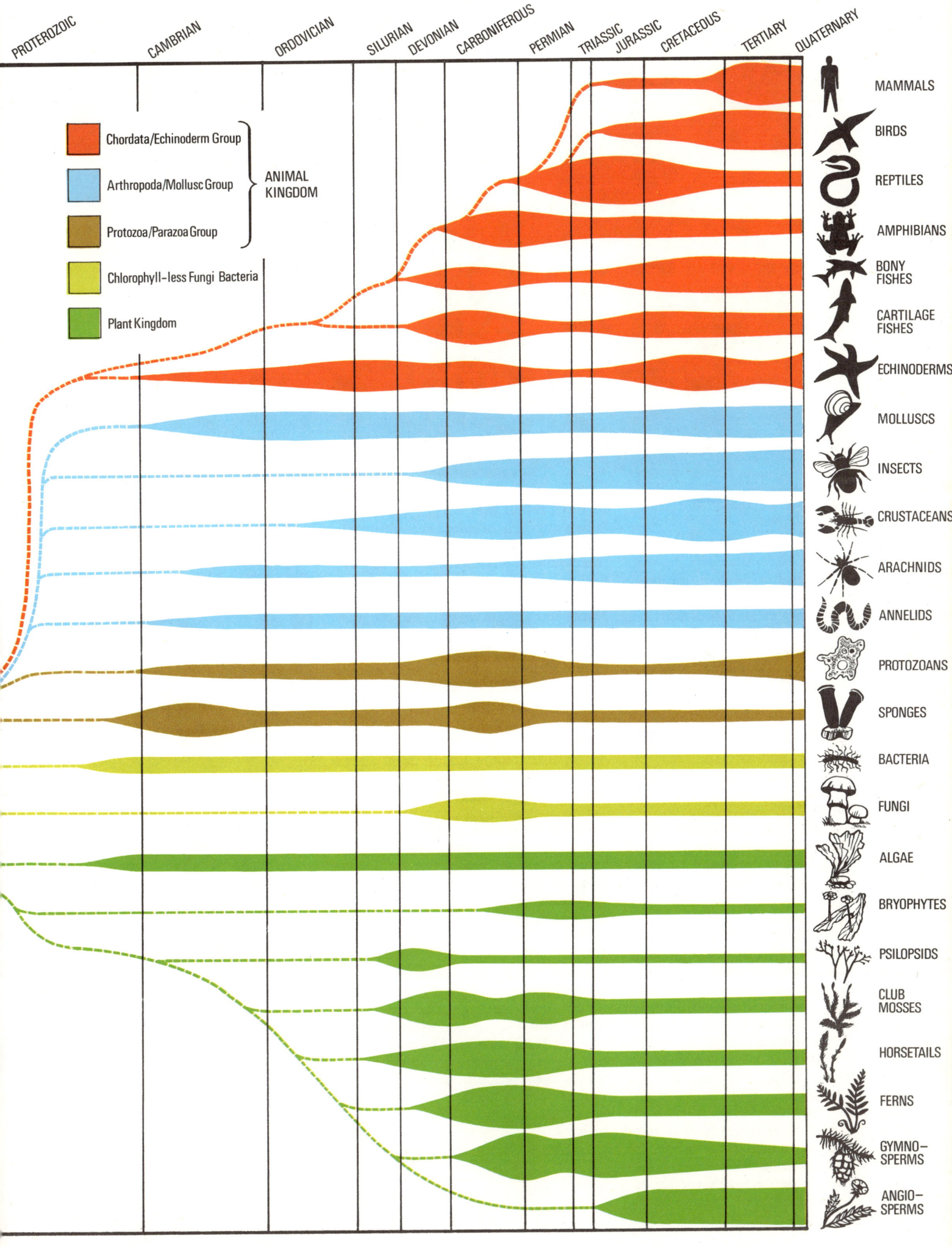

The compound microscope of the English physicist Robert Hooke (1635–1703), with the aid of which he made many detailed and enlarged drawings of animal and plant life.

they died, forming deposits of peat. When the ground subsided, floods of fresh or salt water laid sediment on top of the peat. As subsidence continued, pressure on the peat layer and chemical change produced seams of the coal we use today.

The Age of Cycads

The Jurassic period, 180 to 135 million years ago, is known as the Age of Cycads. Cycads are palm-like trees, some of them growing flower-like cones. By about 100 million years ago the true flowering plants were established, helped perhaps by pollinating insects in search of honey. This was the period of the dinosaurs, giant, egg-laying reptiles.

Conifers and ferns were common 70 million years ago, but the flowering plants, including deciduous or leaf-shedding trees, had by then become dominant. The world was beginning to look as it does today, although tropical vegetation reached much farther north then. The giant dinosaurs were extinct and the age of mammals, animals who suckle their young, had begun.

None of this development of different species could have happened without substances called deoxyribonucleic acids or DNA for short. The arrangement of amino-acids round a central coiled strand of DNA in the nucleus of a cell determines the sort of protein that will be produced. When the cell divides, this information is passed on to the new cells by these giant DNA molecules. They are thus the 'memory' of the cell, passing on hereditary characteristics to new plants. As a plant adapts and changes over the slow evolution of millions of years, so the DNA stores the new information and passes it on to ensure the continuation of the new features.

Plant Cells

As we learn more about it, it seems that the cells of a plant, however small, are as complex in their organisation as a modern city. The seat of government, the nucleus of the cell, has a library of information which helps to direct the activities of all parts of the cell and even to recall something of its origins thousands of millions of years ago, in the primeval sea. Thus is each cell able to continue its function without reference to other cells, but for the benefit of the whole plant.

By a method of trial and error, the 'tree of life' has grown and developed, learning from its mistakes and building on its successes. Modern techniques are enabling the scientist to enter the city of the living cell and uncover its secrets.

The substance called DNA (deoxyribonucleic acid) is found in the nucleus of all living cells. Shown here is the Watson-Crick model of DNA which is named after Francis Crick and James Watson, the British biologists who shared a Nobel Prize for their discoveries.

Plant or Animal?

In the sea, where so much about the origins of life still waits to be investigated, there lives a plant-cell called *Halosphaera*. It consists of a cell wall containing a central nucleus surrounded by the protoplasmic material called cytoplasm, open watery spaces called vacuoles, and colour-sensitive particles called chromoplasts. It is a plant because it lives by photosynthesis.

As *Halosphaera* grows older, deposits of glass or silica form on the cell walls. This makes the walls harder. As the protoplasm grows still further, the wall splits in half. Inside are two growing cells which, as they separate, often carry away part of the old hard wall as little domes of glass on their outer surfaces.

Zoospores

At stages in its life, the nucleus of *Halosphaera* divides into two parts. These again divide, making four parts, and so on until a large number of small nuclei have formed. Cytoplasm collects round each nucleus to form tiny bodies of protoplasm. When the walls of the cell split open these new plants escape and swim away. They are called zoospores. Each of them has a thin outer membrane but no cell wall, and a tiny red spot at one end with two fine hairs of unequal length. By lashing about with these hairs, the zoospore can swim. The red spot works like an eye, attracting the zoospore towards the light. It may even contain a small lens.

As the zoospore grows, it loses the fine hairs and the red eye-spot and begins to build a cell wall. It is turning into a plant cell again, but for a brief while it has possessed some of the characteristics of an animal.

There are many such tiny organisms in the sea. Some do not use photosynthesis but absorb their food through the thin skin of the outer membrane in a way that resembles an animal feeding. Such creatures are more animal than plant. This suggests that, at the beginning of time, there were organisms in the sea simpler than a single cell, some of which developed into plants and some into animals. A number of them remain today as half plant and half animal.

As life developed to higher forms further up the 'tree of life', the differences between plants and animals became more distinct. An animal must feed on other animals or plants, while a plant makes its own protein food from carbon dioxide, water and other chemicals. Animals generally move about freely, whereas plants, with the exception of those like free-swimming zoospores, are fixed in one place or floating at the mercy of the waves. Animals have a nervous system enabling them to react quickly to any stimulus; plants have no nervous system and react slowly.

Differences in Growth

Growth occurs in all parts of an animal usually until maturity, but sometimes beyond. Plants higher up the evolutionary scale grow mainly at the tips of stems and roots, and in the girth of the main stem or trunk. This growth continues throughout life.

Free-swimming zoospores, called flagellates from the flagella or hairs which propel them, move like animals but feed like plants. Their position in the 'tree of life' is at a point where the differences between plants and animals first began.

Insectivorous plants catch and 'eat' insects. Venus's fly-trap is a tropical plant which attracts its prey on to hinged leaves, which then close and trap the insect. The plant gives off digestive juices which absorb the substance of the insect. These plants obtain most of their food by photosynthesis.

Sea anemones are flower-like animals which live in the sea among the rocks. They catch other animals in waving tentacles, sometimes swallowing them whole in a central mouth which can be stretched to encompass their prey.

Giving Plants Names

Since plant life first appeared on this planet, it has been adapting and developing in countless ways. Many early varieties have disappeared, leaving no trace. But some extinct plants that lived in the sea encased themselves in lime and have been well preserved. Others left impressions of themselves in the mud that has hardened to fossil rock.

Many hundreds of thousands of different plants have survived and still flourish today. Modern horticulturists have improved on the methods of the first farmers and are producing new plants all the time. These are hybrids, two species crossed to produce a new one, perhaps a blue rose or a black tulip.

Every one of these plants must have a name both for the gardener's catalogue and for the student's botany book. Mankind has always been interested in plants as a source of food, as medicines, as fuel to provide heat and light and as an aid to the healing of wounds. From the beginning of language, we have given plants names to distinguish one variety from another.

Descriptive Names

At first, the names of plants were descriptive. They described what the plant looked like or the use to which it could be put, or they identified some feature that was peculiar to that species. Names changed as fashion changed and the old name lost its descriptive value.

A buttercup has a flower the shape of a cup and the colour of butter. Lady's mantle was the name given to this wild flower when ladies wore collars that were pleated and with serrated edges like the leaves of the plant. Honeysuckle has flowers rich in nectar and is therefore popular with bees collecting material for making honey.

Self-heal was the name given to the plant that in olden days was thought useful to wrap around an open wound. Since carpenters may be supposed to cut themselves on sharp tools more often than other people, the plant is also called carpenter's herb. Farm workers using pruning hooks and sickles for cutting hay and corn also used this plant as a bandage. So it has two other names, hook-heal and sickle-wort.

The English names of plants often reflect the languages of that country's many invaders. The Saxon name for a tree was beam and the word for lively was *cwic*. The quickbeam is therefore the 'lively tree', so called because its leaves dance merrily in the slightest breeze. The name dandelion comes from the Norman French *dent-de-lion* or lion's tooth, descriptive of the toothed edge of the leaf.

Names of plants often carry a warning. Deadly nightshade is a poisonous plant that grows often among ruined buildings, supposed to be dangerous to visit at night because of ghosts of the dead and evil spirits. Other names are contemptuous of the ignorant and stupid. Fool's parsley looks rather like the edible herb, but is evil-smelling and said to be poisonous.

It is interesting how some plants have lent their names to places through some forgotten association

The family tree of *Ranunculus repens*, or the creeping buttercup.

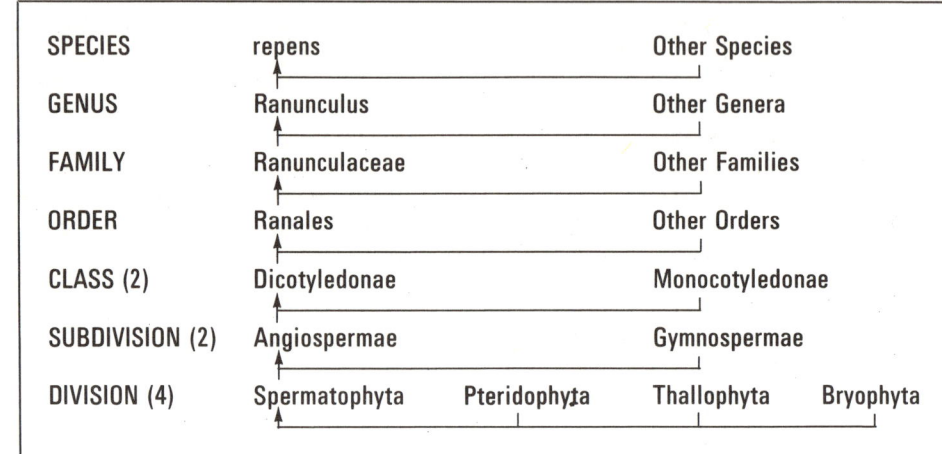

SPECIES	repens	Other Species
GENUS	Ranunculus	Other Genera
FAMILY	Ranunculaceae	Other Families
ORDER	Ranales	Other Orders
CLASS (2)	Dicotyledonae	Monocotyledonae
SUBDIVISION (2)	Angiospermae	Gymnospermae
DIVISION (4)	Spermatophyta	Pteridophyta	Thallophyta	Bryophyta

The main groups of the plant kingdom.

in ancient times. The hawthorn tree was planted to mark a place where people assembled for meetings or to make war. From this custom, the word thorn appears in the names of many villages.

With so many different species of plants and so many languages in the world, the list of common names for plants is endless. Many plants even bear several names in the same language. To enable botanists of all countries to communicate with each other, a common language of plant names had to be devised.

Linnaeus

Carl Linné, the Swedish botanist who lived between 1707 and 1778, realised this. He had a passion for order. From the age of twenty-four, he began to bring order into the naming and classification of plants. Since Latin had been the language of the Roman Empire it had spread throughout Europe. It was still taught in all the schools and colleges of the western world. Linné therefore used Latin as the language for naming plants and it was by the Latin version of his name, Linnaeus, that he became famous.

He invented what is called the binomial system of plant classification. That is to say, he gave each plant two names, like a first name and a surname, though in the reverse order. The first name, in this case, was that of the genus or type to which the plant belonged, and the second name was one given to that particular species or member of its type. Linnaeus's system first divided plants into those that flower and those that do not. The flowering plants he divided into genera (which is the plural of genus) on the basis of the formation and number of pistils and stamens, which are the parts concerned with reproduction.

Genus and Species

The first name or genus of a plant is nowadays usually given a capital letter, whereas the second name of the particular species begins with a small letter. Italics are used for the plant names. Thus the Latin name which Linnaeus gave to the bulbous buttercup is *Ranunculus bulbosus*. Since even Linnaeus could not in his lifetime give names to every plant in the world, it is the modern practice to give the author's name after the name of the plant like this: *Ranunculus bulbosus* Linnaeus. As the Swedish botanist is so famous, often a shortened version of his name, Linn., is written, or even merely the initial L.

Linnaeus made mistakes, placing particular plants in the wrong genus, for instance. In such cases his name is usually put in brackets and followed by the name of the person who corrected the mistake. Linnaeus called the yellow water-lily *Nymphaea lutea*. A botanist named Smith placed this plant in the genus *Nuphar*. The Latin name is therefore now usually written *Nuphar lutea* (L.) Smith. Thus the whole history of the classification of this particular plant is contained in the way the Latin name is written.

Though Linnaeus worked mainly from information obtained by other

Pteridophyta

Gymnospermae

Angiospermae

botanists, his contribution to the study of plants has been invaluable. His system, though corrected and added to, has been broadly followed ever since. It showed botanists the way forward out of the confusion of local plant-names towards a classification understood throughout the world.

The advance in the design of microscopes since Linnaeus's day and improved laboratory techniques have enormously increased our knowledge of plants. Expeditions to remote areas of the world have discovered new species. Today, plants can be more accurately grouped in relation to their form and structure. As far as possible the order of their appearance on earth and their natural origins are indicated in their grouping.

The Main Groups

Plants can now be divided into four main groups: thallophytes, which include algae, fungi, lichens and bacteria; bryophytes, the mosses and liverworts; pteridophytes, ferns and related species; and spermatophytes or seed-plants. Seed plants are again sub-divided into gymnosperms, those with seeds that develop naked as in a pine cone, and angiosperms, those with seeds contained in a seed-vessel or pericarp as in most flowering plants. The differences between plants in these four main divisions are described in the next three chapters.

Divisions and sub-divisions are divided into classes and sometimes sub-classes. Classes are divided into orders, and the larger orders into sub-orders. Orders and sub-orders are divided into families, and again into sub-families, which in their turn are divided into tribes. These are divided into genera (singular, genus) which give the first names of the individual plants. A large genus may be divided into sub-genera. The genus is divided into species which give the second names of the plants.

Thus the common daisy is an angiosperm belonging to the class called dicotyledons or those having two seed-leaves, as compared with the class called monocotyledons, having only one seed-leaf. It belongs to the family of Compositae and is a member of the genus *Bellis*. Linnaeus called it *perennis* so its botanical name is usually written *Bellis perennis* L.

A Common Language

This may seem a complicated way to describe the common daisy but it is understood by botanists all over the world who do not speak the same language and to whom many common flowers might be unknown in the wild state. Once the system of plant grouping has been understood, new discoveries and new hybrids created by crossing existing species can be allotted their appropriate place in the great pattern of plant life.

Of course, mistakes will be made. A greater understanding of how plants live might suggest alterations in their grouping. But this work is vital in spreading new information and in creating order from the apparent chaos of nature.

(Carolus Linnaeus) 1707–78

One of the largest families of flowering plants is the Compositae which includes the daisy, dandelion and thistle. Despite the variety of forms, all members of the group have certain features in common.

gi and Lichens

bacteria live on and break up
aste matter of plants, so do
Much of the forest that once
d large areas of the earth has, in
ed countries, been cleared or
up by man. A wild forest or
is a tangle of trees, creepers and
plants, each struggling upwards
share of light to carry on photo-
esis and to go on living. Many
 fail and die. The lower
es of trees rot and break off.
trees are struck by lightning,
down by the wind or uprooted
imals. Every plant reaches the
of its growth, the span of its
 and dies. The forest floor is
d with debris of past growth and
llen leaves of yesteryear. It is
hat the bacteria and fungi feed.
e main growth of a fungus is out
ht under the surface of the soil,
unk of a tree or other vegetation
ich it grows. What we call the
room, toadstool, puffball or
et fungus is really the fruit-like
h which carries the spores
the surface for disposal in the

Mycelium

ngus is composed of branching
of cells one ten-thousandth of a
metre wide, covered with a firm
 of cellulose. Though often
red, the cells do not contain
oplasts, those organisms that in
plants carry out photosynthesis.
partition walls between cells
 in from the side leaving a tiny
 in the centre for communication
one cell to the next.
ese threads or filaments of cells
lled hyphae. The hyphae are the
ng fingers spreading through the
or the material on which the
s is growing. Like bacteria, they
e enzymes which are injected
 the surrounding material to
pose it. They also inject poisons
might kill the plant or tree they
 in. Through the hyphae walls
bsorbed water and the products

Dogs can be trained to sniff out edible fungi called truffles.

of external digestion brought about by the enzymes, thus feeding the further growth of the fungus. The web of growing hyphae is called the mycelium of the fungus.

Useful Moulds

There are three kinds of fungus. First is the microscopic kind such as moulds in which individual hyphae grow into the air with a tiny container for spores in the tip called a sporangium. *Mucor*, the bread mould, with a black pin-head sporangium on a hypha like a thread of silk, is one example. Penicillin, the fungus that grows on cheese, is another.

The other two kinds of fungus grow hyphae in hundreds or even thousands above the surface to form a large fructification which is the name given to the spore-bearing 'fruit' of a fungus. In one kind the spores form inside an elongated cell called an ascus at the tip of a hypha and are squirted out when they are ripe. In the other kind, the spores form on tiny stalks on the outside of the end cell of a hypha called a basidium and are flicked off when they ripen. Thus there are ascus fungi and basidium fungi. Toadstools, puffballs and large

The fruiting body of the edible mushroom develops underground and grows rapidly to its full size within about seven days. Above right are luminous toadstools which emit light.

bracket fungi are basidium fungi, which have the most vigorous and extensive mycelia growing in soil and the rotting vegetation of tree trunks.

Fungus spores are extremely small and produced in great numbers. A giant puffball will produce perhaps seven million million. A mushroom will produce several thousand million. Yet less than one from each fructification ever settles in a suitable place to grow into a new hypha. Spore production is the most wasteful operation in all nature, though perhaps it is useful in the food chain of some creatures.

Because so many spores land on unsuitable hosts and either never germinate or are killed by antibiotics, fungi never get the upper hand in nature. Among cultivated

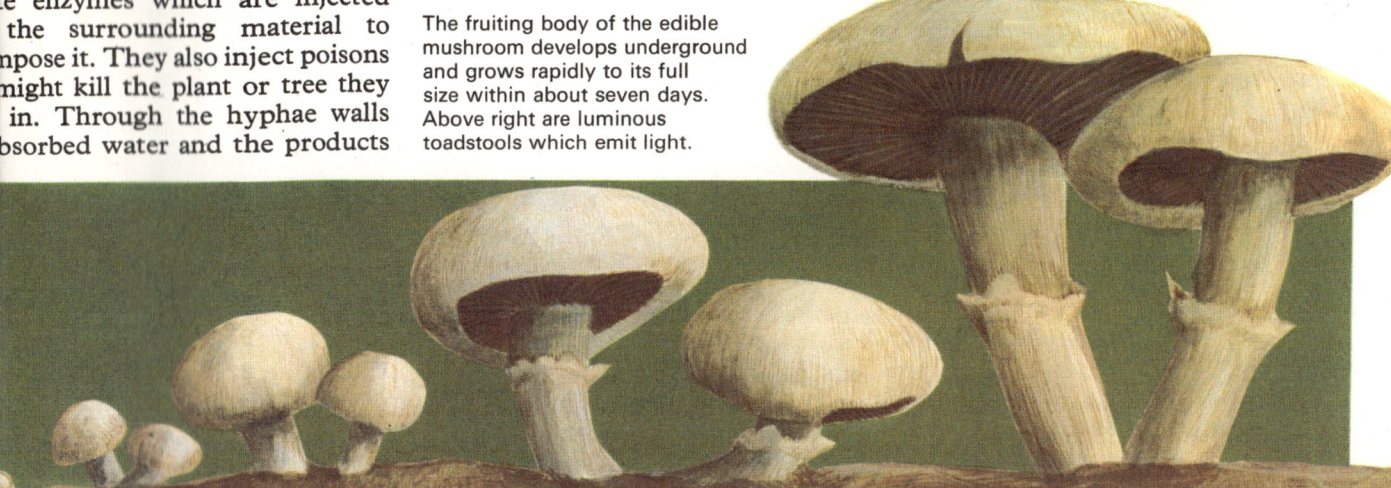

The green scum sometimes seen on ponds is composed of algae

Primitive Plants

Not all plants use photosynthesis to create the proteins of their food supply. Instead, they live off other plants and animals, working in the darkness. Some can even be killed by too much exposure to light. Such plants are the bacteria and the fungi. They are nature's rubbish disposal operatives.

A study of bacteria and fungi may one day lead us to solve the two great mysteries of how life began in the sea and how plants first invaded the land. Some species of bacteria are able to build up protoplasm, the living matter of a cell, from carbon dioxide and chemical salts by a process called chemosynthesis. This is similar to photosynthesis, but takes place in the absence of light. Such bacteria may be not unlike the primitive forms of life first produced on earth.

Fungi, on the other hand, in their structure and behaviour resemble seaweeds and may be a development from the first plants to climb ashore and adapt themselves to life on the land. The question of which came first, the photosynthesising green plants or the seaweed-like fungi that learned to live off them, remains unanswered.

Bacteria

Bacteria have a bad name because of their association with some of the diseases that afflict man. Yet without them nature would not continue to produce the rich variety of life on which we all depend. They are microscopic in size and multiply rapidly, one producing as many as 16 million others in a single day.

Under the microscope, bacteria are seen to be transparent cells usually without colour. They consist of a mass of protoplasm surrounded by a wall which is somewhat different from the cell wall of higher plants. Bacterial cells do not seem to contain an organised nucleus. The cells hold food reserves, grow rapidly and divide almost immediately they have reached their full size. After division, they may separate, cling together in chains or irregular masses or form a series of branches. In extremes of temperature, they form thick-walled spores called endospores which remain until conditions for growth again become favourable.

Bacteria live in or on animals or plants. They secrete enzymes, lifeless substances made out of living matter, which help to break down the tissues of their hosts to feed bacterial growth. When bacteria live as parasites, they harm the host plant or animal and sometimes kill it. In the soil, they extract nitrogen from the air and convert it into nitrates which help to feed plants. When bacteria are thus beneficial to their hosts, they are said to be symbiotic, which means living in partnership. Bacteria that live on and decompose the waste matter of plants and animals are saprophytes.

Among the things for which bacteria are useful to man are separating the fibres of such plants as flax, jute and hemp for making cloth and rope, turning animal dung into nitrate-rich manure, converting wine into vinegar and milk into cream for butter, in the curing of tobacco, and the tanning of leather.

crops, however, once a fungus gets a hold the spread is made easier. Spores can blow immediately from one host to an adjacent plant of the same species. Thus fungi become the pests of agriculture and forestry.

In other ways, fungi are extremely useful to man. For example, there are the yeasts, made up of masses of single cells. Yeasts are rich in vitamins and contain the enzymes which act as catalysts in the chemical breakdown for the release of carbon dioxide which makes dough 'rise' in baking, or to start the process of fermentation in brewing and distilling. They are also used in medicines and in the preparation of food extracts. In the wild state, yeasts appear on the surface of fruits and flowers. The action of enzymes does not seem to depend on the parent plant. In some processes they can be extracted and used on their own.

There are many kinds of algae that have left the sea and adapted to life on land. They can dry out and revive again when wetted. Some of them live in symbiosis or partnership with fungi. A fungus spore develops into a hypha in the same conditions that suit the alga. The two meet and the fungus

Varieties of fungi and lichens are seen in the panel above. At the top (left to right) are rock lichen with reindeer moss growing beneath; field mushrooms; *Amanita*, or death cap; and common morel. Below (left to right) are seen fly agaric; *Clavaria, Bovista* and *Boletus.*

incorporates the alga into its mycelium. Somehow the growing cells of the alga influence the fungal hyphae so that, instead of spreading out into the usual mycelium, they form tough, compact structures that look rather like small seaweeds. Such growths are called lichens.

Living together are two plants, one feeding itself by photosynthesis, and the other by external digestion. During daylight, the alga provides the fungus with oxygen, and the fungus may provide the alga with carbon dioxide. The alga produces excess carbohydrates of use to the fungus, and the fungus produces nitrates that the alga needs. An alga can live without the fungus, but its partner cannot live without the alga.

How the marriage between the two began is a mystery. It seems that, during the struggle of plants to establish themselves on the land, there were three distinct developments. Some ancestor of the mosses fed

itself by photosynthesis, some ancestor of the fungi learned to feed itself from the dead and dying green plants, and some that failed to achieve either combined to form the lichens, which are types of land seaweeds.

Invasion of the Land

When the first seaweeds climbed ashore or were stranded there, many must have died. Their death would have provided a decaying mass in which bacteria and other microscopic saprophytes like moulds could develop. Perhaps these moulds later developed into fungi. Never having inherited the chloroplasts of photosynthesis, they would not need to join the upward struggle for light. Their presence would encourage the growth of new green plants by rotting the previous vegetable matter into fertile soil. The microscopic size and great numbers of their spores would ensure their wide dispersal.

Whatever happened in the land invasion of the plants, it must have been a long, hard struggle. But nature has never been in a hurry. It has had more than four thousand million years for its act of creation.

Some seaweeds form great underwater forests. Travellers claim they grow 600 feet high. A giant seaweed of this size is shown to the same scale as Nelson's Column in London.

Seaweeds

A fungus has no need of roots since the whole of its mycelium is in contact with its food supply. Similarly, a seaweed is in contact with the water all over its surface. The difference is that seaweeds use photosynthesis to extract their food from the chemicals dissolved in seawater, whereas fungi use the action of enzymes to break up soil and vegetation.

The first plants in the sea were single cells, feeding, growing and dividing, or releasing small masses of cytoplasm called zoospores which could grow into new plant cells. They had no need to join together and were virtually immortal. Had some accident not changed their manner of living, life on earth could have remained in this primitive form.

What happened was that some of these plant cells settled on rocks and began to build the complicated structure that has resulted in the plant life in all its forms that we know today.

There are three ways in which a seaweed clings to a rock. Microscopic cells may dovetail into the equally tiny unevennesses of the rock face or cells acquire an adhesive material on their outer walls by which they are gummed to the rock; or cells send out hyphae-like fingers to act as struts and anchors. Any or all of these methods may be used by an individual seaweed.

Together with this clinging to the rock was developed the ability of one cell to remain fixed to another after division. The success of the multi-cellular seaweed has been such that seaweeds include the largest plants on earth. *Macrocystis*, the giant kelp, can rise from a depth of twenty-four metres (eighty feet) and reach a length of 182 metres (600 feet). Japanese oarweeds can grow ninety feet in the space of one year at the rate of fifteen centimetres (six inches) a day. *Nereocystis*, the bull kelp of the North American Pacific coast, produces a stem fifteen metres (fifty feet) long and has fronds of a similar length growing from it.

The Sargasso Sea

Another strange phenomenon of the ocean is the Sargasso Sea of the northern tropical Atlantic. Vast numbers of bits and pieces of the seaweed *Sargassum* have broken away from the shores of South America, the West Indies and perhaps even West Africa. Buoyed up by their air-bladders, they float across the ocean and continue to grow. In places they are so densely entangled they can restrict the passage of ships.

In general, the greater the ebb and flow of the tide, renewing water around the seaweed with the chemicals required for their growth, the bigger will the individual seaweeds become.

The multicellular structure of seaweeds is much the same as that of all plants. The difference is that the cell walls of seaweeds remain soft and do not become woody like the stems of land plants and the trunks of trees. Nor do the interior cells of seaweed stems need to become elongated to conduct water from root to leaf as in land plants. Seaweeds have their water supply all about them. For this

Seaweed contains several substances which are used in the preparation of certain foods. This detail from a Japanese print shows the gathering of cultivated seaweed, used in the East for flavouring soups.

reason, seaweeds dry out and die if left too long above tide level. Modern seaweeds cannot advance up the shore.

Nor can they grow in the darker depths of the ocean where light cannot reach them for the feeding process of photosynthesis. The cells at the 'root' of a seaweed, called the hold-fast, do indeed lose their ability to photosynthesise, but they are fed from photosynthetic cells higher up the stem and closer to the light source.

All the cells on the outer surfaces of stems and fronds continue photosynthesis, growing and dividing. Interior cells, fed from the others, cease to photosynthesise or divide, but grow larger as the seaweed grows. Between these interior cells hyphae-like threads develop and grow downwards, stiffening the stem and feeding the hold-fast.

Seaweeds are green, blue-green, brown or some shade of red, pink or purple, according to the depth of water they inhabit. All these are colours of the chloroplasts which aid the green chlorophyll to do its job of photosynthesis. The red pigment absorbs light at the blue-green end of the spectrum which penetrates most deeply through the water. Brown pigment absorbs the yellow-orange light. The chlorophyll itself is sensitive particularly to red and blue light.

Thus the position of a seaweed in the water determines its colour. The green seaweeds grow generally close inshore in shallow water. The brown seaweeds occupy the middle position, and the red seaweeds develop in deep water.

Air-Bladders

Seaweeds are maintained in the light by the movement of waves bearing them up, and by the penetration of air into the spaces between the larger interior cells which sometimes develop into buoyancy tanks, the characteristic air-bladders of some seaweeds. These air-bladders contain a high proportion of lighter-than-air carbon dioxide provided in excess by the process of photosynthesis.

Seaweeds develop their fronds either by sideways growth of cells or by the joining together of many filaments within a sheath of jelly-like mucilage. It is this mucilage, common to all seaweeds and continually washing away in minute quantities, that prevents particles in the water from sticking to the seaweed and stopping light from reaching the photosynthetic cells.

High water mark

Littoral zone

Low water mark

Sub-littoral zone

Seaweeds are of three kinds, red, green and brown. Green seaweeds are generally found in shallow water. The brown ones grow at the low tide level and the red ones are usually in deep water.

Early Land Plants

For clues to the land invasion of plants, we must examine the most primitive and oldest group of plants, the thallophytes. They do not have roots, stems or leaves, and most parts look more or less alike. Such a plant body is called a thallus, so a thallophyte is a thallus plant. They include the fungi, lichens and seaweeds already described. Seaweeds come in the group called algae. There are green algae that have adapted to life in fresh water, and in damp soil and other moist places. The green scum that covers a pond in summer is algae, and so is the green coating on damp walls and tree trunks.

Many green algae found in fresh water are single-celled plants such as *Chlamydomonas*, which has thread-like flagella, or 'arms', to help it to swim in the water. Some green algae, like *Pandorina*, have separate cells which join loosely together to form a ball. These are called colonial algae. They may be a stage in the creation of the more complicated multicellular plants.

Other green algae, like Spirogyra, have built delicate threads of cells which form slimy green masses on the surface of water. Some of the blue-green algae exist as single cells, and others are joined in loose chains. Many of the blue-green algae live in damp soil or are found as the photo-synthetic part of a lichen. There are microscopic algae called diatoms which live in fresh water and in the soil. These are single-celled and encased in silica which forms a glass-like box made in two parts that fit together. The boxes come in various shapes and patterns. A diatom reproduces when the box splits in half and each half grows a new half. The green chlorophyll of a diatom is covered with a yellow pigment, so all diatoms are yellowish in colour.

Mosses and Liverworts

The next group in the classification of plants is the bryophytes. They include mosses and liverworts. Mosses and most liverworts have stems and leaves, but some liverworts have a flat body like the hold-fast of a seaweed. Bryophytes have no real roots, though there are hair-like threads thrust into the earth to anchor the plant and to help in taking in water. These are called rhizoids. Bryophytes rarely grow more than seven centimetres (three inches) high.

The life story of a moss or liverwort is in two acts or stages. The first stage is a leafy green plant or, in the case of some liverworts, a thallus-like, flat green body. Such liverworts are not included among the thallophytes because the thallus stage grows rhizoids like the bryophytes. From the first stage grow the male and female reproductive cells called gametes. The male gametes and female gametes develop in separate containers. The female gametes remain in their container where chemicals are produced which somehow attract the male. Male gametes then leave their container and, with the aid of their flagella, swim about in the films of water that cover the plant. For this reason, mosses and liverworts usually grow in damp places where the male and female can come together.

Once male and female gametes have joined in the female container it grows a stem with a capsule at the top containing the fertile spores. This is the second stage. This capsule, or spore case, bursts and the spores are scattered to grow into new plants and begin the process all over again. Mosses and liverworts often grow plant buds in little cups which can be scattered by raindrops and grow into new plants.

The main method of reproduction of ferns is by spores produced on the undersides of the leaves. When they are ripe these spores are ejected as if from a catapult. Some spores germinate where they fall and develop primitive roots and organs of reproduction which are capable of producing a new plant to carry on the cycle. Ferns grow abundantly on hillsides in Europe and are often called bracken.

A fern garden

Every plant has a reproductive stage, and it is most noticeable in bryophytes. In the next group of plants, the pteridophytes, it is very small. The pteridophytes include the ferns, club-mosses and horsetails. Their reproductive stage is called the prothallus and it grows from a spore. In ferns and horsetails, this prothallus is a small green disc from which the female and male gametes join together and grow into a new plant. For a while, the prothallus feeds the young plant, but once the plant can grow by itself, the prothallus usually dies. In club-mosses, the prothallus is a root-like tuber which usually contains no chlorophyll and gets its food from a fungus-root.

Roots and Rhizomes

Pteridophytes are usually much larger than the mosses and liverworts. They have true roots which provide them with water and chemical salts from the soil. Many of them also grow rhizomes or underground stems which can grow new plants even if the rhizome is cut or part of it dies. These rhizomes provide vegetative reproduction and also store food for the winter. Ferns carry their spores usually in a little cluster called a sorus on the underside or edge of the leaf. The spores of horsetails are carried in cones at the tips of the stems. Each spore has four straps which coil and uncoil as the humidity changes, helping to scatter them. Club-mosses have spores on special leaves grouped into cone-shaped clusters at the tips of the stems.

Pteridophytes that live today are fairly small plants. They were the first plants to grow woody stems, about 350 million years ago. Some reached heights of thirty metres (a hundred feet) or more. There are still about 10,000 species left, but once there were many more. Some of them helped to make the seams of coal we use today. Fossils of *Calamites*, a giant, extinct horsetail, are common in the rocks of coal measures.

A cycad is the most primitive plant to reproduce by means of seeds. The seeds of a ginkgo or maidenhair tree are seen in close-up.

Cycads and Conifers

In adapting to life on dry land, plants developed four major changes in their structure which do not exist in seaweed. The first was the establishment of internal air spaces between the cells. The second was the waterproof layer of 'skin' called a cuticle which covers leaves and stems. This consists of transparent cells which hold in a 'sea' of water providing chemical salts to the photosynthetic cells within the cuticle. The third invention was the production of lignin, the material which forms the woody parts of stems and branches, and which gives the necessary structural strength for a plant to grow into something as large as a tree. The fourth and most complicated advance, occurring last in geological time, was the seed.

How all these inventions work and aid the success of the land plant is explained in the following chapters. Here are considered the plants that have descended from the ones which invented the seed as the most effective means of plant reproduction.

Thallophytes, bryophytes and pteridophytes all produce spores as part of their reproductive cycle. Generally speaking, all spores of a particular species are alike. In land plants, they consist of a single microscopic cell with a thick wall and waterproofed by the cuticle against evaporation. Seaweed spores, floating in water, do not need the cuticle and are surrounded merely by a soft mucilage.

Spores of land plants are like dust, blowing about until they settle into a suitably moist place to grow into a new plant. The beginning of a moss or fern cannot be seen by the naked eye. It might be days or even weeks before the tiny spore has grown into something that can be seen as a new plant. The gametes, or male and female reproductive cells, must then grow from the green plant, come together and produce the new spore for dispersal.

Reproduction by Seeds

A seed is a much larger and more complicated structure. It contains within itself the embryo plant and some food to continue its growth. Even without absorbing any more water, a seed can sometimes put forth roots and leaves to establish itself as a new plant. Seedlings overshadow and crowd out the young spores. Only by their minute size and large numbers are spores able to find places where seeds cannot go, to ensure the survival of their own species. In competition, the more self-contained seed will win every time.

In the life-cycle of a plant, the seed is the equivalent of the spore with the one essential difference that it contains the characteristics of male and female. The beginning of this process can be seen in certain club-mosses, water quillworts and in marsh or water ferns. They do not have seeds, but their spores are of two kinds which are distinctly male or female. The male spores, called microspores

Tree silhouettes in winter; from left to right, Norway spruce, silver fir, larch, Scots pine, Douglas fir.

Fir trees are distinguished from pines and larches by the way in which their needle-like leaves grow singly on the shoots rather than in clusters. One of the most important fir trees is the Norway spruce (right) which grows in northern and central Europe. Cones and seeds (left) are of the Noble fir.

because of their small size, on being released from the parent plant, develop and release a few male gametes or sperms. The female spore, called a megaspore because of its larger size, is set free and, on wet ground or in water, forms a small green prothallus which grows containers holding the female gametes. The spores of some club-mosses are blown about by the wind. The spores of other related plants are carried by water, when the sperms swim their way into the female containers.

In some species of club-moss, slender cones grow at the tips of the leafy branches. Some leaves of the cone hold female spores, others of the same cone hold male spores. Where the female spore is too big for the cone-leaf to release it, the female prothallus is produced where it is, and the male sperm swims to it from the male prothallus in a film of rain. This process is beginning to look like that of the female seed fertilised by the male pollen-grain of a flowering plant. The essential difference is that the female spore growing into a prothallus is not being fed from the parent plant.

Seed Plants

The seed plants come in the group called spermatophytes. These are subdivided into the gymnosperms and angiosperms. Gymnosperm is a word meaning naked seeds for those plants that develop without an enclosing ovary. Angiosperms have a seed-vessel called a pericarp or carpel, which is usual with most flowering plants. Gymnosperms, which include the cycads and conifers, do not have real flowers.

A cycad looks like a tree-fern with large leaves composed of many smaller leaves which carry male and female cones resembling giant pine-cones. As plants, cycads seem to be midway between ferns and conifers. They probably represent the earliest seed plants. They cannot, however, be regarded as direct ancestors of the flowering plants. The exact chain of progress from the earliest primitive land plants to the modern flowering plants has not yet been established. The cycads, once existing in great forests, but now rather rare, are just one of the many developments plants have been through to adapt to life on land.

The conifers include the biggest of all trees, the *Sequoia*, or redwood.

The female cones of the cycad produce the egg, the male cones produce pollen. In the flowering plant, a pollen grain produces a thread-like growth which is inserted into the female ovary to fertilise the egg. In cycads, the pollen tubes are very short and produce sperms with many flagella. The sperms use these to swim into the ovary, rather in the manner of the male gametes of the fern. The cycad genus *Cycas* is even more like a fern in that the female seeds are not produced in a cone, but on short, imperfectly developed leaves.

Another oddity is the ginkgo, or maidenhair tree. It is the sole surviving species of another line of seed-producing plants. It has fern-like foliage, spreading branches like a flowering tree, yet the pollen produces sperms to fertilise the female egg in the manner of the *Cycas*.

Cycad eggs are among the largest in the plant world. The sperms may take up to two months to navigate the tiny ocean which leads them to the egg. From pollination to the joining together of male and female cells might take up to six months. These are trees that live for hundreds, even thousands of years.

Fertilisation

The conifers take the production of seeds a stage further in that the methods of fertilisation are quicker and less wasteful. Their cones produce either seeds or pollen, never both, and indeed male and female are sometimes on separate trees. The pollen sacs are on the underside of the scales of the male cone. The female spores, called ovules, are exposed on the upperside of the scales of the female cone. Pollen is blown on to a small aperture called the micropyle of the ovule, where it is caught by a drop of sugary liquid. As this liquid dries, the pollen grains are drawn inside towards the central body of the ovule

Distinctive features of conifers are their cones. Seen here are cones from 1 cedar of Lebanon, 2 Weymouth pine, 3 larch, 4 Douglas fir, 5 Corsican pine.

A branch of the Chilean pine, better known by its popular name, the monkey puzzle tree.

called the nucellus. Tubes grow from the pollen grains to penetrate the nucellus, inside which are several containers of female gametes. Pines have two to five of these containers in each ovule. Giant redwoods or *sequoia* can have as many as sixty.

The structure inside the nucellus is the equivalent of the prothallus of a fern. It is embedded in the tissue from which the female spore was formed and from which it gets its food and water supply. After fertilisation, the future food supply of the seed, called the endosperm, grows. More than one embryo plant may begin to grow in the seed. However, as rivals for the available food and water supply, only the most vigorous survive.

The Embryo Plant

Thus the female gamete joins with the male gamete to develop into a young plant. This embryo plant with its food supply of endosperm and its protective covering, together with a part of the cone scale often forming a wing for flight in dispersal, is the seed as we know it when it leaves the tree.

These seeds are quite different from the fertilised spores of a club-moss in that they have been fed from their parent plant. They carry away with them an embryo plant already growing and supplied with sufficient food and water to begin life in a new location. Their chances of survival are therefore that much greater. This explains why the cycads and conifers were able to dominate the ferns and mosses, and spread great forests across the land as long as 250 million years ago.

Yet within another 100 million years of the establishment of cycads and conifers, the buzz of insects was to sound a warning note to the flower-less plants. With insects aiding pollination, and by devising many other ways of seed dispersal, the flowering plant was to become dominant. Today, there are about 350,000 different species of plants in the world. Of these about 125,000 are thallophytes, bryophytes, pteridophytes or gymnosperms. The remaining 225,000 separate species, of all sizes and shapes, living in all climatic conditions from the tropical rain forests to the windswept tundra, are the angiosperms, or flowering plants. It is they who represent the highest form of plant life and have produced so many varieties to delight us.

Flowering Plants

All seed plants produce two kinds of buds. The first is a leaf-bud, a form of vegetative reproduction repeating the foliage habit of the species. Some leaf buds have continuous growth, the outer adult leaves protecting the inner younger ones. The growth of these is checked only when weather conditions are against it. Most leaf buds have protective scales within which the bud can either lie dormant or form itself into a whole series of overlapping young leaves ready to open out when they are needed or the season is appropriate.

The second kind of bud is sexually reproductive. The simplest of these is made when some of the inner bud scales become fertile by carrying pollen sacs or ovules. These open out into cones whose job is not to add growth to the plant but to produce new plant seeds from it. Once that job is done, the cones die and fall off the plant. In the biggest of the conifers it may take many years before the first seed cones are produced. Once the process has begun it may be continuous during the remaining life of the plant, as in many palms. It may also be a seasonal phenomenon, or it may end the life of a plant.

The Flower Head

A flower is a more highly organised reproductive bud. Its scales are of five kinds, developing in succession each new kind within the previous one. The outermost scales are called the bracts and are the most leaf-like. Next come the outer green sepals which form what is called the calyx. Inside them are the petals forming what is called the corolla. Within the corolla are the male scales or stamens, and right in the centre the female scales or carpels. The stamens are the equivalent to the male spores and the carpels to the female spores of the club-mosses.

In most flowers these five parts remain close together throughout the life of this reproductive unit, except that there is often a length of stem separating the bracts from the rest of the flower. Since horticulture has aimed over the years at producing long-lasting blooms for our delight, it is often forgotten that, in the wild, flowers last only as long as it takes them to do their job, that of producing a seed. When that job is over, the

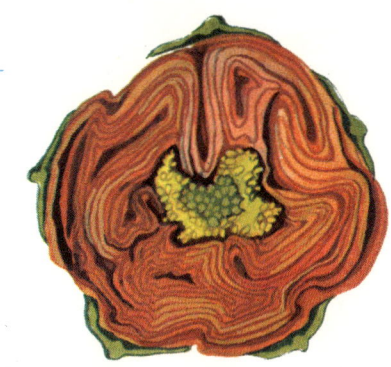

Cross section of a rose bud which is actually an unlengthened shoot with leaves closely packed around it.

flower withers away and dies. As a 'die-away' structure, it reaches its characteristic size and shape and then stops growing.

In addition to the five parts already mentioned, flowers contain patches of tissue called nectaries in various parts of the flower. These secrete the sugary nectar that attracts insects and other animals to aid the process of pollination.

The female part of a flower, called the ovary, completely encloses the ovules, the parts destined to grow into the seeds. This is quite unlike the female cones of cycads and conifers where ovules are exposed and pollen is able to settle directly on them. Flowering plants are therefore called angiosperms, which means with seeds or ovules boxed in. There are three distinct ways in which this ovule box is formed.

The Ovule Box

The first and simplest way is by the folding of the carpel to form a purse-like structure, the edges of which stick together. On these edges, the ovules grow alternately so that they fit together into a continuous row. The tip of this folded carpel is where the pollen grains arrive and begin to grow into the ovary towards the ovules. This tip is called the stigma, and it is often separated from the ovary by a more or less slender stem called the style. When the pollen grain lands on the stigma, its cells divide and lengthen, sending out a tube which reaches down through the style towards an ovule. As many pollen grains as there are ovules are required to fertilise them, and to fill the pod with fertile seeds.

All sorts of pollen from different plant species may land on the stigma, but for both chemical and physical reasons foreign pollen cannot enter the style, which thus acts as a sort of filter. The style has another effect. It has been found that pollen from the same flower landing on the stigma

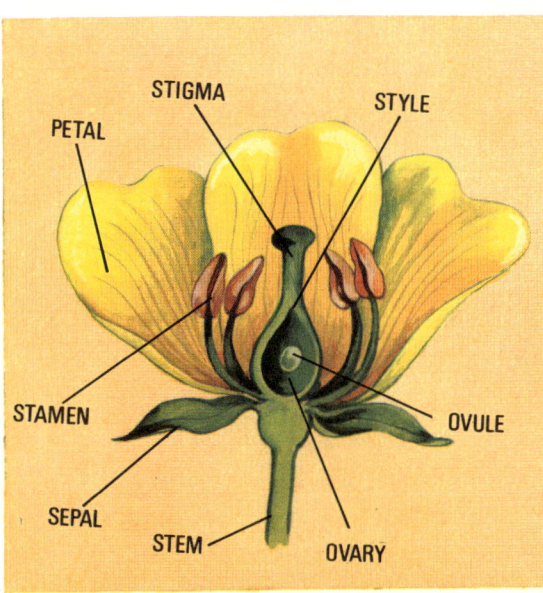

The flower is the part of a flowering plant concerned with its reproduction. On the left is a diagram of a typical flower head. The stamens are the organs which produce pollen. The male cell from the pollen grain reaches the ovule through the stigma.

Monocotyledon plants include grasses, lilies and daffodils. The tulip (right) is typical of the class. Its leaves are long and narrow with parallel veins growing from its base. The term monocotyledon is derived from the presence of only a single seed leaf (cotyledon) within the seed. Dicotyledon plants have two seed leaves and their leaves have nets of veins, like the primrose (far right).

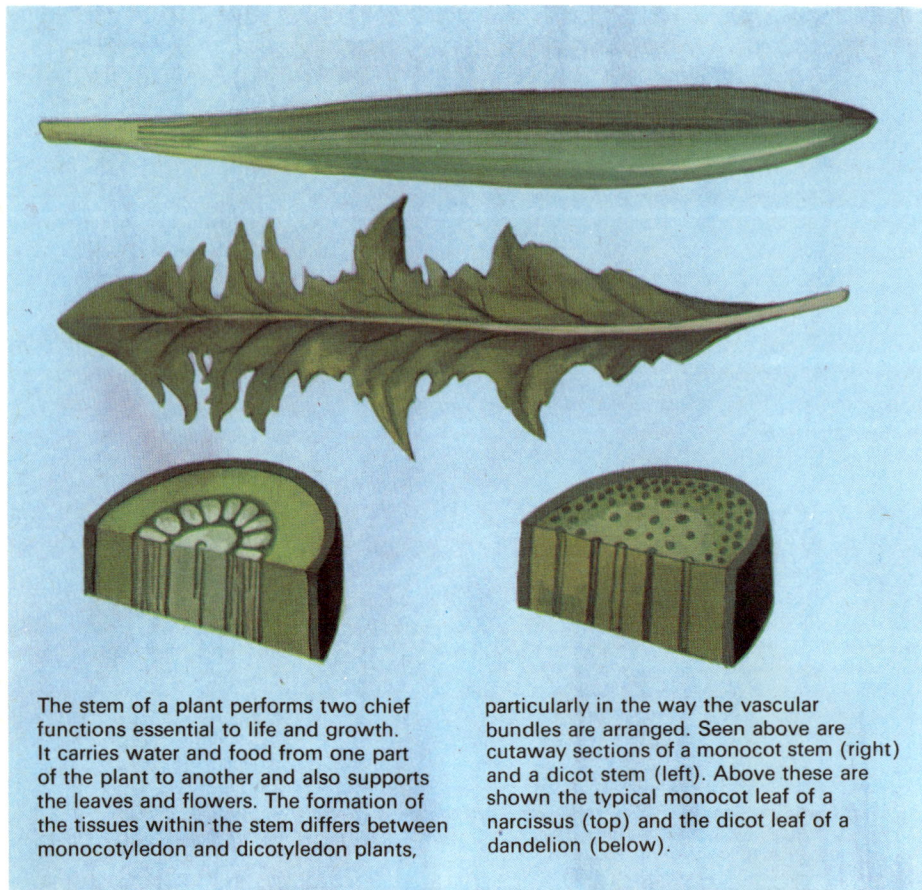

The stem of a plant performs two chief functions essential to life and growth. It carries water and food from one part of the plant to another and also supports the leaves and flowers. The formation of the tissues within the stem differs between monocotyledon and dicotyledon plants, particularly in the way the vascular bundles are arranged. Seen above are cutaway sections of a monocot stem (right) and a dicot stem (left). Above these are shown the typical monocot leaf of a narcissus (top) and the dicot leaf of a dandelion (below).

grows more slowly than pollen from another plant of the same species. Thus, it is more likely for the ovules of one flower to be fertilised from the pollen of another plant of the same species than from its own pollen. This suggests that cross-pollination is the rule and produces the most healthy seed. Inbreeding, as with animals, is something a flower avoids.

The second way in which the ovule box is formed does away with the carpels almost entirely. The carpels begin to form inside the bud at the tip of the flower stem, but only far enough to make the stigmas and their styles. Beneath them, a ring of growth appears which becomes longer by cell division until it has grown into a hollow cylinder inside which the ovules appear. This type of ovary is called a pistil. It is green in colour because it must use photosynthesis to feed the growing seed.

In the third type of ovary box the stem itself becomes wider and hollow to form a chamber for the ovules. This type of ovary is not on the same level as the other parts of the flower, as in the two previous cases, but below them. It is therefore called an inferior ovary whereas the other two kinds are known as superior ovaries. A good example is the crocus whose inferior ovary is actually underground with several inches of style leading up to the stigmas within the flower centre.

An ovule begins to form as a microscopic lump on the wall of the ovary. Within it appears one cell with denser contents and a larger nucleus. This nucleus divides until four cells are formed. Three of these are usually crushed out of existence by the fourth which grows into a mass of protoplasm. Its nucleus again divides, usually into eight nuclei, one of which with some cytoplasm becomes an egg. This whole structure is called the embryo sac.

Pollen Sacs

At the tip of a stamen can be seen the pollen-producing growth called the anther. The pollen sacs in which the pollen grains form are embedded in the tissue of the anther. When these sacs burst, the pollen is carried by wind, or by an animal or some other agency to the stigma of the female ovary. There it grows a filament called the pollen tube which thrusts its way down the style and enters one of the ovules. There are three nuclei in the pollen tube, one of which dies while the other two enter the embryo sac. One of these joins with the egg and grows into the embryo plant with a root and one or two seed leaves.

The remaining pollen nucleus joins with two nuclei from the embryo sac. This new nucleus goes on dividing to form a mass of cells filled with food reserves which is called the endosperm of the seed. From this endosperm, the embryo plant takes food for its further growth and, in many cases, for germination after the mature seed has left the parent plant. As the embryo and its endosperm enlarge, so does the wall of the ovule and also the wall of the ovary to accommodate the growing ovules. The stalk of the flower thickens to provide more food and water to the developing fruit and its seeds.

The embryo plant includes one or two seed leaves. A seed leaf is called a cotyledon. A plant growing from a seed with only one cotyledon is called a monocotyledon. A plant growing from a seed with two cotyledons is called a dicotyledon. The distinction was first noticed by John Ray at the end of the seventeenth century, but it took another hundred years before other botanists appreciated the discovery. Though there are exceptions, monocotyledons generally have many tufted roots of equal length, while

The Madonna lily may claim to be the oldest domesticated flower. The drawing above is based on a mural found in Crete which dates from the middle Minoan period, about 1700 B.C. Its history as a flower cultivated by man because of its beauty can be dated back to the Assyrians, possibly 5,000 years ago. Its original home was probably the Balkans, but due to its cultivation by the Romans it spread throughout their empire and eventually grew wild in many parts of Europe and Asia. The association of the flower with the Virgin dates from the second century A.D.

Some examples of the variety of form and colour in flowers.

dicotyledons have a main tap root with side roots branching from it. Monocotyledons have leaf veins running parallel to each other and equal in thickness. Dicotyledons have a main leaf vein with smaller branching veins making a network within the leaf. Again there are exceptions to this rule.

Flower Stems
The stem of a dicotyledon is composed of the epidermis, a single layer of cells whose outer walls are covered with a tough waterproof cuticle. Inside this is the cortex in which are long tough strands of cells running from roots to leaves called vascular bundles. Each of these is made up of different kinds of cells running alongside each other. The inner cells of the vascular bundle are long cells with woody walls which make up the parts called the xylem, meaning wood. These cells have lost their protoplasm and the walls at either end have opened out to make one long tube of each strand. It is along these tubes that the water climbs from the soil up to the leaves, and the woody texture helps to support the stem in an upright position.

The outer cells of the vascular bundle are long, soft and full of protoplasm, the walls between them pierced with holes. These cells carry the sugar and other foods manufactured by the leaves to all the other parts of the plant. They are called the phloem. Between the xylem and the phloem is a ring of young cells called the cambium. As these young cells grow, the inner ones become xylem cells and the outer ones become phloem cells.

In the centre of a young stem is a mass of soft, thin-walled large cells called the pith. This helps in the conduction of water until the cells die and dry out as in the soft centre of a willow stem; or disappear to form a hollow stem as in the delphinium; or harden into the heartwood of some trees. Connecting pith and cortex are narrow sections of cells running between and at right angles to the vascular bundles. These are called medullar rays. They help to give firmness to the stem structure and also store food and water.

The structure of monocotyledons is less complicated. Their stems have all the different parts of the dicotyledons except the cambium. The vascular bundles are scattered throughout the stem, including the pith. They do not form rings as in the dicotyledon stem. Because there is no cambium, the stems do not grow thicker or become stronger each year. For this reason, most monocotyledons are herbaceous plants, which means that the parts above ground die down each year. Typical monocotyledons are the grasses, including cereals, sedges and rushes, lilies, daffodils and other bulbs.

Dicotyledons mostly grow from their tips outwards. Monocotyledons grow from the base, pushing the older parts upwards. Thus a grass lawn can be mown without destroying the monocotyledonous plants of which it is composed. Mowing or grazing merely crops the older parts of the plant. The new growth springs from the short underground stem. When the young growth at the top of a dicotyledon is eaten by an animal, that part of the plant dies. New growth must appear from a dormant bud lower down.

Formation of Trees
Many monocotyledons are temperate plants, such as the grasses and bulbous plants like onions. But some tropical species, like palms, screw pines, and bananas and their related

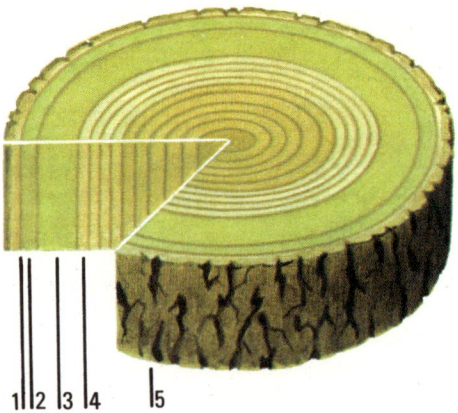

Wide rings in a tree trunk show good growing years. Above: 1, sap line. 2, latest growth. 3, heavy growth. 4, small growth. 5, outer bark.

species, produce massive growth, A palm can take up to five years to grow a leaf nine metres (thirty feet) long. It can therefore never be a deciduous tree (one which sheds its leaves) and very few species can withstand frost.

Another feature is demonstrated by the bamboo, a member of the grass family. The point along a stem from which a leaf grows is called a node, and the length of stem between leaves is called the internode. The leaves of bamboo, like all grasses, are in two rows and such a simple arrangement appears to make it easy to produce long internodes. The Malayan bamboo can have an internode as long as three metres (nine feet). Such structures have found a use among the natives as blowpipes. A bamboo shoot can grow as much as twenty-five centimetres (ten inches)

in twenty-four hours. In a few months it can reach a height of thirty metres (100 feet). As it grows, the stem becomes thinner and begins to branch. As these branches branch again, the leaves on them become smaller until a minimum size is reached and that particular species of bamboo can go no higher.

This indicates how trees were first formed. Palms, screw pines and bananas grow in the wild in the swampy flood zones of tropical rivers where newly formed soil is deposited. Perhaps this is how the flowering forest began.

An annual plant passes through the whole cycle of its life from seed to flower and final death in a single year. A biennial has two years of life, producing its photosynthetic growth the first year, its flowers and seeds the second. Such plants are necessarily in a hurry to reproduce themselves. A perennial plant may die down each year having produced that year's quota of seeds. A flowering tree, on the other hand, is aiming at massive growth. Trees which are dicotyledons produce cells in the cambium to thicken the trunk. The tree divides into branches and spreads a massive head of more and more leaves to feed more and more growth. It is in no hurry to reproduce itself by seeding. It might be twenty years or more before a tree produces its first flowers. Yet the massiveness of its overall growth does not mean that its individual parts are massive. The largest tree can have quite small leaves and even smaller flowers.

The evolution of the flower appears to have been one of reduction. A 'primitive' tree like a magnolia has a flower resembling a cone in that it is composed of many bud scales. The lowest of these may be greenish but they are little different from the next petal-like ones so that calyx can hardly be distinguished from corolla. There are many stamens and many carpels each with two to twelve ovules. Such large complex structures can be compared with flowers of the *Compositae* family which includes daisies, sunflowers, dahlias, lettuce and thistles.

Flowering Heads
In evolutionary terms, these are among the advanced flowers. As the name implies, their flowering heads are a composite of many small flowers, each with an inferior ovary set in the short stem and carrying one ovule. The slender corolla bears five thin stamens through which pass a slender style with two stigmas. The calyx is merely the silk of the seed. The most advanced of the monocotyledons is the grass flower. It has a superior ovary with one ovule, two styles and three slender stamens. There are no petals or sepals, just two small appendages called lodicules that swell and force apart the two green bracts so that stamens and styles may emerge.

Such flowers have evolved by stages to become shorter and more bud-like, less stem-like. The ovary has reduced to a single ring of carpels,

Deciduous trees shown in this scene are (left to right) silver birch, horse chestnut, ash, poplars, elm and oak.

then to an ovary tube and finally to the inferior ovary. The number of parts has even been reduced to only one petal, stamen or carpel. Finally, male and female flowers have become separated as in the catkins of the oak, or grow on separate plants as in the catkins of poplars and willows. The flowers of these latter trees, like the grass flower, have no sepals or petals, stamens and stigmas being protected merely by a leaf scale.

As the flowers become smaller, so their numbers increase. Thus appears the plant with many flowers growing from a single stem. In some cases, as in *Compositae*, these inflorescences, as they are called, form together a compact flowering head called a capitulum.

In others each flower has its separate stem. When these grow alternately up the main stem, the inflorescence is called a raceme. A bluebell is a one-sided raceme. When each flower has a reduced stem it is called a spike or catkin. When the alternate branching stems themselves branch and each branch branches until all the tips flower, as in a privet, it is called a panicle. When the lower alternate stems grow longer than the upper ones so that all the flowers are more or less at the same height as in yarrow, it is called a corymb. When stems of roughly the same length grow from the apex of the principal stem as in wild garlic, it is called an umbel. When the stems of an umbel branch into further stems at their tips before flowering as in hogweed, it is called a combined umbel. When stems grow by repeated branching in a haphazard fashion as in elderberry, it is called a cyme.

Finally, in small plants, the branching inflorescence reduces to fewer flowers until only one grows at the head of the stalk as in tulips and daffodils.

No longer do botanists believe that a single flower with a single stamen or a single carpel is primitive. The flowers of the smallest duckweed, *Wolffia*, with one stamen and one ovary containing one ovule, are a development from a spike-like inflorescence. Its tiny body is without roots or leaves and is reduced to a miniature of sub-seedling life.

The seed of a dandelion hangs from a little parachute of hairs easily detached and carried off by the wind.

Variety of Seeds

Just as nature has produced this enormous variety of flower forms, so it has created a variety of seeds, each designed for its particular means of dispersal and survival of its species. Thus the embryo plant can form part of the head of the dandelion clock with its gossamer parachute to catch the wind. Or it can be contained in the shell of a coconut capable of floating from island to island with enough food to produce several leaves up to thirty centimetres (a foot) in length and a number of strong roots. Between these two extremes are all the varieties of berries, fruits, nuts and grains.

Dwarf trees are usually produced by special treatment. On the left are seen a dwarf pine and juniper growing in pots. The art of flower arranging is one which skilfully combines the colour and shape of plants and relates them to their container.

Plant Behaviour

Such is the variety of plant life that even the general rules of its behaviour can be broken by particular species. Though most plants manufacture their own food by photosynthesis, certain primitive species that lost the art managed to survive. It was perhaps a loss of chlorophyll in some ocean plankton that enabled them to live on the protein content of other plant life. A similar loss in land plants created fungus, able to consume the products of living or dying green vegetation. By the invention of eating, the animal was created.

In the long course of time, the swimming limbs, or flagella, of male reproductive cells became the muscles which made it possible for animals to move about. Although some seaweeds can float freely in the deepest ocean and survive, the first species developed by clinging to rocks to build themselves up. Similarly, on land, plants rooted themselves in the soil to gather the raw materials of their food manufacture. Yet the seeds of some plants grew wings which blew through the air to take root in fresh ground. There are even plants that can send out roots on one side which prosper, while those on the other die away. So the plant can be said to drag itself slowly across the surface of the earth, step by step, in a patient search for nourishment.

Animals feed off plants and each other. Similarly, some species of plants have learned to be parasitic, that is they feed off the tissue of other plants and even off living animals. Bacteria are tiny plants that have invented a means of living that does without light, just as the hyphae of fungus work away in the underground darkness.

If the first form of life on our planet, the single photosynthetic cell, had been a perfect organism, creation would have ended there. Although plant plankton in the sea reproduces itself almost indefinitely for losses in its numbers, primitive life is not perfect. Accidental breakdown has led to change and adaptation.

As a bean seed germinates, the radicle grows downwards and develops into roots. Cotyledons grow upwards and form leaves.

The Plant Cell

The cells that make up the most complicated plant are very similar to the single plant cell in its most primitive form. It seems that the first protoplasm contained all the things needed for development, just as the human brain is capable of being educated and of adapting to changing circumstance. In this way, a plant can 'think' in the sense that it has the power to react to change and adapt its form.

The energy that first created life on earth came from outside the planet. It was light energy from the sun. That energy has continued for millions of years with such strength that many different forms of life have been built up. But our planet has limited resources and it is a continual struggle to make use of them. As long as the earth's resources continue to be renewed with the aid of the sun's energy, life of some kind will continue. Man, as the most greedy form of life, must learn to respect his planet's resources if he is to remain a part of that continuing process.

The Growing Root

The roots of a plant live mainly in darkness underground. They do not have the green chlorophyll colouring of the rest of the plant, which must send down food for the roots to grow. Inside every root are chains of living cells through which the food is carried. At the tip of each growing root is a thimble of cells which protect it as it pushes its way through the soil. These cells are constantly being rubbed off, making the tip slimy as it eases its way between the soil particles. Behind the cap, the cells are continually dividing and lengthening, pushing the tip forward in search of water. Behind these cells is the part of the root which grows fine whitish hairs. These hairs grow longer as they age and then wither away, the shorter hairs growing nearest to the root-cap and the hairy area remaining constant in length along the root.

There are various types of roots. From the left are shown the fibrous roots of a cereal, the adventitious roots of a dahlia, and the tap root of a carrot. Above are a bulb and a rhizome (right). Both of them store food underground as well as being reproductive structures.

The leaves of some plants are sensitive to touch, particularly certain species of mimosa (left). If one end of the leaf is touched, before long the whole leaf is folded. A plant will also wilt if its cells lack water.

It is these root hairs that absorb the water with its dissolved chemical salts which eventually provide the leaves with their material for photosynthesis. It has been estimated that a single wheat plant needs two and a half litres (half a gallon) of water every day, and a mature tree may need this amount every two minutes. The root system of a plant is therefore extremely complex. A single grass plant occupying only sixteen cubic centimetres (one cubic inch) of soil may produce up to 20,000 root hairs with a combined length up to 1,219 metres (4,000 feet). The water is passed up to the rest of the plant through chains of woody cells.

Some of the roots grow through the topsoil where they act as drains removing the material left by fallen leaves and other dying vegetation which has decomposed. Sometimes they are helped by a fungus which grows with them forming a fungus root. The hyphae of the fungus cover the rootlets with their threads or, in some cases, enter the rootlets and establish themselves among their tissues. Oaks, beeches, birches and many conifers have such fungus helping to break up the rotting vegetation so that its salts can be absorbed by the tree roots.

The final job of the root system is to anchor and support the rest of the plant. Usually roots act as stays like the guy ropes of a tent. In some large tropical trees, to do this job, they grow from the trunk high above the ground. In other cases they act as props on one side of a leaning trunk or as stilts lifting the whole trunk above the ground. In the latter case, they help to provide the roots with oxygen when the tree grows in very wet ground. Swamp-dwelling trees such as mangroves solve this problem by sending up breathing roots.

Plant Stems

The stems of plants or trunks of trees continue the passage of water up from the roots and the distribution of food for growth down to the roots. They also provide the plant with the rigidity, or stiffness, necessary to lift the leaves into the light where photosynthesis can take place. In a green or soft stem this rigidity is provided by the water in the cells pressing against their individual walls. Cell walls in their turn press against each other and against the outer cuticle of the stem. When the water supply is cut off, the stems eventually become limp as water evaporates from the breathing pores of the leaves and is drawn out of the cells in both leaf and stem. When the plant is watered again, the cells swell up and the plant regains its rigid, upright posture.

Plants also contain a substance called lignin which is the cause of woodiness. As the cells of a plant become filled with water, lignin is deposited on their inner walls, either in a spiral pattern or in rings or hoops. Each vein in every leaf of a plant is connected to a chain of lignified cells which act as a water pipe to that vein. Because the walls separating one cell from another would stop the flow of water, most of the upper and lower ones dissolve away, making the pipe continuous. In some trees, these pipes, called vessels, are very short. In others, they can be several metres long. The longest vessels, up to six metres (twenty feet), and the widest, only a fraction of an inch in diameter, occur in climbing plants and can carry water up to the leaves at considerable speed.

Another feature of a woody stem or trunk is the bark. The outer cells of the vascular bundles are the food-carrying cells. They last usually for only one season. When they die, they are squeezed by new cells forming behind them. These squashed, dead cells form the bark. In trees with a smooth bark, the outermost cells become powdery and are blown away or washed off. In other trees, as the trunk grows thicker from within, the bark splits into deep grooves.

In the middle of a tree trunk, the woody substance builds up until the vessels can no longer carry water. They dry out and create what is called the heartwood of the trunk or branch. It is this rigid structure that supports the weight of the tree.

Working Leaves

Though the green stems of plants contain photosynthetic cells, it is the leaves that do most of this work. Leaves have an epidermis, or skin,

Mangroves are tropical trees which grow in quiet ocean waters, particularly along the American coastline from Florida to the northern parts of South America. As they grow mainly in swampy water the trees have developed breathing roots. In some species these grow upwards and in others the roots curve out of the water. In both cases the exposed parts of the roots are able to absorb oxygen. Another function of projecting roots is to anchor the tree and keep it upright by acting as props.

The process of photosynthesis is carried out in a plant's leaves, which are arranged on the stem so that no leaf completely obscures light from another.

forming the waterproof cuticle with, on the underside, tiny holes called stomata. Each one of these stomata has a pair of guard cells which fill with water pressed from the cells of the epidermis so that the stoma opens. Through these tiny holes carbon dioxide from the air enters during daylight and excess oxygen escapes. The concentration of water vapour inside the leaf is usually greater than in the air outside. So when the stomata open, the leaf begins to dry out. Moisture must be replaced from the veins. The veins are the irrigation system of the leaf, receiving their supply of water and dissolved salts from the tubes of the stems.

Within the epidermis of the leaf is a row or a series of rows of long cells set at right angles to the epidermis like the palings of a fence. They are lined with chloroplasts sensitive to light and have air spaces between them connected with the stomata. Between the top and bottom layers of cells there are more or less shapeless cells with fewer chloroplasts and larger air spaces between them giving the heart of the leaf a spongy texture. These air spaces were the first new invention of the land plant after invading the earth. With them and the leaf veins, all the parts of a plant are supplied with air and water, the raw materials of photosynthesis.

How Plants Live

The smallest living part of a plant is the cell. Leaf, stem, root and flower are all built up from collections of cells. A cell consists of an outer wall forming a capsule and its contents called protoplasm. No particular part of the protoplasm can be thought of as more alive than any other. If the parts are separated or removed from the cell they die as does the rest of the deprived cell. How the various parts of the protoplasm come together to make a living thing is the mystery of life itself.

The cells of all green plants contain chloroplasts, usually minute, disc-shaped bodies. These contain pigments, mostly green chlorophyll with others coloured orange-yellow or yellow. The two last pigments cause the yellow colour of those parts of a variegated leaf unable to make chlorophyll. Some seaweeds contain other pigments of yellowish-brown, deep brown, pink, red or purple. In this case the chloroplasts are called chromoplasts. The essential ingredient in all of them is the chlorophyll, which absorbs the red, orange and blue rays of sunlight and turns their light energy into chemical energy. This energy is used to convert the water and carbon dioxide within the cell into sugar and oxygen. The process is called photosynthesis.

Chloroplasts

The electron microscope shows the chloroplasts to be complicated structures. They resemble microscopic accumulators filled with the molecules of chlorophyll which are themselves made up of atoms of carbon, hydrogen, oxygen and nitrogen on one atom of magnesium.

The sugar provided by photosynthesis is needed to grow more protoplasm. Sugar is made up of carbon, hydrogen and oxygen. Protoplasm contains many more elements, principally nitrogen, phosphorus, sulphur, calcium, magnesium, potassium and iron. Traces of chlorine, iodine, boron, cobalt and manganese are also present. All these elements are contained in the salts of the water which occupies the spaces in the cells called vacuoles. They are combined with sugar to build up into the large molecules called proteins. The proteins are then built into the other two parts of the protoplasm, the cytoplasm and the nucleus. The nucleus is the 'brain' of the protoplasm, directing and controlling all these operations according to an inherited 'memory' stored in its D.N.A. molecules. So do the total contents of a cell form the living organism.

Photosynthesis is thus the beginning of the manufacture of protein which is the essential food of all living matter, plant or animal. Since the cells of animals cannot photosynthesise or produce their own protein, they must absorb it by feeding on plants or other animals. As the primary source of protein, plants are the beginning of life.

Cell Activity

By absorbing carbon dioxide and expelling excess oxygen during photosynthesis, a plant cell can be said to be breathing. During daylight, carbon dioxide is consumed and oxygen expelled. The weaker the light, the less sugar and oxygen are formed. At night, photosynthesis stops. Then the cell gives out carbon dioxide and consumes oxygen just as an animal cell does. The oxygen is used to burn up some of the excess sugar made by photosynthesis during the day. This releases energy which is used to shift chemicals about for further growth.

So the life of a plant cell can be divided into five activities. These are photosynthesis, breathing or respiration, the making of protein, taking in water and letting out excess products.

Cross-section of the flower of a plant, containing the reproductive organs:
1 anther, 2 stigma, 3 style, 4 pollen tube, 5 ovary, 6 pistil, 7 ovules, 8 filament, 9 sepal, 10 petal

The first three build up the protoplasm of the cell and the last two break down the protoplasm. If a cell is to grow, the building up process must exceed the breaking down. This building up takes place during the day, since photosynthesis requires sunlight. The plant cell survives during the night by the excess of photosynthesis during daylight.

Another activity going on within a plant cell is the building of cell walls. These are made of minute threads of cellulose criss-crossing each other in layers. Cellulose is made up of sugar molecules strung together by the removal of the molecules of water. As the protoplasm grows, the cell expands and more cellulose fibres are fitted into the wall to extend it. In time, the cell wall becomes too thick to expand any more. Then the cell divides by making new walls between the divided halves of the nucleus. In the case of some plant plankton in the sea, the cell bursts and the protoplasm escapes to begin building new walls. In this case, the old cell walls form a dead shell that is left behind.

The Nucleus

The nucleus, or 'brain', of the plant-cell contains the hereditary material that controls all the activities of the protoplasm. It does this by means of enzymes which are complicated proteins that cause particular chemical reactions, building up or breaking down other proteins, sugar, oil, cellulose and vitamins within the protoplasm. Under the direction of the nucleus, enzymes enter the cytoplasm or return to the nucleus to do their work. The nucleus is separated from the cytoplasm by a very thin membrane which is the means of communication between the ruling body and its subjects, with the enzymes acting as messengers. This makes the membrane one of the most remarkable creations in nature. The nucleus is the first part of a plant cell to divide. First it loses its fine membrane. Then new membranes are formed around the two new nuclei. Another membrane forms across the cytoplasm between the two new nuclei and cell walls begin to build on either side of it. Thus two new cells are formed, each containing within its nucleus the pattern of future growth inherited from the parent nucleus.

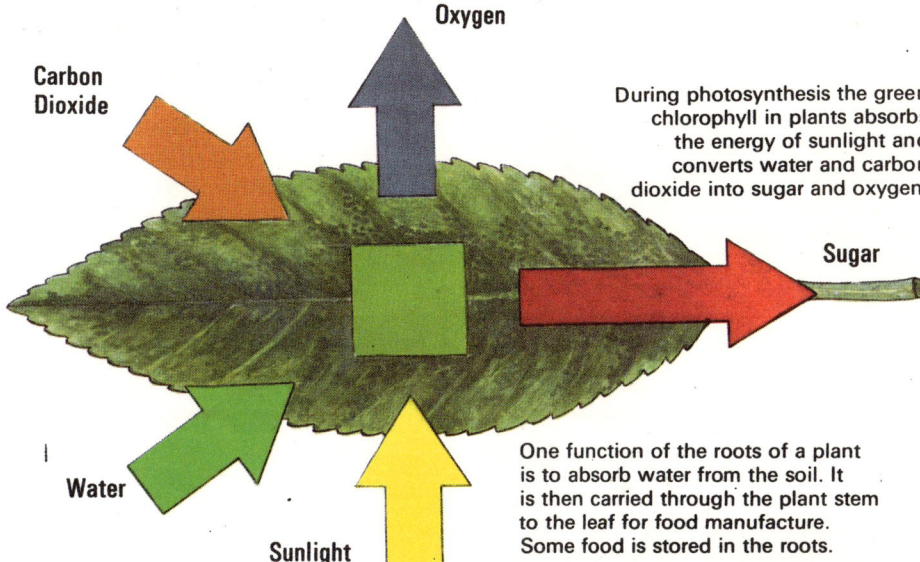

During photosynthesis the green chlorophyll in plants absorbs the energy of sunlight and converts water and carbon dioxide into sugar and oxygen.

One function of the roots of a plant is to absorb water from the soil. It is then carried through the plant stem to the leaf for food manufacture. Some food is stored in the roots.

Examples of seed and spore dispersal: 1 lime sail, 2 mock apple (squirting), 3 cranesbill, 4 dandelion and 5 'old man's beard' (parachute), 6 sycamore (wings), 7 goosegrass (sticking), 8 inkcap (spore drop), 9 poppy (shaking), 10 goatgrass, 11 sporangium, 12 bulrush.

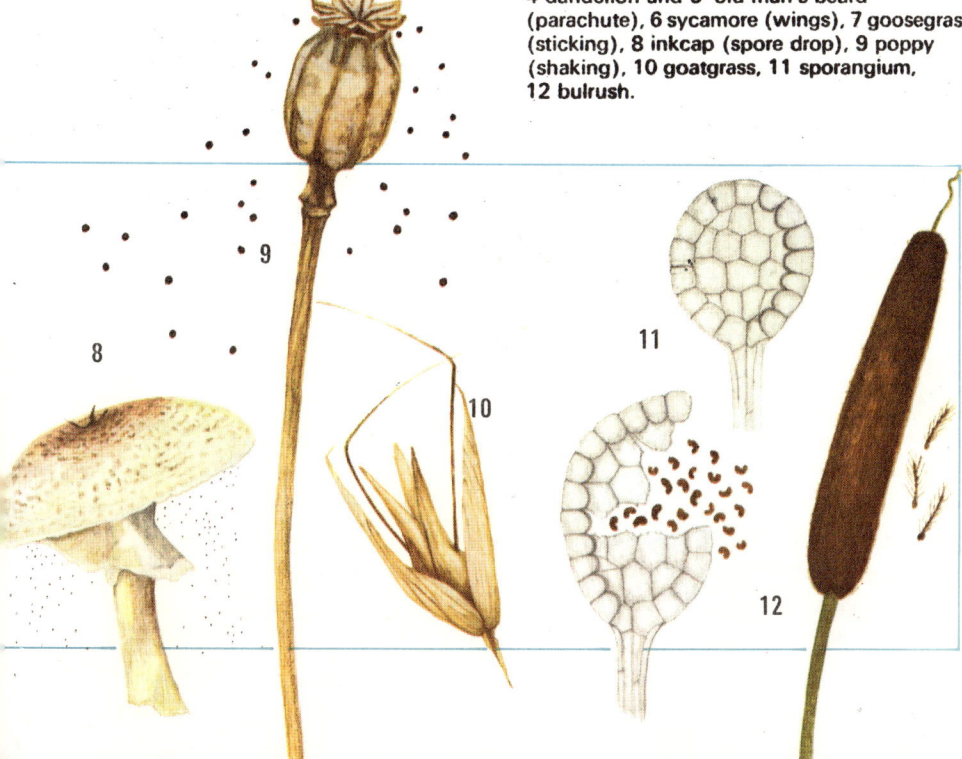

Cell Division

Cell division seems generally to happen at night. Though some flowers close their petals when it is dark, a plant cannot be said to sleep in the way an animal does. After the photosynthetic work of the day, a plant works internally at night when most of its growth may be produced. Cell division is the means by which a plant increases its size. It is the basis of vegetative reproduction.

Sexual reproduction requires external contact between one part of a plant and another, or between separate plants. The gametes, or reproductive cells, of seaweeds, mosses and ferns usually have water as a means of communication. The male gametes use their flagella to swim in search of the female. In seed plants, the male pollen is carried to the female egg by means of the wind or with the help of animals, just as the spores of the lower plants are carried off to find suitable resting places to grow into new plants.

The movement of spores, however, happens by chance and is wasteful, whereas the pollination of flowering plants has achieved varying degrees of specialisation. Flowers have developed colour, shape, scent and the lure of sugary nectar to attract particular creatures to them and, incidentally, to spread the pollen from one flower to another.

Similarly, seed plants have developed various methods of dispersing their seeds in search of fertile ground where they can flourish. If plants are to spread throughout the available soil and to find places where the sunlight is not already hidden by the leaves of other plants, then they must often travel quite long distances. Like spores, they may be carried by the wind. Spores are light and tiny. Seeds containing the embryo plant and its food supply are necessarily larger and heavier. Those that have adapted most successfully to wind dispersal have developed wings or parachutes to catch the wind and bear them up.

Water is still a means of dispersal even among seed plants. The seeds of the alder tree growing by a stream fall into the water and are carried off by the current. A palm tree growing on a sandy shore drops its coconuts into the sea to be carried away by the tide, even to another land mass.

Dispersal by Animals

Spores may lodge in the fur or feathers of an animal to be shaken or washed off later and in some distant location. It is the seed, however, that has found ways to exploit animals for its dispersal. The association between plants and animals has been an important aspect in the development of flowering plants, both through pollination and seed dispersal. It is the association that has developed the great variety of fruiting plants. The tasty outer covering of the fruit attracts the animal to pick and eat it. The seed inside is protected by a firm coating that can pass undamaged through the animal, or is contained in a woody shell forming the nut or stone of the fruit which is discarded by the animal. Of course, some seeds are eaten and digested by the animal, but enough are knocked down or removed and mislaid by his activities to ensure the survival and spread of the plant species..

This association of plant and animal has led even to the carnivorous plant which eats insects. The spores of some fungi are capable of sending their hyphae into the body of an insect until they fill out and mummify the whole body. Others set up growths within the stomachs of larger animals. There is even a yeast that grows in the dead and dying outer skin cells of humans. Among flowering plants, the butterwort has sticky hairs on its leaves that attract insects. When an insect becomes attached to the sticky fluid, an irritation is set up in the leaf which slowly folds around its victim, releasing acids to dissolve

All green plants are capable of manufacturing their own food by photosynthesis, including the carnivorous plants which 'eat' insects. These plants gain some nourishment by absorbing the proteins of animal life. Shown here are the pitcher plant (above) and the butterwort (below).

The English chemist and clergyman, Joseph Priestley, was once described as a man who had the art of making important discoveries by following the wrong theories. He was born near Leeds in 1733. Priestley was a nonconformist minister with an intense interest in science. A lasting friendship with the American statesman and scientist Benjamin Franklin led to his experiments in electricity. Then he turned to chemistry and discovered several gases, the most notable being oxygen. Priestley called it dephlogisticated air. It was the French chemist Antoine Lavoisier who later gave it the name of oxygen. Priestley was a careless and unmethodical worker, with flashes of brilliance which inspired other men to follow up and complete his experiments. His political views were in advance of his time and found little support. His sympathies with the French revolutionary movement won him many enemies. In 1795 he left England and settled in America.

and digest it. The Venus's fly-trap has a sensitive trigger mechanism within its leaf which snaps it shut like a man-trap. Members of the large family of tropical pitcher plants all have alternate leaves formed into jug-like containers which hold a sugary fluid to attract the insect and other juices to digest it.

Colour and Shape

The nucleus of a plant cell determines through the inherited arrangement of its DNA molecules what job that cell is destined to do—whether it will form part of the leaf, flower, stem or root. According to its predetermined instructions, the cell will form a wall suited to its place in the plant. It is the cell walls that determine the overall shape of the plant. In their minute construction, they will build the characteristic shape of the leaf, the curl of the petal, the spread of the branches. Some will die and become filled with the deposits of lignin that form the woody fabric of the giant tree. It is lignin that provides the gritty texture of the pear and the hard seed-case of a nutty fruit.

By a process of selection and adaptation, each species has found a shape and structure to secure its survival. The arrangement of leaves in each species has been arrived at during its evolution to capture the maximum of sunlight. The extent of its growth depends on its success in photosynthesis. The great tree spreads its massive head of leaves to the sun. Enough of the sun's rays pierce through to alight on the leaves of the more modest plant below with its lesser growth.

The bird of paradise flower grows in South Africa. Its orange and blue flowers look like the feathers of a brightly coloured bird.

The enormous variety of colour and shape in flowers has been achieved over a long period to suit the particular pollination needs of each plant. The hibiscus (above) and a species of *Aristolochia* are examples.

Pollination

The colour and shape of each flower has been arrived at to suit the particular animal that aids in its pollination. Once attracted by the bright colour and perfume of a flower, an insect must penetrate deeply to reach the nectar, thus covering its body with pollen or depositing pollen from another flower. Some flowers gently hold the insect so that it must shake itself free and, in doing so, dislodge the pollen. There are tiny flowers to exploit the tiny insects, large flowers to attract larger insects and birds. There are some flowers, such as orchids, that provide a landing stage or front doorstep to welcome in the pollinating agent. There are hanging flowers that attract the hanging bat to their sugary secretion. There are flowers that provide certain beetles with sleeping or mating chambers. There are underwater plants whose flowers form tall trumpets opening out on the upper air, inviting beetles into a warm, safe bedroom and a dusting of pollen. The flower lures and uses the animal, then abandons it by fading and withering once its pollination has been effected.

Lastly, the shape of a plant depends upon its situation. Its roots spread towards its water source and through the soil particles of least resistance. Its stem or trunk bends to the prevailing wind. The leaves turn towards the source of light. Its roots and stems are controlled by growth substances which affect the rate at which cells lengthen. Very little growth is made in strong sunlight. A stem grows less on its sunny side so that it bends towards the light. The growth substances drain down to the lower side of a stem which thus grows more and turns the stem upwards. In roots, there is an opposite effect. In the lower side, growth slows down so that the upper side grows more and the root is bent downwards. Such growth movements, or tropisms, cause the tendril or stem of a climbing plant to coil round its support, the leaf of such plants as mimosa to droop when touched and the corolla of some plants to close at night or according to a predetermined rhythm.

Plant Ecology

This is the branch of study concerned with plants and their environment. Seven-tenths of the earth's surface is covered by the oceans. Since they are daily exposed to most of the light energy that reaches us from the sun, it is not surprising that photosynthetic life began here. The great mass of plant plankton has continued in the sea virtually unchanged for millions of years. In the shallower water, close to the shores, the seaweeds have developed, each species in its particular habitat and water-depth.

Land Masses

The land masses have created the land plants according to temperature and rainfall. Around the equator is a belt of tropical rain forest. Here there is warmth and rain all the year round. Growth is not affected by seasonal changes. Most of the trees are evergreen. They spread such a canopy of leaves to the sunlight that the forest floor is in almost perpetual darkness where no photosynthetic plant can grow. This is the home of the epiphyte, the plant that grows on another taller plant to share its sunlight. Many tropical orchids are epiphytes. Tropical epiphytes often have trailing roots that never reach the ground but gather their moisture from the humid atmosphere. The common epiphytes of the temperate regions are the lichens, mosses and ferns that grow on trees. An epiphyte gets none of its nourishment from the host plant, but only from the air and water around it. In this respect it differs from the parasite that drains nourishment from its host to the detriment of that plant.

To the north and south of the rain forest belt are areas of high temperature and low rainfall. Here very few trees grow. It is mostly grassland called savannah and, in the driest areas of all, desert. A few plants have adapted to life even in the desert. These are the xerophytes such as succulents and cacti. Desert plants plunge their roots deep into the ground in search of water or spread them widely to capture as much water as possible when it does rain. They have found new ways to retain the water. They usually have small leaves to cut down on evaporation. Many of the leaves are waxed or rolled as a further protection. Cacti have no real leaves at all. They photosynthesise through their green stems and store water in their spongy tissues. Even after being uprooted, some cacti can continue growth for several years.

In the temperate zones, where temperature varies from summer heat to winter cold, the deciduous forest is to be found. Trees and plants here shed their leaves in winter. Except in the roots, all growth stops for a time until the warmer weather of spring starts the buds bursting. Here sunlight can reach the forest floor before the leafy canopy is restored, so early flowering plants can flourish. The falling leaves provide a carpet of dying vegetation on which the saprophytes can feed. Saprophytes are such plants as bacteria and fungi which feed on and break down the rotting vegetation. They provide a humus, a soil rich in nitrates in which many small flowering plants can grow. It is difficult to walk through a deciduous forest because of the lush undergrowth.

Water Supply

By capturing the available supply of water with their extensive roots and by spreading out their canopies of leaves in summertime, the deciduous trees have pushed the conifer forest into the colder northern climates and into the more mountainous regions of the world. The conifers came first and then the flowering trees took over. Conifers are more primitive trees and have suffered from the success of the flowering trees. Most conifers are evergreen and capture much of the

The falling leaves of autumn provide a rich golden carpet of vegetation which rots down to form a valuable plant food.

The fruit of the baobab tree (far left) is sometimes used as a flavouring for cool drinks. The traveller's tree (left) has leaf stalks which contain a drinkable water-like liquid.

rain and sunlight. Very few plants can grow around them. The conifer forest is dark with a thick carpet of small leaves and dead needles on a dry floor where their decomposition is slow.

Lastly, there is the tundra of the far north. Here the summer days are long, but the summer is short-lived. The winter days are short and the ground in winter is often frozen. Plants reach the limits of their endurance here. What does grow can achieve only modest size. Even the tree species tend to adopt a creeping habit to protect themselves from the wind. As with the tundra, so with the mountainside just below the permanent snow line, the so-called alpine regions. Here again the plants are small and sparse. Mosses and liverworts like the tundra or highland bogs.

The height to which plants grow is greater in tropical climates than in polar areas. Seen below are typical plants ranging from reindeer moss of the polar zones (far left) to conifers of temperate areas and palms of tropical countries.

Tumbleweed (left) is a plant which in dry weather may detach itself from the ground and be blown by the wind to scatter its seeds over a wide area. A cactus plant (right) often has colourful flowers.

Thus can the world be divided into its five belts of tropical rain forest, savannah or desert, deciduous forest, conifer forest, and tundra. Within these belts some blending is possible. There are conifers in the tropical rain forests, for instance. Also the geological circumstances vary the communities of plants inhabiting a particular area within one of the belts. Beech trees like shallow, chalky soil and are found often over downs and hillsides. Oak trees prefer low-lying, heavy clay soils. Oaks are not as greedy for sunlight as beeches. They permit the associated growth of the evergreen holly, and many flowers such as bluebells grow in oak woods. The ash likes the same chalky soil as the beech but does not cast such dense shade. Shrubs and flowers grow thickly in ash woods.

Marram Grass

Wherever the sea recedes, providing a new area of land, plants seize their opportunity. The sea throws up a sand dune which is eventually left above high tide. First the sand couch grass binds the dune together with its rhizomes and roots, then the

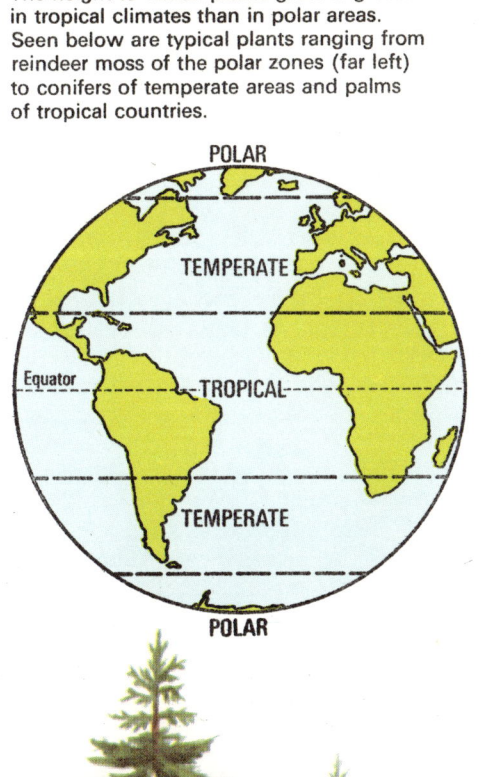

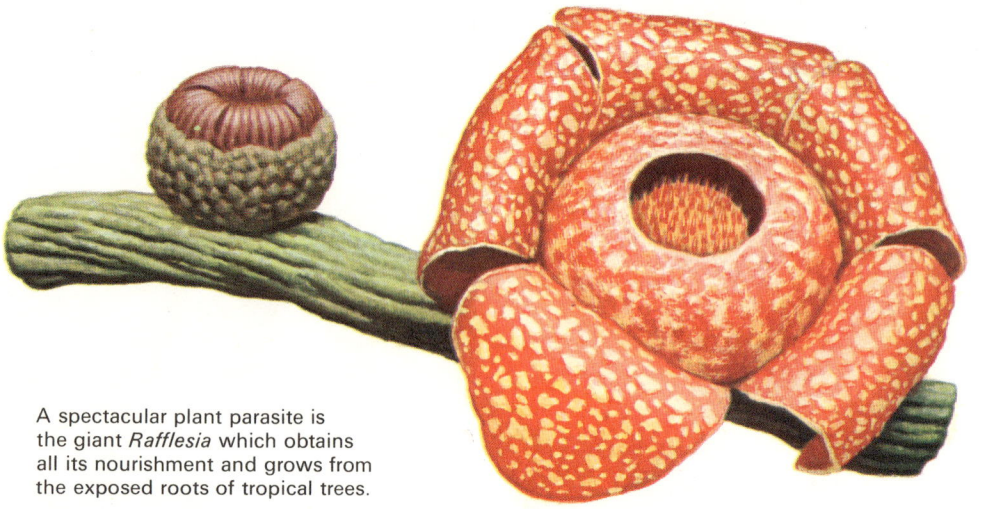

A spectacular plant parasite is the giant *Rafflesia* which obtains all its nourishment and grows from the exposed roots of tropical trees.

marram grass arrives. Marram grass can roll up its leaves with all the stomata inside. Thus it avoids water loss and can survive dry periods, unrolling its leaves again when it rains. Marram pushes its roots deep into the sand in search of water, incidentally helping to hold the growing dune together. More sand is deposited around the marram which continually throws up new shoots to keep its head in the air. The dying parts of vegetation add humus to the sand, darkening it. The humus holds water, making it possible for mosses, liverworts and lichens to grow in it. Then come such plants as the sea holly and wild carrot.

There are many plants called halophytes adapted to life in soils containing a lot of salt, such as sand-dunes and salt-marshes. They have many of the xerophyte characteristics such as a thick, waxy cuticle that prevents water loss. Gradually, as plants live out their span and deposit more humus, soil builds up on the sand-dunes until the ridges can support the forest growth of oak, birch or beech. Such coastal forest is widespread in Holland, a country which was once smaller than now and still would be except for the marram grass holding up the dunes as a defence against the sea.

Influence of Animals

Animals have had considerable influence on the life and environment of plants. The success of flowering plants, and certainly their variety, could not have come about without the unconscious participation of animals in the work of pollination and seed dispersal. Of course, animals do damage to plants, but plants seem to have been well able to take care of themselves. For instance, the leaves of the holly tree are prickly up to the height which a grazing animal can reach. Above that, their edges are smoother. It seems that, in this case, the tree could 'out-think' the animal.

One animal, however, has done permanent harm to areas of the world where plants once flourished. That animal is man. One tenth of the land surfaces of the world is at present under cultivation. Some areas, like Europe, have been continuously cultivated for centuries with a due regard for the soil that has kept it fertile. Earlier civilisations took more from the land than it could give without deteriorating. The result was erosion and the creation of the desert.

Erosion

There are three main kinds of erosion. Over-cultivation makes the soil lose its ability to absorb water and hold together. Rainwater that previously soaked in runs off a sloping surface carrying soil with it. This is called sheet erosion. The area from which the topsoil has been run off becomes incapable of sustaining anything more than the most scrubby growth. Robbed of the humus provided by growing and dying plants, the soil returns to a sandy consistency at the mercy of the wind. Gully erosion occurs when too many trees are felled and storm water runs downhill, cutting channels which widen and deepen with every downpour. Thirdly, soil that has lost its fertility becomes pulverised and powdery in times of drought. Then the wind can lift it and carry it for great distances in enormous dust clouds. The land left behind again becomes useless, and even previously beneficial irrigation channels become choked.

Fortunately, man is now attempting to put right the mistakes of the past. Forestry, reclaiming of desert land, great dam and irrigation schemes, the use of chemical fertilisers and, above all, a clearer understanding of plants and their needs are having their effect. The deserts are in retreat, the trees are on the march again and the encroaching ocean tide is being beaten back.

Dodder is a destructive weed which twines itself around another plant and feeds on it through little suckers. When it is secure its original root dies away.

Ancient Egyptian wall painting from a tomb, depicting corn reaping; and a figurine (right) kneeding dough.

Man and Plants

Man may be the most adaptable of all the animals on earth, but his adaptability cannot compare with the way in which plants will change to survive in a world controlled by men. When anyone who lives in a modern industrialised country comes face to face with a land plant, he can be almost certain that it is not entirely as nature would have it, but what man has made it. Only the plants in the oceans have lived and developed throughout time more or less untroubled by the ambitions of mankind.

When you look at a field of waving corn, it is not the original wild corn from the upland slopes of Asia Minor. It is a new species developed by selection and cross-fertilisation to produce a bigger grain for the feeding of men and their domestic animals. Even the grass of meadow and pasture is not the wild scrub of the tundra. It has grown from selected seed, cleaned of the interloping weed and the fungal pest.

The potted plant so carefully watered and tended, even the flowers in parks and gardens, are not wild species. They are hybrids of hybrids, fed with nitrate and phosphate to bring forth the size and colour of bloom that men have decided should be their aim in life. The fruits and vegetables on your table would not have existed had men not altered the course of their development. Even the wild fruit trees and the wild vegetable plants growing in the countryside are discarded stages in that development.

Wild Plants

Many of the wayside wild flowers found themselves where they are because men brought the first seeds to the area, and some of their descendants escaped and flourished where they fell. The wild parsley, the wild garlic and the wild mustard all have relations producing their spices and flavours for the modern cook. The wild vine once produced its fruit to fill the wine bottles of a vanished society. The wild flax once gave seed oil to fill the lamps of long ago: its cousin still provides fine linen for your home. The foxglove and the deadly nightshade have cured men's ills, the madder and the now wild woad have dyed his raiment.

Even the mighty trees of the forest can live only where man permits them. They may stand proudly erect only as long as man finds them useful for his own devices. The history of their coming and going is told now only in the microscopic pollen grains buried deep in the layers of peat where once the wild, free forest grew.

There is no part of any civilised countryside where the plants have not felt the influence of man. In the past, he may have used them with scant respect. That they have survived in such profusion reflects less credit on him than on their own cunning. Perhaps plants cannot think, but plants have the knowledge to survive.

The breadfruit is one of the most important foods of islanders in the south Pacific. The drawing above is based on one made by the botanist Joseph Banks, one of the scientists who accompanied Cook on his expedition to Australia and New Zealand. At Cook's suggestion the breadfruit was introduced to the West Indies where it was fed to slave workers. Other plants, as well as the breadfruit, have been transported from one part of the world to another, as the map on the left illustrates. Examples are the potato, which travelled from the New World to the Old World and back again; coffee, which spread from Africa to Asia and the New World; and rubber, which was taken from Brazil to Malaya by British traders in the nineteenth century.

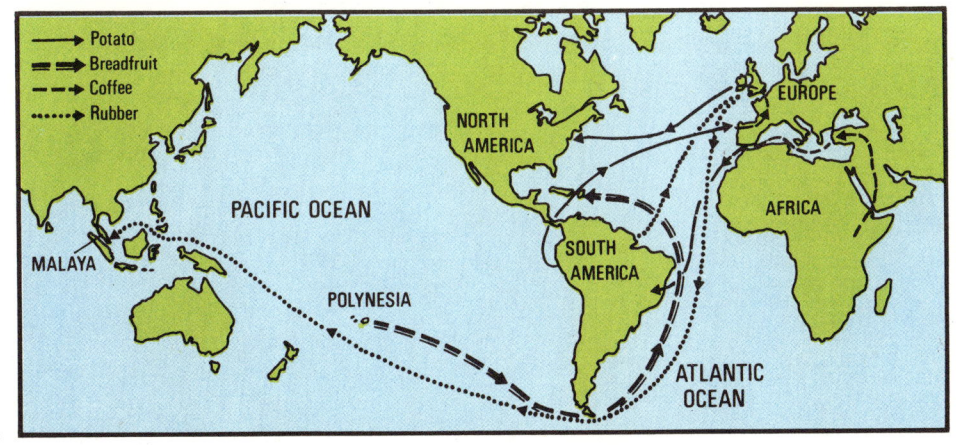

43

Food Crops

The great variety of plants that make up the family of grasses has been of prime importance to the development of man. Grass made possible the growth of civilisation. Without an understanding of grass plants, man may never have learned how to dominate the living world.

Many animals depend upon the great grasslands of the world for their food. Early man was quick to learn the importance of grass to the herds of animals he hunted. Copying the animals he probably tasted the grass and discovered the value in the seeds which he chewed. Early forms of wheat and barley growing wild in the grassy uplands of the Middle East were found to be especially nutritious.

Early and middle Stone Age men knew the importance of a settled base for their tribal operations. They needed caves or stone-roofed pits for shelter in the winter. They needed to mine flintstones for the manufacture of their weapons. But, as hunters, they had to follow the migrations of the animals that provided them with food throughout the year. Only those who lived by fishing or amid such lush tropical vegetation that their food of meat and fruit was always about them, managed to settle in one place.

People always on the move, hunting and gathering food and seed-grain as they go, must travel light. They cannot make decorative things for mere pleasure. They cannot improve their standard of living by building permanent homes. They can never become civilised.

The grasses could be used to alter the wandering way of life and by the late Stone Age, at least ten thousand years ago, man had discovered how.

The First Farmers

The first farmers gave up hunting to collect wild cattle, sheep and goats, and to herd them from pasture to pasture. Their life was still a wandering one, but at least by keeping their animals with them they were more in control of their wanderings. This new life taught them to examine the grasslands more closely.

They would have learned to collect and carry handfuls of grain with them on their herding trips. Perhaps some of the seeds from the most nutritious of the grain they gathered fell to the ground where they sheltered in bad weather. It would sprout and thus food appeared magically on their own doorstep. From this it was but a step to the planting, watering and tending of crops in one settled community. Before long pits would have been dug for the storing of grain during the winter and the selection of the best seeds for planting in the spring.

This may have been the way in which wheat, barley, millet, rice and maize were 'invented' as food crops by early man. Seed selection over thousands of years have provided the species we know today. Carbonised grains and clay impressions of the spikelets of early cultivated species

Cereals are members of the grass family and the seeds are used as food. From left to right are: wheat, rye, oats, maize, rice and three millets.

Many early coins were decorated by the images of food crops, which underlines their importance. This Greek stater (c. 500 B.C.) bears a barley ear.

have been found in modern times on Stone Age sites. They tell us a lot about how these grasses have been developed through cultivation for the benefit of man.

The grains of primitive wheat, for instance, fall and scatter soon after they are ripe since the spikes are brittle and break easily. The kernels cannot be threshed easily from the chaff. These are called hulled wheats. A later development, produced by natural selection and crossing, produced the so-called 'naked' wheats where it is easier to separate chaff and kernel, and where the grain does not fall off during harvesting.

Harvesting Grain

The first planted fields of grain were little more than rough gardens. Communities still continued to hunt, to

herd domestic animals or to fish. The grain harvest was put by as a store of winter food for men and animals at a time when the preserving of meat was unknown. Planting and harvesting held a community to one locality. It gave man the leisure to become the greatest of thinking animals, to pursue the arts of civilisation and to create the man-dominated world of today.

This development of the cereal grasses, as they are called, enabled the civilisations of ancient Egypt and the Middle East to begin. They were based on wheat and barley; whereas the Far Eastern civilisations of India, China and Malaysia were based on rice; and the civilisations of Central America and Peru on maize. Maize, or Indian corn, is unique among the cereals in that the male tassels of the plant are so far from the female ears that it cannot reproduce itself without human aid. The true wild ancestor of this purely cultivated species is not known for certain. Modern maize, along with many foods we take for granted today, was 'invented' by people clever enough to cultivate grasses and build elaborate cities but who had not yet developed the wheel. For them cultivation and building were of prime importance.

One other grass crop that began to be cultivated in the late Stone Age should be mentioned. This is *Sorghum*, the ancestor of modern sugar canes. It grew wild and was cultivated in tropical Africa, south of the Sahara. Some forms were introduced into southern Arabia and thence to India. It does not appear to have reached the Mediterranean until more recent, historic times. The growing of sugar cane and, indeed, the general use of refined sugar throughout the world has been only during the last three or four centuries.

Over Cultivation

It was early recognised that the growing of crops could quickly exhaust the soil of the food chemicals the plants needed. The annual flooding of the river Nile brought new richness to the land along its banks from silts carried downstream. Irrigation systems aided the spread of this fertilising flood. In other, less fortunate places, over-cultivation produced dust bowls from which the topsoil was blown away.

In medieval Europe, the three-field village system of agriculture was developed. The people lived in cottages clustered in the centre of an area partly composed of pasture for their animals. The remainder was divided into three fields, one growing grain, another growing peas, beans or grain, and the third lying fallow, or resting, and being prepared for a crop in its turn. Each year, the crop in the fields was changed, and each year a different field lay fallow.

The intricate patterns made on the natural landscape by man's cultivation of plants are seen in sugar cane fields (left), rice paddies (centre) and wheatfields.

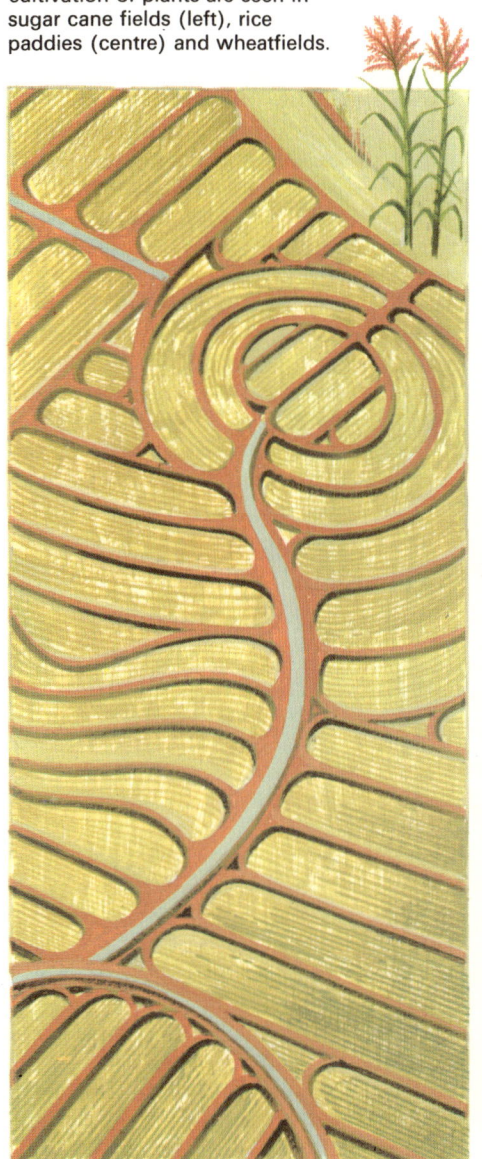

Medieval ploughing as illustrated in the Luttrell Psalter, a fourteenth-century English manuscript.

This method of agriculture was wasteful of land. By the seventeenth century, the inclusion of potatoes, red clover and turnips provided a better rotation of crops, one crop succeeding another and each replenishing the soil for the next. Important in these developments were two men both born in 1674. Jethro Tull invented the first practical seed drill which made sowing in rows possible. Hoeing between the rows kept the crop free from weeds and the soil aerated. Charles, second Viscount Townshend, introduced the four-crop rotation system and the use of turnips as winter feed for cattle.

The three-field system, whereby one field lay fallow each year, tended to be wasteful. The introduction of a better rotation of root crops enabled farmers to use their land more effectively.

Clean Seed

In the nineteenth century, the importance of 'clean' seed free of weeds, parasitic fungi and bacteria, was recognised first in Denmark. The great improvement in microscopes encouraged a study of bacteriology, especially in the work of Louis Pasteur. New machines were invented for ploughing, harrowing, hoeing, sowing, reaping and binding the sheaves of corn, some powered by animals, others using the new steam engines. Concentrated cattle foods were developed, the first of these, linseed cake, as early as 1795.

Nowadays, farming has become a science. The laboratory technician has become as important as the farm worker, and governments have taken a hand in research. Different mixtures of grass seeds are used according to whether permanent or temporary grassland is required. If permanent then the seed is chosen either for pasture, which is grazed by animals but not mown, or meadow, which is mown for hay every year or at less frequent intervals.

Artificial as well as natural fertilisers are used for higher yields of grain. Pesticides are sprayed on the crops to prevent the spread of damage from insects, fungi and parasitic bacteria. New species of cereal crops have been developed and seeds made more resistant to disease.

Agricultural Machinery

The engineer, too, has put his knowledge and inventions at the service of the farmer. Huge machines clear the land. Great dams are built to irrigate it. Combine harvesters reap and thresh the corn and bale the straw in one operation. Only for rice and sugar cane, in some parts of the world, are armies of workers still employed to plant and reap them.

To provide the ever increasing populations of the world with bread, beer and breakfast cereals, whole landscapes have been changed, even to the extent of influencing climate. Deserts have been made to bloom again. Experiments have succeeded in doing what the courtiers of King Canute failed to do by holding back the ravages of tidal waters. In this age, when land is becoming more precious, ways have been found to bind the shifting sand dunes with living grass and to turn the salt marsh into pasture for cattle to graze.

The bamboo furniture of China and the fine turf of an English lawn may be thousands of miles apart and seem to have little in common. Yet both are products of high civilisations, and both are made from members of the great family of grasses.

In 1849 a steam plough was patented in England by James Usher. The power produced by the engine was transmitted by a system of gears to the plough shares which helped to push the machine along.

Formal gardens were very popular in France and Italy in the eighteenth century.

Gardens for Pleasure

When the early wandering tribes first settled in one place, they grew hedges around their homes and their herds to protect them from wild beasts. Within the hedges, they planted fruit trees and vegetables. These were the first gardens.

From earliest times, man was not content with something that was useful. He decorated his body, his clothing and his home. A painting in a tomb of ancient Thebes shows cornflowers, poppies and papyrus plants adding colour to the banks of a canal. Among the Seven Wonders of the ancient world were the Hanging Gardens of Babylon. They were described as terraces built one above the other and supported by great stone arches. They covered an area 122 metres (400 feet) square rising from the river in the north of the city. Legend says that they were built for Queen Nitocris, wife of Nebuchadnezzar II, in the sixth century B.C. because she wearied of the flat plains of Babylon and longed for her native hills of Media.

Before that, Tiglathpileser, King of the Assyrians who lived about 1100 B.C., was bringing trees from foreign lands to decorate his parks and gardens. The Greeks were the first to grow decorative and useful plants in pots. The Romans spread their love of gardens throughout their Empire. Both Greeks and Romans introduced statues and fountains into their garden designs.

In medieval Britain, such purely decorative flowers as roses and lilies were considered heathenish. The ladies tended herb gardens and were skilled in the making of healing potions from them. An early garden was called *Ortus sanitatis*, the place of health. Later, flowers were planted among the grass, trees were clipped and arbours constructed where meals might be taken out of doors.

Formal Gardens

During the Renaissance, formal gardens laid out in strict geometrical patterns became commonplace. In the Age of Discovery botanists brought back exotic blooms from their voyages. In seventeenth-century France, André le Nôtre was employed by Louis XIV to design the gardens of Chantilly, St Cloud, the Trianon, St Germain and Versailles. He came to Britain and laid out the gardens in St James's Park, Kensington Gardens and Greenwich Park around the growing city of London. In Rome, he designed gardens in the Quirinal and the Vatican.

The British reacted against the formal gardens of France and Italy. Their particular contribution to the gardening art has been in landscaping. The architect, William Kent (1685–1748), considered the whole of the environment in his designs for great houses, including interior decoration and the laying out of gardens and parkland. He can be said to be the father of landscape gardening in which a natural appearance was aimed at. Prospects of rolling lawns led to groves of trees with summerhouses or even fake ruins nestling among them. Sometimes a church steeple without a church may have been included purely to enhance the view.

Kent was, for a time, in partnership with the famous 'Capability' Brown who began his working life as a gardener and later became an architect. Brown brought landscape gardening to its most beautiful. His clients were men who had grown rich in trade and were so full of self-confidence they imagined the world they were creating would go on for ever. They built family mansions and laid out parkland that would not reach its full beauty until they and its designers had long passed away.

Men like Kent and Brown were creating a countryside for future generations to enjoy. Theirs is the legacy of city parks and country estates open for the enjoyment and

recreation of people in the noisy bustle of today. The modern suburban garden with its lawns and herbaceous borders, its fishponds with water plants and rock gardens filled with alpine plants, is in miniature the descendant of the work of the eighteenth-century landscape gardeners.

Garden Plants

What is a garden plant? It can be any plant that is grown in a garden for use or pleasure. A weed may be defined as any plant that has arrived self-sown and uninvited into the garden and spoils the planned arrangement. What may grow as a weed in one place may be a carefully nurtured and highly regarded garden plant in another.

The California poppy is a popular garden plant in Britain. In California, its native home, it is a common weed. Golden rod grows wild in Canada but is much cultivated in gardens in Europe. Where a wild flower is imported from abroad for cultivation in another country, the expert horticulturists usually get to work on it, improving the size and colour of its blooms.

One of the methods of making these improvements is by cross-pollination. The pollen grains formed in the stamens of one plant are transferred to the stigma of another, usually closely related species. The seeds produced by such crossing of species grow into a new plant called a hybrid, which will have some of the characteristics of both parent plants, but may look very different from either.

Most garden roses, for instance, have been developed by hybridisation. Many early types were a dull red or pink until wild yellow roses were introduced from Persia. From cross-pollination over many generations, a wide variety of colours has been introduced. By now, the most sought after rose species are probably hybrids of hybrids. Roses with different habits have also been created. There are climbing briar roses, standard roses like miniature trees, and bush roses growing many blooms on a single stem called floribundas.

Growing New Plants

Selection from wild plants has created many of our finest garden blooms. Species of particular colour and vigorous growth are planted in ideal

A formal garden in the Japanese style, which is cool and elegant.

These border flowers are 1 wistaria, 2 lonicera, 3 fuchsia, 4 clematis, 5 hosta, 6 filipendula, 7 hemerocallis, 8 gypsophila, 9 lupinus, 10 erigeron, 11 gaillardia, 12 armeria, 13 kniphofia, 14 lavendula.

conditions to increase size and number of blooms. For this, the root of the wild plant might be divided, or a cutting taken from it. A cutting is a suitable young shoot cut from the parent plant and planted separately where it will grow its own roots and become an individual plant. Special growing compounds are often used for this, and the cutting dusted with hormone powder to promote the growth of strong roots.

Grafting can also be used to grow one plant from the rootstock of another. A leaf bud, with some of the bark or outer skin of the stem it was growing from, is tied to a scar cut in a branch of the foster-plant. The bud retains most of its original characteristics but may become larger or more vigorous in growth from the feeding provided by its foster-parent's rootstock. The whole character of a plant may be changed by grafting. Even apples and pears may grow together from the same tree.

Garden plants are divided into groups according to their life cycles. An annual is a plant that lives through its whole existence in one year. A seed is planted. Stem and leaves grow from it. Flowers bloom, seeds fall and the plant dies. Next year's plants must be grown from the seeds produced in the previous year.

A biennial has a life of two years. The seeds grow into the leafy plant during the first year. The plant then winters, to flower and seed again for the first time during the second year of its life.

Perennial Plants

Perennials are plants that go on year after year. They grow to flowering size in one or more years, then die down. They lose their leaves and sometimes their stalks in winter, but store food for the next year's growth in the crown at the top of their roots. Bulbs, shrubs and trees are all perennial, storing energy through the winter in different ways. Bulbs are really enlarged underground leaves used as food stores. After one year, they divide to produce a double plant the next year, and so on, so that 'naturalised' daffodils and crocuses, for instance, can spread in the course of years over a wide area.

Deciduous or leaf-shedding trees are perennials that lose their leaves in winter but retain their trunks and branches. Evergreens lose their older leaves, too, but are constantly replacing them so that the plant remains 'green'. Some spring-flowering shrubs grow their buds in the autumn. They remain dormant through the winter storing energy for producing their blooms the following year.

Often, when the first cold weather appears to 'kill' a plant, heat retained in the soil is warming the roots so that they continue to grow underground. Many plants, however, are killed by the first frost in temperate climates. They need to be taken indoors or into a greenhouse for protection through the winter. These are plants imported from a warmer land and not adapted to cold winters.

Plants can thus also be divided into hardy, half-hardy and tender groups. Hardy plants grow almost anywhere and survive severe frosts. Tender plants need some protection such as covering with a layer of peat or straw in the coldest weather. Half-hardy plants are usually annuals which need to be sown and the seedlings developed indoors before planting outside when the danger from frost is over.

Two common garden weeds are stinging nettle and ground elder. The term weed has no exact meaning and can be applied to almost any plant which is growing where it is not wanted by the gardener.

The banana plant (left) originated in the East. The pineapple (above) is a native of South America.

Fruit and Vegetables

All flowering plants have fruits but only comparatively few of them have been cultivated as food. Nuts are woody fruits and such varieties as hazels have been a valuable winter food and are now sold principally at Christmas-time. Acorns are another example of a woody fruit. They have not usually been eaten by man, but pigs have been allowed to graze in oak forests and forage for acorns.

Juicy fruits come in three kinds. Berries are usually juicy all the way through and contain a number of seeds or pips. Redcurrants and gooseberries are particular examples.

Drupe is the name given to a fruit with a fleshy outer layer and a woody stone in the middle. The seed of the plant is inside the stone and called the kernel. Plums and cherries are drupes. Sometimes, as in walnuts and almonds, it is the kernel of the stone that is eaten. Unripe walnuts can be pickled, or the ripe nut split open and the kernel eaten.

The third kind of juicy fruit is called a pome. A pome is made largely from a swelling of the flower stalk and not just from the carpels which are the parts of the flower containing the seed eggs. For this reason, the pome is also called a false fruit. Apples and pears are pomes.

Fruit trees and shrubs have been cultivated and improved since man first began to farm. There are many examples of primitive fruit trees, abandoned or self-sown, growing wild in Europe. Their small and rather bitter-tasting fruits show how the horticulturists have improved fruit growing. In temperate countries like Britain there are orchards of apples, pears, plums and cherries. Usually these are not the only crop the farmer or nurseryman grows since the price of fruit to the grower can vary so much from year to year. A moderate crop in a bad year can often yield a better profit than a good crop in a good year, when the price is lowered by a glut. Apples, pears, plums, cherries, peaches, raspberries and strawberries all belong to the rose family, *Rosaceae*.

In Warmer Climates

Some hot countries have groves of citrus fruits like oranges, lemons, grapefruit and limes. They also grow olives for pickling and for the manufacture of oil. In more tropical areas, bananas are grown, not on trees but on large plants up to seven and a half metres (twenty-five feet) tall. These have a 'trunk' composed of bundles of leaf-stalks from the top of which emerge oblong or elliptical leaves. From the centre of these comes a long spike of flowers from which grow the bundles of fruit which are seedless berries.

The palm family, of which there are more than four thousand different kinds, contains the trees which, after the grasses, are most useful to man. In fact, palms are closely related to grasses. Most of them grow in tropical climates and flower and fruit continuously. A coconut palm can produce up to a hundred fruits during the course of a year. Dates, coconuts, oil for soap, margarine, cooking and salad oils, fibres for matting, sugar,

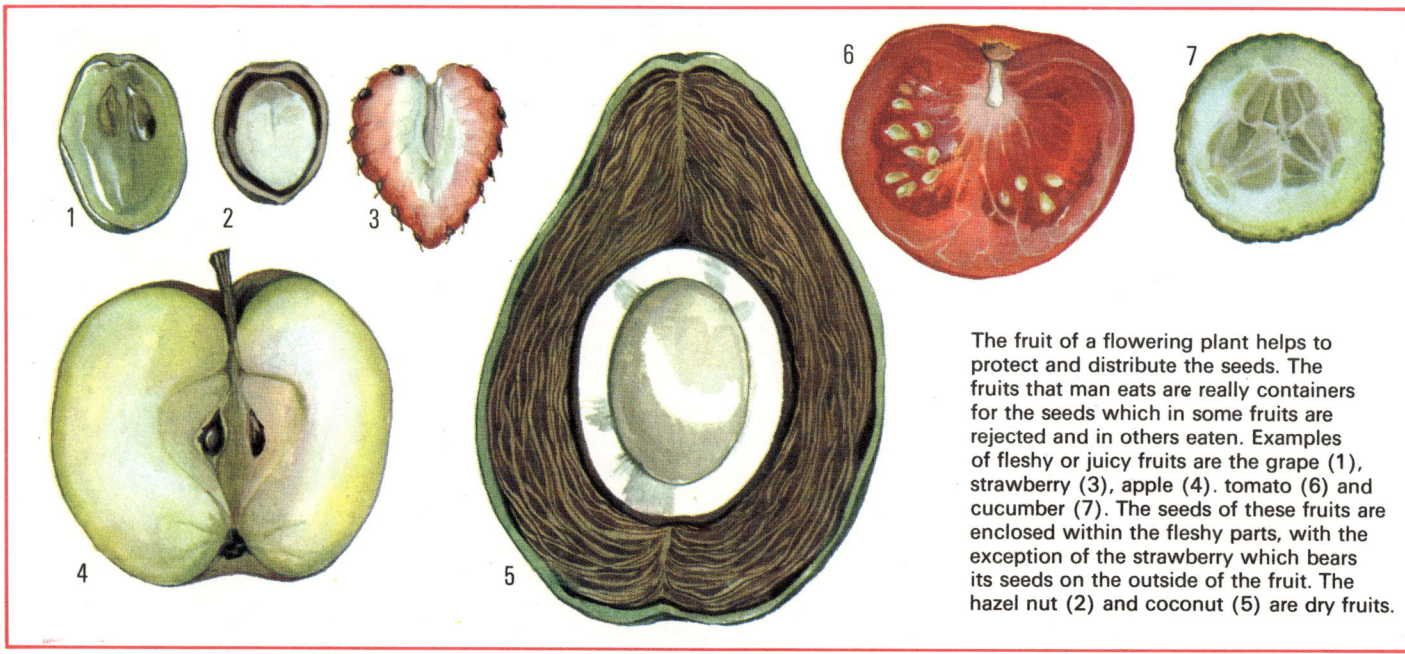

The fruit of a flowering plant helps to protect and distribute the seeds. The fruits that man eats are really containers for the seeds which in some fruits are rejected and in others eaten. Examples of fleshy or juicy fruits are the grape (1), strawberry (3), apple (4), tomato (6) and cucumber (7). The seeds of these fruits are enclosed within the fleshy parts, with the exception of the strawberry which bears its seeds on the outside of the fruit. The hazel nut (2) and coconut (5) are dry fruits.

The drawing on the right is based on a seventeenth-century engraving from a book on vegetable growing which illustrates and describes eight different cabbages.

sago and various building materials are all obtained from palms.

The fruit or pods of the cocoa tree grow on the trunks not the smaller branches. The pods are about 305 millimetres (twelve inches) long and contain the seeds which are crushed to make cocoa powder. In the wild, the tree will grow to twelve metres (forty feet) but in cocoa plantations it is kept to four and a half metres (fifteen feet) for easy harvesting of the pods.

The coffee plant is a small tree or bush, the most useful species of which is called *Coffea arabica*. It first grew in Africa and Asia, but is now planted in the tropical zones of the American continents. It bears dense clusters of white flowers that grow into fruit rather like cherries. Inside the fleshy skin are two seeds which are the coffee bean. They are dried, roasted and ground into powder to make the coffee we drink.

The various kinds of beans, peas, vegetable marrow, cucumber and tomatoes are fruits which we cook as vegetables or eat raw. With peas and broad beans we eat only the seeds. In other cases, we eat the whole pod or fruit. Peas and beans are grown extensively for feeding cattle. Many of our vegetables are pre-cooked and canned or frozen so that they are available to us all year round instead of just once a year.

The Soya Bean

The soya bean is likely to become one of the most important vegetables grown in the world. The plant was cultivated in China more than 4,800 years ago but it was not until 1908 that soya beans were first shipped to Britain and began to arouse worldwide attention. Now they are grown all over the world, principally in China, Manchuria, the United States and Japan. As well as being eaten as a vegetable, the soya bean produces oil and is made into flour, soya sauce, synthetic meats, milk and cheese-like products. The textile industry has become involved in using adaptations of their machinery for producing man-made fibres to spin textures from the soya bean which look and taste like meat. The product is rich in protein, costs less than meat and, for the production of the raw material, is less wasteful in space than the grazing of animals.

Root-crops have long been cultivated for the feeding of people and animals. Since they extract different chemicals from the soil than grain crops, they have proved useful in crop-rotation systems. Mangels and fodder-beet, a cross between the mangel and the sugar-beet, have proved to be valuable animal foodstuffs. Swedes, turnips, carrots and parsnips can be used for both animal and human consumption. The development of sugarbeet for the manufacture of refined sugar has been encouraged by the governments of many countries in temperate climates unsuitable for the growing of sugar canes. Since its introduction into Europe from America in the sixteenth century, the potato has become a staple food.

Lastly, the growing of plants whose leaves and flowers are used for food continues throughout the world. Among these are cabbages, kale, cauliflower, sprouts, broccoli and salad plants. They lead naturally into a study of the greatly expanding industry of herb-growing.

Herbs, Flavours and Spices

Herbs can be defined as soft-stemmed plants with fragrant leaves, the young ones of which are gathered for the flavouring of food and the making of medicines or perfumes. They can be used fresh, or dried by hanging in the shade, when the stems usually go hard and the dried leaves are rubbed off and stored in airtight containers to preserve the aroma. Herbs grow wild in temperate climates, especially round the Mediterranean and on the North American continent where they are grown commercially in large quantities. They can be eaten raw in salads or cooked with food.

Spices, on the other hand, are the dried parts of plants, such as seeds, fruits, buds, bark and roots, used to disguise or enhance the taste of food. They usually grow in tropical climates. The condiments, such as pepper but excluding salt, are spices. A condiment is usually added to food after cooking, whereas a spice is used during the cooking, pickling or preserving process.

Flavouring

Flavours are manufactured vegetable products added to commercially prepared food in the canning, bottling and preserving industries. A typical flavouring is monosodium glutamate, made from sugarbeet pulp and wheat gluten, which is a rubbery, elastic material obtained by washing the starch out of a dough of wheat flour and water. The glutamates are not nutritional in themselves and do not add a new taste to food. They seem to work by stimulating the taste buds in the mouth.

The seasoning of food has probably gone on for tens of thousands of years, though the earliest known reference to it was carved in stone about five thousand years ago in the Assyrian version of the Creation. It was discovered that salt could be used to preserve meat when animals were killed, and so make the small stocks of cattle food last the winter. Salt meat and fish lose their taste, so herbs and spices were needed to enliven the dishes when the food was eventually cooked. During religious fasts, such as Lent when only fish could be eaten, herbs and spices did much to vary the taste of a monotonous diet.

The trade in spices between East and West has continued since Old Testament times. The routes of the camel caravans were largely established by the spice trade which continued through the Mediterranean

Lavender is a shrub which grows wild in parts of Europe and it is also cultivated as a garden plant. In France lavender fields provide oils for use in the manufacture of perfume.

as far as Britain and Scandinavia. When the Romans first invaded Britain, they are said to have carried with them more than four hundred varieties of herbs and spices for planting there.

The Spice Trade

For years the Moslems monopolised the trade. They kept secret the places where spices came from and told exaggerated stories of the dangers and hardships of bringing them to the West, thus inflating the prices. Many of the great voyages of discovery were financed because their backers hoped for sea routes to the East to be established and for rich cargoes of spices to be their reward.

Queen Elizabeth I of England granted a charter to the East India Company to exploit these routes and carry on the spice trade. From such profitable enterprises, later including the tea and rubber trades, the building of the British Empire was begun. Nowadays, with the great increase in canning and deep-freezing and the consequent loss of flavour in much of our food, the use of herbs, spices and flavours has taken on a new lease of life.

One of the most important herbs in cooking is basil. It came originally from India where it has been treated as sacred and used in religious rites. For many centuries it has grown wild around the Mediterranean.

Chives have an onion flavour and can be eaten fresh in salads or cooked

The inside of a cocoa pod showing the beans which are protected by pulp.

in other food. They were known in China five thousand years ago but apparently did not appear in Europe until the sixteenth century. Garlic is a near relation with a much stronger flavour. It is not the leaves but the bulbs which are used in cooking. These bulbs are made up of smaller ones, each called a clove.

Dill and fennel are two closely related herbs that should not be planted together because they will cross-pollinate. They have a slight aniseed flavour. In America, their seeds were known as 'meeting seed' because they were given to children to ward off hunger during long church sermons.

The tea plant grows in many places in east Asia. Here, tea pickers are seen in Indonesia gathering the young leaves.

The origin of mint is a mystery. It has never been found in the wild state, though it is used all over the world. The usual variety is spearmint or *spicata*. Parsley is native to the Mediterranean area. The Greek gods were said to feed it to their horses to give them speed and spirit. It is rich in vitamins A and C, iron and valuable salts.

These are just a few of the many hundreds of herbs used in food and drink. Tea also might be described as a herb since it is made from the top sprig of leaves plucked from the plant, dried, rolled and infused with boiling water.

One of the most commonly used spices is pepper. Black pepper is the berry when not yet ripe, which is dried so that the outer flesh shrivels and turns black. White pepper is the ripe berry with the outer covering soaked off. Capsicums from South America come in different varieties, the fruits of which when dried produce chilli powder, red pepper or cayenne, paprika and sweet pepper. Caraway is a seed with a liquorice flavour. Cloves, from the Latin *clavus*, a nail, are the dried, unopened flower buds of the tropical clove tree. Ginger is obtained from the root of the plant. It can be bought peeled, unpeeled, dried or preserved. Saffron comes from the stigma of the mauve-flowering autumnal crocus.

Three varieties of the grape species *Vitis vinifera:* Riesling (left), Grenache (centre), Pinot Noir (right).

Wine and Vineyards

Wine can be made from many different fruits, vegetables and flowers, but the most important plant in wine making is the grapevine, which came originally from Asia. There are many different species of grapevine grown commercially for their fruits. Hamburg, Muscat, Muscadine, Sweetwater and Alicante are the names of dessert grapes eaten as fruit. Malaga, Sultana, Alexandria and Gordo Blanco are types of grapes dried to produce raisins and currants. The great wine grapes belong particularly to the regions where the famous wines are made. Such grapes are the black Cabernet Sauvignon of Bordeaux, and the black and white Pinot of Burgundy and Champagne, all three districts of France; the Riesling of the Rivers Rhine and Moselle; the Pedro Ximenez of Jerez in Spain; and the Furmint of Tokay in Hungary.

All these wine-growing districts have developed their own particular grapes which produce wines distinctive to each district. An expert taster can tell not only where a wine comes from but often the year in which it was made. The name of each district has made famous its own particular type of wine, Burgundy, Champagne or Sherry (Jerez), for instance.

The Colour of Wine

When grapes are crushed, the juice can be run off at once for the making of white wine, or it can be left to ferment in the presence of the stalks, skins and pips of the grapes to make red wine. A pink or rosé wine can be produced by allowing the juice to ferment for a short while with the skins of the grapes, which contain the colouring matter. Or it can be produced as white wine and poured back on the marc, as the crushed grape clusters are called, until the faint rose colour has appeared. All the colouring of table wines comes from the skins of the grapes and has nothing to do with the colour of the growing fruit.

The juice of a grape contains sugar. This sugar is broken down by the enzymes in the microscopic yeast which grows on the grape and can be seen as its 'bloom'. This fermentation turns most of the sugar into alcohol, though a little of both sugar and yeast is left for further fermentation after the wine has been put in casks or bottled, which is how a wine mellows or ages.

Champagne

Something of the care and pride taken in the making of wine can be illustrated by describing one particular type. What better to choose than the sparkling white wine known throughout the world as champagne? True champagne is made only in the Champagne region of France, which is an old province about 145 kilometres (90 miles) north-east of Paris. The vine-growing area is strictly limited by law to an area of about 30,000 hectares (74,000 acres) of which only 17,800 (44,000) are at present occupied by vineyards, the name given to wine-growing plantations. The area includes 250 villages spread over the highlands of Rheims, the valley of the River Marne, the so-called Slopes of the White Grapes (*Côte des Blancs*) and parts of the Departments of Aube and Aisne.

The vineyards of that area have a mere 30 centimetres (12 inches) or so of topsoil over a deep layer of limestone in which the roots of the vines spread. It is this soil to which the champagne grapes owe their particular flavour. Only three types of grapes can be used for champagne, the Pinot Noir, the Pinot Meunier, both black grapes, and the Chardonnay, a white grape. The juice from all three, in equal quantities, goes into every bottle of champagne. The vines bear fruit four years after planting and live about thirty years before needing to be replaced.

The vines are pruned every year according to very precise rules to limit the quantity of fruit and increase the quality. They flower in June, and the grapes are ready for picking towards the end of September. Then follows a process called *epluchage*, which is the sorting and examination of the grapes and the rejection of imperfect ones. According to the condition of the crop, a maximum yield per hectare is fixed each year by law and anything over this is also rejected.

The grapes are pressed and the juice run off quickly so that it will not have time to absorb any red colouring from the skins. Each press takes 4,000 kilograms (8,800 pounds) of grapes, producing 2,710 litres (596 gallons) of juice. Surplus juice may not be labelled champagne.

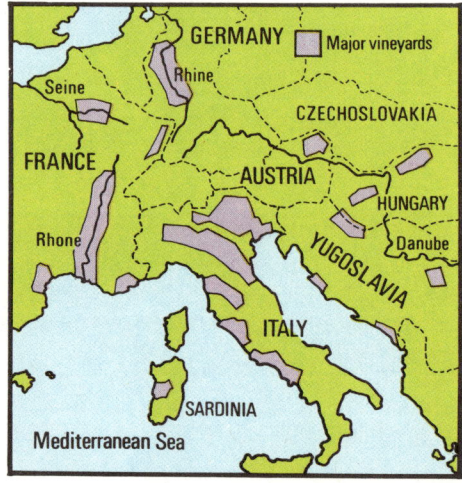

Fermentation

The first fermentation takes place in vats or casks, starting the day after the grapes are picked and continuing for several weeks. At this stage, a still, white wine has been produced. During the winter, it becomes perfectly clear and is tasted by the firm's experts to determine its particular qualities. Sometimes as many as thirty wines from different vineyards are mixed together to produce the well-balanced wine that is aimed at. Each firm jealously guards the secret of its own formula. If some wine held back from previous years is included, then the result is a non-vintage champagne. If one year's product has exceptional quality and no addition from other years is made, then it is a *champagne millesime* or vintage champagne.

The next operation is to add a small quantity of cane sugar and some fermenting agent, then to put the wine in bottles and lay them in a cool cellar. There follows a second fermentation lasting several months, turning the sugar into alcohol and carbonic gas which gives the wine its 'fizz'. During this second fermentation, a deposit forms on the lower side of the bottle. Every day, over a period of several months, each bottle is shaken gently, turned through an angle of forty-five degrees and tilted a little farther down until, at the end of this treatment, it is standing vertically with the cork downwards. This makes the deposit slide towards the neck of the bottle and collect on the cork. The neck of the bottle is then dipped into a freezing solution and a block of ice, containing the deposit, forms. The bottle is turned smartly, the cork removed, and out shoots the block of ice. The space left is filled with a liqueur of an old champagne mixed with cane sugar, the amount varying according to the dryness of wine required. This operation is called the dosage.

A new cork is inserted with a wire cage to hold it in position. The wine is now ready to be drunk. The second cork bears the name champagne, as must the label on the bottle. By law, this process must have taken place within the legal boundaries of the wine-growing area of Champagne and in cellars into which no wine of any other origin has been admitted.

Many of the best wine-growing districts of France, Germany and Italy are hilly, and terraced vineyards are common. On the right are seen typical wine bottle labels and three of the traditional bottle shapes.

Oil Crops and Rubber

The seeds of many plants are rich enough in oil to make its extraction commercially worthwhile. Although nuts and seeds were at one time gathered from trees and plants growing wild, nowadays most come from plantations that have been cultivated all over the world.

From West Africa comes most of the world's supply of coconut oil. It is taken from the dried kernel of the nut called copra which consists of 70 per cent oil. Also from West Africa and from South-east Asia comes palm oil, taken from the outer pulpy layer of the fruit, and palm-kernel oil from the nut kernel. These oils are produced in a hard, fatty form called stearine which is used in the manufacture of chocolate and cooking fats and in the preparation of medicine. In liquid form it is called oleine and is used in baking fats for biscuits and cakes, and in toffee, caramels and salad dressing. The crude, unrefined oil can be used in solid soaps, liquid soaps and shampoos.

The cotton plant, grown commercially in the United States, India and Egypt, has a fruit called a boll which splits open to reveal the fluffy white fibres and a number of black seeds each about six millimetres (a quarter of an inch) long, the kernels of which are about 37 per cent oil. Cottonseed

Sunflower seeds yield oil for cooking. The cake left after the extraction of oil can be used as cattle food. Seeds of the groundnut also produce valuable oil.

oil is used in margarine, cooking fat, salad oil and mayonnaise as well as in soaps, resins, grease and lubricants. It is used also for frying and as a preservative in tinned foods such as sardines.

Linseed Oil

Linseed is the seed of the flax plant which is grown principally in the United States, Russia, the Argentine, India and Canada. Flax fibres are woven into linen cloth. As a by-product, the seeds produce oil for oil paints, varnishes, printing and lithographic inks, linoleum, oilcloth and as a waterproofing agent. The cake, which is the residue after extracting most of the oil, is a valuable cattle food.

The groundnut, earth-nut or peanut is the seed of the plant *Arachis hypogea*. After the flowers have been fertilised, they turn downwards so that the young pod is forced into the ground where it matures and ripens. The pods hold up to four seeds and a fully-grown plant produces forty or more pods. The seeds yield a valuable oil and are cultivated mainly in India, China, West Africa, the United States and South-east Asia.

Other valuable oil-producing seeds come from the safflower, or *Carthamus tinctorius*, grown especially in India, the flowers of which also produce a yellow dye; and the soya bean grown extensively in China and the Far East. Two other plants grown in China are called *Aleurites fordii* and *Aleurites montana* and they produce Tung or Chinese wood oil, the cake from which is poisonous and used only for manure. Also important is the sunflower, a native of Mexico and now grown in Russia, Yugoslavia, Turkey and South Africa.

Rubber latex is the milky juice found in many species of trees, shrubs and herbs. It consists of a rubber hydrocarbon with varying amounts of other substances, depending on the plant source, dispersed in water. The latex can be clotted and dried to give the raw rubber which has many uses.

Vase from ancient Greece showing olive gatherers

A sprig of olive

Invention of Rubber

It is said that Christopher Columbus found the natives of Haiti playing with a ball made from the gum of a tree. The ball was lighter and bounced better than any known to him. This gum was called rubber because an early use of it was the rubbing out of pencil marks. India-rubber comes from the old Spanish word for South America, *Indias*.

Although known from the sixteenth century onwards, rubber did not appear in quantity in Europe or the United States until the nineteenth century. At first, all the rubber came from trees growing wild in the Brazilian jungle. Then in 1876, the

British planter Sir Henry Wickham collected some seeds from the Brazilian rubber tree, *Hevea brasiliensis*, which produced 2,700 plants in Kew Gardens, London. Nearly two thousand of the plants were shipped to Ceylon, and all the vast rubber plantations of Asia sprang from these original specimens.

The trees are planted one hundred to an acre and eventually grow to a height of 30 metres (100 feet) with a girth of 914 millimetres (36 inches). The latex-bearing tubes are in the bark, which is cut to sever them but not so deeply that the cambium, a thin skin between bark and wood, is damaged. An average 128 grammes (four and a half ounces) of latex flows from each tapping, and about 2,700 litres (600 gallons) can be expected per half hectare of trees each year.

The Uses of Rubber
One of the disadvantages of rubber was that it hardened in winter and became sticky in summer. The Scotsman, Charles Macintosh, tried to overcome this by making a sandwich of rubber between two layers of cloth to make the waterproof material that bears his name. A much better solution to the problem came from Charles Goodyear, an American inventor who heated rubber with sulphur to provide a material that retained its flexibility in low temperatures and did not become sticky in the summer heat. Thomas Hancock in London also discovered this effect and gave it the name vulcanisation. The addition of between 5 and 10 per cent sulphur gave a soft, flexible rubber, while the addition of a greater amount of sulphur produced a hard, brittle substance called vulcanite.

During the Second World War an attempt was made both in Russia and the United States to grow the Russian dandelion, *kok-saghyz*, for its latex content. Nowadays synthetic rubbers are widely used, mainly to meet the need for an oil-resistant elastic material in car and aeroplane parts. There are many examples of synthetic rubbers. Plastics, too, are taking the place of rubber in many manufacturing industries. They can be made in a range of attractive colours and finishes and, with the use of PVC for conveyor belts, can reduce the risk of fire in such places as mines. The development of synthetic rubbers and plastics has been encouraged by the dislike of non rubber-growing countries of becoming dependent upon a product growing in an area where the political situation can be unstable. Thus an industry barely a hundred years old already shows signs of decline.

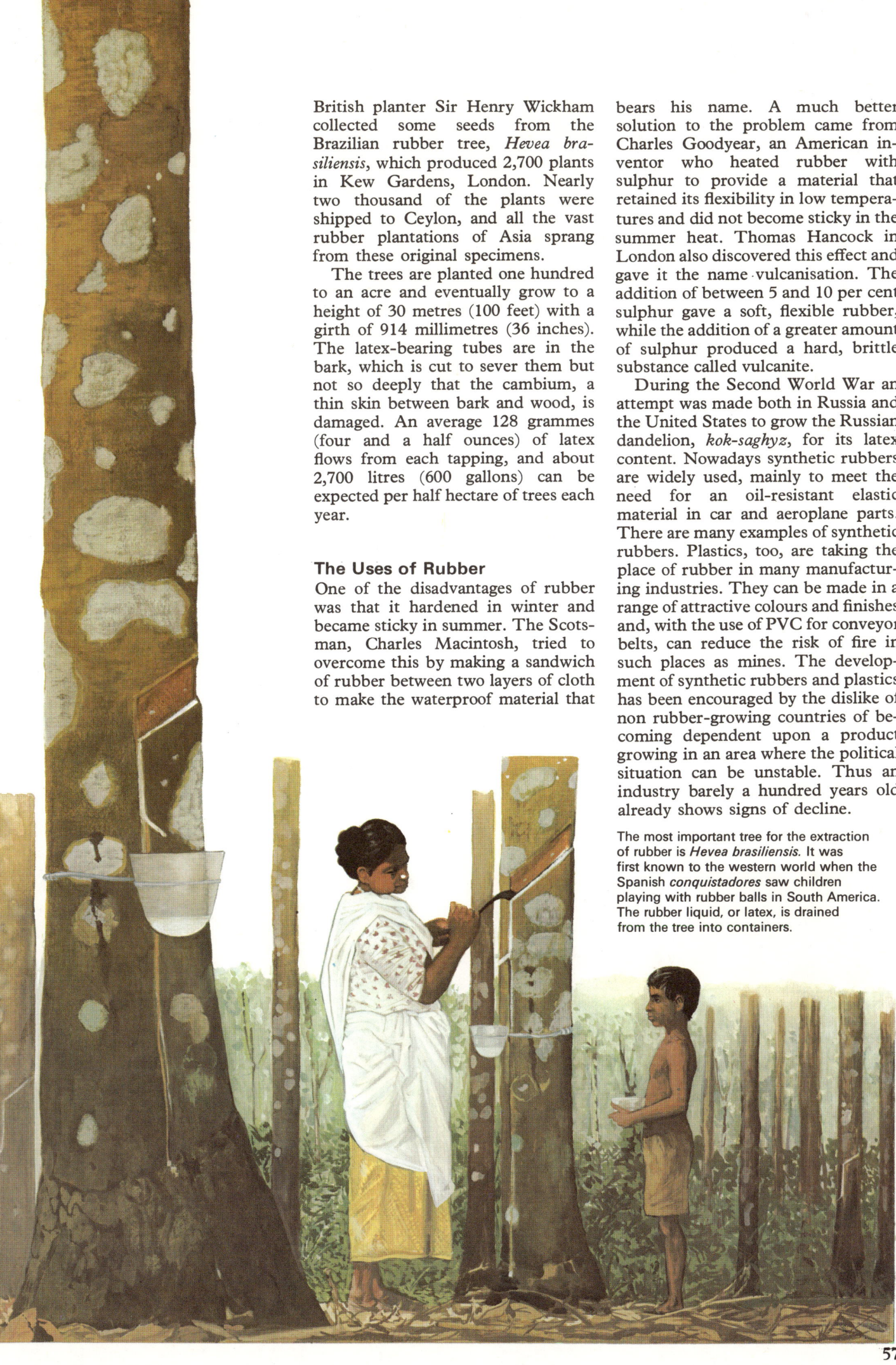

The most important tree for the extraction of rubber is *Hevea brasiliensis*. It was first known to the western world when the Spanish *conquistadores* saw children playing with rubber balls in South America. The rubber liquid, or latex, is drained from the tree into containers.

Timber and its Uses

Since he first learned to make tools, man has been clearing forests to make room for planting other crops and for pasture. He burned the wood on his fires, and used it for essential parts of his many inventions. Wood is a useful material. It can be easily cut and shaped. It is also simple to fasten pieces of it together by jointing, gluing, nailing and screwing. In parts of the world it grows abundantly. Even today, about one-fifth of the land surface of the earth is covered by trees.

The many uses to which wood can be put are the forests' undoing. In modern times, the amount of timber felled increases each year. It may take 7,000 trees to produce 400 tons of paper, sufficient only for a single edition of a daily newspaper. In the eighteenth and nineteenth centuries great forests of English oak disappeared to provide the wood to build ships for the British Navy. During the seventeenth century the techniques of shipbuilding developed rapidly. Proper plans and models were made. Timber was selected from trees by matching up wooden templates of the size required with the shape of the tree.

New Forests

Only in recent times has man begun to replace the forests he destroys. Afforestation (or the planting of trees) of areas unsuitable for other uses, and reafforestation of areas where the timber has been cut, are now carried out on a large scale throughout the world. Tree nurseries have been established where seedlings can be tended and grow into young trees for transplanting elsewhere. Foresters nurture the naturally seeded trees that appear where the old timber has been removed.

For the first few years of re-afforestation, the weeds that grow round the seedling trees must be cut down. Once the new trees have grown above the weeds, nature can be left for a while to get on with the job. After about eight or ten years, the lower branches of the new trees begin to grow across each other. Then the operation called cleaning and brashing must be carried out. Cleaning is the removal of all unwanted young trees, either those that have not developed vigorous growth or ones of a species not required. Brashing is the pruning away of lower branches up to head height so that the trees can be selected for the next operation, which is thinning.

Trees are allowed to grow or are planted close together to encourage straight growth and to discourage weeds. Later, misshapen or diseased trees can be removed and only the best left for the final crop. The thinnings can also be sold for such things as pit props or household Christmas trees to provide some income before the new forest reaches maturity. Also, 'rides' or paths between the trees can be created by thinning. The rides provide access through the forest and also act as barriers to prevent the spread of a forest fire.

In large timber-producing countries one method of transporting felled trees from the forest to the factory is by water. One ship can tow a vast number of logs along rivers in this way.

The Forester

It takes up to fifty years for even the quick-growing conifers or softwood trees to be ready for felling as timber. Hence, the forester is working for future generations. Most of the timber we use today comes from ancient forests.

Nowadays, petrol-driven chain saws are used to fell the trees and to trim off side branches. After the feller has done his work, a man called the

The trees in this panel and examples of the timber obtained from them are
1 Californian redwood, 2 eucalyptus, 3 spruce, 4 rosewood, 5 oak, 6 ash, 7 sapele, 8 walnut, 9 pine, 10 beech.

bucker cuts the trunk into suitable lengths to drag away. Fellers and buckers are together called lumberjacks. The logs are first moved to a convenient central point called a landing. This operation is called extraction.

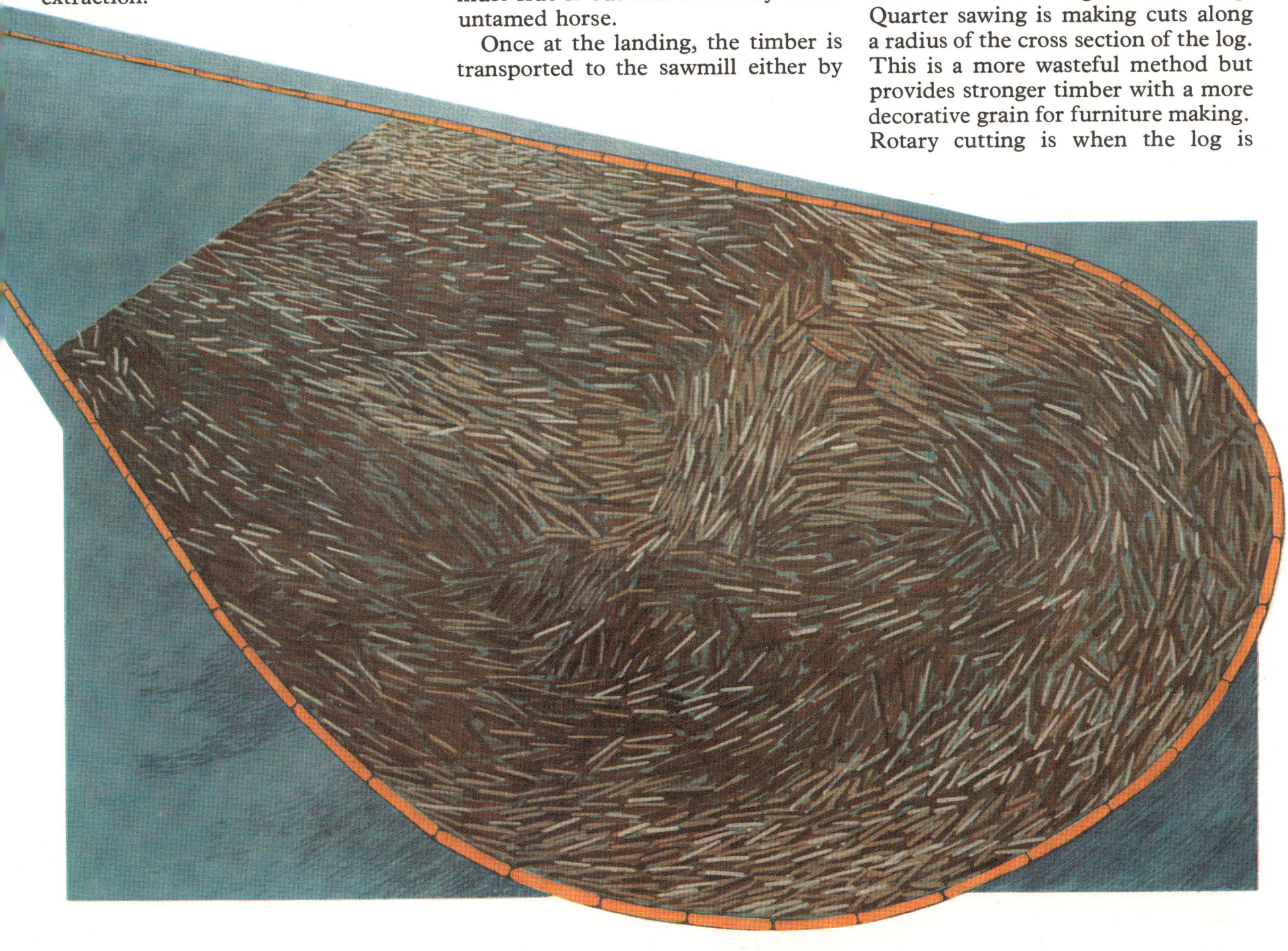

Extraction can be achieved in several ways. Sometimes the logs are simply dragged by horse or tractor. Sometimes tractor-drawn arches and sulkies are used. These are wheeled frames that lift one end of the log off the ground for easier dragging. Sometimes the logs are hauled on long cables attached to winches. In this case, pulleys are often attached to the tops of the so-called spar trees, the tallest trees in the area. To get the pulley up is one of the most dangerous jobs in lumberjacking. A man has to climb the tree with spiked boots and lop off the top of the tree. He is attached to the tree by a special belt. If the tree splits, the tension on the belt can break his back. In any case, as the top falls, the tree whips madly and the man can be thrown off. He must ride it out like a cowboy on an untamed horse.

Once at the landing, the timber is transported to the sawmill either by truck or rail, or by floating it down river. If the timber is sent by water, teams of drivers with long, spiked poles travel with it to prevent log jams. Quite often logs are tied into rafts on which the drivers live, sometimes with their families. The logs are slid into the river down chutes called slides. A slide with water flowing down it is called a flume. In the far north where the rivers freeze solid during the winter, the logs are kept piled on the bank until the thaw. Then the great rush of water as snow and ice melt is used to speed them on their way.

At the sawmill, the logs undergo conversion, the cutting of them into suitable shapes and sizes. Plain or flat sawing is cutting along parallel lines down the length of the log. Quarter sawing is making cuts along a radius of the cross section of the log. This is a more wasteful method but provides stronger timber with a more decorative grain for furniture making. Rotary cutting is when the log is rotated against a sharp knife to cut a spiral of thin wood called a veneer.

After cutting into planks, the wood is seasoned or dried in kilns. In the kilns the temperature is increased to dry out the moisture content. This seasons the wood quickly and uniformly, the operation taking from one to twelve weeks. Seasoned wood is used for making furniture, and in the building trade for flooring, windows, roof joists, staircases, doors and so on.

Veneers are made from expensive woods to cover and give an attractively grained finish to furniture and

In some areas of Scandinavia logs are manhandled across snow on sledges.

Composite timbers are greatly used in the building trade. Seen above are plywood, blockboard and chipboard.

other articles made from cheaper wood. Cheaper veneers are made into plywood by gluing sheets together with the grain in each sheet running at right angles to that of the next sheet. This makes thin board that is stronger than the same thickness of the ordinary timber would be. Another kind of plywood, called blockboard, has a sandwich of two veneers with a filling of strips of softwood. It is often used for making doors. Cheap veneers are also used for making shallow baskets called punnets and for boxes such as matchboxes.

Chipboard is made from chips of wood mixed with glue or resin, rolled into sheets and allowed to harden. Insulation board is made by subjecting wood chips to high pressure which breaks them down into fibres that bind together into a fluffy mass. This can then be heated again under pressure to make hardboard which has a smooth, water resistant surface.

Paper-making

Wood can also be ground with water into a pulp which is then mixed with other things such as clay, size and dyes, rolled out and dried to make cheap paper like newsprint. By 'cooking' wood with certain chemicals in a pressure cooker called a digester, another kind of wood pulp can be made. According to the chemicals used, this produces finer quality writing or art paper, or the strong kinds such as brown wrapping paper and cardboard. This chemical wood pulp can also be forced out through tiny holes of a spinneret to produce thin threads which harden in a chemical solution. These threads are then spun together to produce the man-made fibre known as rayon.

Wood that is heated in the absence of air, in the process called distillation, breaks down into other substances. The charred wood left behind is called charcoal which is used in the smelting and refining of metals, the removal of impurities from chemicals or in the manufacture of gunpowder. Other products of distillation are a valuable industrial solvent called wood alcohol, oils used in disinfectants, tar and creosote. Distilling the sap from pinewood gives turpentine and rosin used in making paint, varnish and polish.

Hard and Soft Woods

Timber trees are traditionally divided into conifers providing softwoods, and the deciduous trees or hardwoods. The names are not very apt since the softest wood of all, balsa, is a hardwood timber, and the softwood yew is almost as hard as oak. Generally speaking, the softwoods are quicker growing and therefore cheaper. Hardwoods have a more attractive grain and polish to a finer surface. They are therefore used in the more expensive furniture. Softwoods tend to be rather similar in appearance and colour, whereas hardwoods vary from the white wood of holly to the black of ebony with every shade of red, brown and yellow in between.

Both softwoods and hardwoods are used for furniture and in the building trade. Certain species, however, have specific uses, such as ebony for piano keys, cedar for cigar boxes, ash for hockey sticks and tennis racquets, willow for cricket bats, elm for coffins, pine for matches, firs and larches for telegraph poles, softwood cedar for pencils, and so on.

The bark of a species of oak provides us with cork. Maples give sugar and maple syrup. The oil of eucalyptus leaves is used in medicines. Rubber comes from trees. Trees give us a more even climate, reduce flooding, prevent erosion, landslides and avalanches, beautify the countryside, and protect and enrich the soil. We must never run short of trees.

Drawing based on a seventeenth-century Chinese woodcut of paper being made by hand. A form of papermaking from cotton rags or grass fibres was invented by the Chinese over 2,000 years ago. The manufacture of paper from wood developed later, when the demand in Europe and America increased rapidly in the eighteenth century. In the diagram below the process of machine papermaking is illustrated. From the mixer the paper pulp is fed across a series of rollers by which it is dried and pressed.

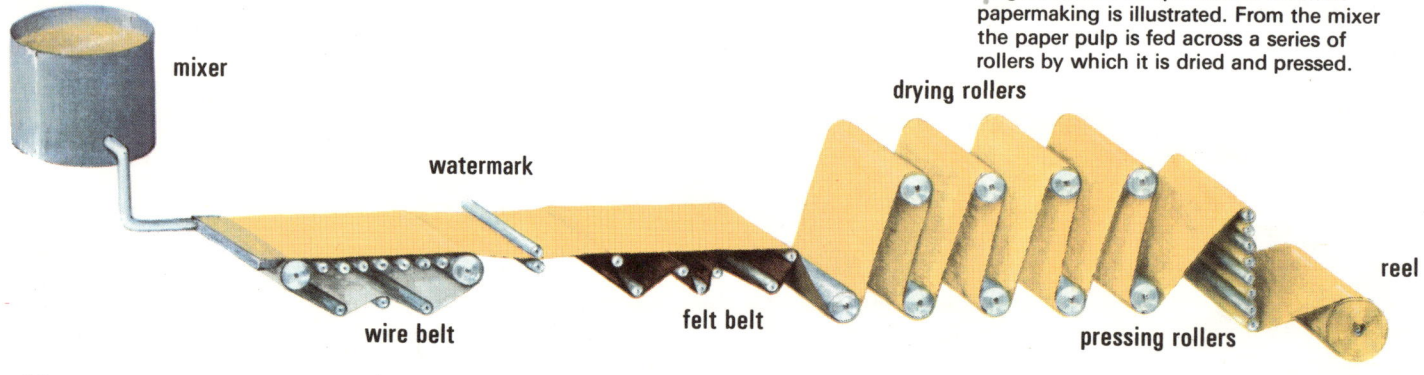

Medicines and Drugs

Probably by trial and error primitive man learned something of the medical properties of wild plants. He discovered that some plants are poisonous, and that others can stimulate or dull the mind, inducing wild dreams or hallucinations. Some he found beneficial as bandages for wounds, or as aids to digestion, some calmed the nervous system. Ancient Egyptian, Chinese and Japanese writings cover extensively the healing properties of plants. Dioscorides, a Greek physician from Cilicia who lived during the first century A.D., published a book called *De Materia Medica* which described more than 600 plants and their properties. It has been treated since as the most authoritative of the ancient books on medicine.

It was not the first *materia medica*, or book which studies the use of drugs in the curing of disease. One is said to have been prepared in China by the emperor Shen Nung as long ago as 2000 B.C. An Egyptian work on medicine, the Ebers papyrus, was written about 500 B.C. Theophrastus, who lived between 380 and 286 B.C., wrote a medical book. Since then, books containing formulae for the preparation of medicines, called pharmacopoeiae, have been more or less officially recognised through the centuries.

Herb Gardens

The earlier works were concerned with preparations made from natural things, particularly plants. It was the religious orders in the Middle Ages who took on the responsibility of founding hospitals in Europe. The Romans had planted gardens of herbs for medical purposes, and the monks followed their example. The first public herb gardens were founded in Padua in 1533, and by then every large house grew its own medicinal herbs. John Gerard, the English herbalist and surgeon, published his *Herball* in 1597. It was the first really comprehensive book on the properties of herbs, all of which were illustrated and given their origins, methods of cultivation and the best type of soil for each. His own herbal garden was in London, on the banks of the river Fleet. He became apothecary to King James I, during whose reign the

The parts of medicinal plants shown in this panel are 1 cinchona bark, 2 nux-vomica seeds, 3 coca leaves, 4 poppy capsules, 5 belladonna plant, 6 foxglove, 7 belladonna root.

Worshipful Company of Apothecaries founded their famous Physic Garden.

Many of the old herbal remedies linger, for example those two Victorian favourites, castor oil and senna pods. The former is the oil from the beans of the plant *Ricinus communis* which grows wild in most tropical and sub-tropical areas and is cultivated in Brazil and India. It was used as a non-irritant laxative, particularly for children. Nowadays its use as a cure for constipation, especially when abdominal pains are present, is frowned upon except under medical advice.

Primitive people living in the tropical jungles of South America have long known the art of preparing poisons with which to tip the arrows and blowpipe darts with which they hunt.

Senna pods come from several species of the genus *Cassia* and are still considered valuable as a gentle laxative.

Today, the preparation of drugs and medicines is strictly supervised and comes under much more stringent government and international control. The damage that can be done by the misuse of or over-indulgence in drugs is a matter of concern for all responsible people. Yet many of the dangerous herbal drugs are invaluable to the medical profession, and the plants from which they come are grown commercially under careful control.

Herbal Drugs

An example is the opium poppy, *Papaver somniferum*, grown extensively in India, Asia Minor, Egypt, Iran and China. The opium is obtained by drying the juice from the unripe capsules of the poppy. Opium contains several valuable alkaloids, notably morphine, which is a very effective pain killer, or analgesic, acting on the brain or influencing the sensory nerve fibres. Foxgloves still provide us with digitalin, used in cases of heart disease. It stimulates the heart muscles, thus improving blood circulation. *Atropa belladonna*, the deadly nightshade, contains the poison atropine from which belladonna, for use in nervous diseases, is made.

Some bacteria and fungi have poisonous effects on other plant life. The most recent development in medicine makes use of the wars waged between microscopic plants. Antibiotics, which are substances produced from bacteria and fungi, are used to kill or limit the growth of bacteria injurious to humans, animals and plants. Most of the bacteria and fungi now used as antibiotics were already known to science. It was an accident that first illustrated their value.

Sir Alexander Fleming in 1928 had a culture of *Staphylococcus* bacteria growing in his laboratory when he noticed it had become contaminated by a colony of *Penicillium*, a green mould or fungus common on decaying or damaged fruit such as oranges, and

Illustration from a medieval manuscript showing Mercury carrying a healing herb.

on cheese. Fleming further noticed that the growth of the bacteria was slowed down close to the mould. Later experiment showed that *Penicillium* had the same effect on other bacteria such as *Streptococcus* and the organisms of pneumonia and diphtheria, though it had no effect on the bacteria of tuberculosis, for instance. Another antibiotic, *streptomycin*, was found to be particularly effective against certain forms of tuberculosis.

From this chance discovery by Fleming a whole study of antibiotics has grown up. In 1944, the first effective control of a plant disease was achieved when a form of *Penicillium notatum*, the very species Fleming found in his bacteria culture, was used to control crowngall disease. Since then, antibiotics, particularly *streptomycin*, sometimes in combination with *Terramycin*, have been found effective against many of the bacterial diseases of fruits, tomatoes, vegetable crops and flowers. Other antibiotics have shown promise in the control of the fungal diseases of plants. It is also now common practice to include regular doses of antibiotics in food given to pigs and poultry. They help to reduce losses in infancy and increase the rate of putting on weight by stemming the growth of harmful bacteria.

Fibres and Dyes

Despite the growth of man-made or synthetic fibres, many plant crops are still used for the manufacture of fabrics. Even the man-made fibre, rayon, is made from wood pulp; and some nylon is made from coal which is the dead plant life of many millions of years ago.

One of the most important plant crops used for textiles is flax. The flax plant contains in its stalks bundles of fibres from which linen is made. The plant grows to a height of about one metre (three feet), and produces blue flowers from which grow round pods containing flat brown seeds. The seeds provide linseed oil. Flax may be grown for the textile fibre or for the seed or both, though the best fibre is obtained before the seeds have ripened.

Harvesting Flax
The flax is harvested by pulling the plant from the ground, either by hand or with machinery. Pulling is better than cutting, since the full length of the stalks, including the part closest to the ground, can be gathered. The stalks are bound together, stacked and allowed to dry in the air.

The next stage is called rippling when the seed heads are combed from the stalks. Then follows the process called retting when the stalks are laid in shallow pools of water or in tanks and allowed to rot a little. Retting helps to separate the fibres and is followed by scutching, which is drying and beating to separate the fibres from the unwanted parts of the stalk. After treatment in the scutching machine, the fibres go into a hackling machine to remove all remaining woody bits and to comb the fibres straight. The hackling machine produces fibres up to one metre (three feet) long, separating out the shorter fibres which are used to make a cheaper yarn called tow.

Linen yarn is woven into a cloth with a crisp feel and a shiny appearance which is also very strong. It is used for fine quality table and bed linen, as a dress material and, because it absorbs water well, for towels and handkerchiefs.

Hemp and Jute
A similar plant crop to flax is hemp. The coarse fibres are obtained from this plant in a similar manner to flax and are used in the making of canvas and sailcloth. Since hemp grows up to six metres (twenty feet) high, its fibres are longer than flax and are particularly useful in the making of heavy rope. Waste fibres from processing are used as oakum to fill in or

Since very early times man has used dyes obtained from natural sources to colour cloth. Two of the most ancient are indigo (blue) and madder (red), both from plants.

The cotton gin was invented by the American Eli Whitney (1765–1825). It was a machine which employed a simple principle but was capable of cleaning cotton fifty times faster than a man working by hand. As a boy Whitney showed great mechanical ingenuity. He made a violin when he was twelve and began a business making hand-wrought nails while still in his teens. He was also one of the first people to use mass production.

caulk the spaces between planks on the decks and sides of wooden boats. Flax can grow in quite cold climates, but hemp requires warmth. It is widely grown in Asia, Europe and North America.

A textile that grows in tropical regions, especially India and Pakistan, is jute. Jute is processed like flax but provides coarser fabrics such as sacking and hessian. Jute cloth is also used as a base for linoleum and as a backing for carpets.

Agave is another tropical plant cultivated for the fibres in its leaves. The leaves of the agave grow up to two metres (six feet) long and contain bundles of thin, cream-coloured fibres that are called sisal. They are too coarse for making clothing but are used in ropes, twines, sacking and matting. Sisal is produced mainly in East Africa, Java and tropical America.

Ramie, or Chinese grass, a member of the nettle family, is cultivated in China and Japan. Its stalk fibres make a linen-like cloth which is strong and shiny.

Cotton Growing

Cotton fibres come from the seed pod, or boll, of the cotton plant. Cotton thrives in humid tropical and subtropical regions. The southern states of the United States produce about a third of the world's crop of cotton. The remainder is grown in Russia, India and Egypt. There are a number of different cotton plants which grow from 30 centimetres (twelve inches) to 2·4 metres (eight feet) high, depending on the variety. After flowering, they produce the bolls which burst to reveal the seeds covered in a fluffy mass of fine white fibres.

The bolls are harvested mainly by machinery, though some are still picked by hand. They are first put into a machine called a cotton gin which separates the long fibres from the seeds. The raw cotton is then baled and sent to the spinning mill. There it is fed into a bale-breaker which breaks up the bales, an opener which beats the fibres and sucks out the dirt,

Man's search for fibres began in prehistoric times. Four of the most ancient natural fibres are flax, hemp, jute and sisal. Flax provides a strong thread or fabric: fishing lines and linen are typical products. Hemp is used for making ropes, and jute for coarse fabrics. Sisal provides strong twine.

and then into a scutcher which fluffs the fibres out and spreads them into a continuous fleecy blanket which is called the lap.

The length of the fibres depends on the variety of cotton grown. Sea Island cotton, which is the finest, has fibres about five centimetres (two inches) long, but the average is less than four centimetres (one and a half inches). The short downy fibres left on the seeds by the gin are called linters. They are too short for spinning but are bleached and sterilised to be made into cotton wool, or used as the raw material for rayon and in some plastics and varnishes.

Spinning Cotton

The cotton lap is put first into a carding machine which has rollers covered in wire teeth. These open out and disentangle the fibres, and remove those remaining that are too short for spinning. A combing machine with finer teeth is then used to comb the fibres even straighter. From this machine, the web of fibres is gathered up into loose ropes called slivers from which the final cotton thread is spun.

Colours for dyeing cloth were once obtained from animals, or from plants such as the madder root which provided the red dye called alizarin. The blue dye called indigo comes from, among others, the woad plant. This can still be found growing wild where it has escaped from one-time general cultivation. Nowadays, however, commercial dyes are almost entirely synthetic, though seed-oil is often an important ingredient in their manufacture. In 1856, William Perkins produced the first synthetic dye, a mauve colour derived from coal-tar. Since then many thousands of dyes have been produced from that useful material. And coal-tar was once a living plant.

Seed farm beds, where new strains of flower seed are developed, make a colourful patchwork.

Science and Plants

Botany is one of the most ancient of the sciences. According to the Old Testament, King Solomon studied plant life. The ancient Greeks, Herodotus, Plato and Aristotle, all attempted to classify them. In the first century A.D., Pliny the Elder wrote about grafting and budding, and the propagation of plants.

The belief in the value of plants for the curing of disease, and in the compounding of medicines and tonics, encouraged the study of medicine. The first school of medicine in Europe was at Salerno in Italy, and there are records of the medical garden of Matthaeus Sylvaticus as far back as 1309. The republic of Venice planted a similar botanical garden in 1333.

Botanical Gardens

By the sixteenth century, most Italian cities had botanical gardens, as did the universities of Leiden, Leipzig, Breslau and Heidelberg. Paris had its famous *Jardin des Plantes*. In 1655, the town of Uppsala in Sweden founded a botanical garden that became famous for its association with Carl Linnaeus. The botanical gardens at Kew in London were founded in 1759 and are now among the largest and most comprehensive in the world. Oxford and Cambridge, Edinburgh, Glasgow and Dublin all have their botanical gardens, as do Missouri, New York, Washington, Montreal and Ottawa.

There are tropical botanical gardens at Pamplemousses, Mauritius, at Sibpur, India, at Singapore and Rio de Janeiro. In Australia they are at Sydney, Melbourne, Adelaide and Hobart, Tasmania; in New Zealand at Christchurch and Dunedin; in South Africa at Kirstenbosch.

Most of the modern botanical gardens include museums, places for research and schools for students. Throughout the years the important studies have been the propagation of plants and the fight against pests and diseases. There are five methods of propagation: the collection and sowing of seeds; the taking of cuttings from a parent plant; the division of parent plants; a process known as layering; and finally, budding and grafting.

Sowing seeds is nature's own way of plant propagation. It is also the only way of propagating annuals and biennials which flower, seed, and die in one or two years. Successful germination of a seed requires darkness, moisture, warmth and air. Nature can be assisted by providing any or all of these requirements under ideal conditions. Planting at the appropriate depth provides darkness and the right amount of air. Moisture can be controlled by correct watering, and warmth maintained in cold frames, greenhouses or propagation frames.

Using Hormones

For propagation of plants by cuttings, a suitable rooting material such as silver sand is required, and science has produced chemical growth substances called hormones in liquid or powder form, to encourage root growth. New shoots, leaf buds, young leaves and cuttings from roots are all used for propagation by this method, according to the suitability of the plant in question.

Division, as the name implies, involves the breaking apart of a parent plant into two or more plants, each with buds and at least the rudiments of roots, to be planted out separately to grow into new plants. This should be carried out for most plants in the spring when the growth is most active.

Layering can happen naturally in a number of plants. It is a term applied to the rooting of the stem of a plant while it is still attached to the parent. The runners of strawberries

Artificial pollination is necessary with some plants, especially when plant breeders are trying to establish a new hybrid, with one variety being fertilised by the pollen of another.

Gregor Johann Mendel 1822–84

was investigated by the Austrian biologist Gregor Johann Mendel (1822–84) whose observations resulted in the publication in 1866 of his famous theory known today as Mendelism.

will root themselves, so will low branches of beeches and horse chestnuts. Layering can be artificially achieved by making a cut in a low branch and pegging it into a specially prepared soil; roots will strike down from the injured portion of the branch. Once it is well rooted, the new growth can be severed from the parent.

Budding and grafting are methods of propagation that involve the joining together of two living portions of two separate plants. The part of one plant with roots is called the stock. The part of the other plant, a piece of the previous year's wood, is called the scion. The stock supplies the root growth, and the scion supplies the branches, leaves, buds and so on of the new plant. For budding, a single bud with a bit of the bark or rind is required for joining on to the stock. With grafting, a whole shoot is used. A suitable cut is made in the stock, and the scion is fastened to it, usually with a binding of raffia.

By these various methods of propagation, vigorous new plant growths can be achieved. Often the result is a hybrid, or the production of blooms or fruit giving a new colour, a better flavour or a bigger yield. What happens to the heredity of different plant species that have been crossed

Mendelism

After taking his degree at Vienna university, Mendel joined the order of Augustinian monks and taught natural physics in the monastery school of Brno where he eventually became abbot. By the time of his death his contribution to the science of heredity had not been recognised. It was only when his writings were translated by Professor William Bateson in 1902 that the scientific possibilities were developed.

In his garden at the monastery, Mendel spent a good deal of time cultivating the edible pea and the sweet pea, and kept careful records of the characteristics of about 10,000 plants. He found that if the two parents of a hybrid showed a marked difference in certain characteristics—for instance if one was tall and the other short—then the hybrid offspring in the first generation was always tall. This tallness was termed the dominant characteristic, while shortness was termed the recessive characteristic.

In the next generation, produced either by self-fertilisation or fertilising the first generation hybrid with another, he found one form with the dominant characteristic pure and another with the recessive characteristic pure. These two forms occurred on average in two out of every four, while the other two exhibited the dominant characteristic, but also had the recessive characteristic latent in them. Mendel compared several pairs of alternatives in peas, such as tallness or shortness, yellow seeds or green seeds, round peas or wrinkled peas. From his results, he compiled his law of the purity of the gametes. This states that any gamete, that is, the male or female reproductive cell, can carry the determining factor or gene of only one of the pair of alternative characteristics.

From Mendel's work, it became apparent that it was only necessary to find out which of the characteristics of a chosen plant were dominant and which recessive in order to breed them permanently into a hybrid. Of course, matters are not quite as simple as that, since new and undesirable characteristics are liable to assert themselves, and these have to be bred out. Mendel's Law however gave the horticulturist a direction in which to work. There is no doubt that his discoveries are among the most important in science.

Pests and Diseases

In modern times, science has turned its attention more and more to wiping out pests and plant diseases. The production of new varieties of food plants and flowers by the various methods of selection and interbreeding have resulted in species not

necessarily highly resistant to diseases. Thus the prevention of disease has become extremely important.

Plant failure can be due to some lack in the soil or climate. For this, good husbandry, such as proper drainage, adequate water supply, correct rotation of crops, proper spacing and weeding, all play an important part, as do the provision of natural manures or chemical fertilisers.

Parasitic diseases are those caused by fungi, bacteria and viruses. For these, science has developed a whole armoury of fungicides, disinfectants and antibiotics. Yet the problem continues to require research. Diseases can create their own immunity to the antibodies used against them. New preparations are being tried out all the time. These, together with the pesticides used against animal pests, must be investigated thoroughly to ensure that they do not create effects harmful to the people or animals who consume the plant food.

Their effect, too, on the whole balance of nature must be assessed. A pesticide that also incidentally destroys animals which might keep down other pests, merely makes the problem worse. Nor does man always know the long-term effect on himself of the use of toxic chemicals on food crops. Whatever science does to affect one aspect of nature can have unknown and perhaps unpleasant side effects in another aspect.

For the business of nature is to survive. It has millions of years of success and adaptation behind it to support its future survival. If man, in his arrogance, tries to hurry it in one direction or another, nature is likely to exact a terrible revenge. The scientist must always be watchful, both in the laboratory and in the experimental field station, if his work is to have lasting and beneficial results for mankind.

Some of the many pests and diseases which attack plants.

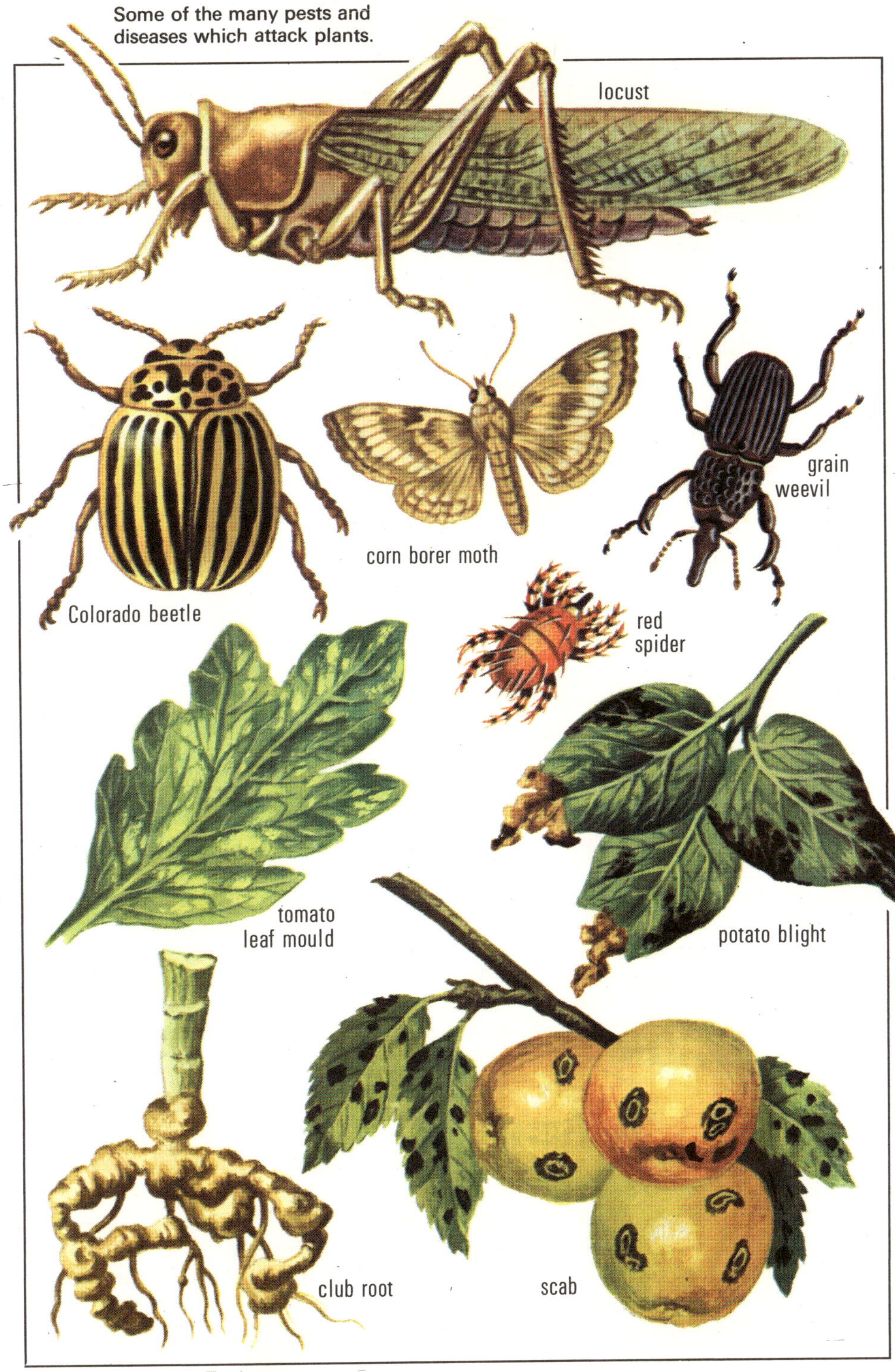

locust

Colorado beetle

corn borer moth

grain weevil

red spider

tomato leaf mould

potato blight

club root

scab

One of the most effective ways of spraying crops with insecticides is from the air.

The Evolution of Animals

Throughout history people have wondered about the origin of life and how it can occur in so many different forms. Have animals always looked as they do today, or could they have altered during the course of time? If so, then why?

In July 1858, two naturalists, Charles Darwin and Alfred Russel Wallace, made a startling announcement at a time when most people believed in the Biblical story of the Creation. This was the theory of evolution, which Darwin explained in his book *The Origin of Species*. In it he sets out how evolution can work, and mentions a number of natural laws which govern the existence of all things.

Population Explosion

Each of the animal species in nature's struggle for existence tends to remain fairly constant in numbers. However, at times, there is a big increase, called a population explosion. The Norway lemming is a good example. This increase does not usually last, and is brought to a halt by some cause, such as disease, starvation, or sterility. At times of high birth rate, there is heavy competition for survival. It is like saying to ourselves, 'there is only so much food to go round, or there are only so many houses to live in—who shall we choose?'

Survival of the Fittest

Darwin's answer, which is nature's way of making life possible, is the survival of the fittest. In order to survive, fitness in the sense of being healthy and strong is a help. More important is the way in which each animal is built and behaves, so that it fits into its surroundings. Human beings specialise in a job or a game. Animals adapt to their surroundings. A woodpecker is a specialist in the tree-tops and belongs to a woodland. It can climb, and in the trees it makes its nest and finds its food. A fish is built for swimming, and in a pond feeds on the plants or small water creatures, and lays its eggs on plants. An earthworm is built for burrowing and feeds on earth and fallen leaves. It lays its eggs in the soil.

Like a key which is made to fit into a certain type of lock, an animal is made to fit into a particular habitat, or natural area: the woodpecker to the trees, the fish to the pond and the earthworm to the soil.

Darwin pointed out that there is far more life produced than can possibly survive. If every animal born were to live to an old age, or every plant reach maturity and live out its full life-span, then the population of both animals and plants would become enormous, with hardly room to move and not enough food to go round. As an example Darwin chose the elephant, which is a slow breeder. Starting with a pair he worked out that, in 750 years, they could result in 19 million elephants alive. With a single pair of mice, the successive offspring could end up with some 200,000 mice after a period of only two years.

Life can vary and these variations can be inherited. Although identical twins may look alike we all know that no two humans are exactly alike. And the same applies to animals. These variations are important because they allow changes to take place in successive generations. This must occur if a species is to survive, because habitats and climates are changing all the time. Land is slowly replaced by sea, and sea by land, climates alter, and food supplies change. This is like changing the lock. The key must then be changed in order to fit the new lock. When we breed animals and cultivate plants we are doing this all the time. By picking out those animals or plants which have the qualities we desire, we can change a species to suit our needs. Sheep are bred for wool or meat, roses for their colour and scent, and greyhounds for their speed. Years ago we took animals and plants from the wild in order to put them to our own use. This is called artificial selection. Nature does this all the time, by natural selection.

Here is an example of natural selection at work. There are many snails living in a wood. They vary a lot in colour and markings. Snails are hunted by the sharp-eyed thrush. Those snails which stand out from their background will be found by the thrush, but it will miss the ones which are well camouflaged. In this way the snails are sorted out and those that thrive are the dark ones hidden on tree-trunks and dead leaves, or the pale ones in the dry grass, or striped ones in the bushes. In this manner a colony of snails is separated into isolated groups. On a much bigger scale one species of animal could become separated into isolated areas, kept apart perhaps by mountains or sea, so that from the one species two separate ones will eventually evolve. This is natural selection, and it depends on the survival of the fittest.

The Peppered Moth

Another example of change, in which camouflage can be a life-saver, has taken place over the past hundred years or so. It is due to the pollution of the atmosphere. The peppered moth is a common woodland insect which rests on the bark of trees during daytime. Its pale, speckled wings matched perfectly the growth of lichens normally found on trees. Then, in 1848, a black specimen was found near Manchester, possibly due to a mutation, or natural variation. In those days black, or melanic, moths were rare. They did not match the trees, and were picked off by sharp-eyed birds. Since then they have greatly increased. With the growth of industry during the Industrial Revolution, coal smoke from factory and domestic chimneys has killed off the lichens and darkened the trees with soot. Today, in Europe, there are large industrial areas where only dark moths occur. They match the tree-trunks better than the normal moths do. Today many insects, including ladybirds, are much darker than before; all have been affected by this industrial melanism, as it is called.

It is interesting to imagine what could happen if the world became a cleaner place, and pollution was ended. Would the lichens then return, and would the dark coloured moths die out because they no longer fitted?

Primitive forms of jellyfish date from Cambrian times

Prehistoric Animals

A primitive lemur, one of man's ancestors.

The fossilised skeleton of an ichthyosaur.

Beneath our feet, buried in the earth's crust, lies a graveyard of animal and plant remains, called fossils. Students of the crust (geologists), and of the fossils it contains (palaeontologists), have worked out a story of life on earth—a story of change and progression down the ages. The picture that emerges resembles that of a growing tree. We and other living animals form the tips of the branches.

Working back through the past it is possible to trace the origins of animals and see how they have altered. At one time they looked quite different from the animals we know today. A well documented example is the horse. The original ancestral type was a midget, called *Eohippus* (the 'Dawn horse'), no bigger than a fox-terrier. On each front foot it had four separate toes, and on each hind foot it had three. It was found in the rocks of the Eocene or Dawn Period, some 50 million years ago. From this early beginning horses have gradually increased in size and risen on to the middle toe, to become the modern horse, *Equus*. This still survives as a rare wild animal on the Mongolian steppes. From this wild horse we have bred a whole range of domestic horses, from ponies to draught horses.

Not only have horses increased in size, they have also changed their habits. The tiny first horses were forest dwellers that could avoid danger by slipping away through the undergrowth. The toes of their feet spread out to support their weight on the soft forest floor. They also had shallow teeth, all that was needed for browsing on soft leaves. Much later, more modern horses turned to open grassland. They were bigger and stronger and built for speed. With no places to hide they had to run from danger, and their slender, single-toed legs were well suited for speed. By then, they had developed deep-rooted teeth for chewing tough grass, not leaves. Modern horses, zebras and wild asses are built in this way, and live in open countryside.

Dating the Past

Information like this, which has been gained from the study of fossils, is similar to the evidence which a detective gathers from clues he finds. It is helpful in our exploration of the past. Dating the past is also possible by examining the rock layers in which fossils are formed. From this we know that life may have commenced over 3,000 million years ago. Unfortunately, little is known about early forms of life since they were very small and had soft bodies which left behind few traces. It is only from the Cambrian Period, 600 million years ago that fossils begin to turn up clearly, and from then onwards a 'story in the rocks' has been worked out, starting with these ancient creatures, and ending up with modern man.

This gradual process of change is called evolution. Like the horse, most animals have altered in the course of time, but there are interesting exceptions. Some animals alive today are called 'living fossils' because they have remained very much the same as their distant ancestors. One of these is a large fish called a coelacanth. As a fossil this goes back as far as the Devonian Period, some 300 million years ago. It appeared in later rocks up until the Cretaceous Period about 70 million years ago. Then it disappeared and was assumed to have died out.

In 1938 some fisherman landed a strange fish on the beach of East London in South Africa. The curator of a local museum, Miss Latimer, took charge of the remains and passed them to Professor Smith, an expert on fishes, who immediately recognised them as belonging to a

The kraken was a legendary sea monster like an enormous octopus which was supposed to drag ships down into the depths of the ocean.

The only wild relative of the domestic horse is Przewalsky's horse. A small number of them survive in Mongolia.

Ancestors of the horse (left) lived about 70 million years ago. Horses increased in size as they evolved.

modern coelacanth, hardly different from its ancestors. He named it *Latimeria*, after Miss Latimer.

Another, better known living fossil, is the odd-looking duck-billed platypus of Australia, a mammal with a mole-like body, flat beaver-like tail, webbed feet, and a mouth shaped like a duck's beak. When the eggs of the duck-billed platypus hatch out, the young are fed on milk. The early settlers were puzzled that such an animal could exist. Somehow it did not fit in, for birds lay eggs, not mammals. However, fossils have shown that early mammals were egg-layers, like the reptiles from which they evolved.

The platypus is a precious link with the past, as is the New Zealand tuatara, a lizard-like reptile. The tuatara is the sole survivor of a group that was alive during the Age of Reptiles. As living animals, these and other fossils have taught us much about life in the past.

The Land Invasion

The step from fish to amphibian required limbs to walk with, and lungs for breathing. As a result amphibians emerged from the water, but were largely confined to the water's edge. So far as we know they laid their eggs in water, and these hatched into young with gills. Next came the reptiles, whose young also hatched from eggs. Since reptile eggs were covered with a shell they could be laid on land.

Following on from this some reptiles gave rise to birds, and others to mammals. Both are warm-blooded animals covered in feathers or hair, but whereas birds still lay eggs, as did their reptile ancestors, mammals have progressed from egg-laying to producing living young. From the mammals man evolved about two million years ago. With his superior brain and skilled handiwork man now dominates the world in which, some 300 million years ago, fishes were the highest form of life.

These early fishes included a group of so-called lobe-finned fishes, to which *Latimeria* belongs. In the Devonian lakes lived *Eusthenopteron*, one of the most likely fish ancestors of the amphibians. It looked fish-like but could breathe air. By late Devonian times amphibians had developed limbs. One of these, *Ichthyostega*, walked on land but still had a fish-like tail supported by fin rays. Amphibians flourished during the Carboniferous or Coal Age. By the time of the Permian Period some had become giants and almost entirely land dwellers, like the two-metre (six-foot) *Eryops*. Of special interest is *Seymouria*, another land dweller, whose skeleton was part amphibian and part reptilian.

The link between reptiles and birds is well shown in the famous fossil of archaeopteryx (the 'ancient wing'). It could well be described as a lizard in bird's clothing. It lived during the Jurassic. Earliest mammals have now been traced as far back as the Triassic. The few remains of them reveal tiny, shrew-like creatures, such as *Megazostrodon*.

The latest step in vertebrate evolution was the tool-making animal, man. His earliest remains were discovered in Africa.

Jean Lamarck was a French naturalist who proposed a theory of evolution before the publication of Darwin's books. As an officer in the French army he became interested in natural history when stationed in the Mediterranean. After leaving the army he wrote books on botany and in 1774 became keeper of the royal gardens. He stayed there for over twenty years, lecturing on zoology. He was very interested in the origin and evolution of animals and his books on the subject, which were published between 1809–22, paved the way for Darwin's theories. These are now universally accepted but Lamarck died blind and poor, unaware that his revolutionary ideas would succeed.

Fossils and First Animals

In early times, strange looking objects we now know to be fossils were picked up or found stuck to rocks by our ancestors. They believed that they had fallen from the sky, or that they were made inside the rocks, and even had magical properties. Later on, as the formation of rock became better understood, it was said that fossils were animals or plants which had turned into stone. They were given fanciful names, like 'snake-stones' for the curled up shells of ammonites, and 'swallow-stones' for the wing-like shells of brachiopods. The pointed shells of belemnites (meaning dart stones) were looked upon as

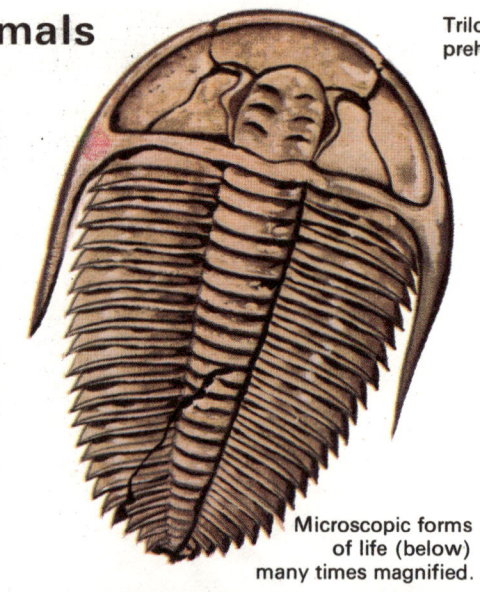

Trilobite, an early prehistoric animal.

Microscopic forms of life (below) many times magnified.

thunderbolts shot from the sky. Fossil sponges were seen as stony mushrooms.

How do fossils get into the rocks? During the late seventeenth century it was widely believed that the story of the Biblical Flood explained the drowning of many creatures which then turned into stone. One scientist even described a fossil skeleton as a man who had drowned in the Flood, and actually described him as *homo deluvii testis* the 'man who witnessed the flood'. It turned out to be a salamander.

Fossils in Water

There is a half-truth in these beliefs of drowning and rock forming. Most fossils are laid down in water. A dead animal sinks to the seabed, or is washed along a river until it gets caught up in the mud and is slowly covered by sediment. The soft parts decay, but hard parts like bone, shell and teeth are preserved. The mud hardens into rock, and thus a fossil is preserved.

Rocks formed in water are called sedimentary. As the earth's crust is gradually worn away or eroded by rain, wind and frost, particles of rock are carried down to the sea, or a lake, and settle on the bottom. When the water is filled up and the sediment hardens, a rock layer is formed. Smooth and soft rocks like clay and chalk are composed of fine particles, whereas coarse rocks like sandstone are formed of larger pieces. These sedimentary rocks can be seen as layers along the cliffs of the sea shore, or on the face of a man-made earthwork, such as a quarry, clay or chalk pit. Fossils may sometimes be seen on the surface. Other fossils can be noticed in building stone or even on pavements.

Certain types of rock rarely contain fossils. One of these, called igneous (meaning fiery) rock, comes from the lava cast up from beneath the earth's crust during a volcanic eruption. As it cools the molten lava or its ash hardens and crystallises into igneous rock, usually destroying any plant or animal which gets trapped. Granite and basalt are common examples of igneous rock. Where eruptions occur or where there is earth movement, heat and pressure on the neighbouring sedimentary rocks cause chemical changes. These make a third kind of rock, called metamorphic (meaning

Fossils are the actual remains of plants or animals from prehistoric times, or impressions of them on a rock face or in a hollow mould left after the original shell has dissolved away. People who study fossils are called palaeontologists and one of their most important tasks is to relate different strata of rock to each other by comparing the fossils embedded in them.

changed in form), which tends to form into layers.

During the early part of the last century an engineer called William Smith made a valuable discovery. He was a surveyor of canals and coal mines. He noticed that certain kinds of fossils always turned up in the same layer of rock. From this he deduced that rocks containing similar fossils, although miles apart, were of the same age.

Rocks belong to different ages which have been given names. From this we can construct a time chart. A palaeontologist can examine a fossil and say, for example, 'this is the leg bone of a dinosaur which lived during the Jurassic Period, 150 million years ago'. He can even tell from its shape that the dinosaur was slow and clumsy, or lively, that it walked on two or four legs, and how big it was. The teeth might tell him what it fed on, whether it was a flesh-eater or ate plants. Even footprints tell their story.

Fossils are formed in different ways. In rare cases the soft parts form an impression in the rock. Even jellyfishes have been preserved in this way. Hard parts are partly strengthened by minerals or entirely replaced by them, that is, they become petrified (turned into stone). The famous Petrified Forest in Arizona, U.S.A., is an example. If a fossil disintegrates altogether, the space which it leaves becomes filled in with the surrounding minerals. This forms a fossil cast. Ammonites and sea urchin fossils are commonly formed in this way, out of chalk or flint.

Sometimes entire plants or animals are preserved. Insects and other small creatures were trapped in the gum which oozed out of a prehistoric tree. This gum hardened into amber which preserved the creature. In the far north, in Siberia and Alaska, tusks, teeth, and even bodies of mammoths and woolly rhinoceroses have been found in the frozen ground. Flesh, skin and hair are still present. It is like being preserved in the deep-freeze.

Pre-Cambrian Rocks

Some of the first animals found in the oldest rocks date from well over 2,600 million years ago. In these Pre-Cambrian rocks nodules and layers of a limey substance have been discovered. These could have been formed by tiny water plants, called blue-green algae, in the same way that they do today. The same material is made by one-celled sea animals, called *Foraminifera*, which form limey shells. One scientist even gave a name to one of these first animals, discovered in some ancient Canadian rocks. He called it *Eozoon canadense*—'the dawn-animal of Canada'. Apart from these puzzling discoveries, pre-Cambrian rocks have also revealed traces of what might have been sponges, anemones and other worm-like creatures, but nobody is really certain what they are.

The picture of this early life is much clearer when we reach the Cambrian Period, about 600 million

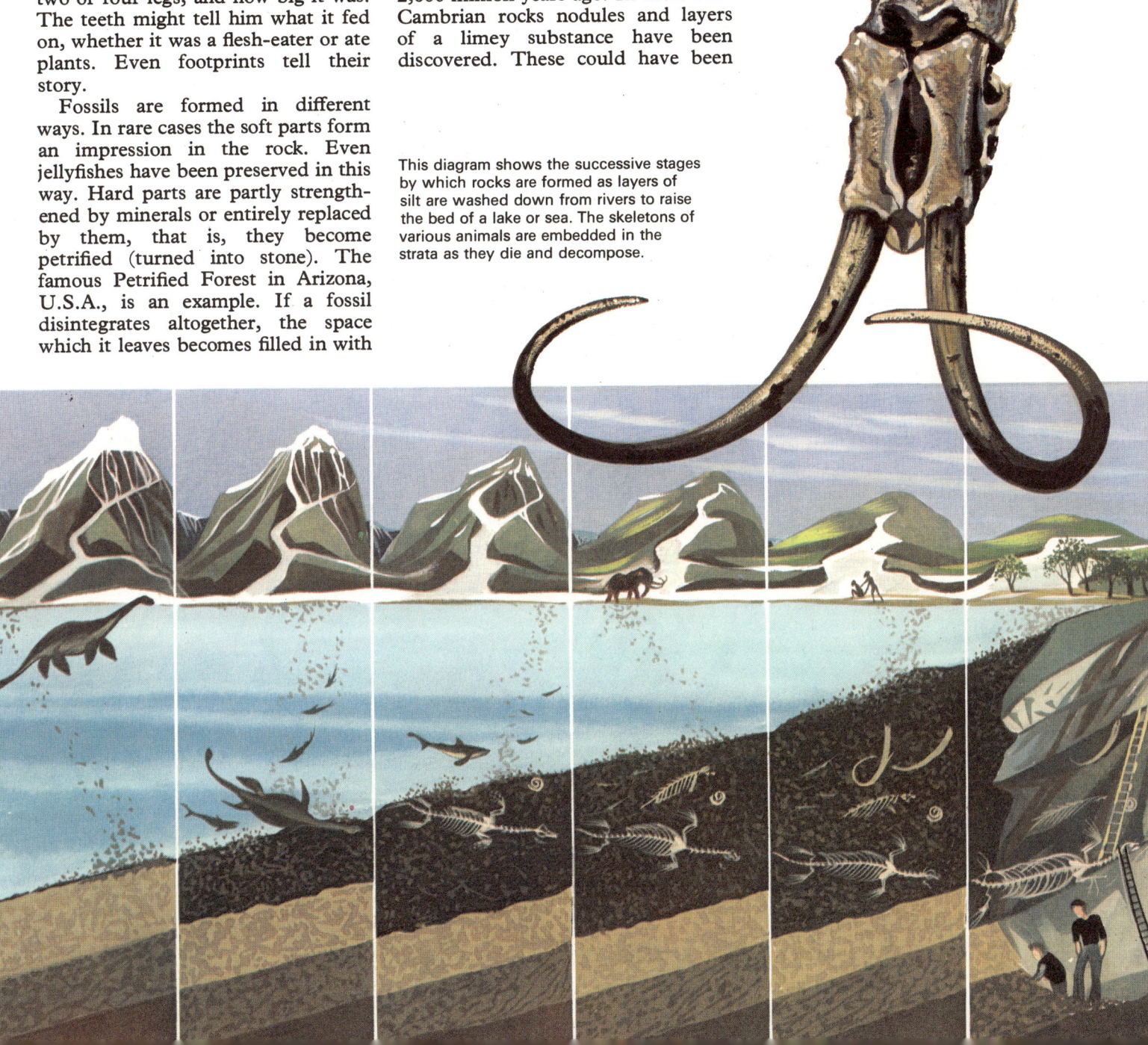

This diagram shows the successive stages by which rocks are formed as layers of silt are washed down from rivers to raise the bed of a lake or sea. The skeletons of various animals are embedded in the strata as they die and decompose.

years ago. The rocks from this period were first studied in Wales, which the Romans called Cambria. They contain various invertebrate animals of different groups, many now extinct, but some which still exist.

The scene we look upon is under the sea, for there is little to find on land. Fixed to the ancient seabed are numbers of seaweeds and sponges. Moving slowly over the bottom are different kinds of worms. There are also starfishes, some free-living and others fixed to stalks. Shrimp-like creatures swim above, joined by shoals of jellyfish. There are many trilobites, some swimming, others crawling. There is even one attempting to roll into a ball. This so-called 'woodlouse' trilobite is avoiding an enemy, in a similar way to the woodlouse of today. Trilobites, which are now extinct, get their name from the way in which their hard shells are divided into three sections, or lobes.

Written on Stone

Many of these first animals are beautifully preserved as fossils, even showing markings of their soft parts. Jellyfishes, too, show up clearly as fossils. It is thought that the bottom of the sea was unsuitable for the bacteria which normally cause decay, so that the bodies of dead animals were buried intact in the mud before they decayed. Fine specimens have been found in Cambrian rocks in Canada. Another extinct group are the graptolites, colonies of simple animals living in cups attached to branching rods. As fossils they look like pencil markings on the rock. Their name means 'written on stone'. All these ancient animals were invertebrates. Many were protected with a shell, but none possessed a backbone.

Some minute fossils are of extreme value in prospecting for oil and coal. When an oil company searches for oil a test boring is made. This could pass through a number of rock layers containing various fossils. A palaeontologist takes sections of the core and examines the contents. Some of these, called indicator fossils, belong to certain rock layers which also bear oil or coal. This helps the miners to decide where to dig their shafts or place their pipes, and how deep to go, in order to reach the mineral.

Tiny fossils of ancient one-celled sea creatures are useful for this kind of search, as are the shells of copepods, or water fleas. Each tiny shell has its individual shape and is recognisable to the expert.

Another useful indicator, this time in determining prehistoric climates and vegetation, can be found in the peat soils of moorlands. The acid conditions of peat help to preserve fossil remains of plants, especially the minute pollen grains. A sample of peat from different levels is removed by boring with an instrument called an auger. A botanist examines the peat and notes the various kinds of pollen grains, each of which has its distinctive shape and pattern. If most of the grains should come from grasses this would suggest a countryside of grassland such as now occurs in the north—an arctic countryside and a cold climate. If the grains are mostly from conifers like the pine and larch, this would indicate a cool climate of coniferous forest, such as in Russia and Canada today. Oak and beech grains would mean a temperate climate.

Changes of Climate

This interesting study shows how much climates have changed in the past, especially during the Ice Ages. At one particular level in peat the remains of cultivated plants have been found. This level is the result of a period when prehistoric man was in the area, farming the land to grow his crops. During Neolithic times he did this for a number of years, first clearing the forest, then growing his crops, and finally moving on to another area.

In Ordovician and Silurian times the seas were filled with invertebrate life. Typical were the two large creatures seen here, a cephalopod (left) and an eurypterid (right).

Fishes and Amphibians

In the two Periods following the Cambrian, the Ordovician and the Silurian (both studied in Wales and named after old Welsh tribes), the invertebrates continued to dominate the seas. Trilobites and graptolites were numerous. There were also brachiopods, small animals with lamp-shaped shells, so numerous that they formed shell beaches when they died and were washed up. These were joined by sea molluscs (from the Latin word for soft) which also had protective shells, like the snails and mussels of today. There were univalves, animals resembling snails and limpets, and bivalves, like oysters and mussels. Also, there were other molluscs called cephalopods, which means a 'head-foot'. The foot normally used by a snail is divided into long arms surrounding the head. The octopus and squid are modern examples. Their prehistoric cousins wore shells, some curled up like a ram's horn (ammonites), others straight and pointed (belemnites).

Among the most important discoveries from this ancient world are some fragments of an animal with bone, found in Colorado, in the United States. This is the earliest sign of a vertebrate animal, from the Ordovician Period, 500 million years ago.

The 'Bony Skins'
Better examples of these backboned creatures are found in Silurian rocks 400 million years old. These creatures were small fishes, called ostracoderms, meaning 'bony skins'. They had thick bony armour around the head and thick scales on the body. They could not move their mouths and had no paired fins. Mostly they lived on the sea bed and fed by sifting food out of the mud. A few of them had slender bodies and chased after smaller prey. They escaped enemies by wriggling into the mud and cracks in the rocks. A few ostracoderms still exist today. They are called lampreys and hagfishes. They attack other animals by clinging on with a sucker-like mouth and rasping at the flesh with a horny tongue.

By the Devonian Period, 300 million years ago, more fishes had appeared. In fact, this Period is known as the Age of Fishes. Some of them, called placoderms, meaning 'plated skins', also had a bony covering, jaws with teeth that moved and paired fins like modern fishes. Many were powerful giants up to six metres (twenty feet) long, with strong, crushing jaws. Despite this, the placoderms finally died out.

One of the earliest amphibians was *Ichthyostega*, which lived in the Devonian Period.

Another group managed to live on, and they are well known today. These are the catilaginous fishes such as sharks, skates and rays. They have a soft skeleton and the only hard parts are the teeth and spines in the fins. This is why they do not fossilise well, and some prehistoric sharks are known only from their teeth. Some were extremely large.

A third group had hard, bony skeletons. Descendants of this group are the most numerous fishes today. Well known modern examples are the goldfish, herring, salmon and stickleback. They occur almost everywhere, in the sea, in ponds, rivers and lakes, and are called ray-finned fishes. Their fins are spread like a fan over rows of bones. Large numbers of prehistoric fishes of this group are known from well-preserved fossils.

Lobe-finned Fishes
Within this large bony group is a smaller one of great importance, consisting of lobe-finned fishes. Their fins formed a kind of lobe or fringe around a central column of bones. An example is the famous coelacanth, already mentioned, whose fins appear to grow on short stalks. Other lobe-fins alive today are the lung-fishes. They belong to warm places, and can actually survive out of water during the dry season. When the swamp in which they live dries up, they burrow into the mud and form hard cocoons, using their lungs to breathe. When the water returns with the rain, they swim out and behave like normal fishes.

What we have learned from these lung-fishes and the coelacanth is that their Devonian ancestors had the right equipment for making life possible on land—lungs to breathe air with, and 'walking' fins for crawling about. It was in the late Devonian that these vertebrates made the first hesitant steps on to the dry land. By this time plants had already made a bridgehead, and all animals depend on plants for survival.

In this manner, the lobe-fins evolved into the first amphibians. Today these animals consist of frogs, toads, newts and salamanders. Most of them have limbs for crawling or hopping, and lungs for breathing air.

The placoderms were fishes which had paired fins and properly developed jaws. They lived during the 'Age of Fishes'.

They live mainly in damp places or in water, coming out in wet weather or at night to hunt food. Their naked and sensitive skins give little protection in dry surroundings. They lay their eggs in water to produce young, called tadpoles, which swim with their tails and use gills to breathe. This is why amphibians need ponds and lakes in which to lay their spawn.

The early amphibians lived in a similar fashion, especially during the late Carboniferous Period, 250 million years ago. At that time large areas of the northern hemisphere were covered by tropical forests in swampy surroundings. The amphibians wallowed and splashed around between the ferns and beneath the strange trees called giant horsetails and clubmosses.

The earliest traces of amphibians are their footprints, preserved in hardened mud. They all appear similar, apart from size. Each one shows an imprint of five toes. This five-toed, or pentadactyl, plan is the kind of limb structure which all land vertebrates possess, whether they walk, run, swim, hop or fly. In course of time, as amphibians evolved into reptiles and then into birds and mammals, vertebrates have adapted themselves to different ways of movement.

The Coal Age

During the Carboniferous Age, when amphibians had reached the land, there was much variation in their development. Conditions were ideal for their preservation. The Upper Carboniferous, meaning 'coal-bearing', was the time of coal formation. Great forests and swamps flourished in the northern hemisphere, in North America as well as in Europe. Coal is mostly carbon, but at first it consisted of dying trees, leaves, ferns and other vegetation which became buried in the mud. Next it turned into peat, then soft brown coal, and finally into black coal. This takes a long time during which many living things are buried.

The reason why coal-bearing rock comes in layers is due to earth movement. During the Upper Carboniferous the land sank so that the swamps became flooded by the sea. The land then rose again, so that fresh forests formed. In between two

The Devonian Period lasted about 40 million years. During this time the first air-breathing animals appeared on land.

coal layers, or seams, lies a rock deposit containing sea creatures.

Masses of plant remains have been uncovered during coal mining, beautifully preserved as impressions in the hardened mud, even on the coal itself. There are fern prints, bark patterns, marks where an insect has crawled over the mud, tracks of amphibians, and skeletons of fish and salamanders. Some branches, trees, roots and cones are so well preserved that even the minute cell structure of the original wood can be seen clearly under the microscope.

Giant Dragonflies

For neighbours, the amphibians had around them snails, centipedes, scorpions, spiders and cockroaches. Few of them could fly, except for dragonflies. Some of these were giants with a wing-span nearly one metre (three feet) across. These, and the various fishes, were preyed upon by the amphibians. Some of these resembled newts in size and shape, others were more worm-like and had no legs. There were also a number of giant salamanders, as big as crocodiles. Unlike modern amphibians, many had scaly skins. Some of them evolved into reptiles, but to begin with they all dwelt in the steamy jungles of the Coal Age. No forest today looks the same. Instead of flowers and trees like oak, beech and pine, there were groves of tree ferns and rushes, stretches of giant horsetails and, towering over all, the 30-metre (100-foot) club-mosses and other scaly trees.

A section of a modern tree will reveal the annual rings which are formed each summer and which occur only in climates with warm and cold seasons. There are no rings in the Coal Age trees, since there were no seasons. The scene would be the same, year by year, a permanent landscape of lush vegetation.

Winged insects first appeared in great numbers and variety during the Upper Carboniferous Period. There were many species which are now extinct, notably giant dragonflies. From impressions found in coal deposits, these had wingspans up to 76 centimetres (30 inches). At the same time there were arthropods including spiders, scorpions and millipedes. During the Permian Period, about 200 million years ago, most modern types of insect came into being and by the time of the Tertiary Period nearly all present-day insects existed. Today scientists have identified over 800,000 varied species of insects. But this is believed to be only a part of the final total of different types. Some estimates place the actual number as high as four million. Most insects live on land and only a few have adapted themselves to life in water.

The Carboniferous Period followed the Devonian and great forests of fern-like plants and horsetails grew up.

Reptiles and Birds

The Permian Period, 270 million years ago, was a time of great change, both in earth movement and in life. The rocks give us information about volcanic activity and mountain formation, and of a dry climate in the north. The southern hemisphere was in the grip of an Ice Age. The seas swarmed with bony fishes and sharks, but the placoderms had died out. By now some amphibians had reached a large size, like the heavily built *Eryops*. This creature showed certain reptilian features, and was almost entirely a land animal.

What makes a reptile? Apart from the way its skeleton differs from that of an amphibian, the most important contrast is seen in the way in which it reproduces. Amphibians lay jelly-covered eggs in water, which then hatch into gilled tadpoles. In evolving into reptiles some amphibians went a stage farther. They began laying eggs on land, which were covered with a shell, containing yolk and water. Inside this the embryo could grow up in a kind of 'private pond'. This method of reproduction still goes on today. Unlike the open water in which amphibians lay their eggs, reptiles provide their young with miniature ponds inside the shell-egg, which the mother can then carry around with her.

Land Invasion

This step, more than anything else, gave reptiles an opportunity to invade the land. So began a great animal invasion which was to last from the Permian Period to the later Cretaceous, a span of nearly 200 million years. Reptiles swarmed everywhere; in the swamps, in deserts, on lakes, and in the trees. There were heavy and clumsy plant-eaters and active flesh-eaters. There were very small reptiles and giants like the dinosaurs. Some reptiles lived in the sea, and some even flew.

A curious feature of Permian reptiles is the sail-like fin which some of them carried on their backs, a web of skin stretched over long upright spines. These 'sail backs' probably used it as a kind of radiator to avoid overheating in their dry surroundings. Others, called mammal-like reptiles, had dog-shaped canine teeth. In reptiles the teeth are mostly of similar shape and size.

During the Period which followed the Permian, 225 million years ago, called the Triassic, the continents were largely deserts of shifting sand, where reptiles could survive, but not amphibians. As a class reptiles are protected by having some kind of scaly covering to help them endure hot and dry climates. Many can bask for hours in the sun. Some of these Triassic reptiles deserve mentioning, for they were the ancestors of later reptiles, some of which are still alive today. One group, the Rhynchocephalia, have a single survivor, the tuatara, one of the 'living fossils'. Another small, lizard-like kind gave rise to the modern crocodiles. A third, the thecodonts, were small, active two-legged reptiles. Surprisingly, these were the ancestors of the dinosaurs. Imagine a slender goose covered in scales, with a mouth full of teeth, arms in place of wings, chasing after an insect. This is what a thecodont probably looked like.

In the seas were more reptiles, even turtles much like those of today. Turtles, and their land cousins the tortoises, are unique in having a bony shell built around the body. From early fossils we can deduce how this came about. By flattening the ribs so that they join together, and placing the limb girdles inside we get an animal which lives inside its rib cage.

By the time of the Jurassic Period, 195 million years ago, the high mountains which were formed long before had been worn down to low-lying plains. The land was covered with swamps and lakes, around which grew a lush vegetation of palm-like trees and plants called cycads, as well as tree ferns, conifers and maidenhair trees. One of these, called a ginkgo, still survives today. There were as yet no flowers, and the seasons did not exist. A tropical climate lasted all the year round.

The long-necked *Diplodocus* reached a length of 25 metres (84 feet). It was a vegetable-feeder and probably spent a lot of its time wading about in water, which supported its body.

This was the world of the dinosaurs. From their modest beginnings during the Triassic they had evolved into long-necked monsters like the *Brontosaurus*, *Diplodocus* and *Brachiosaurus*. Measuring up to 25 metres (eighty feet) long and weighing twenty tons or more, these awkward giants must have found it difficult to move about on land, having to carry so much weight.

A piece of detective work on their skeletons makes the idea possible that they spent much of the time in water. There were plenty of lakes and marshes to live in. The water would help to support their massive bodies, by taking the weight off their feet.

Amphibious Life

Various interesting features in the skeleton make the idea of an amphibious life possible. The skeleton can be compared to the structure of a boat. The heavy legs would give the body a low centre of gravity. As with the keel of a ship or the heavy boots of a diver, the legs would act as

a steadying influence. These would keep the cumbersome body upright as the animal made its way through the water.

There was always a danger of being caught up in a current or being swept out to sea and drowning. The long neck could operate as a kind of periscope, and the long tail would give the body balance. Eyes and nostrils were placed on top of the head. This is a common feature among water animals, such as the crocodile and frog. The curious peg-like teeth at the front of the jaw could be used for raking and sifting the soft, aquatic plants on which these animals fed. The small size of the head, containing a brain no larger than a man's fist, would seem to suggest that dinosaurs were rather dull-witted giants. The so-called second brain in the hips was really a swelling in the spinal cord and gave automatic control to the legs and tail.

Spending much of their time in water would also mean that *Brontosaurus* and its dinosaur cousins were safe from their enemies, the hunting dinosaurs such as *Allosaurus*. This swift, two-legged creature had sharp, saw-edged teeth and massive hind claws. With these it could leap on to its prey and tear it apart.

Other bulky plant-eaters were heavily armoured and covered with bony plates. Such was *Scelidosaurus* which lumbered about like an animated tank. Another well-known giant is *Stegosaurus*, which had a rounded back protected by a double row of bony plates and a tail with large spikes.

Jurassic Seas

The Jurassic seas swarmed with life. Ammonites were everywhere, so were sharks, rays and cuttlefish. These were preyed upon by giant sea reptiles called plesiosaurs, some as long as 10 metres (30 feet). Long-necked, with small heads, they had torpedo-shaped bodies ending in a tail. Paddle-shaped limbs helped them to swim and turn swiftly so as to catch elusive fishes. The way in which their limbs are attached to the body shows us how they could twist and turn them in every direction. They could paddle forward on one side and back-paddle on the other, rather like we can do with oars when turning a boat.

Plesiosaurs probably hauled themselves on to the rocks now and then, rather like seals do. This would not have been possible for their cousins, the ichthyosaurs (meaning 'fish-lizards'). In appearance, ichthyosaurs could have been mistaken for large fishes, since they had streamlined bodies, a fin on the back, a fish-like tail, and hands and feet which looked like fins.

Usually the soft parts of an animal do not show up in a fossil, but in the case of the ichthyosaur some beautifully preserved remains have been found in some quarries in Germany. The soft parts of their bodies were clearly marked on slabs of limestone which was once the soft mud at the bottom of an inland Jurassic sea. Some of these fossils even show the remains of embryos inside the mother's body. From this we know that the ichthyosaurs bore live young, as one would expect from air-breathing animals which spent all their lives in water. Ichthyosaurs were fast swimmers and hunted fish, ammonites and turtles, competing with long-nosed sea-crocodiles for possession of their watery world.

Winged Lizards

In the skies flew strange, bat-like creatures called pterosaurs, or 'winged lizards'. These reptiles were built in an unusual manner. Fossil remains of many have been uncovered in the same limestone quarries in Germany. Each wing had a greatly elongated fourth finger. Along the body, from this finger-tip to the ankle of the hind limb, stretched the wing. A popular name for these flying reptiles is pterodactyl, meaning 'wing-finger'. It seems doubtful whether they had the strength to fly like a bird, by flapping their wings, and they probably glided rather than flew. To do so they needed plenty of open space, and a wind current in order to take off. So they may have lived in high places, clinging to cliffs and tall trees from which they could launch themselves into the air. Soaring over the land and sea they swooped down to catch food, like sea birds do, catching small animals or fish with their sharp teeth.

Some fine specimens of sea reptiles have been found on the coast of England, especially in Dorset. It was here, at Lyme Regis, that a fossil hunter and his daughter, Mary Anning, used to collect specimens and sell them to scientists. It was Mary who discovered the first remains of an ichthyosaur, and later the first complete skeleton of a plesiosaur.

During the Cretaceous Period which followed the Jurassic, reptiles still flourished, but of a different kind. There was little mountain formation, and the land was still low-lying and swampy. The shallow seas were full of life, especially fishes, ammonites and belemnites, but reptiles were still dominant. A few ichthyosaurs still existed, but by now the plesiosaurs were in command. One of these, *Elasmosaurus*, was six metres (twenty feet) long. Even this giant was dwarfed by a huge kind of sea serpent, *Mosasaurus*, up to fifteen metres (fifty feet) long. It was found in Belgium, near the River Meuse.

Pterodactyls had also reached a huge size. One of these, *Pteranodon*, had a wing span of eight and a half metres (twenty-eight feet). Although large and heavy, it was probably light for its size. Like modern birds

Fin-backed reptiles had sail-like backbones.

these flying reptiles had hollow bones filled with air. They probably spent days at sea, soaring and drifting over the waves like albatrosses.

The Duckbills

On land, in the swamps and along the seashore lived different kinds of dinosaurs. The giant swamp-dwellers had died out and were replaced by two-legged waterside dwellers, called duckbills or hadrosaurs. They had webbed feet and tails flattened sideways which would have helped in swimming. One of these, called *Trachodon*, had rows of teeth, as many as 2,400, in its duck-like mouth. These were used to sift and grind the waterside rushes on which it fed. Some hadrosaurs had bony swellings or long horns on top of the head, which were hollow and filled with air. This would have helped them to stay under water for long periods when searching for water plants.

Plesiosaurs were long-necked reptiles which lived in the sea. Some were over twelve metres (40 feet) long and looked like giant sea serpents. They fought the flying pterosaurs.

On land lived other kinds of two-legged plant-eaters, such as *Iguanodon*. This was one of the first dinosaurs to be discovered. In 1822, at Cuckfield, a village near Horsham in England, the wife of a doctor named Mantell found some teeth. Dr Mantell, also a palaeontologist, made further discoveries in a nearby quarry. With these and the teeth, he tried to reconstruct the creature they belonged to. Because the teeth looked like those of modern lizards, called iguanas, he named it *Iguanodon* (meaning 'iguana tooth'). This dinosaur had a peculiar feature, a spiky thumb on each hand, which was probably used for defence, or for tearing down branches of cycads to get at the leaves. The *Iguanodon* probably lived in herds, roaming the Cretaceous forests, browsing on plants. In a coal mine in Belgium a whole group of them was found, all buried together. They are now on display in a museum in Brussels.

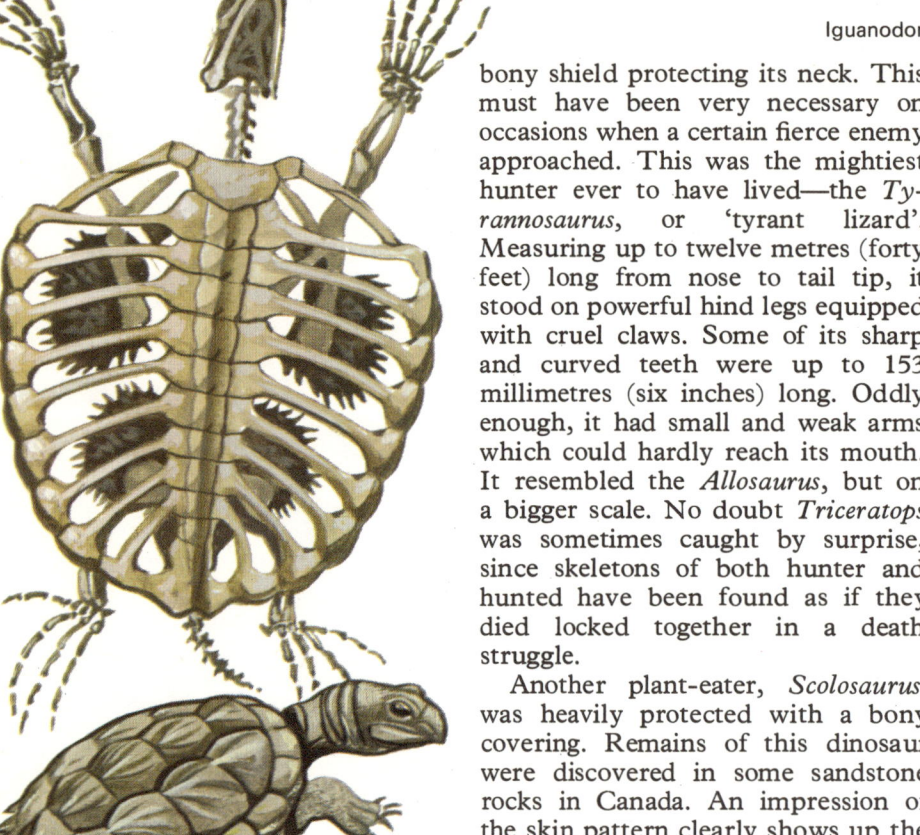

Iguanodon

The skeletons of prehistoric turtles show them to have been heavily armoured.

bony shield protecting its neck. This must have been very necessary on occasions when a certain fierce enemy approached. This was the mightiest hunter ever to have lived—the *Tyrannosaurus*, or 'tyrant lizard'. Measuring up to twelve metres (forty feet) long from nose to tail tip, it stood on powerful hind legs equipped with cruel claws. Some of its sharp and curved teeth were up to 153 millimetres (six inches) long. Oddly enough, it had small and weak arms which could hardly reach its mouth. It resembled the *Allosaurus*, but on a bigger scale. No doubt *Triceratops* was sometimes caught by surprise, since skeletons of both hunter and hunted have been found as if they died locked together in a death struggle.

Another plant-eater, *Scolosaurus*, was heavily protected with a bony covering. Remains of this dinosaur were discovered in some sandstone rocks in Canada. An impression of the skin pattern clearly shows up the thick scales. When danger threatened, all these plant-eaters relied either on their speed or their armour to protect them, or dived into the water.

The word Cretaceous comes from the Latin *creta* for chalk. This was formed in the sea, from calcium carbonate and from the shells of countless minute sea creatures. Parts of the seas eventually filled up and turned into chalk. In places where chalk ridges reach the sea, white cliffs hundreds of metres thick can be seen, as at Dover and Beachy Head in Britain. Below the chalk lies another rock, the Wealden clay, in which dinosaur remains are preserved.

The Dinosaurs' End
Plant remains from this time show that changes were taking place. The climate was cooler, and the tropical vegetation of cycads and conifers was being replaced by plants of a more modern kind. For the first time flowers existed, together with trees like the oak, elm and maple. Water lilies grew in the lakes. Modern plants of this kind lose their leaves in wintertime, and this could have meant a shortage of food for the dinosaurs. This may be one of the reasons why they began to die off. The earlier evergreen plants had provided them with food all the year round. Another reason could have been their size and poor brains. Maybe a disease wiped them out, or they could not adapt themselves to a changing world. It is still a mystery why so many reptiles disappeared, after having ruled the world for so many millions of years. By the end of the Cretaceous, some 70 million years ago, the great Age of Reptiles had come to an end.

The word dinosaur was first coined in the nineteenth century by Sir Richard Owen, a British palaeontologist, and has long been in everyday use. In fact, the dinosaurs consist of two separate groups of reptiles, depending on the shape of their hip bones and teeth. Hips are composed of six bones, three on each side. In one group, called Saurischia, or

Armoured Dinosaurs
Other Cretaceous dinosaurs were protected with armour and spikes. One of the largest was *Triceratops*, the 'three-horned face'. It had a horn on its nose, and one above each eye. Behind the head was a large,

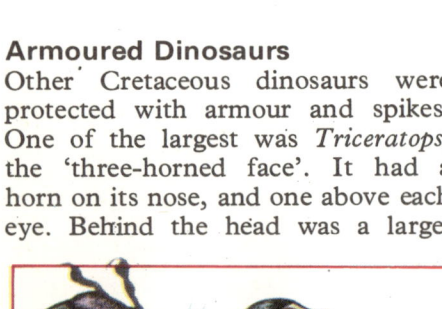

The *Archaeopteryx* was a creature which developed in Jurassic times about 150 million years ago. It is an important link between reptiles and birds as it combines characteristics of both. It represents a vital evolutionary stage in the development of birds. Limestone slabs showing almost complete skeletons of *Archaeopteryx* have been found in Germany with the impression of feathers. It was a little larger than a pigeon and probably did not fly very well. It glided from one tree to another and could even climb using the clawed digits on its wings. Despite its rather fierce head it was not a bird of prey but lived on fruit and berries. *Archaeopteryx* comes from the Greek, meaning 'ancient wing'.

'lizard-hipped', the ischium and pubis bones are placed wide apart. *Brontosaurus* and *Tyrannosaurus* belong to this group. In the other, the Ornithischia, or 'bird-hipped', they are close together. This is where *Triceratops* and *Stegosaurus* fit in. At first, when bird-hipped dinosaurs were being discovered, it was thought from the shape of their hips that they were huge prehistoric birds. But it is now known that they were reptiles which laid eggs.

Dinosaur Eggs

The discovery of dinosaur eggs is a rarity, but we do know something about them. During the early 1920s, a team of scientists from the American Museum of Natural History in New York made an expedition to the Gobi Desert in Mongolia. Here they uncovered the remains of a small dinosaur, called *Protoceratops*, together with nests of eggs. These were so well preserved in the sandstone rocks that by cutting sections in order to look inside, it was possible to reconstruct models showing baby dinosaurs hatching from their eggs. These eggs were more than 80 million years old.

The fearsome flesh-eater *Tyrannosaurus* fights with *Triceratops*.

The story of birds and their evolution is rather sketchy. Bird skeletons made of slender and hollow bones do not fossilise well. However, we do have some idea how they originated. During excavations at the German limestone quarries where so many reptiles have been found, a puzzling discovery was made. This quarry dates from the Jurassic Period, some 150 million years ago, when the Age of Reptiles was at its height. On a piece of stone the workmen found the imprint of a feather. Was this from a bird, and what was it doing among all these reptiles? The idea that it came from a bird was confirmed shortly afterwards when a finely preserved skeleton turned up, on which the feathers of the wings and tail were clearly marked. This is the earliest known feathered creature, called *Archaeopteryx* (the 'ancient wing'), of which three specimens have been found.

This rook-sized creature turned out to be a kind of reptile covered in feathers. It had teeth, a long tail and claws on its wings. In fact, the actual skeleton was very much like that of a lizard. Modern birds have no teeth or claws on their wings, and a short tail. Rarely do we find such precious fossils which form a link between two different groups of animals.

By the Cretaceous Period, a number of true birds had evolved, the ancestors of our modern birds. They were mostly water birds. From these we can recognise a large diving bird, called *Hesperornis*. It had no wings and was shaped like a large grebe. Another, called *Ichthyornis*, could fly, and resembled a tern.

Sabre-tooths were small tiger-like mammals which survived for a long period in the Americas.

The Age of Mammals

The skulls below show the development of the elephant. From the top: *Moeritherium, Palaeomastodon, Tetrabelodon, Mastodon* and the modern elephant.

The origin of mammals is a little uncertain. Throughout the Age of Reptiles there existed very small and insignificant mammals which evolved side by side with reptiles. A few precious fragments of jaw bones and teeth show that they existed as far back as the Triassic Period, as the structure of a mammal's jaw and teeth is quite different from that of reptiles. Also the limb bones of mammals are placed underneath so that the body can be lifted off the ground. In reptiles the limbs sprawl out sideways, and a reptile tends to drag itself along on its belly, rather than walk.

As recently as 1966 a fine fossil mammal, called *Megazostrodon*, was found in South Africa. A reconstruction shows a tiny, shrew-like creature, which probably had a warm furry body and actively hunted insects. Shrews are among the most primitive of modern mammals.

Whereas the cold-blooded, mammal-like reptiles died out, the true mammals continued to exist. For millions of years, from the Triassic onwards, these tiny mammals lived literally under the very feet of the giant reptiles, and made very little progress.

A New World

By the end of the Cretaceous Period a new world was in the making. The great reptiles were no longer dominant and mammals were taking over. Changes in climate, geography and plant life contributed to the dinosaurs' downfall. Disease may have helped, or else the reptiles wore themselves out through what is called racial sterility, that is they simply failed to go on reproducing.

As the climate cooled, new mountain chains were formed, such as the Alps, Rockies and Himalayas. Flowering plants increased, and the winter and summer seasons came about. Warm-blooded mammals and birds could more easily adapt to these changes, and were even able to live through the great Ice Ages.

Changes came about slowly during the Age of Mammals, from the Eocene Period about 70 million years ago until the present day. Although mammals had existed as far back as the Triassic, they remained small and obscure during the reptile age. However, by the Eocene a whole range of mammals had evolved, and from them can be traced the ancestry of modern mammals. Little *Eohippus* has already been mentioned. Then

The woolly mammoth lived in the Ice Ages.

there was the dawn-elephant *Phiomia*, no bigger than a small pig, and with a short trunk. Many mammals were shrew-like in build and behaviour and hunted insects and other small prey with their sharp teeth. The distant ancestor of man leaped about in trees. This was a small lemur called a tarsioid, very little different from the modern tarsier. Lemurs, monkeys, apes and man have hands for gripping things and for climbing, and are called primates, or hand mammals.

One feature of a mammal is that the mother feeds her baby on milk (*mamma* is Latin for a breast). She takes care of it and teaches it the way to live. Reptiles never do this; the young receive no training and they are ignored. However, not all mammals are born in the same way. One primitive group lays eggs. Such mammals were quite common in Jurassic times but today are almost extinct. The only survivors of these monotremes, as they are called, are the platypus (duckbill) and the echidna (spiny anteater) of Australia and New Guinea. Little better equipped for life are the marsupials or pouched mammals. Today they are confined to Australia and the warmer parts of America. This group includes a whole range of kangaroos and opossums, a pouched wolf, cat and mole, the wombat, phalanger and the lovable koala.

Early Marsupials

Early marsupials lived side by side with the last dinosaurs during the Cretaceous Period and looked much like the Virginia opossum, the only marsupial still living in North America. Baby marsupials are born when they are still very immature. Even the infant of the large grey kangaroo is less than twenty-five millimetres (one inch) long at birth. It spends many months in the safety and warmth of its mother's pouch, feeding on her milk. At one time a number of large marsupials existed, such as a giant kangaroo, *Sthenurus*, and a large wombat, *Diprotodon*, as much as three metres (eleven feet) long. There was also a kind of sabre-toothed cat, the size of a modern puma.

The decline of monotremes and marsupials is probably due to competition between them for living space. Their place was taken by modern mammals, called placentals. The placenta is a delicate filter inside the mother's body, through which blood and food is passed to the growing embryo. At birth the baby is well-grown and some, such as lambs, fawns and calves, may even start running about in a few hours. In this history of mammals' evolution we can see a pattern of change which produced more efficient methods of reproduction. A baby carried in its mother's womb has a greater chance of survival than one which is hatched from an egg. It enters the world better equipped to grow up and compete with nature.

The Age of Mammals has lasted for some 70 million years. During this time there have been many giants among the plant-eaters, as there were with reptiles. Among hoofed mammals there existed a long-necked rhinoceros, *Baluchitherium*, which was over three and a half metres (twelve feet) tall and the biggest land mammal ever to have existed. A two-horned beast, *Arsinoitherium*, was about three and a half metres long. During the last Ice Age there were other giants, such as the largest elephant, nearly four metres (thirteen feet) tall, and a kind of

Arsinoitherium was a fierce prehistoric mammal with large tusks like a rhinoceros. It lived in Africa where it was hunted by packs of dog-like creatures called hyaenodonts, which are now also extinct.

Oreopithecus, one of man's primate ancestors.

giant fallow deer with antlers nearly three and a half metres (11 feet) across.

Among the hunters were sabre-toothed cats, bigger than modern tigers. Many sabre-tooths and other animals have been uncovered in the famous tar pits of California. Today, a few pools still exist at Rancho la Brea, now part of the city of Los Angeles. These pools once lay in the middle of an open plain. When it rained in those ancient times the water settled on top of the liquid tar and attracted animals which came down to drink. Many were caught in the tar and drowned. When the Americans started using this tar for lining their roadways, thousands of fossils were found, such as mammoths and mastodons, sabre-tooths, wolves, ground sloths, and many different kinds of birds and insects, animals all now extinct.

Mammals have evolved, competed with one another, and moved from continent to continent, at times when the land was joined together. In this coming and going, the placentals finally drove out the egg-layers and marsupials into corners of the earth where they managed to live on until today—to South America and Australia. Australia, the great 'southern land', is sometimes described as a 'museum of living fossils'.

Meanwhile, many different kinds of birds were evolving. Their story is less well known, since the fragile and often hollow bones of birds do not fossilise well. The ancestors of many modern birds already existed in the Cretaceous Period. Some were swimmers and fish-hunters, others were birds of prey. Some, such as prehistoric mammals and reptiles, were giants. In New Zealand lived the great ostrich-like moas, which died out not so long ago. A large ground running bird, called *Aepyornis*, is linked with the mythical Arabian roc bird.

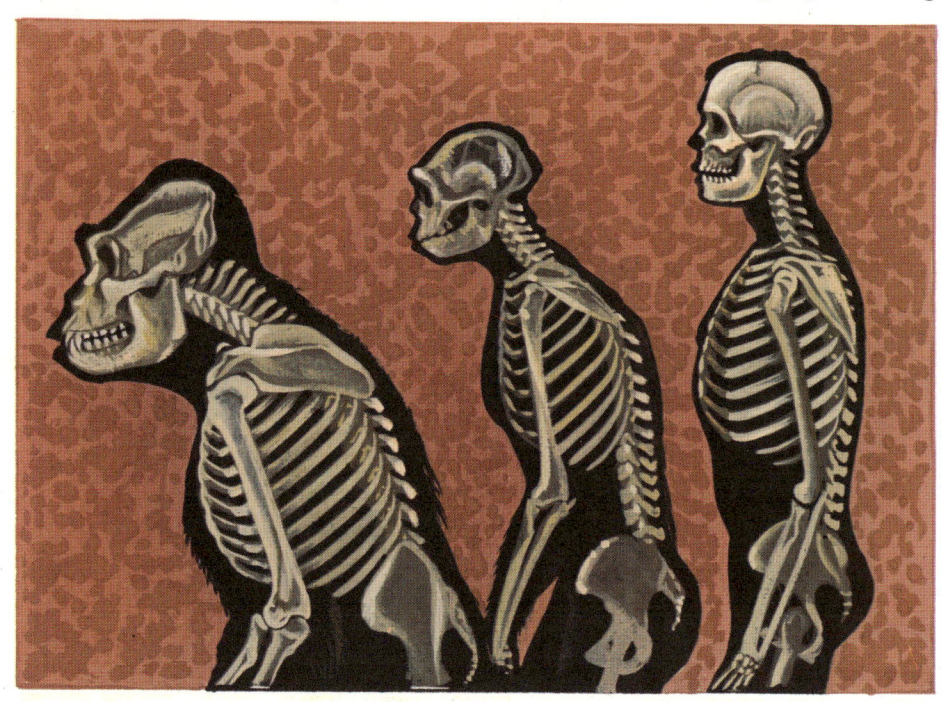

The backbone of an ape has a pronounced curve but it is constructed to allow an upright stance. Neanderthal man (centre) has a straighter backbone although it lacks the distinctive triple curve of modern man's skeleton (left) which makes his normal upright stance possible. The changing shape of the head is also clearly seen.

The Ice Ages

The great Ice Age is the final chapter in fossil history. Several Ice Ages occurred in places where there is now a tropical climate. The one we know best started about 600,000 years ago, during the Pleistocene Period. It was not continuous, but ebbed and flowed in slow and ponderous waves of ice. During a cold or glacial stage, snow fell and packed into ice which then spread slowly southwards from the Arctic. It moved off the mountain tops and covered the northern parts of America, Europe and Asia with a layer of ice, in some places hundreds of metres thick. Even the North Sea was filled with ice, and glaciers ground their way along the valleys. In Britain the ice sheet came to a halt just north of the River Thames.

All living things were pushed south as the ice advanced. The Arctic countryside was almost barren except for lowly lichens and mosses, Arctic flowers and stunted willows and birches. Across this bleak landscape roamed the mammoth, protected from the icy wind by a thick coat of hair, sometimes accompanied by the woolly rhinoceros. We know about the hair of these animals from frozen carcasses which have been found in the permafrost ground of Alaska and

Some idea of the primitive domestic family life led by cave-dwelling Neanderthal man can be gathered from reconstructions of their human remains and tools and weapons.

Siberia. Whole carcasses of mammoth and rhino have been preserved for thousands of years in a kind of deep freeze. Even traces of colour can be seen in the hair of the mammoth, from which we believe that it was auburn haired.

Neanderthal Man

There were herds of reindeer feeding on reindeer moss. The Arctic fox competed with the snowy owl in hunting the Arctic hare. The massive cavebear and packs of hyenas lived in caves. Here, too, lived Neanderthal Man, a cave man of the Old Stone Age. His remains were first identified with a discovery made in a cave along the valley of a little stream in Germany, the Neander. Somehow this tough, stocky man managed to live off the land by hunting the mammoth, rhino, reindeer and wolf. He made his tools and weapons out of flint and from the ivory, bone and antlers of the animals he killed. These have been found in many caves and in the gravel along river valleys.

When the ice melted and retreated with the return of warmer weather, the mammoth and other cold-weather animals moved north, and Mediterranean animals came up from the south to take their place. If you were standing on the banks of a river in northern Europe during such a warm interglacial stage you might have seen hippopotamuses wallowing in the mud, and a lion or two lurking in the undergrowth. Each time the ice melted and retreated the sea level rose as rivers carried the water away. Rocks, gravel and sand deposits were left behind, in which the Pleistocene mammals are buried. Remains of mammoth and reindeer, even Neanderthal man, are usually found in gravel pits or in caves. Britain was not always an island. There were times when the North Sea was low-lying land, so that animals could wander across from France. The well-known Dogger Bank fishing grounds were at one time a range of hills. From these the fishermen sometimes dredge up fossil remains.

The pre-human creature *Australopithecus* may have been the first tool-maker.

Cro-Magnon man lived in caves during the Ice Ages about 30,000 years ago.

As the fourth wave of ice retreated, some 20,000 years ago, Neanderthal Man died out, to be replaced by our own direct ancestor, a *Homo sapiens* like ourselves. We call him Cro-Magnon Man after some caves in the district of France where he was first discovered. This intelligent Stone Age hunter was a skilled worker of stone tools and carvings, also a fine artist. The animals he painted can still be seen on cave walls.

Today the ice has retreated to the Arctic Circle, and Cro-Magnon has died out. Modern man has taken his place, the last creature in a long line of vertebrate evolution which started 500 million years ago with the little lobe-finned fishes of the Devonian. What comes next?

Animals of Today

Animal groups are classified according to their basic structure. By finding out from fossil remains about the ancestors of today's animals we can see how they originated from simple beginnings. They have kept certain features by which we can recognise them. For example, all mammals have backbones and are warm-blooded, features they share with birds. But an obvious difference between the two groups is that mammals are hairy and suckle their young, whereas birds are feathered and lay eggs.

Within any particular group of animals there is great variety in size, shape and habit. Mammals range in size from the minute pygmy shrew to the 30-metre (100-foot) blue whale, mightiest animal that has ever lived. A monkey lives in the trees and a mole lives underground. An antelope runs very fast, a seal swims, and a bat flies. A fox is a meat-eater, but a rabbit feeds on grass. All are mammals, and these differences are due to the way in which each has adapted to its surroundings.

The chimpanzee is one of the primates closest to man in his behaviour. Chimpanzees live in small communities and spend much of their time in trees.

The Mighty Whale

A whale is a special case. Originally all mammals lived on land. Their bodies were kept warm by a covering of hair, and they ran about on four legs. They breathed air through nostrils into their lungs. A whale looks so different that at first glance it might be mistaken for a fish. Indeed, the old whalers used to call it a 'big fish'. A closer look will show that it is still a mammal, but has become adapted to living in water. Apart from a few whiskers on its nose a whale is naked. A full covering of hair would be useless, since it would soon become soaked with water. Only dry hair, like dry clothing, keeps the body warm. Instead, a whale has a thick 'overcoat' of fat, or blubber, to keep in the warmth. This is one reason why whales are hunted, to obtain whale oil from the blubber. This is used for many purposes, such as in the making of soap and margarine.

The two flippers, which look more like fins, are not so different from our own hands. Inside are rows of finger bones which are covered with flesh and skin to form useful paddles for swimming. A whale's nostrils, called the blow hole, are situated on top of the head. This makes it easier for the whale to breathe when it comes to the surface to blow. With its enormous bulk and weight a whale could not possibly live on land. In the water this giant is light and buoyant, and able to carry a baby calf which is up to eight metres (twenty-five feet) long at birth.

The Tiny Amoeba

At the other end of the scale of life in the animal kingdom is a minute single-celled creature, called amoeba. It lives in almost every pond and ditch. Its living contents are enclosed in an elastic membrane whose shape

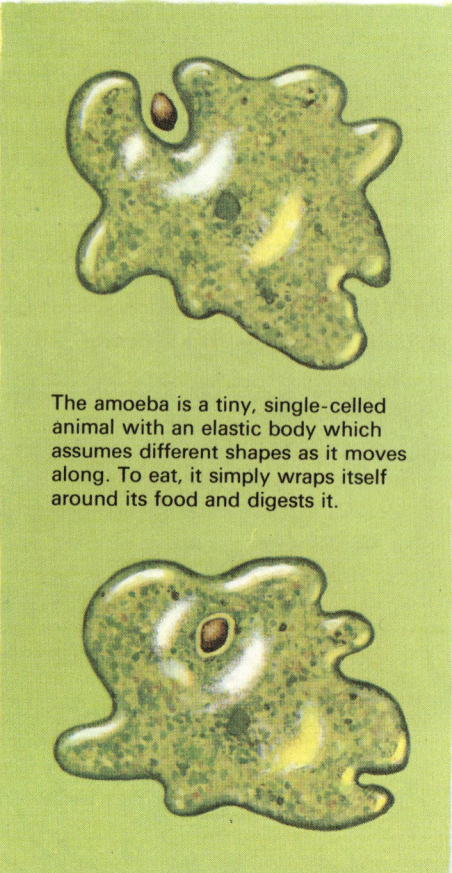

The amoeba is a tiny, single-celled animal with an elastic body which assumes different shapes as it moves along. To eat, it simply wraps itself around its food and digests it.

is constantly changing as it creeps about in a ghostly manner. The cell contents flow out into a finger-like process, called a false foot or pseudopod. Whichever way it turns it can produce these false feet, and it will move away from bright light or water which contains anything unpleasant. During hard times such as a drought when the puddle dries up, or during winter frost, it shuts into a tight ball and rests until better weather returns. To feed, amoeba simply wraps itself around its prey to form a kind of temporary stomach. Inside this the digestive juices break up the meal. Any waste products are released from the cell. To reproduce itself amoeba merely divides into two.

The blue whale roams the oceans— the minute amoeba lives in a drop of water. These are two extremes and yet like all other animals they have certain things in common. Because they are unable to make food in the way that plants do, animals need to search for it, or catch it in some way, and this means movement. To control this, and to know what is going on, animals have a nervous system. Food is taken in through a mouth into a food canal where it is digested and absorbed into the body. Any waste is passed out, or excreted. Since animals must eventually die they reproduce themselves. This, broadly, is what animals are capable of—movement, awareness, feeding, digestion, excretion and reproduction. They use these functions in different ways according to where they live, and what kind of food is available.

Animal Skeletons
A main difference in animals is the support given to the body. In vertebrates the skeleton is internal, as in mammals, birds, reptiles, amphibians and fishes. In all other animals, called invertebrates, there may or may not be some kind of support. If it exists, then it is always outside the body, as a hardened skin in insects and crustaceans, or as a shell in molluscs such as snails. This difference of skeleton may have something to do with the fact that vertebrates include the largest animals, like the whale and elephant, and the prehistoric dinosaurs, whereas invertebrates include the smallest, like the one-celled protozoans. In comparing buildings with animals we can look on a tall building with an internal 'skeleton' of girders as a vertebrate, and a small dome of a church with an outside 'skeleton' as an invertebrate.

Animals today occupy almost every corner of the planet, each one adapted to its surroundings. The only limitation to life would seem to be extremes of temperature and places which are completely dry or lacking air. Even so there are creatures which can exist in snow or in hot-water springs, on the tallest mountains or in the driest deserts. Any vacant space caused by fire, or volcanic eruption, or ploughed-up ground will soon be reoccupied by plants and animals. They fill up what is called a biological vacuum.

Male and female lions usually mate for life and in the wild the lioness produces no more than two or three cubs at a time.

Animal Classification

In order to study and understand any kind of animal it is first necessary to identify it, so that it can be recognised from all other kinds. Collections of animals and plants preserved in museums are arranged into their different groups, that is, they are classified. In a similar way a collection of records, stamps or books is sorted out. With animals there is a difference. They have a blood-relationship.

Among humans the nearest relationship is between parents and children, then between cousins, nephews, uncles and aunts. Scientists search for these relationships in animals. The lowest unit in classification is called a species, described looked alike. It would seem that a bat and a bird, because they both have wings and fly, should be related. Similarly, as a fish and a whale both swim they might be thought to belong together. Is the bat a kind of bird with fur—a flitter-mouse? And is the whale a kind of big fish? In fact, they are constructed quite differently. A bat is a mammal—not a bird—and the whale is a mammal—not a big fish. This method of classifying plants and animals according to their structure was first worked out during the eighteenth century by a Swedish botanist Carl von Linné, better known by his Latin name Linnaeus. He called it *Systema Naturae*, or Nature's System.

Linnaeus's System

With this method Linnaeus slowly built up his famous system of classification, based on structure, and applied it to both plants and animals. An example of how it works can be seen in the common frog and the successive groups into which it is placed. To this amphibian Linnaeus gave the species name *Rana temporaria*. These are Latin words, *Rana* meaning frog, and *temporaria* meaning temperate, for the common frog lives only in the temperate climates of northern countries.

There are many other species of closely related frogs. One of these is the edible frog, called *Rana esculenta*. Both frogs have the same first name,

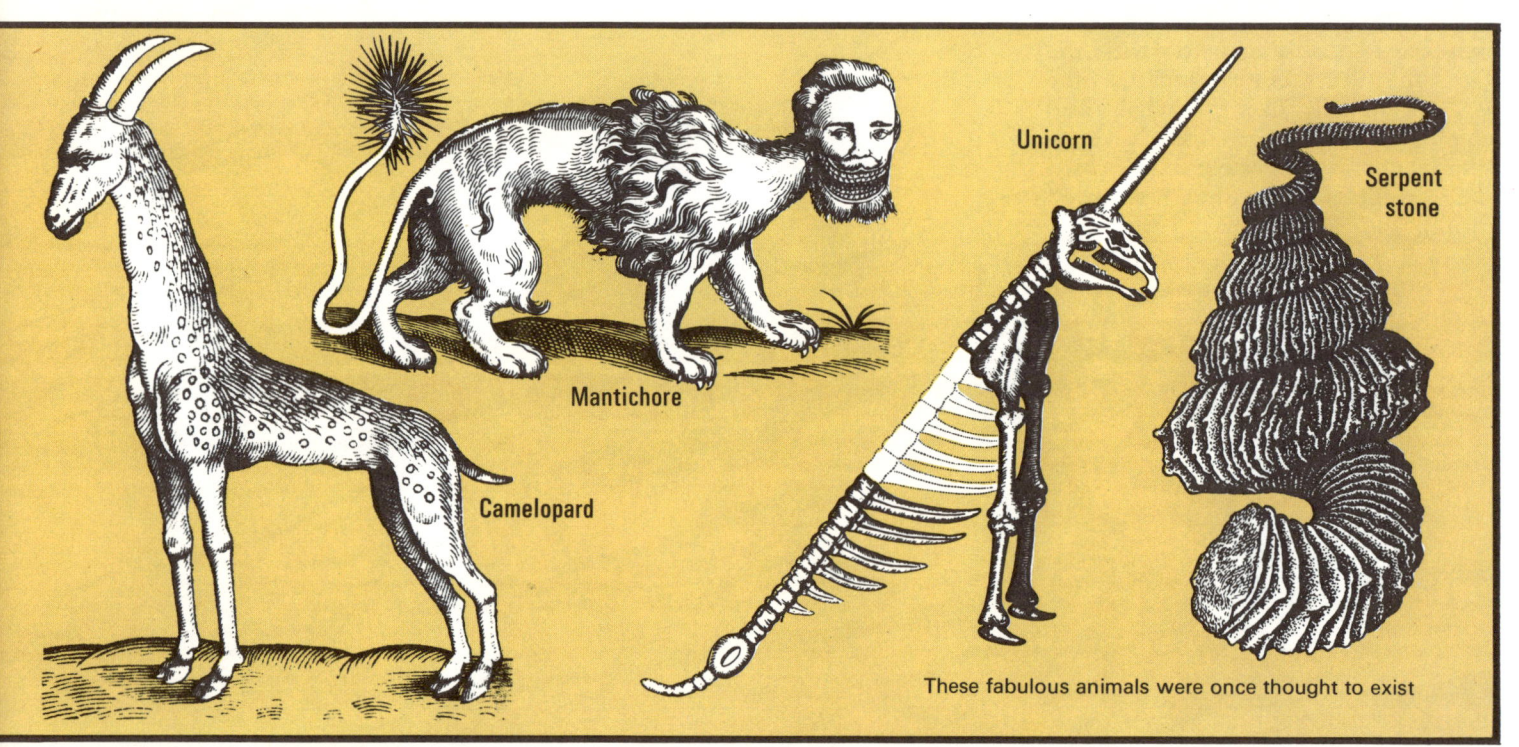
These fabulous animals were once thought to exist

broadly as 'a population of animals or plants which interbreed'. Human beings, whatever their colour, class or religion can do this, and together form a species *Homo sapiens*. The general rule is that separate species do not interbreed. If they do, then the offspring is mostly unable to reproduce itself. The best known example is the cross between a horse and donkey which produces a mule, called a hybrid. This cross-breeding has also occurred in cage-birds and tropical fishes. In zoos a lion sometimes mates with a tiger, and produces a liger.

Grouping Animals

At one time naturalists grouped animals together simply because they Linnaeus was born in 1707 in southern Sweden. His father was a country parson and he encouraged young Carl to study the wildlife of the lovely Swedish countryside. After his schooling Carl went to university, and later became a lecturer in botany at Uppsala. During his studies Carl began to classify the plants he collected by looking at the structure of their flowers, rather than their shape and colour. He examined the male and female organs, called stamens and pistils. Flowers with one stamen he called *Monandria*, those with two *Diandria*, and those with three *Triandria*, and so on. This is how a botanist recognises a flower today, by looking at the flowering parts.

Rana. This is the name of the genus to which each belongs. A bigger group, called a family, contains all the related genera of frogs and is called the Ranidae. Another family called Bufonidae contains all the toads. Frogs, toads and some other families make up an order called Anura, meaning 'without a tail'. The next higher group is the Amphibia. This is known as a class, and it also includes the order Urodela, that is amphibians with tails, such as newts and salamanders. All these animals—frogs, toads, newts and salamanders—have a backbone, so the Amphibia are placed in the phylum Vertebrata, or backboned animals. Finally the Vertebrata and all other phyla make up the entire animal kingdom.

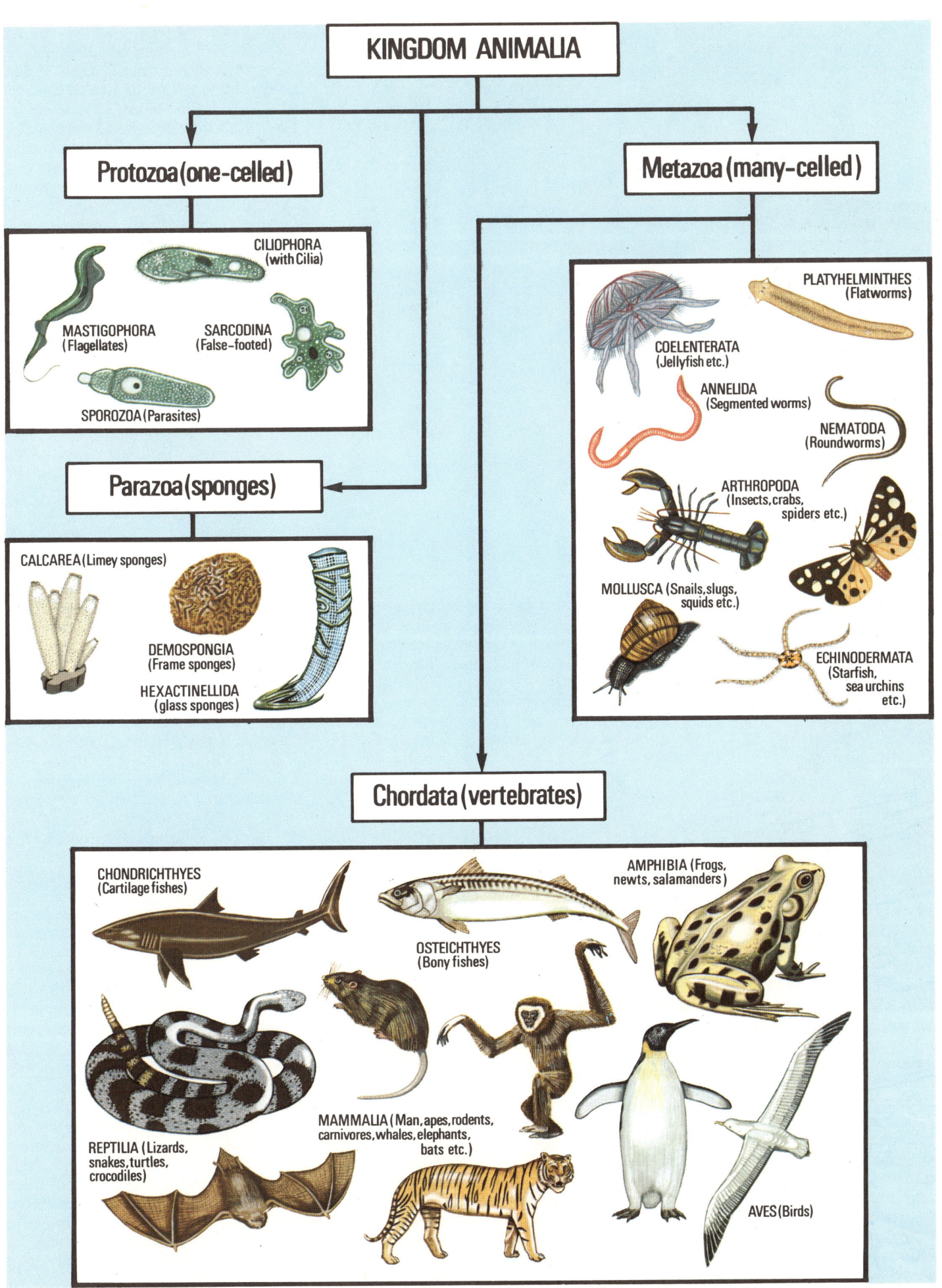
This classification chart sets out the most important and more familiar divisions of the animal kingdom.

At least seventy species of birds have been observed on the islands of Hawaii. Over half of them belonging to the remarkably varied family of honeycreepers.

The classification table for the common frog and the common toad is set out like this:

	Frog	Toad
Species	*Rana temporaria*	*Bufo bufo*
Genus	*Rana*	*Bufo*
Family	Ranidae	Bufonidae
Order		Anura
Class		Amphibia
Phylum		Vertebrata
Kingdom		Animalia

Notice that genus and species names are put into italics. Also the genus name has a capital letter, and the second, descriptive name of the species a small one. These are the rules of classification which are followed by all naturalists. In the case of the common frog it should be written in full as *Rana temporaria* Linnaeus, 1758. This tells us that Linnaeus named this species of frog in 1758. You can find it written down in his *Systema Naturae*.

Mistakes are sometimes made in classification. Linnaeus named the common toad *Rana bufo* thinking it was a close relative of the common frog. Actually it belongs to a different family. A later naturalist changed the name and called it *Bufo bufo* (Linnaeus 1758). Linnaeus's name is placed in brackets to tell us that his original name is no longer used. This may seem rather complicated, but it is necessary if each species is to go into its correct place in the animal kingdom. Since 1758 hundreds of thousands of animals have been discovered and named, from microscopic animals to the giant blue whale. In the most successful class of animals, the insects (class Insecta) some 800,000 species have so far been named.

Scientific names are always in Latin, or in Latinised Greek. This is because the earlier naturalists wrote in Latin. It is a common language which is used all over the world. Ordinary local names can lead to confusion. The frog, called the common frog in English, is known in French as *grenouille rousse*, meaning red frog. In German it is *grasfrosch* or grass frog. But in all three countries naturalists call it *Rana temporaria* and know exactly which frog it is.

Naming Species

Sometimes naturalists name a plant or animal they have discovered after themselves. During his student days Linnaeus was sent to Lapland in the far north to collect the beautiful Arctic flowers which were so little known in those days. One of these he named *Linnaea borealis*, meaning 'Linnaeus's little flower of the north'. He described it as 'lowly, insignificant, flowering for a brief spell—it is named after Linnaeus who resembles it'. This little plant is known in English as twinflower and it grows on the floor of pinewoods in the Scottish Highlands. The very descriptive way in which Linnaeus described an animal is seen in his entry for the domestic cat, *Felis domesticus*. It reads: 'A lion to the mice; moves its tail while intent on its prey, seeks its mate with querulous cries of misery; when storms threaten washes its face; buries its dung; when thrown from a height falls on its feet'. Linnaeus was a very observant naturalist.

Law of Priority

It sometimes happens that a new species receives different names when it is discovered independently by more than one scientist. To avoid confusion there is an international law which states that the first name given to a species is the one which must remain. This is known as the Law of Priority. With every new discovery the first specimen is known as the type specimen, and the place from which it came the type locality. When Linnaeus described and named the human being *Homo sapiens* he chose himself as the type specimen! This would make the type locality Sweden. Type specimens are valuable and need to be carefully preserved. They are usually kept in museums or scientific institutes, and are referred to by specialists who may be studying the group of animals to which the specimens belong.

Sometimes, in making a study of a certain animal or plant, the scientist may decide to split up the species into sub-species or races. This is helpful so long as the racial differences are constant and can be recognised. It can happen where a species becomes separated by such things as the sea, or a mountain barrier or a difference in climate. Island races are common where the animals have been separated from the mainland for a long period. Darwin noticed this when he visited the Galapagos Islands. He wrote a scientific account of the finches, and described how they varied in their beak structure, according to whether they fed on insects or on fruit. It is this kind of separation of a species into isolated groups which may eventually give rise to further species.

Animal Behaviour

One obvious difference between plants and animals is that animals move about. The main reason for this is that animals need to search for food, whereas plants can make it themselves. Most plants remain in one position all their lives, and take their food from nature. The main ingredients are carbon dioxide, water, and mineral salts from the soil. With the aid of sunlight and a green plant substance called chlorophyll, they manufacture their own foodstuffs. These are the sugars, starches, fats and proteins. Animals have no chlorophyll, so cannot do this. Instead they must eat the plants, or one another if they are hunters, in order to live. Animals have to find food, and avoid being caught to provide food for others. They search for a mate and protect their young. They must be aware of their surroundings and know what is happening around them. This is why they have a brain and a nervous system.

The study of animal behaviour, called ethology, is an attempt to find out how and why animals behave in the way they do. Since earliest times we humans have hunted animals, and have needed to know their habits and movements. A trained naturalist or hunter is experienced in this, but when it comes to understanding why they act in different ways, this is not always easy. This is because we are also animals, and sometimes make the mistake of thinking that animals behave in the same way as we do. For example, a dog sits up and opens its mouth as if it were laughing. But is this really so? We often compare ourselves to animals by using such expressions as cheeky monkey, greedy pig, vain peacock, sly fox and wise owl, when people seem to behave like them. Actually a monkey is behaving like a monkey, and a pig like a pig. In fact the animals are simply being themselves. This is their natural way, and has nothing to do with us.

Reflex Actions

However, there are many actions which we share with them. Some of these occur automatically, and others are controlled by the brain. A common automatic reaction is called a reflex. With our senses we pick up some sensation. This passes as a signal along a nerve to the central nervous system. Instead of continuing to the brain the message comes straight back from the spinal cord and operates a muscle or a gland. It is like a short circuit in which the brain is left out.

An example is a pleasant smell of food cooking, which reaches the nose and starts the salivary glands working so that the mouth waters with digestive juices. It is a way of preparing for a meal. A hand accidentally touches a hot stove and the arm muscles jerk it away. An object suddenly appears in front of the eyes, so we blink. A loud bang makes us jump. In this way messages run backwards and forwards helping us to recognise food, or jump away from danger, and generally protect our bodies from harm. All this goes on automatically, and helps other animals in the same way.

Another automatic behaviour is called instinct. Whereas reflexes are

A great eagle owl spreads its wings and rushes with flaming eyes at an attacker.

Hippopotamuses live in family groups, the males remaining in company with the females. They spend much of their time wallowing in marshy swamps.

common to different animals, an instinct is special to each species of animal. Also, it is inborn and does not have to be learned. It just happens, as we say, by instinct.

Mating Instinct

One example is called the mating instinct. This usually takes place in spring, especially among birds. It is believed to have something to do with the increase in hours of daylight as the days lengthen. This causes chemicals called hormones to circulate in the body, and to bring the reproductive organs into breeding condition. Male birds colour up and start to sing. They fight rivals and court the females until mating takes place. What is so remarkable is that a bird can build its nest without any training. When the babies hatch, the mother feeds them with the correct food. Her mother instinct is so strong that she will even sit on imitation eggs made of stone. What seems very sad is that she ignores a baby if it falls from the nest—it is no longer part of the family. All this is done by instinct.

Some very interesting studies have been made on this kind of animal behaviour, showing how animals do things by instinct. There is one elaborate mating story which is easily watched—the breeding behaviour of the stickleback. This common little fish is easy to find.

The Stickleback

To reproduce its natural habitat artificially an aquarium would be required, containing water plants in a layer of aquarium sand, so as to represent a miniature pond. The male comes into breeding condition in late spring, and colours up with red on its throat. It then selects a gap in the water plants and guards this territory from all intruders, especially a rival male. Battles take place in which the owner stickleback nearly always wins. By placing model sticklebacks in the aquarium, some with red throats and some without we know that the colour is important. This is the warning signal—red for danger.

Meanwhile a nest is built by the male. He collects bits of debris and pulls off pieces of plants and pushes them into the sand. This is bound together with a sticky substance from his kidneys. Also, mouthfuls of sand are picked up and deposited on the nest to hold it down. If a female approaches she is recognised by her dull colours and the shape of her swollen body full of eggs. The male will then perform the 'zig-zag' dance, swimming backwards and forwards and moving towards the nest so that the female can follow. She enters the nest and lays her eggs. The male then fertilises them. From that moment on he takes charge and even drives away the female. The nest is now protected vigorously as the plucky little male fights off all invaders. Extra care is needed when the eggs hatch. If a baby strays too far away, the male will pick it up in his mouth and put it back into the shoal. When old enough to fend for themselves the young scatter,

Despite their plant-like appearance, sea anemones were recognised as animals by the ancient Greeks. Some of them resemble colourful flowers and are voracious hunters of small fish.

and the male takes no further interest in them.

This remarkable performance by a small fish is only one of the many ways in which animals behave by instinct. But first, they have to be put 'in the mood', as it were. This is where the hormones play their part. One of these is called the 'fear' hormone which works when an animal is angry, tensed up or frightened. In man this hormone comes from the adrenal gland near the kidneys, passes through the blood, and releases sugar from the liver. It gives us added energy, and sometimes leads to a sweet taste in the mouth. The energy helps us to run from danger, or to stand up to an enemy. This is what might give a soldier courage in wartime.

Release of Tension

Animals behave in this way all the time, but in a normal, peaceful life man cannot always react instinctively. In fact, we are trained to control our immediate instincts. Yet it often seems cowardly to run, and not to fight back. In this situation a strange thing sometimes happens. Imagine a

The domestic cat is a typical carnivorous animal and it is its natural habit to hunt. However well fed, it will rarely lose the tendency to chase other small animals.

schoolboy who has done wrong and is facing his master. He feels guilty and perhaps is frightened, but he cannot run away or fight. He is full of energy because the 'fear' hormone is working, and he must get rid of it somehow. So he does something ridiculous, like scratching his head or blowing his nose—anything to release the tension.

In the same way, a mouse which is cornered by a cat and cannot get away, will sit up and wash its face. Or a bird that is frightened will start to make pecking movements, as if it were catching insects. All these actions are ways of getting rid of bottled-up energy, and they are called displacement activities. They make up for normal behaviour. Sometimes they can do harm and cause a nervous upset because we cannot do what nature intends.

To demonstrate the strange things that can happen with a reflex action, a famous experiment was carried out with some dogs by the celebrated Russian scientist Ivan Pavlov. When he showed them food their mouths watered—a normal reflex. At the same time he rang a bell. He did this many times and then began to ring the bell without showing the food. The dogs were so used to the association of the sound of the bell and the sight of the food that their mouths still watered. This is called a conditioned reflex.

All these ways of behaving go on automatically. In addition, we and other animals do things deliberately with the help of our brains. Much of this is the result of teaching or is due to experience. We go to school to learn. We can read, write and make conversation. With animals it is different, and they learn mostly by copying their parents, or by finding out for themselves. Memory then

The tiny stickleback takes its name from the isolated spines on its back, which vary in number. They are very fierce little fish and fight among themselves.

helps them to do the correct thing. A mother hen pretends to pick up food for pecking. The chicks copy her and so learn to find food for themselves. The young of hunting animals play a lot. It is like going to school to learn how to hunt. A puppy or kitten cannot resist chasing a ball.

In many cases animals grow up without help from the parents, and have to rely on reflexes and instincts. Others grow up with a family and learn by imitating. Still others live in family groups, or societies, as we do. Examples of animal societies are

The ring-tailed lemur has a distinctive tail with black-and-white markings which it uses to spread its scent during mating.

those of monkeys, wolves, jackdaws, deer, geese and hens. Many of these animals are kept in captivity or as pets, and have been closely studied.

Pack Leaders

In every society there is a leader, a certain wolf, jackdaw, deer or monkey. He or she can order the others about, even punish them, but they must not retaliate. The next in command bosses the rest, but respects the leader. So it goes right down the ranks to the lowest position. Everyone keeps to his rank. This condition was first studied among farmyard hens, and is called the 'pecking order'.

All the time, however, the young males keep on challenging the leader, and try to take his place. Sometimes there are serious fights between rival wolves and deer, but deaths are rare. It would be foolish to kill one another, because the strength of a social group is in its numbers, and the way in which it bands together to face danger from outside.

Dogs are descended from wolves and are also pack animals. A dog treats its human family as a pack, and its master becomes the pack leader. If well trained it will obey its leader or master, and even fight to defend him. This attachment to a master is so strong in some dogs that they have been known to travel for miles when lost in order to find their way home.

The habit of protecting a territory can be seen almost every day in the way a dog behaves. It is guarding its home and master, so when a stranger arrives it barks furiously and may even bite, as every postman knows. Man will defend his chosen territory in just the same way. A small nation will bravely fight a much bigger one which invades its country. The pages of history are filled with tales of such bravery of countries and soldiers who, with their 'backs to the wall', would rather die than give in.

Migration

Wild animals can travel great distances when they migrate to their breeding grounds. A special study has been made on the migration of birds. Rings are placed on their legs, which carry a number and an address. When a ringed bird is caught it is possible to tell how far it has come from its original home. One of the longest journeys is made each year by the Arctic tern. It breeds in the north, and travels to and fro across the world to winter in the south, a round journey of some 32,000 kilometres (20,000 miles). Even tiny humming birds can fly over the sea, from Florida in the United States to the island of Cuba, some 800 kilometres (500 miles) away. Passenger or racing pigeons can find their way back to their lofts when released far away from them. They have been used for carrying messages. Even some butterflies and moths migrate. Each summer a number come to northern Europe from north Africa.

Young salmon go down to the sea to grow up, then return to spawn in the rivers in which they were born. Eels start their lives in the Sargasso Sea in the mid-Atlantic Ocean. The tiny larva of the eels are then carried by sea currents to the shores of

Queen bee surrounded by attendant workers. Bees live in a highly complex society in which the bees are divided into groups each with its own function within the hive.

Young birds wait impatiently to be fed

Female pig-tailed monkey with its young. This breed comes from east Asia and is so named because of its short tail.

Europe on a 3,200-kilometre (2,000-mile) journey which takes nearly three years. Every spring, giant whales travel south to the Antarctic to feed on the plankton, then go north again to have their calves. Herds of antelopes go on migrations across the African plains, and reindeer move south as the Arctic winter closes in.

There is still a great deal of mystery attached to these animal journeys and little is yet known about the way in which so many different creatures find their way across the world.

Survival Instinct

Behaviour helps an animal to survive, whether it acts automatically or from teaching or experience. The behaviour will depend on how and where the animal lives, what it comes into contact with, and what kind of brain it uses. Much of the behaviour of lower animals is automatic. Marvellous as the community life of ants and bees may seem, it is not thought out, but instinctive. In a beehive, life is centred around the queen bee. She is an egg-producing machine from which the working colony is born. As more and more workers appear they take on different duties to keep the beehive going. Some tend their queen, others feed the grubs, build or repair the nest, gather food, remove debris, and even act as guards at the hive entrance. By vibrating their wings at the doorway some help to ventilate the interior.

Feeding is automatic, and food passes from one worker to the next. Food gatherers give it to the hive nurses who then feed the grubs. Food exchange is made by tapping the head with the antennae. A worker will even do this to a model head made out of Plasticine. Even more remarkable is the bee 'dance'. A food gatherer brings back nectar or pollen to the hive and performs a figure-of-eight dance on the comb. The angle of this dance in relation to the sun, and the number of times it wags its tail will tell other workers how far away the food source is, and in which direction to go. This has been tested by marking bees with spots of paint, so as to follow their journeys.

Mother and Child

Among animals which care for their young it is important for the mother and child to recognise each other, so that they do not lose contact. This can be done through one of the senses, through smell, sound, sight or touch. Among a flock of sheep with new-born lambs every mother recognises her baby by smell, and will ignore other lambs. If a mother has a still-born lamb the shepherd will take another lamb from a mother who has had twins, and place the skin of the dead lamb over it. In most cases the bereaved mother will accept it, although it is really a foster child. This recognition by smell is common among social mammals, such as deer, horses and seals, and can be watched wherever there is a group of such animals with young.

The sea horse has a prehensile tail with which it can hold on to water plants.

Among birds recognition is more by sound. Each parent bird has her own special 'mother' call which the baby immediately recognises on hatching. Dr Konrad Lorenz, the Austrian

Pigeons were probably the first birds to be domesticated by man. They have been used for thousands of years to carry messages. The birds which are commonly seen in many large cities are descended from the wild rock dove.

Rajah Brooke's birdwing butterfly

The antennae of moths are usually more elaborate and feathery than those of butterflies, which are slender and end in characteristic knobs. The male luna moth (above) has remarkable antennae which are capable of picking up the scent of a female over a distance of several miles.

naturalist, has made a special study of geese. Just when some goslings were about to hatch he removed the mother goose and sat by the eggs. As the babies hatched he gave the mother call. As a result they followed him everywhere. Unfortunately he was too big for a goose, and they became bewildered when he stood up, but were quite happy to follow him when he crawled about on hands and knees!

Shape, Size and Touch

To some young animals shape and size are important. When a mother bird approaches the nest to feed her young they automatically open their beaks, but she must be the correct size. If too big or too small they ignore her. Some birds swallow food and half digest it in their crops, then cough it up to feed the young. To make the parent open her beak the babies peck at it. But two things are important—the beak must be the correct shape and colour. The beak of the herring gull is yellow, and has a red spot near the tip of the lower part. This is what the babies peck at—a kind of target. Parents who place food into the mouths of their young are helped by the wide gap and bright colours inside the babies' mouths.

Touch plays a big part in the behaviour of some young mammals, including ourselves. We like to feel something soft and furry, and cannot resist stroking a cat or a rabbit. Young children like to play with cuddly toys, and will cling to mother when frightened. Most mammals are hairy, and hair is one of the first things which a baby touches. Also it feels warm. If a baby monkey is taken from its mother and placed by itself on the ground it will huddle up and show signs of distress. If we pick it up it will cling to our clothing. Place this baby on a model of a mother monkey made of something cold like wire or wood, and again it will seem upset. On the other hand it will cling to a 'mother' made of cloth or wool. Many mammal mothers will pluck hair from their bodies, or gather soft plant material, in order to make a comfortable nest for their newborn family.

Change of Habit

There are a number of animals which have managed to change their habits and can now live successfully in artificial habitats, such as man-made towns or in houses. Everyone is familiar with the town pigeon. This bird has descended from the wild rock dove which lives and nests on sea cliffs. In towns it nests and roosts on buildings. It seems that old habits die hard. The familiar birds like the robin, thrush and chaffinch, which are really woodland birds, have readily taken over parks and gardens, and will even use the homes we provide for them. A blue tit uses a nest-box, and a robin an old tin kettle.

Some dogs in our streets have even learned a kind of traffic drill, and can be trained to use a pedestrian crossing. Unfortunately for them, hedgehogs have not yet got used to traffic in country lanes, and many are run over at night.

The handsome plumage of the greater sun-bittern, when displayed, gives the bird the appearance of a broad-winged butterfly.

Animals and Man

At one time humans were an insignificant part of the animal world, and lived in natural surroundings. Man went about his business in small bands, searching for plants and animals to eat, and sheltering in caves. He gathered wild fruits and dug up grubs, caught fish and managed to kill the occasional large animal. All the time he was alert to danger, since he was just as likely to be caught and eaten himself.

This hand-to-mouth existence worked reasonably well so long as there was food to be had. In times of hardship man may well have died from starvation. This is probably why he moved about so much in a restless way, ever searching for food. Neanderthal and Cro-Magnon man behaved in this way, and the tools and drawings they left behind tell their story. Even today there are some

became farmers. This was during the Neolithic or New Stone Age. They tamed the animals which we now breed and use on our farms—cattle, pigs, sheep and goats—to provide themselves with meat, wool, milk and leather. Even before this the dog had been tamed to help in the hunt and to act as a guard. Much later came the taming of the horse. The origin of most domestic animals is known, and many of their ancestors may still be alive today. The remains of the dog have been found in the burial mounds of Stone Age hunters. Its ancestor is almost certainly the wolf, but the jackal may also be involved. Both these animals can be interbred with the dog.

Detail from a medieval manuscript of a hunting party. The chase was the most popular recreation of the nobility.

The use of armorial bearings began in the twelfth century when knights started to wear helmets which completely covered the face. So that they could be recognised by their followers and readily distinguished from the enemy, individual designs or 'devices' were placed on their shields and as lance pennons. Each knight chose a badge of recognition which became his personal arms or bearings. Animals often appeared in heraldry as the distinctive emblem of a family crest or as supporters of shields on the royal arms of British sovereigns.

places where modern man lives in a kind of Stone Age. The little bushmen of the Kalahari Desert, and the aborigines of Australia still make stone tools and go hunting in search of food.

Farm Animals

Over 10,000 years ago a revolution took place. In the fertile valleys of the Middle East our ancestors settled down in village communities and

It is easy to imagine how a loose alliance built up between wolf and man. The food remains of Stone Age man would have attracted wolves looking for food. Today, in the streets of eastern countries, pariah dogs roam about as scavengers in the same way. Also, a pack of wolves might corner a deer or bear and attract the attention of the human hunters, thus making a kill easier for them. No doubt the occasional wolf cub would have been brought back

to camp and reared as a pet. A social animal like a wolf will readily join a human family if taken young enough. In this way man and dog came to rely on one another, both as companions and as hunters.

Cattle have descended from a magnificent animal called the aurochs, which finally died out in Poland in 1827. This large woodland beast roamed the forests of Europe and Asia and is well known from cave paintings. It stood nearly two metres

This bison from a Stone Age cave painting is typical of the animals depicted in primitive art.

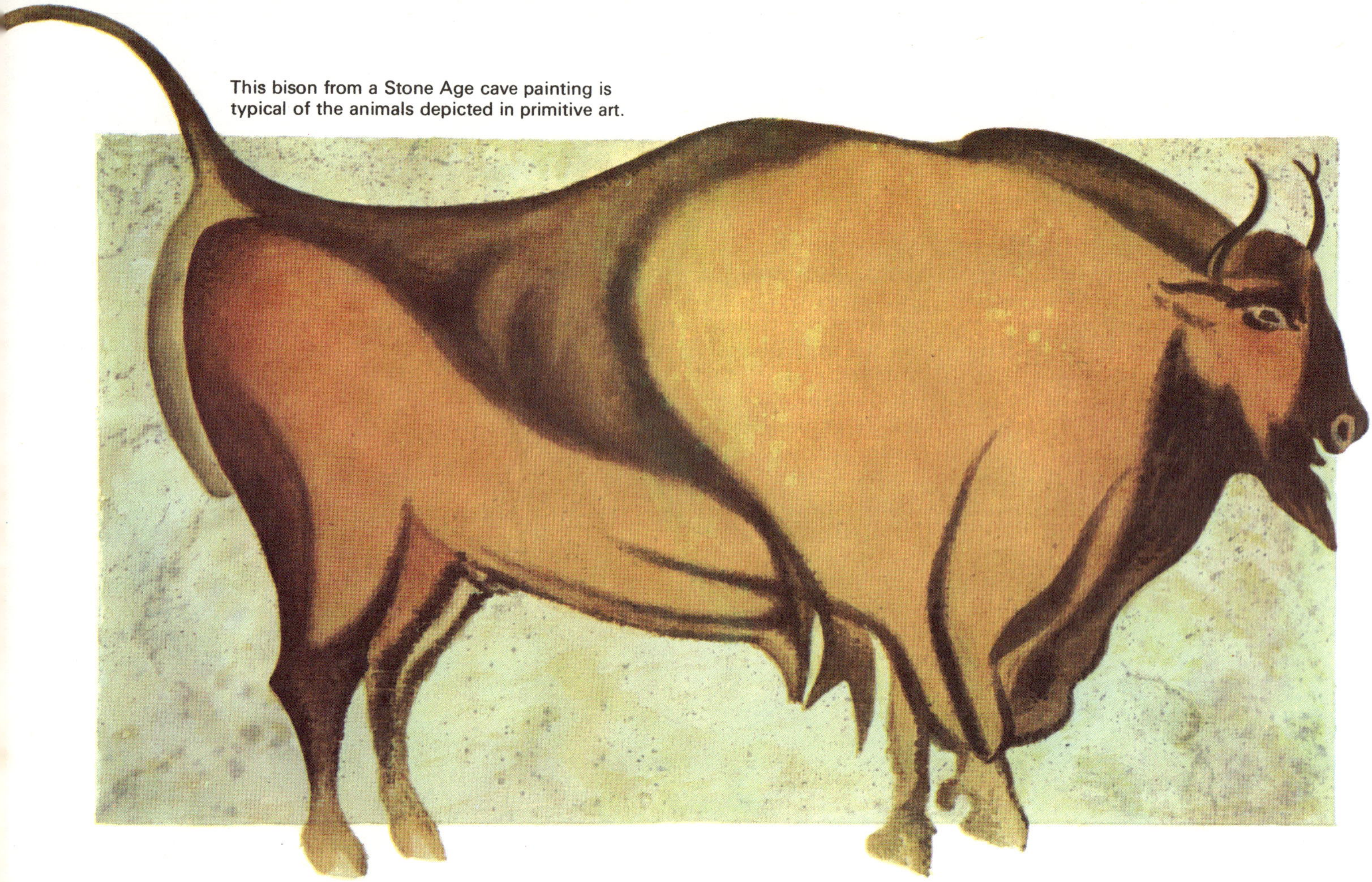

(six feet) at the shoulders, was dark coloured, and had large and sharp upturned horns. The famous white cattle in parks in Britain resemble it in shape and size. A successful attempt to revive the aurochs as a breed by crossing various domestic animals was carried out at Munich Zoo in Germany. The result was an animal closely resembling the one seen in ancient cave paintings.

There is no problem in tracing the origin of pigs, which are descended from the wild boar. Today this animal is widely scattered in forests and parks in Europe and north Africa, and eastwards through Asia as far as India.

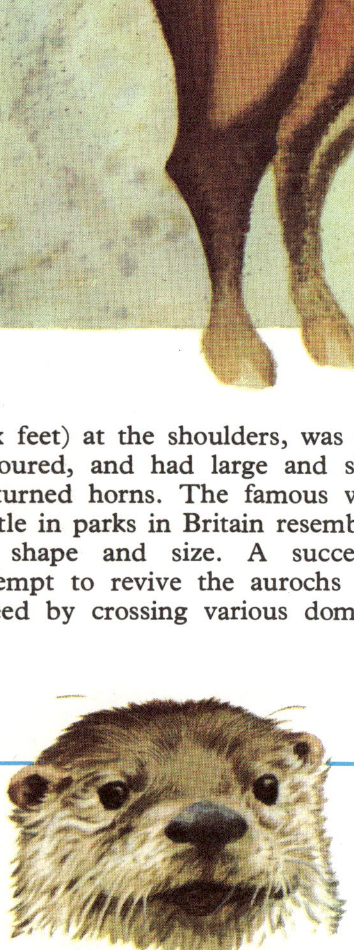

Sheep and Goats

With sheep and goats there is some difficulty in separating and identifying their remains. These have been uncovered in Neolithic settlements going back some 8,000 years. In sheep the horns of the wild ram form a spiral, but in the billygoat they are more scimitar-shaped. Domesticated sheep probably come from three wild kinds—the mouflon, argali and urial. All three belong to mountainous country in south-west Asia. In Europe the mouflon survives in Turkey and in some of the Mediterranean islands. The Soay sheep which live on Scottish islands and on the Isle of Lundy are closest to the original sheep brought there by the Neolithic farmers.

The goat, which was domesticated at about the same time as the sheep, has a probable ancestor still living—the bezoar goat of mountain country in the Middle East. Horns of domestic breeds do not always resemble those of their ancestors, but there are some helpful distinctions. A 'goatee' beard is worn by the billygoat, and both male and female carry horns. In sheep only the ram has them. Both sheep and goats retain the habits of their ancestors. They are good at climbing and if let loose prefer the hilly countryside.

The turkey comes not from the country after which it is named but from the mountains of Mexico. The

The otter is an attractive water creature which man has learned to tame and train. In its natural state the otter is found throughout Europe and in North America, a quiet, shy animal who hunts at night. It is incredibly agile in the water, turns somersaults, dives and performs impressive water acrobatics which are fascinating to watch. An otter will also enjoy playing with toys, such as marbles, rubber balls and other small objects, and chatters happily to itself while it plays. Gavin Maxwell, the Scottish writer and naturalist, lived for years in a remote Highland cottage with otters as his constant companions. The most famous of his otter friends were Mijbil and Edal. These he trained to live side by side with him, like any other domestic pet, sleeping in the same bed, eating from his hand, and greeting him with affection.

Indian jungle fowl is the ancestor of the barnyard hen, and the wild mallard has produced the duck. Farm geese are bred from the greylag goose.

The Domestic Cat

The domestic cat originated in North Africa from a race of wildcat. It was tamed when farming first started, in order to keep the rats and mice from raiding stores of grain and fruit. The European wildcat, which also lived in the Scottish Highlands, is not the ancestor of the domestic cat, and has never been tamed. Although it looks very much like a pet tabby, it is larger, with a thicker, more bottle-shaped tail, and prominent stripes. In a tabby the markings tend to be blotched and the tail thinner. Domestic cats slowly spread through Europe, and in Britain were a novelty for many years.

Tamed horses arrived late, well into the Bronze Age. Over the grassland steppes of Asia roamed herds of wild horses which are now almost extinct. They were caught and tamed by the nomads, and to the civilised world must have been a strange sight. This may account for the appearance of the centaur in Greek mythology—a kind of half man, half beast. Today only a few of these wild horses exist in Mongolia. They are called tarpans, horses of stocky build, mouse-grey in colour, with dark lower legs and a short, stiff mane. There is a black stripe along the back, and zebra stripes behind each foreleg. Ponies have run wild for many years in such places as the Camargue in France, the Pyrenees in Spain, Westphalia in Germany, and in many parts of Britain. Among British breeds the nearest to a wild ancestor is the Exmoor pony.

Hunting Animals

Man has always kept in close touch with animals to suit his various needs. With the coming of domestication (from the Latin word *domus*, a house) the need to hunt for food lessened. But hunting is a deep-rooted instinct in man and he continued to chase animals for sport. The horses which man first killed for food became his companions in the hunt.

In Europe the 'sport of kings', or the pursuit of wild deer, became the fashion among the rich. The Normans introduced a strict code of hunting, governed by laws which gave protection to the 'royal beasts'. More important, large areas of woodland were set aside as hunting forests in which the deer could live and breed. The ordinary folk, or commoners, who lived in isolated cottages and hamlets within the forest boundaries were permitted to carry on their daily lives. Cattle, ponies and pigs were allowed to wander about and feed on the forest leaves, grass and acorns as they had always done. Firewood could be gathered, and timber cut or lopped from the trees. Some of these ancient commoner's rights are still protected today, particularly in Britain. Ponies and cattle can be seen on open grassy places in the New Forest, Epping Forest and Dartmoor, which are all that remain of some of the old hunting forests. The royal

Often described as 'man's best friend', the dog has been trained to obey man and to work for him. A gun dog, for instance, such as the retriever pictured above, can be trained to fetch and bring back in perfect condition birds and game shot by its owner.

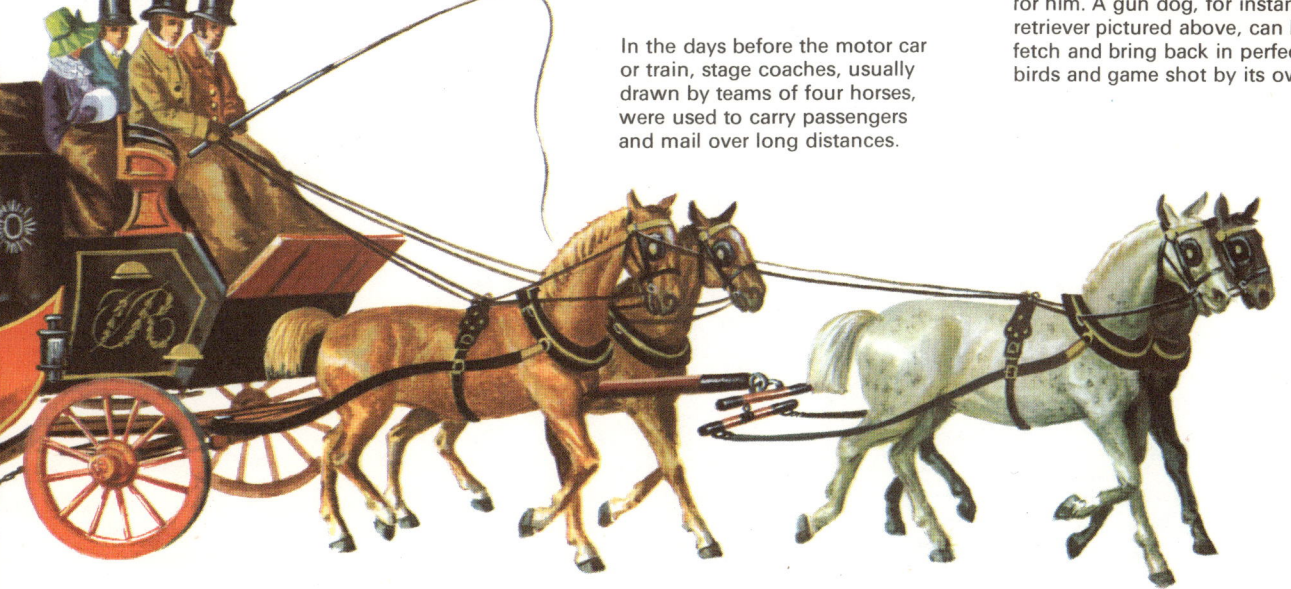

In the days before the motor car or train, stage coaches, usually drawn by teams of four horses, were used to carry passengers and mail over long distances.

On the grazing lands of the western highlands and islands of Scotland, a family such as this of West Highland cattle is a familiar sight. Framed against a background of heather-clad mountains and still, blue lochs, the cattle with their shaggy brown coats and wide horns make an impressive picture. These cattle are closer to the original wild cattle of Britain than any other breed; they are rarely found outside Scotland. The beef from West Highland stock is renowned throughout the world for its tenderness and flavour.

courts of Europe continued to hunt until the end of the nineteenth century. Today deer hunting still goes on in some places but mostly it has been replaced by fox hunting which, in its turn, is dying out.

New sports have come into fashion with the arrival of firearms. Pheasants, grouse and other game birds are shot for pleasure. The hare is pursued by hounds. One of the most ancient sports is hawking. A bird of prey such as a falcon is trained to fly at other birds. It is now even used to scare away birds from airfields where they might be a danger to aircraft. Many people dislike blood sports and condemn them as barbaric. Even so, the ancient urge to hunt still lingers on in man. An outlet for this instinct can perhaps be found in games such as football, hockey and cricket. Chasing after a ball is really not so very different from chasing an animal.

Animals in Combat

Athletics started with the Olympic Games in ancient Greece, which were a test of skill and endurance between men. At that time also, animals were used in combat with one another, and with men, in order to provide a holiday spectacle for the public. This was continued in the time of the Roman Empire, when gladiators were trained to fight animals. On a smaller scale cock-fighting and the baiting of bulls and bears went on all over Europe. Bull fighting still continues in Spain. To add to the excitement, betting on the winner of a race between animals was introduced, especially those involving horses and greyhounds. Dogs and horses, man's 'best friends', have been bred for racing and other pursuits for many years. For hunting with dogs there is the greyhound, deerhound and wolfhound, all very old breeds. The bloodhound, once a guard dog, is now used in tracking. The little dachshund was actually bred to help in hunting the badger (*dachs* is German for badger). The basset hound is trained to hunt the hare.

Gun dogs, which include the pointer, retriever, setter and spaniel, help in finding game and collecting the kill. Terriers, from the French word *terre*, meaning earth, are sturdy dogs used for digging and creeping underground to flush out foxes and to catch rats and other vermin. Special breeds for controlling farm animals are the sheep dog and the corgi, a cattle dog. Of special service to man are the Alsatian as a guard dog, the Newfoundland for rescue work, and the husky for pulling the sledge.

The Horse in Battle

Horses have also played their part with man, and even changed the course of history. First tamed by the nomads of the Asiatic plains the horse was used for travelling and hunting. Before the arrival of railways and cars it was the main means of transport. When carts and chariots came into use, during the Iron Age, horses were bred for strength and endurance and used in fighting. The menial tasks of pulling the plough and carrying loads were left to cattle.

The sturdy shire horse (top) is one of the strongest horses in the world, and bred to work in the fields, pulling ploughs and heavy carts. The beautiful thoroughbred (centre), bred from Arab stock, is used for racing and hunting. The tiny pony (below) was once a worker, but now is seen mainly in circuses and as a children's mount.

Many animals have been domesticated, sometimes as pets and sometimes for ornament. The pet rabbit (left) is descended from the wild European rabbit. The golden hamster (above left) is a popular pet, now almost extinct in its wild state and existing mainly in captivity. The goldfish (above) was domesticated from a dull-coloured wild carp in Asia. The canary (above right) has been bred from the wild finch of the Canary Islands, and the budgerigar (right) from a small Australian parrot. Shown below is the cat, perhaps the most aristocratic of our domestic pets.

The use of the horse in battle has changed with the times. Nomadic tribes, the 'barbarians' of Asia, used swift horses in making raids and advances into Europe in Roman times. During the Dark Ages heavier horses were used by the knights of old on crusades and pilgrimages. Wars were fought in heavy armour. From these powerful horses are descended the shire and farm horses. At the battle of Agincourt the clumsy cavalry proved a poor match against the English bowmen. Horses were used right up until the First World War, mainly in transport. Today they would be no use against armoured tanks. Horses arrived late in America, and were taken over by the early settlers, such as the Spanish. Those that escaped made for the open plains and hills. These mustangs which had gone wild helped to write a new chapter in the history of America. They were soon captured and tamed by the American Indians, who had never before seen a horse. They were used during the days of the Wild West, particularly for buffalo hunting and for pulling the wagon trains westward.

Today dogs and horses are used mainly for racing and hunting, or kept as pets, although in some countries they are still beasts of burden. Other servants of man are the Indian elephant, the yak of Tibet, the camel in the Sahara and Asia, and the reindeer in the north.

Animals have also helped man in education and research. In universities, museums, zoos, research institutes and schools, animals are studied for a variety of reasons. One important aspect of this research is concerned with animals that do us harm, by causing damage or spreading disease. Because we live artificial lives these animals take advantage of the things we build and grow. If we neglect our homes or food we may expect unwelcome visitors like mice, rats and house flies. Slugs attack garden plants, squirrels damage trees, and mosquitos bring malaria. All have to be controlled.

Animals in Art

Animals also play their part in poetry, art and story telling, and in entertainment. Many of the oldest books, such as the Bible, often mention animals. The first drawings of animals were produced by our cave ancestors and are supposed to be a form of magic, or religion. If man could steal the shadow of the animal which he hunted, and place this on the cave wall, then he had some kind of power over it. This is one possible reason for cave paintings.

Another is that these drawings were the beginning of writing. For example, a drawing of a snake as a simple curved line would form a letter 's', which makes the snake's hissing sound when pronounced. By Egyptian times the hieroglyphics cut on to stone were being used as a language. Many of the oldest natural sounds we make—like a baby's cry of 'ma-ma' for its mother—are now part of language. *Mamma* is Latin for breast, and mammal is the English word for a breast-feeding animal.

Zoos and Nature Reserves

Since 1900 as many as a hundred different species of animals have been exterminated by man. During the nineteenth century there was mass slaughter by big game hunters in Africa and India, and in America the buffalo was nearly wiped out by hunters. Throughout the Middle Ages the Norman kings and barons hunted red deer and wild boar. Such royal sports must have accounted for the lives of countless numbers of birds and beasts. In Biblical times the Assyrian kings hunted lions and gazelles, and the Romans killed all kinds of animals to please their emperors and the mass of the people on holidays. Even from the very earliest times, before he hunted and killed for pleasure, man pursued wild animals for food. Today we are beginning to realise that this cannot go on and that the slaughter must end before all wild animal life is wiped out.

But hunting is not the only danger to wildlife. The human population is increasing and expanding rapidly, people are living longer, and they are travelling about more than ever before. This means there are more mouths to be filled, more homes and roads to be built, and more food to be grown. Everywhere more space is needed. As a result we are steadily invading the homes of wild animals and disturbing the countryside in which they live.

Natural Habitats

This is the real problem—the destruction of natural habitats. Animals are more specialised than we are, and can only live properly in the right surroundings. Their homes may be in woodland, on a mountain, in a pond, along the sea shore, or in the sea. Different sorts of ground—soft or rocky, flat or hilly, wet or dry, acid or chalky—will support different communities of plants and animals. Wherever possible, land is now set aside to provide nature reserves in which animals may be protected.

On a bigger scale national parks and game reserves are created by governments, such as the Buffalo Park in Canada and the Kruger National Park in South Africa. These special areas are very necessary. Whereas man can adapt himself to all sorts of surroundings, and may one day even live on the moon, animals can live only in places to which they are naturally suited.

From the level of governments down to each individual person all can play a part in helping to preserve animals. Even the creation of a local park or a simple garden is a help. Such places attract insects and birds which are often encouraged by the provision of bird tables and nest boxes. Flowers are grown not only for their scent and beauty, but also to attract bees and butterflies. A garden pond becomes a kind of miniature reserve for water creatures such as fish, frogs and many kinds of water insects. In a surprising way nature is quick to take advantage of these places, and a naturalist can find as much going on in a town garden as in a wild place. Even so there are constant dangers which animals have to face, such as pesticides, pollution of water, damage from oil and the attentions of poachers. To save the rarer animals laws are passed to protect them.

In conserving animals zoos can be a help. At one time they were run just for amusement, and sometimes kept in poor condition. Today many

Some species of animals have been saved from extinction by the creation of nature reserves and national parks, where the natural balance of life is encouraged and preserved.

of the best zoos care for rare animals in the hope that they will breed and increase. Some species have even been saved from extinction, and have been returned to the wild. The European bison, Père David's deer and the Hawaiian goose have all been saved in this way. Many countries now have organisations whose aim is to protect animals and their homes, by providing trained scientists to study them and to give money towards the upkeep of nature parks and game reserves.

The Study of Ecology

The study of animals and plants in their natural surroundings, and how they relate to one another, is called ecology. It shows how dependent one form of life is upon another, and upon the nature of its environment. There is a delicate balance within nature so that each animal in a community gets its proper share of food and living space. Much of this is linked with what is called the food chain. For example, in a hedgerow there are many leaves which are eaten by insects. These insects are then fed upon by songbirds. These in turn provide food for a family of sparrow hawks. Working along such a food chain the number of animals gets less and less as they get bigger. If it is a poor year for insects then the song birds may suffer, and the sparrow hawks will have fewer birds to hunt. If there is an insect increase, songbirds will benefit, and the sparrow hawk family may be larger than usual.

When man interferes with these food chains he may also suffer. Killing off predators like birds of prey, or hunters like the stoat and fox, may start an increase in rodents, resulting in damage to crops and trees. In parts of Africa crocodiles are shot for their skins, and have been exterminated from some rivers and lakes. As a result the lake-side villagers who depend on fishing have gone short.

Man has kept animals in zoological gardens or parks since the days of ancient Egypt. Many great kings and queens throughout history have maintained private collections of animals. One of the earliest zoos set up for the general public was in London at Regent's Park in 1826, when the Zoological Society of London took over the royal collection of animals from the Tower of London. Other famous zoos are the Jardin des Plantes in Paris and the first zoos in Russia (Moscow 1864) and the United States (Philadelphia 1859).

This is because young crocodiles live in the shallows and feed on small waterside creatures such as catfish and crayfish. Because there are no crocodiles to keep these creatures down they have increased and so raided the spawning beds of other fish to eat their eggs. This means there are fewer fish for the fishermen to catch.

Science and Animals

Geese can be conditioned to adopt a human 'mother'.

Animals have greatly helped man's search for knowledge and discovery in many ways. Through them he has learned much about behaviour and intelligence, about sickness and disease, about how the human body works, and about such things as flight, space travel and direction finding.

In the fight against disease little was known about its cause until Anton van Leeuwenhoek discovered the use of the magnifying glass in 1675. Today the microscope and the more powerful electron microscope are uncovering a whole world of minute plants and animals we call germs, which are responsible for disease.

For centuries it was thought that a killer disease, called malaria (from the Italian for bad air), came from the unpleasant smell which hangs over marshes and stagnant water. Scientists then discovered that the real danger comes from a minute germ carried by a female mosquito. The insect feeds on human blood so that the germs enter the body and attack the blood cells. This causes bouts of fever. In Britain, where malaria was once common, it was called the ague, or shivering disease. A careful study of mosquitos and how they live and breed in water has helped to fight this problem. One method is to drain away the stagnant water where they live, or treat the water with chemicals so that the mosquitos cannot breed.

Blood Transfusion

When a person has an accident and loses blood a transfusion may be necessary. A blood donor volunteers his own blood to help the patient. But there are different types of blood, and those of the donor and the patient must match. Yet even when the blood groups matched, there were times when the patient became worse and even died. To find out why this happened experiments were carried out on Rhesus monkeys. As a result of these experiments it is now known that most people have in their blood a special chemical. It is called the Rhesus positive factor, or Rh+, named after the monkey. A few people without this chemical are Rhesus negative or Rh−. When giving a transfusion, in addition to seeing that the blood groups match, it is most important that Rh+ blood is not given to a Rh− patient.

Fighting Illness

Some diseases such as smallpox, tetanus and typhoid can be prevented or cured by giving an injection. The disease germs give off a poison called a toxin. The body fights back to try to kill off the germs and stop the poison. In a mammal such as man there are special cells in the glands called lymphatic organs, situated in the armpits and groin. These sometimes swell up when we are poisoned. The lymphatic glands make a chemical called an antibody which helps in fighting the germs. If these antibodies cannot work fast enough to kill the germs, the patient may die. So, to help our bodies keep healthy, we can be vaccinated. This is like being given a mild dose of the disease. A large animal like a cow or horse is injected with the toxin and starts to make its own antibodies. Being a large animal it is not harmed. The serum which is formed is taken from the horse and injected into the patient. His body is then prepared to fight the disease, should he happen to catch it. He is immunised, or not liable to the danger of infection.

Poisonous snakes and spiders are also used in fighting illness. A person bitten by a snake can be given an anti-venom serum. There are special snake farms in parts of the tropics where poisonous snakes are 'milked' of their poison, which is then prepared into a serum and injected into a patient.

One of the most common ways to study trial and error behaviour in animals is to place a creature such as a rat in what is called a puzzle box. This may contain a lever which, when properly operated by the animal, releases a pellet of food or turns on a light or a current of heat. The animal thus learns to make the correct movement in order to gain some reward which is pleasing. It often takes a long time for an 'inexperienced' rat to learn the correct action so that it will repeat it as a conditioned reflex. There is another form of experiment which involves the use of a maze, through which the animal must find its way in order to obtain the reward of food.

Exploration

In exploring, and more recently in space travel, animals have played

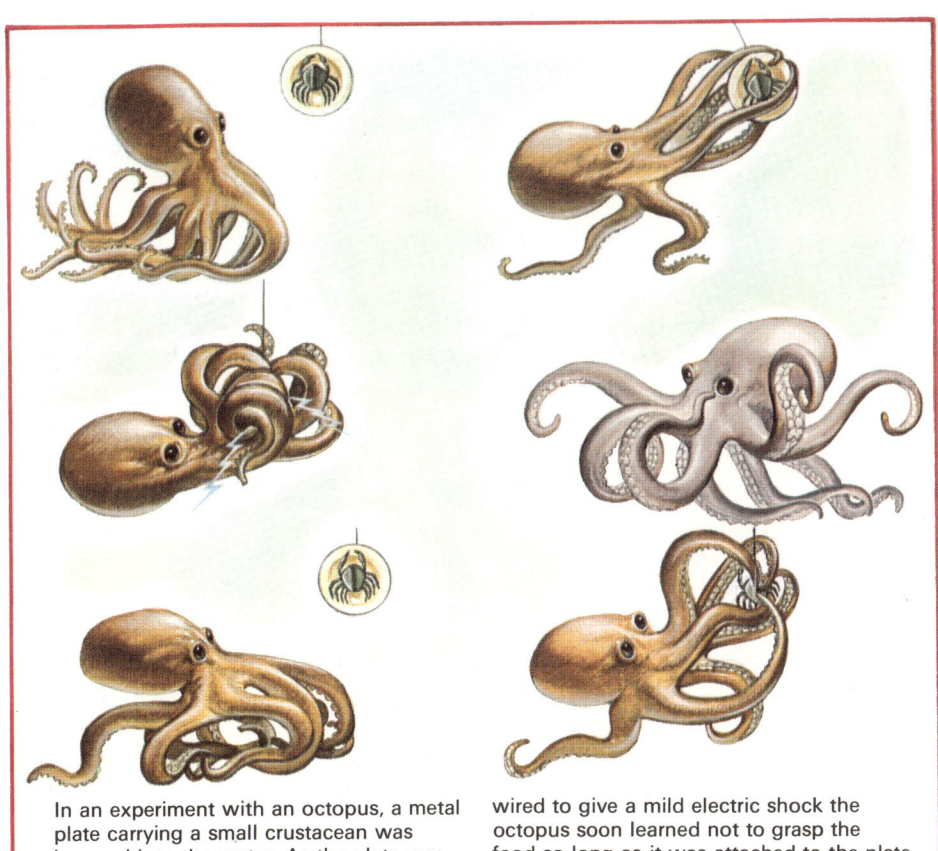

In an experiment with an octopus, a metal plate carrying a small crustacean was lowered into the water. As the plate was wired to give a mild electric shock the octopus soon learned not to grasp the food so long as it was attached to the plate.

their part. Dogs and monkeys were among the first astronauts to travel in space. Dogs have taken man to the north and south poles. Canaries have been taken down coal mines to test for gas, and pigeons used to carry messages long before wireless was invented. Bats and dolphins have taught us much about direction finding. Both can find their way even when blindfolded, by sending out very high-pitched sounds, which bounce off objects as an echo. This echo-location, called sonar, is similar to the radar equipment which was first used in the Second World War to search out enemy aircraft and trace their movements.

Many animals have been used to test their intelligence. Most of what they can do, however remarkable, is due to their highly developed senses, rather than to the powers of reasoning such as man uses. A simple story will illustrate the point. A boy misbehaves, so his mother scolds him in a cross voice. 'You are a naughty boy,' she says. If she had used a cross voice to say 'You are a good boy', he would have been puzzled. But if she said to her dog, 'You are a bad dog' and used a gentle voice, the dog would probably wag its tail. It would not understand the words but would react only to the tone of voice.

Designing Machinery

Much of the machinery which we depend upon works with levers and joints. In designing machinery scientists can learn from the way in which an animal's skeleton is built, and how its legs and wings operate.

To keep airborne a bird can hang on the wind in an almost stationary position, merely by adjusting the position of its wings. The hind edge is tilted downwards, so that pressure of air is built up on the underside. This forces the wing upwards, and by overcoming the force of gravity keeps the bird in the air. A kangaroo leaping at full speed can make a sudden, sharp turn without falling over. You or I would probably tumble head over heels. In this case it is the tail which acts as a counterweight. In the turning movement it is swung round to keep the kangaroo from over-balancing. A fish has a swim bladder filled with air. The pressure inside can be varied according to the depth of water, and so made equal to the pressure outside. In this way a fish can hang in the water at different depths, as if floating in air, and without the need to swim. These three principles of flight, balance and water pressure have been applied to the building of machines such as aircraft, cranes and submarines.

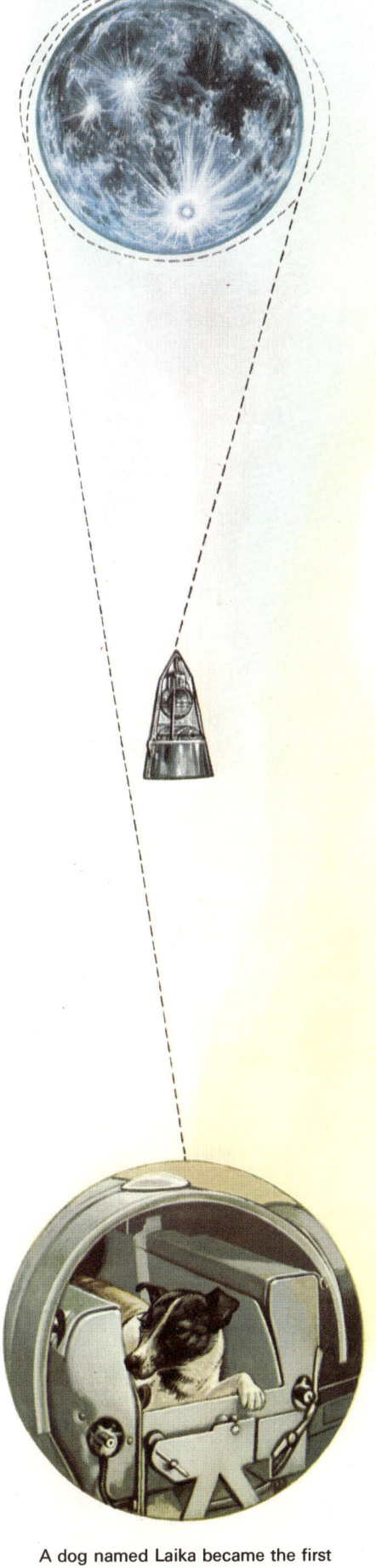

A dog named Laika became the first creature to travel in space when she was launched in the Russian Sputnik 2 in 1957.

Animals without Backbones

By far the majority of animals are small and have no backbone. These are called invertebrates—animals without backbones. Insects alone number over 800,000 species. They swarm everywhere, and live on the highest mountains and down the deepest mines. They can be found in the ground, on bushes and trees, in rivers, ponds and lakes; some even in deepest snow and others in hot springs. Insects spread right down to the sea shore and only then are they halted. They are not sea creatures. Even so there are one or two water bugs which manage to live on the ocean surface.

Not surprisingly, insects can be destructive and harmful to man. They invade crops and attack farm animals. They kill garden plants and do damage in our homes. We may even suffer in our bodies from their unwanted attentions. Some insects cause disease, such as the mosquito which carries the malaria germ.

Insects are readily recognised by having six legs, a body divided into three parts—head, thorax and abdomen—and most are winged. Also, they pass through stages that progress, with some exceptions, from an egg to a larva which feeds and grows, shedding its outer skin from time to time. The larva then changes into a pupa and finally into an adult creature. The adult does not grow and usually lives a short life. Insects like grasshoppers and dragonflies pass direct from larva, called a hopper or nymph, into an adult.

Arachnids

Arachnids are invertebrates which are sometimes confused with insects. They consist of spiders, scorpions and mites. In their case the combined head and thorax is joined to the abdomen. The adult arachnid has eight legs and biting jaws. Scorpions have elongated bodies and a sting on the 'tail'. Mites are small and occur in the ground, on plants and animals, and can be harmful.

Millipedes

Soil is the main home of another group of invertebrates, the millipedes and centipedes, which have long bodies and numerous legs. Millipedes are plant-eaters and have rounded bodies and a double pair of legs to each segment. Centipedes have biting jaws, a flattened body, and are hunters. There is a single pair of legs to each segment.

Crustaceans

Some invertebrates live in the sea. These are the crustaceans. They have a hardened shell-like body, and many pairs of legs which operate in different ways. They may be used for walking, feeding, swimming, catching food, or even for breathing. The best known crustaceans are the lobster, shrimp and crab, but there are a great number of smaller kinds. Some live in freshwater, like the water flea, *Daphnia*, and many tiny creatures in the sea drift about as plankton.

Molluscs

Molluscs include the familiar slug, snail and mussel. As many live in the sea as on land. Some are naked, others have a shell. The shell can be single, as in the snail, which is called a univalve. The mussel with its hinged double shell is known as a bivalve. Looking very different, yet still molluscs, are the octopus, squid and cuttlefish, which all have tentacles. These take the place of the foot which a snail uses for crawling.

This diagram illustrates some typical representatives of the principal phyla or groups of invertebrates. The protozoans (1) are simple single-celled animals. Coelenterates (2) include jellyfish, sea anemones and corals. Annelids (3) are worms and leeches. Molluscs (4) are snails, oysters and octopuses. Echinoderms (5) are starfishes and sea urchins. Arthropods are one phylum which includes arachnids, or spiders and scorpions (6), insects (7), crustaceans (8) and millipedes (9).

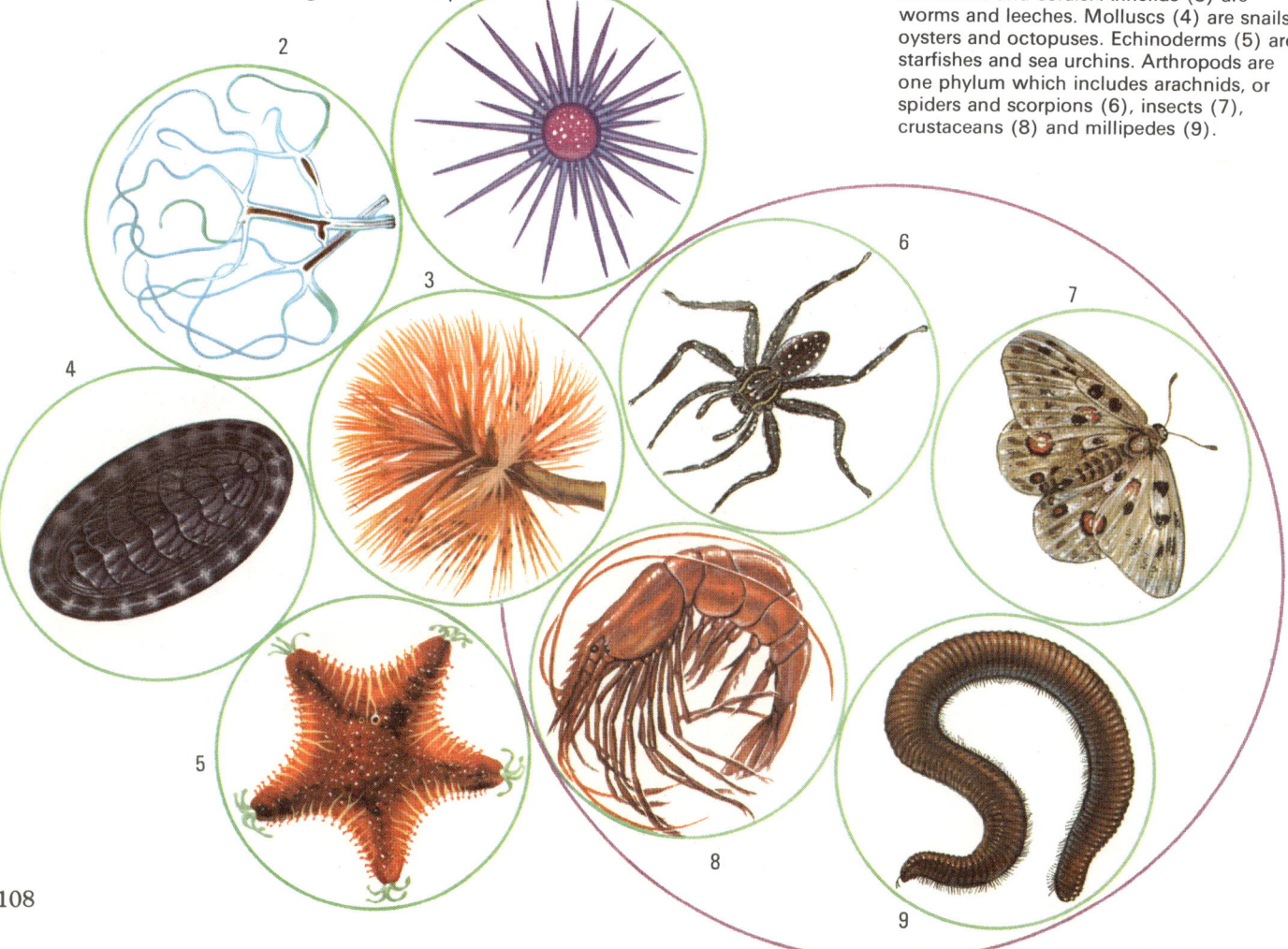

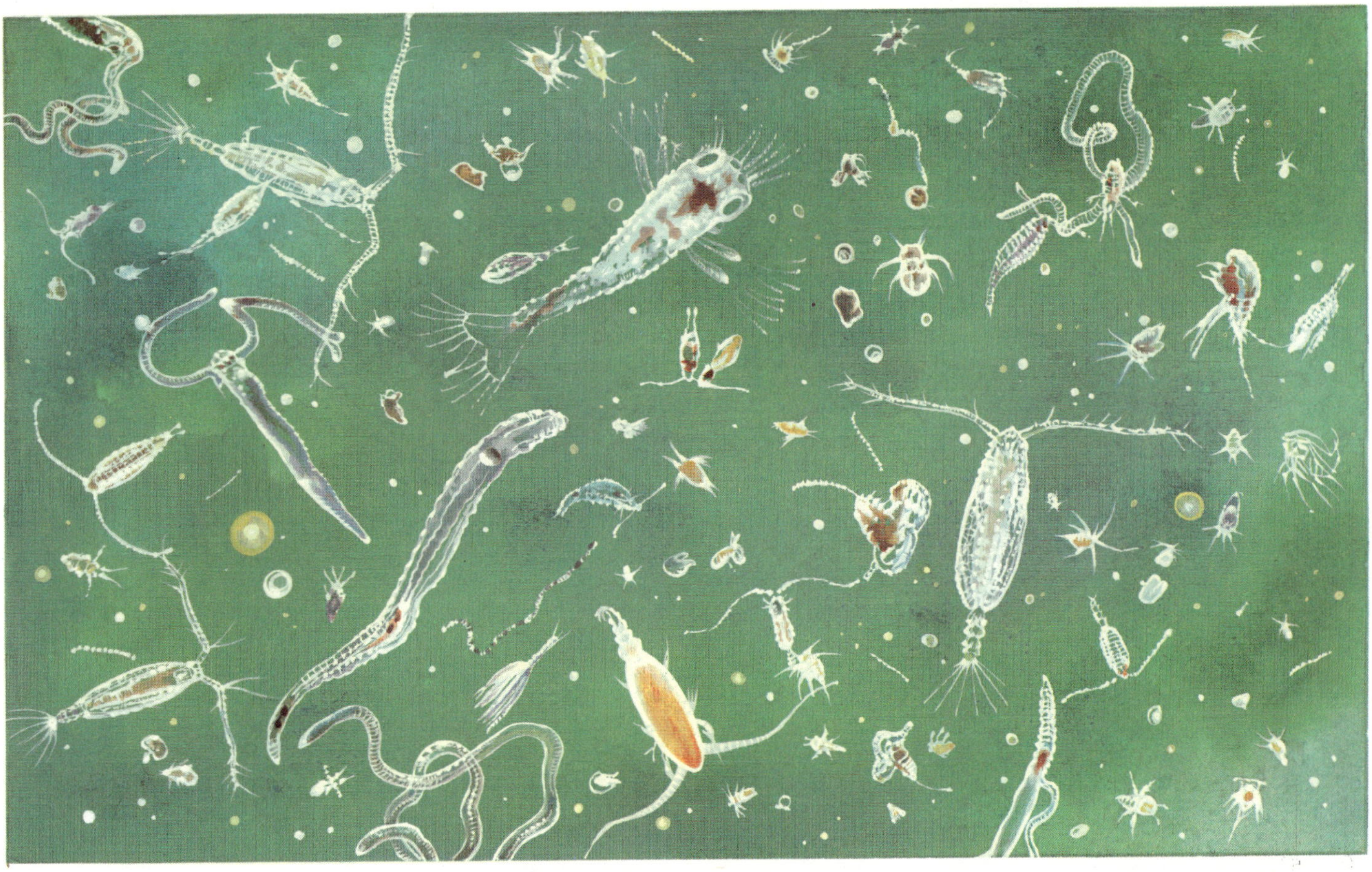

Worms

What is usually known as a worm could mean anything which is long and crawls. There are a number of 'worm' groups. The well-known earthworm belongs to a group called Annelida (Latin *annulus*—a ring). Its body is divided into segments. There are many kinds living in tubes in the mud and sand on the sea bottom. Fishermen dig them up for bait. Some have fan-shaped gills which are used to breathe with and to comb the water for food. Roundworms, or nematodes, on the other hand, have no segments and are pale in colour. They live in darkness, either in the soil or as parasites in plants and animals, including man. A person suffering from 'worms' has probably become a victim. Eggs which pass through the mouth develop into nematodes which settle in the intestine, and cause weakness by stealing food. Their eggs then pass out. Clean habits and proper sanitation help to avoid this kind of illness. There are about 10,000 species of roundworms.

Flatworms, which belong to the phylum Platyhelminthes, are of two kinds. Some, called flukes, are leaf-shaped and again are often parasitic. Here, the life story is more complicated. A well-known example is the liver fluke of sheep. A swimming larval fluke attacks a water snail, changes its form many times, then swims away to settle on a blade of grass at the water's edge. A sheep eats the grass and the larva ends up in its liver to grow up. The mature fluke lays eggs which pass out as water larvae, and these seek out more snails. This is why liver fluke disease usually occurs in chalk country where there are more snails.

Tapeworms are long, ribbon-like flatworms which live inside animals, sometimes in humans. They are fixed to the wall of the intestine by a tiny head which has suckers or hooks on it. The tape is in segments, and the ripe ones at the end of the tape break away to release the eggs. These may be picked up by a smaller animal and will turn into a larval tapeworm. If this smaller animal is then eaten by the larger one a tapeworm will result. In the case of the pork tapeworm the pig swallows an egg, and a larval worm forms in its flesh. A human may then eat this pork and swallow the larval, which then turns into a tapeworm. This is why meat inspection and proper cooking of meat is important so as to make it safer to eat. There are about 6,000 species of flatworms.

Zooplankton or animal plankton are tiny forms of life drifting about in the ocean. They provide food for larger fishes.

The protozoan called *Volvox* is a primitive form of algae found in water. Microscopic in size, it propels itself by waving two thread-like structures on its body, called flagella. The *Volvox* tend to live in colonies and each is a green-coloured, hollow sphere about the size of a small pin's head and may be thought of as either plant or animal.

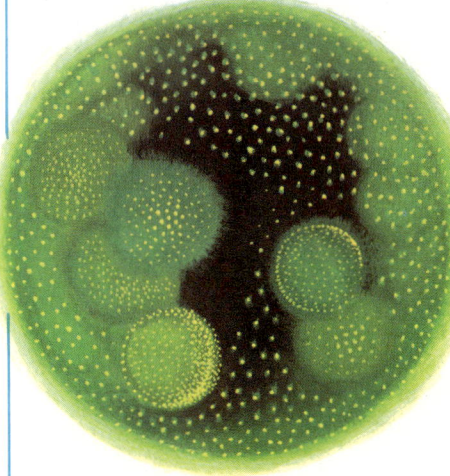

Other Groups

Other groups of invertebrates include the one-celled protozoans, the coelenterates (anemones and jellyfishes), sponges and rotifers.

Primitive Animals

Living in a world which is only visible through the microscope are a host of tiny plants and animals on which so many of the larger animals depend. They live mostly in water, from which all life originated, and are an important link in the food chain. In countries with seasonal changes of climate they lie dormant during the cold winter months. With the coming of spring and longer hours of daylight life is renewed. A pond turns green with the appearance of tiny, swimming plants called algae. These become the food of the protozoans. Water fleas and other small crustaceans eat the protozoans and in turn provide food for small fish, newts and water insects. In this way the larger fish and water birds can get a meal. It is the same in the sea, but on a much bigger scale. Even the mighty blue whale depends on minute sea plants, called diatoms, which bring the food chain to life again every spring.

Protozoans

Protozoans swarm everywhere, even in stagnant puddles, and number some 30,000 species. There are four main kinds which move in different ways. Amoeba belongs to those which creep about with their temporary false feet. In the sea are similar creatures, which build shells around their tiny bodies. They are called foraminifers, and drift among the plankton. When they die their shells sink into the ooze on the sea-bed. In the past whole seas have filled up with these shells, to form the thick layers of chalk which show up along some cliffs.

Flagellates are protozoans which swim with the help of a whip-like thread called a flagellum. A common pond flagellate is *Euglena*. In the sea lives another one, *Noctiluca*, which means 'little nightlight'. If the sea is disturbed by a passing ship swarms of them light up to produce the phosphorescence in the water.

A third group, called ciliates, are covered with whip-like hairs, called cilia. These sweep backwards and forwards in a rhythmic motion, and push the tiny animal along. *Paramecium* the slipper animalcule, is common in ponds. Some ciliates are attached by stalks to water plants.

Protozoans are the simplest organisms alive and they exist in great numbers. They evolved into multi-celled animals, such as jellyfishes, called metazoans.

Worms belong to the group of animals called annelids, which is a word taken from the Latin *annulus*, meaning a ring. Worms have segmented sections which give their bodies a ring-like appearance. The common earthworm is familiar to all gardeners. It burrows its way through the earth by eating the soil, and leaves worm casts of undigested material on the surface of lawns. It feeds on leaves which are pulled into its burrows. The worm has no feet but each ring or segment of its body has pairs of minute bristles which help it to move by contraction and expansion of its body.

Vorticella is bell-shaped and has a ring of cilia which sets up a tiny whirlpool to sweep up food.

The fourth group, called sporozoans, are parasitic and live inside other animals. Some can be dangerous and cause disease. One of these attacks the gums in the mouth of humans and causes gingivitis. Another carried by a mosquito attacks blood and causes malaria. Sleeping sickness, which upsets the nervous system, is caused by a protozoan carried by the tsetse fly.

Rotifers and Sponges

Rotifers are small water animals called wheel animalcules which swim about with the aid of cilia. These are arranged in a ring, and when they vibrate give the impression of a spinning wheel. This 'wheel' is close to the mouth and helps in feeding. The tail end has a sucker or a pair of pincers for holding on to things. The smaller male rotifer mates with a female who then lays eggs. Summer eggs hatch almost at once, but winter eggs rest until the spring before they hatch.

Sponges live in the sea and are not easy to describe. They grow in all shapes and sizes to form a framework made of a chalky or horny substance, or one which contains tiny spicules of silica. Holes on the surface lead into a system of canals which are lined with cilia, so that the sea water is kept flowing throughout the sponge's interior. The way in which a sponge lives and grows is still something of a mystery. The sponge used in the bath is a dead and dried portion.

Coelenterates

The coelenterates are a very large group of simple animals which live mostly in the sea. These consist of sea anemones, jellyfishes and corals. The body of a coelenterate consists of an outside wall with a hollow interior, and a single opening ringed with tentacles. There is no digestive tube or hind opening, as in higher animals like ourselves. These animals come in two shapes. First there are sea anemones which remain fixed to something like a rock, as in a rock pool. They sit upright, with tentacles outstretched, waiting to catch a small animal like a shrimp. These tentacles are covered with stinging cells. Such a shaped coelenterate is called a polyp. Some polyps live in colonies, and are branched. There is a fresh-water species, called *Hydra*, which lives in ponds.

A jellyfish resembles an umbrella in shape and drifts about the sea upside down. This form is called a medusa. The strange thing about coelenterates is that, from generation to generation a polyp stage follows a medusa stage. For example, an anemone as a polyp produces young which at first resemble a medusa and swim about. Then they settle on something and turn into the polyp shape. Corals consist of whole colonies of small polyps which are joined together and supported by a hard outer skeleton. This is made by the polyps from the calcium carbonate in the sea water. A coral colony is born from a single larva which settles on some bare rock to form a polyp. This 'buds' off more polyps, and so the coral colony grows. Coral takes on all shapes. It may be branched or compact, flat or mushroom-shaped. In every case there are holes on the surface through which the polyps emerge after dark, in order to catch food.

Some coral grows to enormous size and forms coral reefs. These only form in the tropics, and in clear water. The main areas are in the West Indies, the Red Sea, the Pacific and along the Queensland coast of Australia. This is where the famous Great Barrier Reef stretches for more than 1,600 kilometres (1,000 miles). A barrier reef stands away from the shore, with a sheltered lagoon on the inside. A fringing reef is joined to the shore. An atoll is coral growing by itself, and usually forms a ring. Coral reefs attract a great number of animals, including fishes, worms, molluscs, sea urchins and crabs. Where there is land on the reef the sea birds and turtles come ashore to lay their eggs.

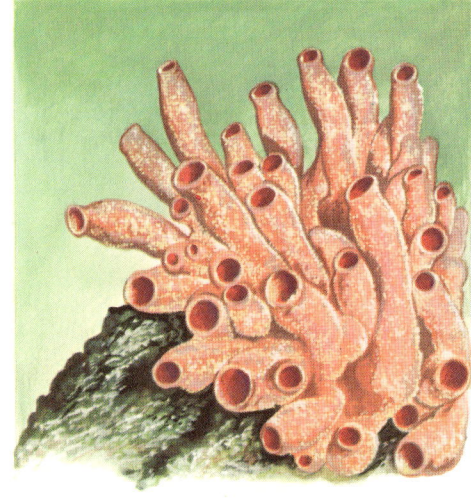

Invertebrates called coelenterates include sea anemones which have a body wall ringed with tentacles. These creatures are called polyps. Coral is made up of a mass of these creatures joined up to form a colony.

The Great Barrier Reef off the coast of eastern Australia is the most famous example of a coral reef. Seen under artificial light, the underwater life is revealed in a rich variety of colour.

Molluscs

Molluscs are animals with soft bodies (Latin *mollis* for soft) which are either naked, such as a slug, or protected by a shell, like a snail. Others, called cephalopods (meaning 'head foot') have tentacles, such as the squid and octopus. There are about 80,000 species of mollusc. A typical mollusc has a muscular underside, called a foot, on which it can crawl. The skin on the back hangs down like a skirt and encloses the mantle cavity in which the breathing organs are situated. This is where the shell is built. The front end has a head with sense organs. Some molluscs breathe air and others have gills. The mouth contains a rasp-like tongue, called a radula.

Depending on where and how they live molluscs vary greatly. The most primitive are the coat-of-mail shells, or chitons. They have a curved shell made of eight rows of plates, and they crawl about on a foot.

Snails and Limpets

Gasteropods, or snails, have a twisted shell containing the body, a well developed head, and a foot. They live on land or in water. In most slugs the shell is missing. The gasteropod most familiar to man is the garden snail which can damage plant life. It leaves behind a slime trail on a path, and will return to the same spot it started from when it woke up at night or after rain. In dry or wintry weather it hides away and seals off the shell with hardened slime. Some snails have a kind of door, the operculum, as in the periwinkle and whelk which can be found in a rock pool. The limpet commonly seen on rocks wanders about when the tide is in, feeding on the soft algae, then returns to the same spot when the tide goes out. You can see exactly where by the round groove on the rock made by its shell. Molluscs like these with one shell are called univalves.

The squid (top) and the octopus (below) belong to the class of cephalopods or head-footed molluscs. The squid has ten tentacles, the octopus eight.

Bivalves have a double, hinged shell. They live in water and are less active. They either remain attached to rocks, like the sea mussel, or live on the sea bed, like the oyster and cockle. Bivalves creep slowly over the sea bed or bottom of a pond or river, pulling themselves along with a tongue-like foot. Some will bury themselves, like the long-shaped razor shell. To feed, these molluscs filter the water for minute life through two openings called siphons. Water passes into one and out of the other. Inside the mantle rows of cilia sweep the water and food towards the mouth.

One unusual mollusc is the piddock which can bore into rock. A baby free-swimming larva settles on stone and grows a shell. The muscular foot rocks the shell which slowly bores into the rock. As it goes deeper the siphons elongate so that the openings are near the hole entrance, and can gather in food. A similar mollusc, the teredo or ship-worm, bores into wood. At one time it caused great damage to the hulls of wooden ships, and hundreds of them have even destroyed a wooden pier. One of the largest bivalves is the giant clam, up to one and a half metres (four and a half feet) across. It has caused people to drown. A bather or diver accidentally puts a hand or foot inside the shell, which then snaps shut so that there is no escape.

Cephalopods

In cephalopods the part which would normally be the foot is lengthened into tentacles which surround the head. These are covered with suckers and are used for catching food. Underneath is the single siphon. Water drawn in can be squirted out, so that the squid or octopus is jerked along backwards in a kind of jet propulsion. The number of tentacles varies. The octopus has eight and is called an octopod. Squids and cuttlefish have ten, and are decapods. The common octopus can grow tentacles up to two and a half metres (eight feet) long. In spite of an evil reputation it is a shy and retiring creature, hiding away among rocks. It uses its tentacles to 'lasso' the crabs on which it feeds. Young octopuses occasionally turn up along the south coast of England. They have been carried across the Channel from the area around the Bay of Biscay, which is their spawning ground.

Squids and other decapods roam freely in the sea, some at great depths. Some squids reach a length of twelve metres (forty feet) or more, and are hunted by the sperm whale. Cuttlefish keep in shoals, usually near the coast. They possess an internal skeleton, the cuttle bone, which can be picked up on the beach, and which is often given to cage birds.

Distant ancestors of cephalopods—the ammonites and belemnites—carried shells. Today this is only found in one species, the pearly nautilus, whose shell is built very much like that of an ammonite. In other living species, the paper nautilus or argonaut, two of the tentacles are curled around a thin, hollow shell of great beauty. It floats at the surface.

In most cases molluscs reproduce themselves from eggs, laid in clumps of spawn. This can be seen stuck to water plants in ponds, or among the seaweeds on rocks along the coast. Snails hatch out as miniatures of their parents. With bivalves which do not move about so easily the babies may be helped on their way. The young of a pond mussel has a gland which forms a sticky thread, so that it can cling to a passing fish. Later on it drops off and settles on the bottom of a pond or stream.

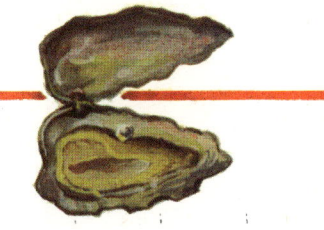

The pearl oyster is a mollusc which produces the pearl. The inside of the oyster is covered with a substance known as mother-of-pearl, and the pearl itself is formed as a result of the entry into the oyster of parasites. These irritate the oyster and it covers them in layers of mother of pearl, or nacre as it is properly called. These layers build up to make pearls of varying shapes and sizes.

The echinoderms, or hedgehog-skinned invertebrates, so named because their skins have spines like a hedgehog, include the sea cucumber (below), sea urchins and scallops (right) and starfishes (below right).

Echinoderms

Echinoderms (meaning 'spiny skins') number about 4,000 species and consist of starfishes, sea urchins, sea cucumbers and sea lilies. They are all sea creatures.

A typical starfish has five arms, and creeps about over rocks, and can burrow into the sand. It holds on by means of many small suckers, called tube feet. Their grip is so strong that a starfish can prize open a bivalve mollusc and get at the contents. Starfishes can be a nuisance in oyster beds. Another serious problem has now arisen among the coral reefs in the Pacific, where a large starfish, called the crown of thorns, is feeding on the coral and killing it off. Normally this starfish is hunted by a large mollusc which has become rare because of its popularity among collectors of shells.

Very unlike a starfish is the sea urchin. It is a kind of closed-up starfish with its arms joined together to form a globe shape. Inside, apart from the organs, is a system of canals containing fluid. By a pumping action this operates the tube feet. Dead sea urchins lose their spines, and make attractive ornaments. Sea cucumbers are sausage-shaped echinoderms, and move about like large slugs. In some countries, particularly China, they are gathered and dried as a delicacy to be eaten, known as bêche-de-mer. Sea lilies are kinds of starfish attached to stalks on the sea bed and are part of an ancient group of animals well known from their fossils.

A collection of common mollusc shells: 1 whelk, 2 mussel, 3 scallop, 4 razor shell, 5 *Aulious* cone, 6 common wentletrap, 7 periwinkle, 8 cockle, 9 limpet, 10 zebra volute.

Sea Shells

The many thousands of sea shells which are washed up daily on our beaches, although vastly different in shape, size, colour and pattern, in fact all belong to a group of animals called the molluscs. This group includes snails, oysters, octopuses, scallops and whelks, most of which—but not all—have shell coverings. Crabs and lobsters are not termed molluscs for their shells are part of their skeletons and not grown as a separate protection.

The word mollusc comes from the Latin *molluscus*, meaning softish. Because these animals are soft and slimy, they usually need some sort of protection against the outside world, and so they exude certain liquids from their glands; these liquids harden into the distinctive shell by which each mollusc is recognised. As the animal grows, so the shell continues to grow too, and even if the shell is damaged in most cases it will repair itself quickly and effectively.

Every mollusc shell has an exact Latin name, although most are known by common or local names as well. In general, the shell-covered molluscs are divided into four distinct classes: the chitons or placophora, which are very small, and have shells made from eight separate plates; the univalves or Gastropoda, which have shells in a single piece, often spiral shaped; the tusk shells or scaphopoda, which have long tubular shells; the bivalves or lamellibranchia, which have their shells divided into two halves, and the halves joined by a muscular hinge. Cockles, mussels and scallops are all examples of bivalve molluscs.

Washed and polished, mollusc shells make attractive ornaments in the home, and many people spend hours scouring beaches in search of unusual and decorative shells. Usually such shells have been cast off from the original molluscs, but sometimes the little creatures are still inside. Live molluscs can often be seen in sheltered rock pools, clinging tightly to the rocks.

Apart from their decorative appeal, shells have many other uses too. In primitive times shells were widely used as money. Today certain types of shells are used for making buttons and jewellery—the button shell, or *Umbonium giganteum*, has a mother-of-pearl type surface which is used for making pearl buttons. The ground-up shell of the cockle is used as a poultry grit, and the ground-up turban shell is used for polishing optical lenses.

Arthropods

Arthropods (meaning 'joined limbs') make up one of the main divisions of the animal kingdom, and contain the largest number of species. These invertebrates have a segmented body which carries numbers of paired limbs used for different purposes, and a body covering of hardened skin made from chitin. As they grow this is shed from time to time. Some pass through various larval stages before becoming adults. Examples can be found almost everywhere. Arthropods include insects, crustaceans (crabs and lobsters), millipedes, centipedes, and arachnids (spiders and scorpions).

Leaf and Stick Insects

The insects which are experts at camouflage are those which resemble sticks and leaves. Their shape makes them easily overlooked by their enemies, chiefly birds. Stick insects, sometimes kept as pets, have elongated twig-shaped bodies and slender legs for climbing about among bushes. They feed on leaves. In the leaf insects the legs, body and forewings are flattened and coloured to resemble leaves. There are even dark patches on the wings to give the impression that the 'leaf' has holes, or is attacked by fungus. These insects are called phasmids, and are vegetable feeders.

Somewhat different, but equally well camouflaged, is the praying mantis which gets its name from the way it sits up in an attitude of prayer. The powerful pincer-like forelegs are folded up in readiness to seize and devour another insect if it comes within range. While it waits, the praying mantis is well hidden from its own enemies. Mantids are mainly tropical insects. So are cockroaches, often called black beetles. They have oval bodies, dark colouring, and leathery forewings which cover the hindwings, as in true beetles. They are mainly nocturnal and can run fast. Numbers have been introduced to Europe by shipping, both from America and the East. They tend to inhabit warm and dark places in kitchens, bakeries, and tropical animal houses. They come out in the dark to feed on scraps of food. If disturbed they will run rapidly for cover.

Stick insects (top) and the leaf insect (above) are remarkable for their resemblance to the plant life from which they take their names. Camouflaged as broken twigs and leaves, they merge completely with their surroundings.

The praying mantis is a carnivorous animal, fierce for its size, and eats large numbers of flies and other small insects which it seizes in its front legs.

Grasshoppers

Grasshoppers belong to the Order Orthoptera, and are insects which are often disturbed in the grass. They also include crickets and locusts, and fall into two groups. Grasshoppers and locusts have short antennae, whereas crickets have long ones. Mostly harmless, these insects with their long legs and jumping ability while away the time chirping, and now and then feeding on plants. The exception is the locust, which can do enormous damage. At one time many different locusts were recognised by their shapes and colouring. Then a curious thing was discovered. For a number of years a particular species of locust would live and behave like

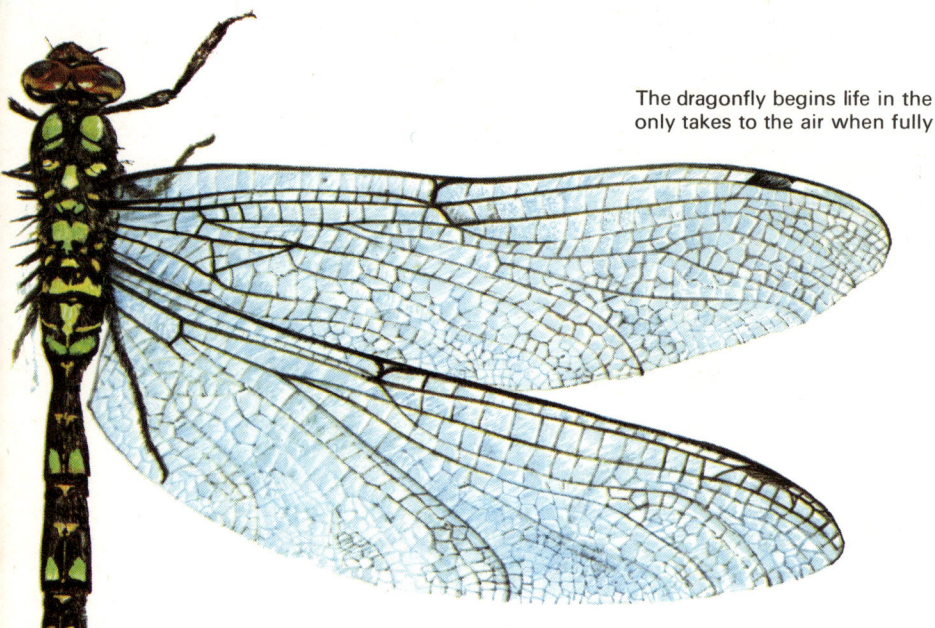

The dragonfly begins life in the water and only takes to the air when fully grown.

harmless grasshoppers. Then gradually these locusts would start banding together, and over a number of generations would change colour, shape, and even their habits.

To lay eggs the female presses her abdomen into soft earth or sand, and as she withdraws it, lays a heap of eggs. A sticky secretion binds the sand around them into a case, called the egg-pod. In this way the harmless 'solitary' locusts turn into 'swarming' or gregarious locusts, and it is the sheer weight of their numbers which does so much harm. As each hatching struggles to the surface it joins its companions and they set off on a deliberate journey, eating every plant in their path.

Young locusts are called hoppers, as they have no developed wings until the last moult. They march off like an army of soldiers, and appear to be under the guidance of the sun. At this hopper stage it is possible to do something to stop the invasion. Poisoned bait is spread in their path. The front ranks eat this and die, and those following behind eat their dead. If taken in time a build-up of such a swarm can be stopped. However, when the adults emerge and can fly, the battle is lost. Although aircraft are used to fly into a swarm and spray it with poison, so that millions are brought down, the rest still get through. Some swarms have covered as much as a thousand miles on one journey.

An adult locust can eat its own weight in one day, and it has been worked out that an average swarm might weigh as much as a thousand tons. Since locusts cross frontiers a number of countries have banded together to fight this menace—what used to be called the 'eighth plague of Egypt'. There are old stories of locust swarms at sea that have settled on sailing ships and eaten every stick of canvas, and of trains brought to a standstill because locusts on the line caused the wheels to skid.

In the Old Testament are a number of very descriptive passages about locusts, especially of the Bible or desert locust of Africa. Of the hoppers it says 'They run like mighty men, they climb the wall like men of war, and they march every one his ways and they break not their ranks. They leap upon the city, they run upon the wall, they climb into the houses, and they enter in at the windows like a thief'. Another passage describes a swarm: 'For they covered the face of the earth so that the land was darkened, and they did eat every herb of the land and every fruit of the trees, and there remained not any green thing'. Crickets, by contrast, are cheerful singers which like warm places, usually in cracks near a fireplace, hence *The Cricket on the Hearth* by Charles Dickens.

Dragonflies

Dragonflies (Order Odonata) are handsome insects of two kinds. The species, Anisoptera, have wings of unequal shape, and keep them spread out when resting. These are the powerful, more robust flyers seen darting about over water. They mate in the air, and sometimes can be seen paired together, the male carrying the female. She lays her eggs on or close to water, and these hatch into a larva called a nymph. The nymph grows and moults a number of times, meanwhile catching food by stealth. The powerful jaws are fixed to a hinge under the head. This is called a mask, and darts out to catch anything within reach. Breathing is through the rectum at the end of the

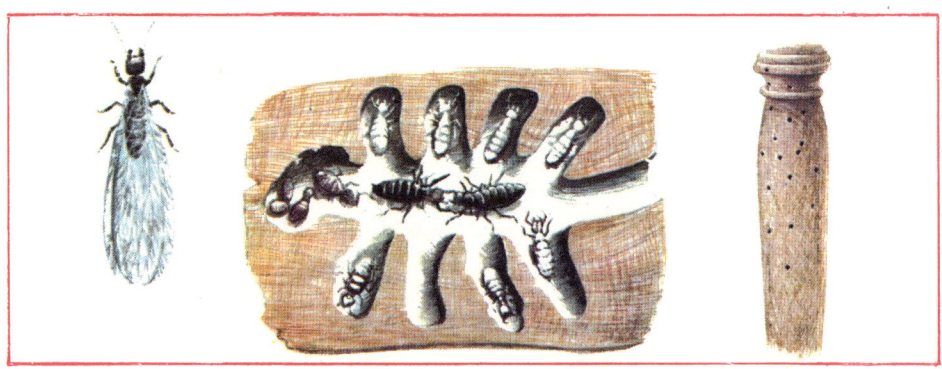

Termites live in galleries made in wood or soil. Like some other insects, termites have a highly organised social life. They are very destructive pests and will bore through the boards of a floor and drive tunnels up the legs of a chair or table.

body. Into this the nymph can draw water and force it out, so that it is shot along in a series of jerks. For the final moult (there is no pupa stage) the nymph crawls up a plant stem out of water, and dries in the air. The skin splits along the back and the adult dragonfly emerges.

Here and there in late summer these empty nymph cases can be found still attached to reed stems.

The mayfly lives on the wing for only one day.

These dragonflies, sometimes called hawks, are expert flyers, and can move in any direction, even hover. They pounce on passing insects and may eat them in mid-air, first biting off the wings and legs before eating the soft parts.

The other group, the Zygoptera, have equally shaped wings, and are called damselflies. They have a rather weak and fluttering flight and can be seen by the waterside, either in pairs or laying eggs. The nymph has three feathery gills at the end of the body, and swims with a wriggling movement.

Butterflies

To our eyes butterflies and moths, which belong to the Order Lepidoptera (meaning 'scale-wings'), are among the most attractive insects. In particular we admire the beauty of their wings. These are covered with minute scales which may brush off as a fine powder. There are many exceptions, but usually butterflies have slender bodies, club-shaped antennae and fly by day, whereas moths are more robust, have feathered antennae and generally fly at night. At rest, butterflies close their wings together over the body. This hides the bright upper sides and shows only the dull undersides. Moths close their wings across the body in a scissors fashion, and this hides the bright hind wings. Both methods help to conceal a butterfly or moth. There are remarkable examples of this form of camouflage. For example, the Indian leaf butterfly resembles a leaf in shape and colour, even imitating the stalk and the veins.

The life of a butterfly is usually short. After pairing the female seeks out a food plant for the caterpillars to feed and grow on. The caterpillar moults a number of times, then turns into a chrysalis, and so into an adult. In some cases the adult will hibernate for the winter period, which explains the early appearance of spring butterflies commonly seen in gardens. The small tortoiseshell, peacock and comma lay their eggs on nettle, and are attracted to garden flowers such as the buddleia, which is sometimes called the butterfly bush. In the adult butterfly a curled up tongue is used to sip moisture and nectar from flowers. One unpopular visitor is the cabbage white. In some seasons big invasions of them do much harm to crops.

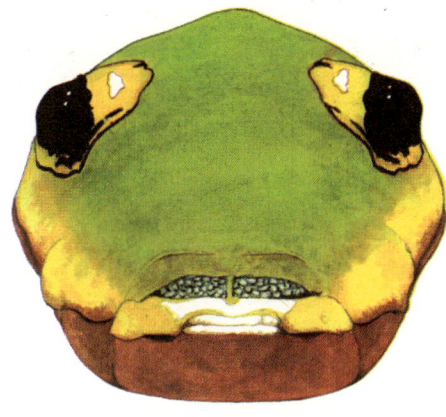

This close-up of a caterpillar head gives an impression of great eyes and a mouth. These are in fact merely coloured markings which help to protect it from its enemies.

Butterflies are to be found in a wide variety of colours and sizes. This is a large tropical species.

Other butterflies, as well as moths, will migrate. The most spectacular journey is that of the monarch butterfly. In autumn it may start from as far north as Canada and end up in the southern part of the United States. Huge swarms have been seen at night silhouetted against the moon as they travel down the coast. They settle for the winter in groves of pine trees. This has become a tourist attraction, and visitors are directed by signs on the road, reading 'To the butterfly trees'.

Although there are some 500 species throughout the world, the swallowtails are some of the rarest butterflies in Europe. One of these lives on the Norfolk Broads in England and lays its eggs on a wild plant called milk parsley. The caterpillar pupates on the reed stems. Also very rare is the Camberwell Beauty, first discovered in Camberwell, once a country village outside London. Originally the word butterfly was used for just one species called the brimstone. It was first known as the butter-coloured fly, and it too lives in Britain.

The largest and most beautiful butterflies live in the tropics. It was in the jungles of Brazil that naturalists, including Charles Darwin, admired such species and discovered an interesting thing about them. Some butterflies are brightly coloured to warn enemies not to catch them, because they have an unpleasant taste. Other butterflies which have a normal taste and can be eaten, mimic the appearance of the distasteful ones and so are avoided by birds. Wings of such butterflies are used for decoration. They are arranged under glass in picture frames or on trays.

Moths

Moths which fly by night are less noticeable, unless attracted to a light trap or an open window. By day they rest on tree trunks and walls, against which they are almost invisible. The stronger night flyers are called hawk moths. They can hover in front of flowers when feeding, in a manner similar to the little humming birds. Some migrate long distances. A summer visitor to Europe is the humming-bird hawk moth, which flies by day. Many hawk moths are named after the plant on which the caterpillar feeds, such as the poplar, lime, privet and convolvulus hawk moths.

Some of the largest moths belong to the silk moth family, such as the giant atlas and lunar moths. Before the caterpillar turns into a chrysalis it weaves a cocoon of silk in which the pupa rests. The silk 'worm' which feeds on mulberry leaves has been bred for centuries in the East to obtain pure silk. A European moth which makes a cocoon is the emperor moth. It lives among the heather on heaths and moors in Britain.

Most moths are small, and some do harm. The clothes moth caterpillar is attracted to animal fibre and will damage furs and woollen goods, but not cotton. Other moth caterpillars, called defoliators, will eat tree leaves. The tortrix moth caterpillars may strip an entire oak tree of leaves. They will pupate inside a curled-up leaf. Apples are harmed by the grub of the codlin moth. Moths and other insects which do harm can be controlled by sprays, but this is expensive and does not always work, since, in time, they become immune.

Another method, called biological control, is to 'set a thief to catch a

Butterflies move through four stages in their life cycle: egg, caterpillar, chrysalis and butterfly. One caterpillar emerges from each egg laid. Seen here are the caterpillars and adult butterflies of the large tortoiseshell (top), adonis blue (centre) and *Parantica sita* (below)

Butterflies are attracted to flowers by their colour and scent.

The tiny eggs laid by butterflies and moths show a great variety of shape and colour when they are studied under a microscope. Shapes may be globular, oval, flat, bottle-shaped, and in colours which usually blend with their backgrounds so that they are not easily visible. The eggs are distributed in many different ways. Most species of butterflies and moths lay their eggs in plants, often on the underside of leaves. Sometimes a single egg is laid and sometimes large clusters of them. The eggs shown on the right, greatly enlarged, are those of the purple hairstreak, vapourer, oak eggar, bath white and the comma. The oak eggar is a type of moth which, unlike most species, flies in daytime and is more brightly coloured than is usual. It relies on its unpleasant taste for protection. The vapourer is also a moth and the other three are species of butterfly.

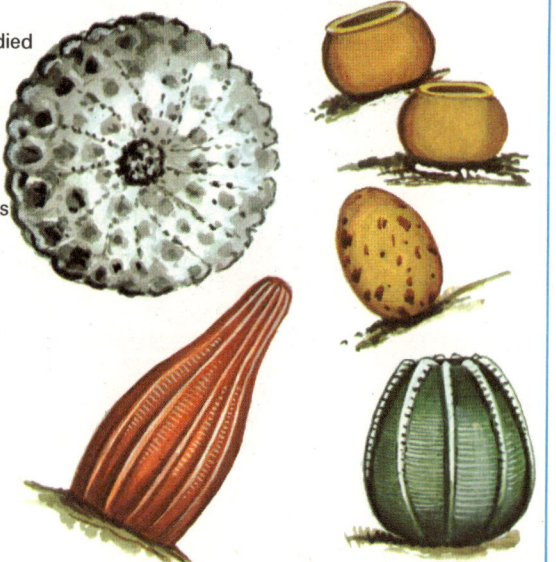

thief'. During the 1920s moths were doing serious harm to the coconut trees on Fiji, where coconuts are grown as a crop to make copra. The caterpillar of the moth *Levuana iridescens* attacks the leaves, which gradually lose colour and fall off. A tree may be entirely stripped of leaves and may take two or more years to recover before it bears more coconuts. This is serious for the industry. One island was already suffering, and it looked as if the caterpillars might spread to others. There seemed to be no natural moth enemies. Then a fly was discovered in Malaya which is a parasite and lays its eggs on a similar kind of moth caterpillar to that of *Levuana*. Infested caterpillars were taken to Fiji, and when the fly larvae emerged from their bodies they immediately attacked the *Levuana* caterpillars. In this way the harmful caterpillars were exterminated. Should any more *Levuana* moths ever turn up in the coconut groves, then the fly will be there, ready to deal with them.

Moths from Europe, Asia and America: 1 *Automeris io*, 2 *Bupalus peniarius*, 3 *Dysphania palmya*, 4 *Eucyane excellens*, 5 emperor, 6 yellow-belted burnet, 7 six-spot burnet, 8 elephant hawk, 9 garden tiger, 10 *Calotaenia celsia*, 11 *Erasmia*.

Ants, Wasps and Bees

The most complex and highly developed insects belong to the order Hymenoptera (meaning 'membrane wing'). Their wings are criss-crossed with veins to form a network of transparent cells. These insects can usually be recognised by their narrow 'wasp waists'. Sawflies, however, have no waist, and get their name from the female's egg-laying tube which has a saw edge, so that eggs can be laid inside leaves and stems. The caterpillar-shaped grub may sometimes do harm, as in the case of the gooseberry sawfly.

Other boring insects, called wood-wasps, are sometimes brightly coloured and mistaken for wasps or hornets, yet they are harmless. A female uses her long egg tube, the ovipositor, to bore into a tree trunk to lay her eggs. The grubs tunnel in the wood and may spoil the timber. For this reason, they are unpopular with foresters. But the foresters have another insect as an ally, a parasitic wasp called an ichneumon. The female is able to find the hidden woodwasp grub, and bores through the bark to lay her eggs on or beside it. The ichneumon grub then feeds on the woodwasp grub. In turn another ichneumon wasp may lay her eggs on the first grub.

Other parasitic wasps, called gall wasps, lay eggs on plants. This causes an irritation, and the plant stem or leaf swells up into a gall. Inside this the grub feeds and grows. Two

common examples seen on oak trees are the marble gall and the oak apple. Bees, wasps and ants have a reputation for stinging or biting, but usually they do this only if disturbed or handled. Among the bees and wasps are a number of solitary kinds which lay their eggs in holes in the ground or in wood and provide the grubs with nectar (in the case of bees) and insects (in the case of wasps).

Some insects, called leaf cutter bees, line their nests with pieces of leaves taken from rose bushes, which can sometimes be seen with neat portions cut out of them. The nest hole is then sealed off and the grubs left to grow up.

The two chief activities of both bees and wasps are those of obtaining food and rearing their young. Social wasps have links with bees, as the structure of their societies is similar. There is a fertile queen and workers and drones. Their nests are formed from a kind of paper which they make from dried parings of wood.

Ants are perhaps the most advanced of all insects, having a well organised social life in underground nests.

Social Groups

Social bees and wasps, and all ants, live a highly organised life in their nests. In each colony their numbers may run into thousands. Egg-laying is done by a fertile female, called a queen, who starts a colony by making a small nest, laying a few eggs, then feeding and tending the grubs. These infertile offspring are the workers. As the colony grows they all take on different duties. Some act as builders, others become nurses to the grubs, and there are food gatherers. Now and then some of the grubs will turn into young queens, or into males called drones. When they mate, new fertilised queens are then able to move away and start new colonies. When kept in hives, the familiar honey bee has a permanent nest. The workers go out to gather pollen and nectar and store it in the hive as honey. The combs in the hive hang down so that the cells where food is stored lie flat. In a wasp's nest the combs are horizontal and the cells point downwards so that no food can be stored. They are only occupied by grubs. In countries of northern Europe where there is a winter season, bees live on through the winter, but wasps die off. Only the young wasp queens survive to hibernate and start a fresh colony the following year. Bumble bees, which live similar lives to honey bees, but on a smaller scale, are common garden insects.

Ants always live in colonies. They are noted for their strength, shown in the way they manage to carry twigs and prey far larger than themselves. Wood ants seen in pine woods carry twigs and needles to build the nest, and follow well-defined paths in search of food. They catch prey and will also climb trees to 'milk' the aphids for their honeydew.

Insects of the Hymenoptera order feed in different ways. A bee sucks nectar from a flower with a long, tongue-like organ. Its sting is mainly for defence. A wasp will use its sting to kill prey, or bite with its jaws to feed on fruit, or to gather nest material. Sometimes you can see

Of all the hundreds of species of bees there are two kinds familiar to most people, the honey bee and the bumble bee, seen on the right taking pollen from a flower.

where a worker has been rasping away wood from a gatepost. Ants usually bite and may squirt formic acid into the wound. This is why their bite stings. Some people can become very ill from a wasp sting or ant bite. In the tropics, driver ants wander about in dense columns, hundreds of yards long, and will kill every living thing that gets in the way. Even a large animal such as a tethered goat or a penned-in cow is not safe.

Termites

Although in a separate order, the termites, or 'white ants', are also social and can build huge nests out of earth, or inside trees. Great damage may be caused to the woodwork of a building by their tunnelling. Termites are among the few animals that can feed on wood. The queen has a greatly swollen body and is simply an egg-laying machine. Among the workers are soldier ants which have large heads and powerful jaws, and act as guards.

With most of these insect colonies there is a mating time when swarming takes place, and the males meet the females. This is the time when on a sultry summer's day there are many flying ants about. On landing a mated female ant bites off her wings and starts a new colony. A bee swarm means that the hive is overcrowded. The old queen leads away the workers to form a new nest. Those left behind rear a young queen who goes off to mate with a drone, then returns to start laying fresh eggs.

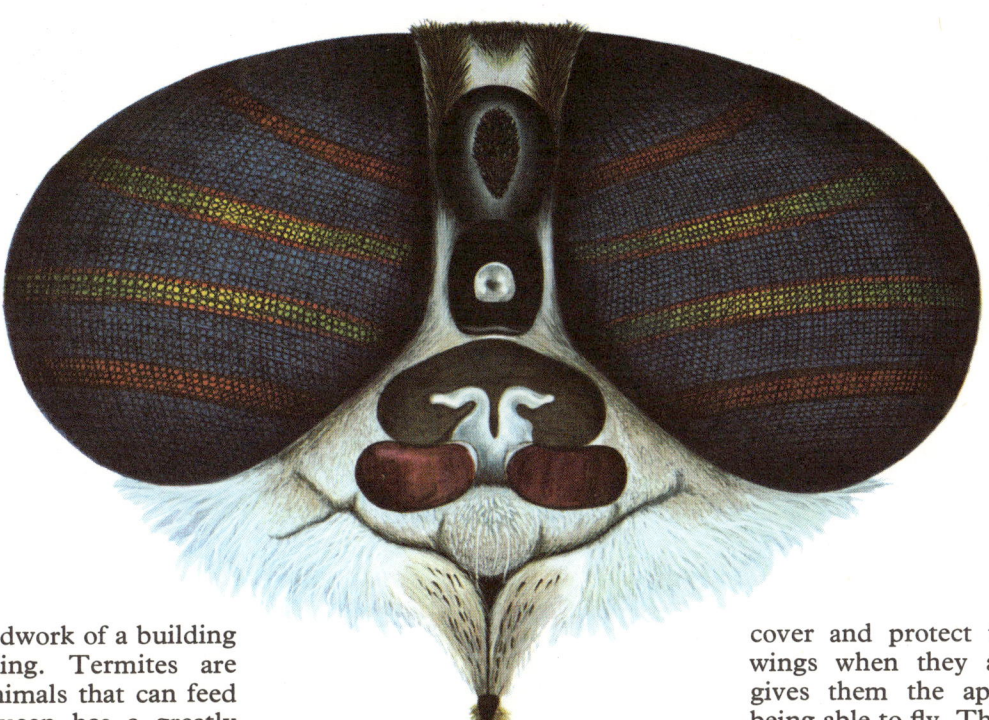

The remarkable structure of a horsefly head seen greatly magnified in this drawing. All horseflies are bloodsuckers and their mouths are delicately-formed piercing instruments. They will attack human beings and other large mammals.

Flies

Flies belong to the order Diptera (meaning 'two-wings'). They use two wings for flying, instead of four. The hind wings are modified as balancing organs, called halteres. This order consists of normally shaped flies, such as the house fly, and those with slender bodies shaped more like the mosquito. Flies suck up soft food, either with a pad-shaped mouth, as in the house fly, or a piercing mouth as in the mosquito.

The mosquito's mouth is also used for sucking up plant juices, or blood from animals. These ways of feeding mean that flies and mosquitos can be dangerous to health, and may pass on germs. A house fly feeding on excreta which contains germs, and then settling on food, can pass on diseases like typhoid and cholera. A mosquito biting a human can transmit malaria. A tsetse fly may spread sleeping sickness, and a small tropical fly transmits elephantiasis. In spite of all the harm they can cause, flies in their enormous numbers are a valuable food supply to other animals, particularly the insectivores, or insect eaters, and birds, amphibians and fish.

Beetles

Beetles are strongly built insects of the order Coleoptera (meaning a 'sheath wing'). The two front wings, called elytra, act as hardened wing cases to cover and protect the normal hind wings when they are closed. This gives them the appearance of not being able to fly. This is true of some ground beetles, which are found in cellars, or hiding under logs. Beetles form the largest order of insects, some 275,000 species, ranging from tiny beetles to giants like the fifteen centi-

Common flea

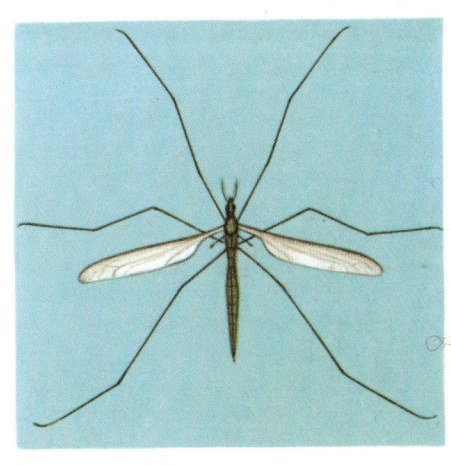

Crane fly or 'Daddy-Long-Legs'

121

metre (six-inch) goliath beetle of the tropics. Most beetles hide away in undergrowth, under bark, in soil and leaf litter, and feed mostly on plant material with their chewing jaws. Some, however, are active hunters or feed on carrion. Dor beetles feed on dung, and the scarab beetle, which was sacred to the ancient Egyptians, collects a ball of food for its young.

Most beetle grubs are fat and clumsy, and feed on plants. It may be three years or more before they pupate. One of Europe's largest species, the stag beetle, grows up in a rotten tree stump. In spite of the large horn-like mandibles of the male the stag beetle is quite harmless. Other wood beetles lay eggs on living trees, and the grubs tunnel under the bark to feed. Where a piece of loose bark is removed different tunnel patterns can be seen, and from these an entomologist (a person who studies insects) can tell which species made them.

A very unpopular borer is the 'wood worm', really the grub of the furniture beetle. Old timber such as the beams in churches and houses may be damaged by the grubs of the death-watch beetle. It can make a tapping sound by beating its head against the sides of the tunnel it bores. Other beetles are a serious problem where food is stored. The 'meal worm' is the grub of a beetle which feeds on grain. As much damage can be done in the warehouse as in the field where corn grows. An interesting beetle is the one which can produce a light—the glow-worm. This peculiarity is confined to the female, which has no wings and attracts a flying male after dark. By controlling the oxygen supply it can switch its light on and off.

There are also beetles which live in ponds and lakes. They are streamlined and have paddle-shaped legs for swimming. Some are fierce hunters, like the *Dytiscus* beetles and their larvae. These grow up in water then crawl out to dig a tunnel in the bankside. After a short pupa stage the adult emerges and returns to the water. Even water beetles can fly, mostly after dark, and are sometimes caught in moth traps, or harm themselves by flying against a window.

Fleas
This order, the Siphonaptera, consists of wingless insects with bodies flattened from side to side. Powerful legs enable them to jump strongly and to remarkable heights considering the size of these insects. They live entirely on mammals and birds, and feed on blood, including that of human beings. The adult flea hangs on to its

The cicada is a large, winged insect, living mainly in warm regions. The male cicadas are famous for their shrill, chirping song.

victim with clawed feet, and having had a meal lays its eggs. When the larva is grown enough it turns into a pupa and finally becomes an adult flea.

Among the primates only man can attract fleas because he lives in groups in the same place. Apes and monkeys which roam about do not have fleas: when they groom one another they are merely cleaning the fur. A strange thing about fleas is that the pupa remains still for long periods unless disturbed, then it changes into a flea. This is why people moving into a long-empty house may suddenly find they have fleas around them. The terrible bubonic plague is caused by a germ carried by the rat flea. Outbreaks of the Black Death were common through the Middle Ages, and during the plague in London in 1665 more than a quarter of the population died. People knew nothing of the disease and believed it came from the air. It was really due to living close to rats encouraged by bad sanitary conditions.

Lice
This order, the Anoplura, also consists of blood-sucking insects, but shaped differently. In their case, the body is flattened downwards. Some are called bird-lice and live in nests where they feed on debris and bits of feathers. Blood-feeding lice live on mammals, including man. They are mainly a nuisance, and the human louse occurs when people do not keep themselves clean, or live in dirty conditions which may not be their own fault. Eggs, called nits, are laid on the hair.

Bugs
This widely used word really applies only to the order Hemiptera (meaning 'half-wing'). It is usual to think of the bed-bug as typical but there are a vast number of other bugs living on animals, on plants, and in the water. They all have a stabbing mouth which sucks up blood or plant juices. There are two groups, the Heteroptera and the Homoptera.

The Heteroptera have half the fore-wing made of hardened chitin like the wing-case of a beetle. These bugs live on land or in water. Bedbugs live in nests, animal dens or in houses which are dirty, and are attracted to a warm place such as a mammal's body. In a neglected

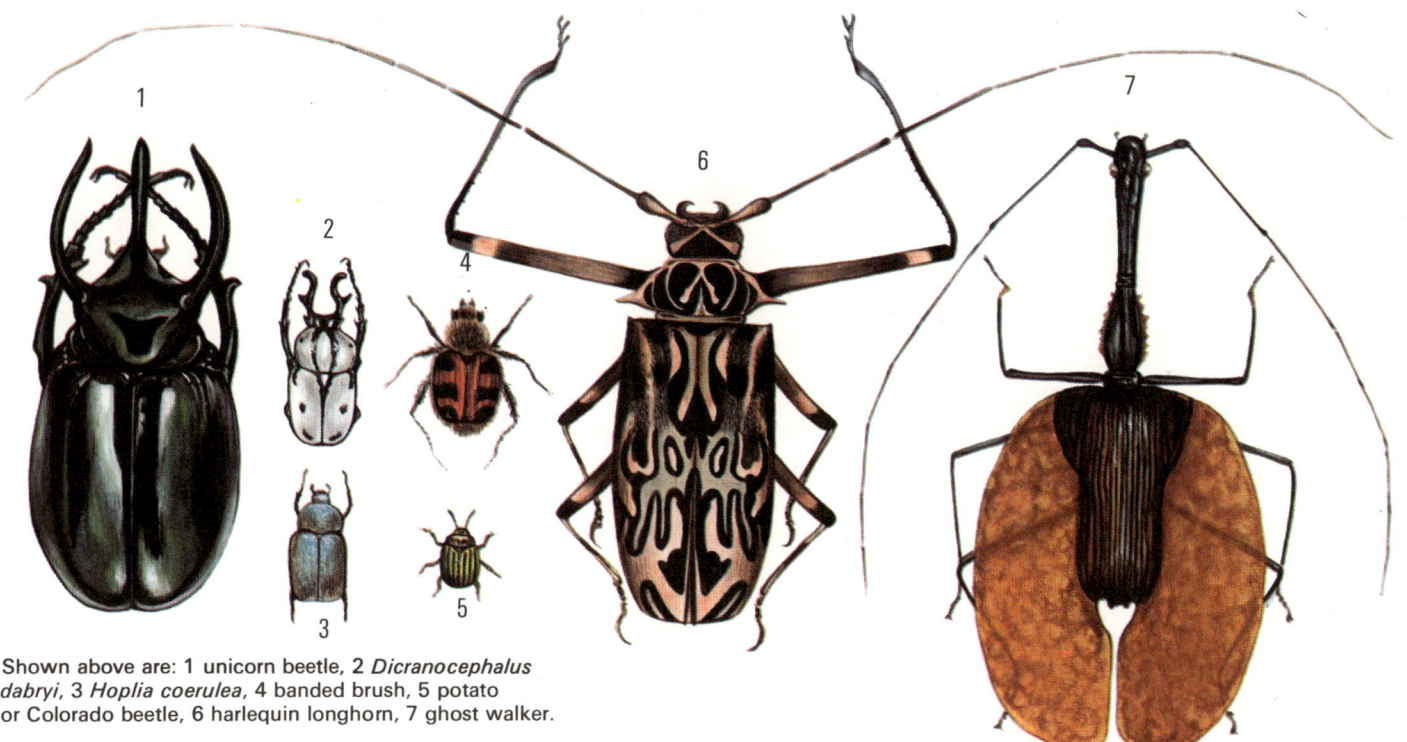

Shown above are: 1 unicorn beetle, 2 *Dicranocephalus dabryi*, 3 *Hoplia coerulea*, 4 banded brush, 5 potato or Colorado beetle, 6 harlequin longhorn, 7 ghost walker.

bedroom they may hide in cracks in the walls and furniture, and come out at night. They may even crawl along the ceiling then drop on to a bed where someone is sleeping. Some of these bugs are carried in the fur of bats. The water bugs, being insects, must come up to the surface now and then for air. A common sight in ponds is the water boatman, an active swimmer. The pond skater is another bug which lives on the surface.

The second group, the Homoptera, have wings which are shaped normally. They are plant-feeders. Most common are the aphids, such as the greenfly which is a pest to gardeners. Some aphids carry virus germs and can infect crops and fruit. The froghopper is a curious bug which feeds on plant juices, blows these into bubbles, and forms the familiar 'cuckoo-spit' seen on grass and other plants. Tropical bugs called cicadas sing loudly at night, and are kept in small cages as pets. There is an Indian bug whose scales are made into shellac, and a Mexican bug which provides a colouring matter called cochineal.

Crustaceans

This is a very large class of invertebrates, some 25,000 species strong, found mainly in the sea. The more familiar ones are those seen along the sea shore, or those which are caught in traps for food. The lobsters, crabs and shrimps seen at the fishmonger are mainly scavenging animals which hide away among rocks or in sand. They are caught with nets or in wicker baskets baited with dead fish. The hardened skin of a crustacean forms a kind of outer skeleton of dead animal matter, called chitin. It is shed

Shown below: 8 longhorn beetle, 9 night hunter, 10 *Megalorrhina harrisii*, 11 goliath beetle, 12 Brazilian weevil, 13 *Mecynorrhina torquata*, 14 Japanese ground beetle.

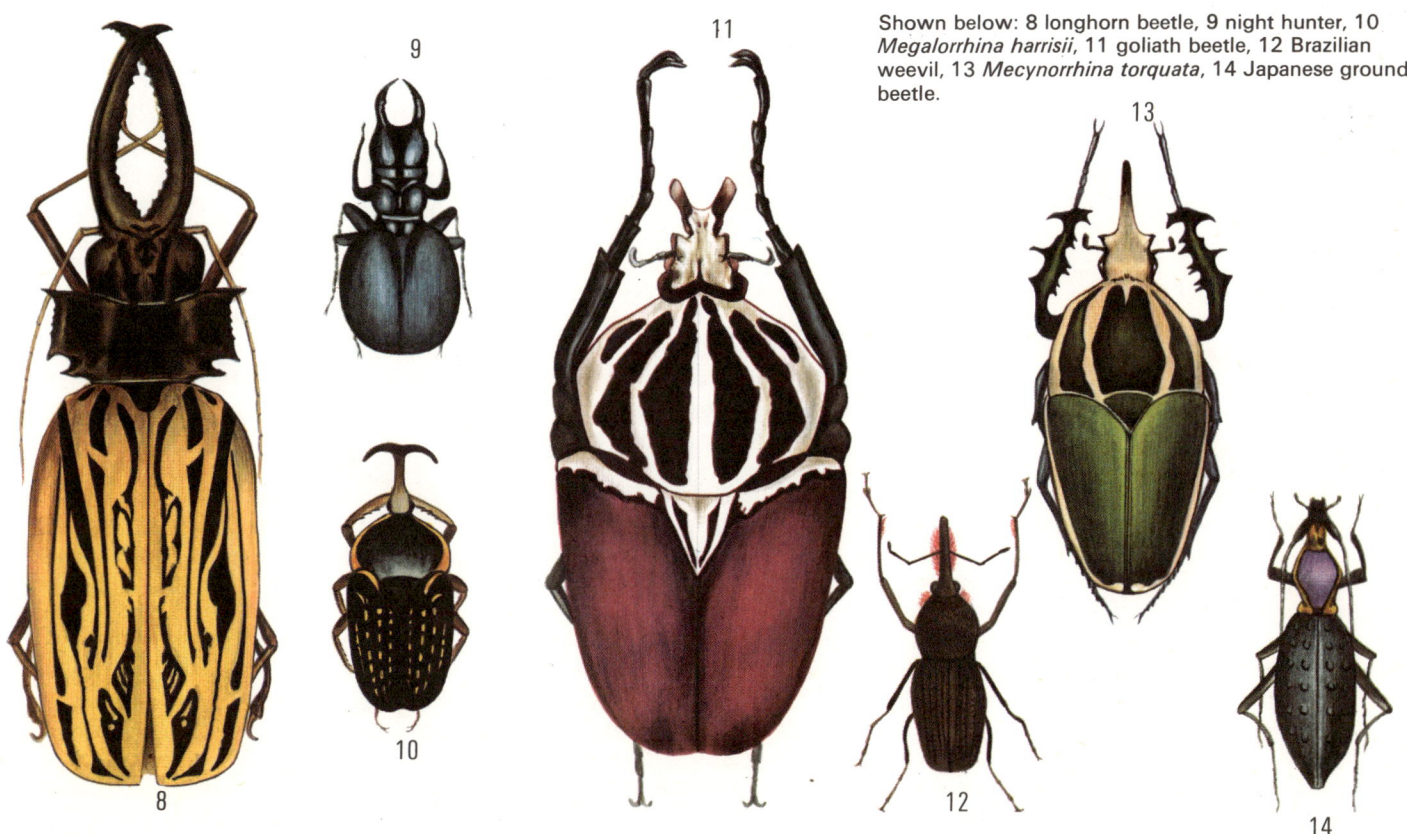

The swimming crab has a pair of legs which are specially equipped for swimming. Segments at the end of the legs are flattened and oar-like.

The male fiddler crab has one outsize claw which he waves to attract female crabs. Shown below this is a long-clawed porcelain crab, a close relation of the hermit crab.

surface of water and drift about as part of the plankton, before settling on the sea bed to grow up. The crayfish is a kind of small freshwater lobster which hides under stones, catching what it can to feed on. Owing to water pollution it has disappeared from a number of rivers and lakes. When its eggs hatch the mother carries her young about for a while before they separate.

Some crabs live on land or in swamps, and make intricate patterns in the sand where they form their burrows. Some, called fiddler crabs, have one very enlarged pincer which they wave about as a kind of signal to their mates. Another crab, the coconut crab, can even climb. It will scuttle up a tree and cut off a coconut so that it falls to the ground. It then are divided into many segments, most of which carry a pair of limbs. According to the number of limbs and the way in which they are used, the crustaceans are divided into groups. They form a very ancient class, going well back into the Cambrian Period, some 500 million years ago, when trilobites existed in the ancient seas. One group, called Malacostraca, includes the lobsters, crabs and shrimps, also the world's biggest species, the Japanese giant spider crab. The male has legs almost two metres (six feet) long. These crustaceans, called decapods, have five pairs of walking legs, and a front pair of pincers used for defence, or for catching food. A lobster or crab will settle into a crack in the rocks and guard the entrance with its pincers.

After mating, the female crustacean produces eggs, called 'berries', which are attached to her underside. They hatch into a minute larva called a nautilus. Some of these float to the descends to break the coconut open and feed on the milk and its flesh.

Sharing a rock pool with crabs is the hermit crab, a crustacean which borrows the empty shell of a dead mollusc so as to cover and protect its soft hind quarters. When it grows too large for its shell it will find another empty one and try it on for size. With some hermit crabs there is a kind of friendship with a sea anemone. The anemone sits on the shell and protects the crab from enemies with its tentacles. In return the anemone picks up the 'crumbs' dropped by the crab while it is feeding. This kind of give-and-take in the animal kingdom is called commensalism, meaning 'off the same table'.

Krill

Among the smaller crustaceans are vast numbers which float near the surface, especially in the sea, or drift about in freshwater ponds. Masses of

from time to time, even down to the legs and antennae, and such empty skins get washed up along the beach. Occasionally a leg may be lost, but it is soon regrown.

A crustacean's body is divided into three main regions as in insects—head, thorax and abdomen—but these shrimp-like kinds, called krill, build up every summer in the Antarctic, and are the food of the giant baleen whales which strain them out of the water. The krill multiplies in sufficient numbers to keep these giants going.

In a similar way, pond crustaceans are a food supply for many animals, and these also multiply during the summer. One of these, a water flea called *Daphnia*, is commonly sold in aquariums and pet-shops as a fish food. Its body is flattened sideways, and it jerks about in a flea-like fashion. Under the outer shell is a space, the brood chamber, where baby water fleas are born and set free. The strange thing is that they are all females, and can grow to produce more females. During summer there is no sign of any males. This kind of 'virgin' birth is a zoological puzzle. Only towards winter or when a drought occurs and the pond dries up, do males appear. They mate with the females, who now lay eggs with hard cases. These are the winter eggs which rest on the pond bottom until the following spring. A similar kind of reproduction takes place among the greenfly in the garden.

Another common freshwater crustacean is called *Cyclops*, after the one-eyed giant in Greek mythology. The two eyes are close together and look like one. It has a pear-shaped body, and the female carries her eggs in two little sacs. The freshwater shrimp, *Gammarus*, is found more in running water, and is a favourite food of trout. Similar crustaceans, called sandhoppers, can be seen along the sea shore. When the tide goes out they hide among the seaweeds and are searched for by sea-birds. *Asellus* is called the freshwater louse, but has no connection with the true insect louse. It lives on the bottom of ponds, and scavenges for its food.

There are only a few kinds of crustaceans which live on land, and then usually in damp places. They are called woodlice and can be found in almost every garden, hiding under stones, flower-pots and in rubbish. They are commonly found in rotten wood, in a log or tree stump, under loose bark and in leaf-mould in woods. If disturbed they immediately run for cover, not so much to escape from danger, but to get away from the light. This is a built-in reaction and a valuable life-saver. Light means an open space where there is a risk of drying up. In fact, a woodlouse placed in a dry tin with no dampness will soon die. Like the ancient trilobite a woodlouse has a shelly covering, and in some cases will curl itself into a tight ball for protection, or to save moisture. This habit of curling up was performed even by some of the trilobites. They have been found as fossils in the curled-up position.

One of the strangest of living creatures is a small arthropod which lives in the tropics, called *Peripatus*. It has a segmented worm-like body but also antennae like an insect, and walks about on many pairs of legs, like a millipede. It is a kind of 'living fossil' which resembles an ancestral type of invertebrate.

Arachnids

Arachnids are a class of arthropods consisting of spiders, scorpions and mites. These are sometimes confused with insects, but the two kinds should be easy to distinguish. Arachnids have eight legs instead of six, as in

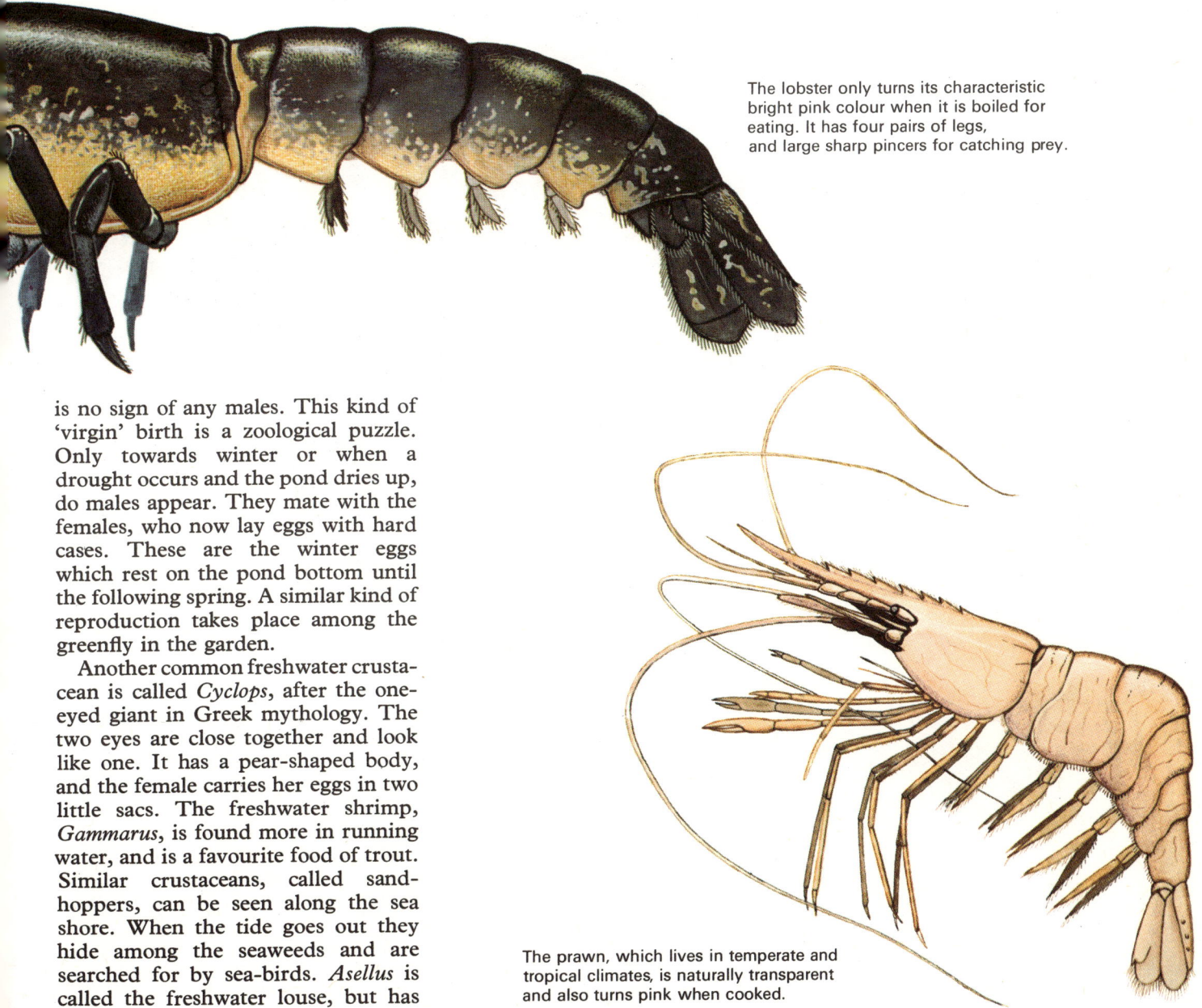

The lobster only turns its characteristic bright pink colour when it is boiled for eating. It has four pairs of legs, and large sharp pincers for catching prey.

The prawn, which lives in temperate and tropical climates, is naturally transparent and also turns pink when cooked.

The common garden spider is an orb-spinner, so named because it produces a wheel-like web made of silk in which to trap its prey.

insects, and the body is in two main divisions instead of three. The joined head and thorax form what is called the cephalothorax, which is attached to the abdomen. There are no antennae as in insects, and the important sense organs are the eyes. Most arachnids live on land, apart from some of the mites which occur in fresh water, or live as parasites. They breathe through layers of plates, called lung-books in land forms, and gill-books in aquatic forms.

One group of primitive arachnids live in the sea, and are called king-crabs or horseshoe crabs. They represent some of the most ancient arachnids known from fossil remains. The body is protected by a curved shell and ends in a long spiny tail. They crawl about the sea bed as they have done for millions of years.

The trapdoor spider lives in warm parts of the world. Instead of spinning webs, this spider digs a burrow in the ground, lines it with silk, and then makes a hinged lid to close the entrance. The spider hides from danger in its burrow.

Spiders

Spiders are mainly hunters, and are divided into two groups according to the position of their biting jaws. Some bite sideways and others bite downwards. A bite injects a poison to paralyse or kill prey. This can sometimes be dangerous to man. In particular the American black widow spider and the Australian Sydney funnel spider may cause death from a poisonous bite. The famous tarantula of the Mediterranean is not necessarily a killer. It was once thought to cause a kind of madness when people were bitten. In order to sweat out the poison an energetic dance was composed called the tarantella, which if performed was supposed to save the patient's life. The bite of the large bird-eating spiders of the tropics, which are often called tarantulas, is less serious. These rather timid spiders may look very fearsome but do not attack. They are often found in ships carrying fruit.

The hunting spiders catch their prey by speed and stealth, and usually lurk in dark corners or in vegetation. The common house spider found in cellars, or which sometimes comes up the plug-hole into the bath is a well-known example. The so-called wolf spiders run about in the undergrowth, catching prey. The female carries a cocoon of eggs with her until they hatch. Other spiders use some kind of trap made of silk, in order to catch prey, or use it as a home. This silk is woven from an organ at the end of the body, called a spinneret. Some spiders make simple webs to hide in—you can see them in the grass or in bushes. Funnel-shaped webs show up after a cold summer's night, when dew has fallen.

Other spiders live in holes. One of the most ingenious homes is that of the trapdoor spider. It uses a hole in a tree or in the ground, and weaves a hinged door which makes a perfect fit, so that the hole is hidden.

The most elaborate webs are made by the orb-web spiders, such as the garden or cross spider, so named because it has a white cross marked on its body. The whole web is made by instinct, starting with a framework inside which the 'spokes' are attached,

There are many different species of scorpions, which vary considerably in size, but all live in warm districts. By day the scorpion hides under rocks and logs, coming out at night to hunt. It has four pairs of legs, a pair of pincers and a poison sting in its tail.

then the spiral to complete the web. This spiral is sticky and becomes a trap for any insect which blunders in. The spider hides nearby and holds a thread with a foot so that it picks up any vibration which tells it there has been a capture. It then darts out, bites its victim, and wraps it up in silk as a future meal. Young spiders when they hatch may travel for miles. They emit a silken thread which is picked up by the passing wind, so that the spider is carried off. This explains the threads of 'gossamer' which can be seen lying about in grass and on bushes.

Very few spiders live under water, although one species actually lives in the sea among sponges. The best known is the freshwater spider found all over Europe and Asia. It can make a web under water, attaching it to the plants. The spider comes to the surface to collect air, and each bubble is placed under the web so that it fills up to form an underwater airbell. This becomes the home of the spider, in which she can breathe, take food, lay her eggs, and even hibernate. Before mating some spiders perform elaborate courtship ceremonies, in which the male even offers his mate a gift of a dead insect. Afterwards, if he is not careful, he may get eaten himself.

Scorpions

Scorpions are easy to recognise, having a body made up of the fused head and thorax, which carries four pairs of walking legs and two powerful pincers in front. The body ends in a long 'tail' which bears a sting. This

Mites are known to attack plants, animals and humans.

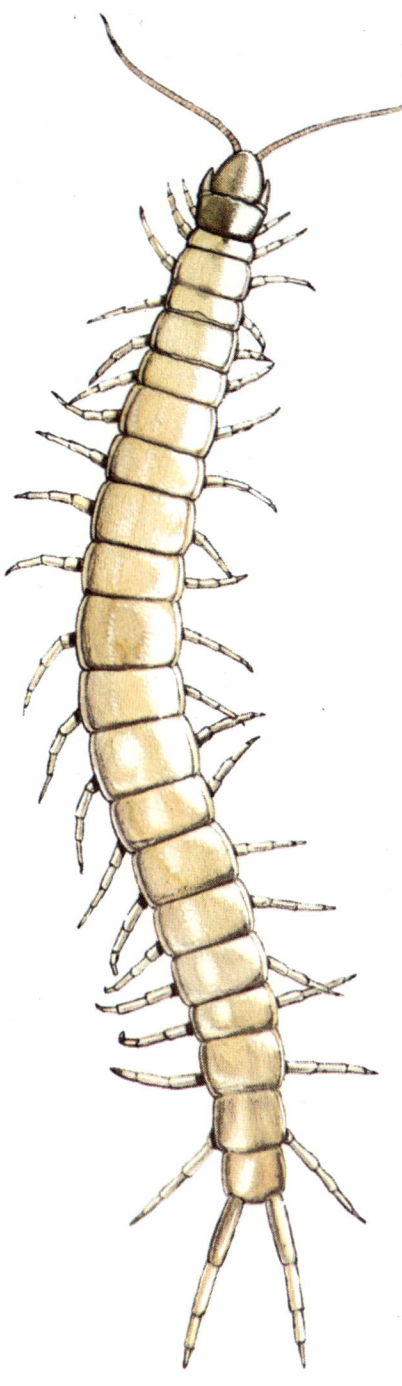

Centipedes occur in many parts of the world and most of them, including the tropical centipede, *Scolopendra morsitans* (shown above), will attack their prey with fangs and a poisonous bite.

is used mainly for defence. Usually a scorpion can deal with its prey by using its pincers. There is no truth in the story that a scorpion will commit suicide by stinging itself to death when in danger. Scorpions live in warm countries, in sandy areas. To avoid hot sun, they hide away under stones or in the sand and come out at night.

They will not normally attack, and a person stung has probably made some kind of mistake, like putting on a shoe containing a scorpion. When mating, a sort of circular dance takes place. The mother's fertilised eggs remain attached to the oviducts, and grow into young scorpions which are then born alive. She may carry them for a while on her back. The size of a large scorpion today is about fifteen centimetres (six inches), which is small compared with the giant sea scorpions of long ago. Some of their fossil remains are up to two metres (six feet) long.

Mites

Mites are small arachnids which exist in huge numbers in the soils and in leaf litter. As many as 175 million have been counted in one acre of a beech wood. They are useful in helping to break down the leaves to form humus. Eggs are laid and pass through a larval stage which at first has only six legs. The adult has the usual eight. Many mites are parasitic on other animals. They live off mammals, birds, reptiles and insects, and can spread diseases which result in fevers or skin diseases. The so-called itch-mites burrow under the skin, and can sometimes attack humans who walk through long grass. As well as these land mites there are many others living in the sea, and in freshwater.

Some parasitic mites which feed on blood have swollen bodies when they have fed. These are usually called ticks. They drop off after feeding, and the females lay eggs. The larva which hatch climb up blades of grass and wave their legs about until they are caught up by a passing animal.

Female ticks are blood-suckers which attack animals and birds and also transmit diseases.

Animals with Backbones

Although the vast majority of creatures in the world belong to the group called invertebrates, that is animals without backbones, it is the vertebrates, or animals with backbones, that command our principal interest. This is understandable because vertebrates include not only man himself but all the more familiar animals, such as lions and tigers, cats and dogs.

For most of us it is difficult enough to think of fishes or frogs as animals, let alone cockroaches or one-celled protozoans. But the fact remains that the animal kingdom is made up of many groups (called phyla) of invertebrates and only one group of vertebrates. However dissimilar fishes, amphibians, reptiles, birds and mammals may seem, they have much more in common with one another than with any of the invertebrates.

The vertebrates, and mammals in particular, clearly represent the highest form of development in the animal kingdom. This has to do chiefly with greater brain power, which has led to man's superior position in the world today, not only over other mammals but over all creatures.

Living in Water
Although the first vertebrates came into being more than 600 million years ago they all lived in water until about 350 million years ago. Even today, all vertebrates at some stage in their development have openings or slits at the side of the throat forming a passage from the exterior to the pharynx, which is the upper part of the passage in the neck through which food is taken. In land mammals, reptiles and birds these slits are present only in the very early stages of the animal embryo. They perform no function, merely indicating that the ancestors of these creatures once had need of them in order to breathe. In fish, they continue to exist as gill-slits.

The true vertebrates consist of a series of classes—fishes, amphibians, reptiles, birds and mammals—which represent successive evolutionary steps from lower to higher orders of animals much more clearly than any links which can be traced between the various groups of invertebrates.

Vertebrates take their name from the vertebral column, or backbone, which all members of the group possess. In the skeleton of an animal the backbone is the jointed rod which extends from the back of the head to the base of the body or, when present, to the tip of the tail.

Within the vertebral column and protected by it, is the spinal cord which connects with the brain. The brain is the chief part of the nervous system, and the organs of sensation, such as the spinal cord, are really outgrowths from it. This arrangement whereby the nervous system is enclosed within a bony tube separate from the rest of the body is peculiar to the vertebrates. The nervous system in invertebrates is enclosed within the general body cavity and is not in any way shut off.

The Vertebral Column
The vertebral column consists of a succession of bony segments each joined to its neighbour in such a way that the animal may flex its body. The segments, or joints, of which the backbone is composed are usually formed of bone in adult animals. Some of the more primitive vertebrates, such as sharks and rays among the fishes, may retain the pliable material, called cartilage, of which the skeleton is first formed and never develop proper bones.

Two other important characteristics of vertebrates are the limbs, which are present in most species and never exceed four in number, and the jaws, which are upper and lower rather than right and left as in insects.

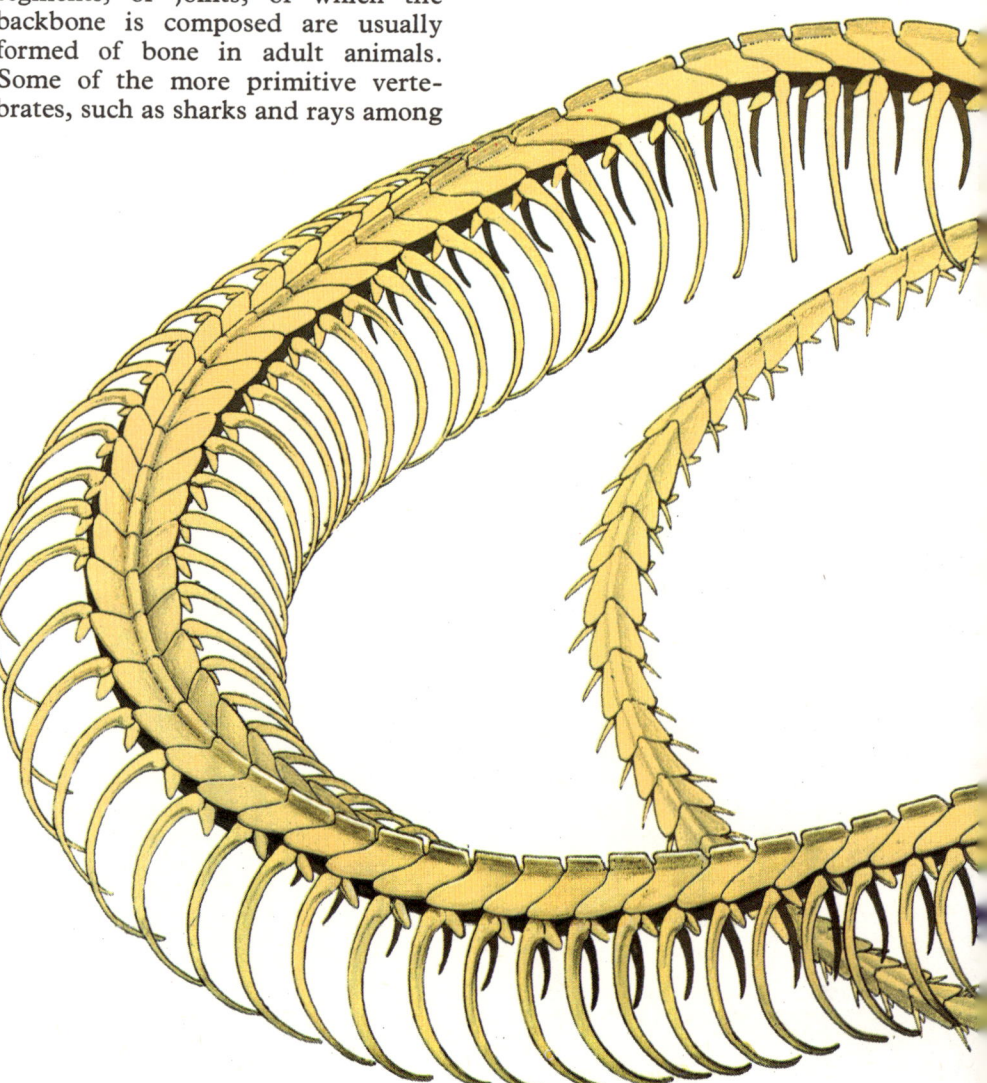

Primitive Chordates

Allied with the vertebrates within the major group called chordates, are a number of very primitive creatures which, although they have no vertebrae, are like the backboned animals in many important ways. They live in or near the sea, the most numerous being the sea-squirts, of which there are no less than 1,200 species.

The Five Classes

Vertebrate animals are divided into five classes and each of these will be looked at in greater detail on the succeeding pages. They are presented in their evolutionary order, beginning with fishes and ending with man.

1. Fishes (scientific name Pisces, from the Latin *piscis*, a fish). Living in water; cold-blooded; mostly breathing through gills; three groups.

2. Amphibians (scientific name Amphibia, from the Greek *amphibios*, having a double life). Fish-like in their early existence; breathing through gills at first, then acquiring lungs; three groups.

3. Reptiles (scientific name Reptilia, from the Latin *repere*, to creep). Bony skeletons; skin clothed with horny plates or scales; most lay eggs but some produce live young; four groups.

4. Birds (scientific name Aves, from the Latin *avis*, a bird). Feathered; warm-blooded; young hatched from eggs; forelimbs developed into wings used in flight; twenty-seven groups.

5. Mammals (scientific name Mammalia, from the Latin *mamma*, the breast). Warm-blooded; producing live young; skin covered usually with hair; breathing air by lungs; young suckled on milk from mother; three groups, egg-laying, marsupial and placental.

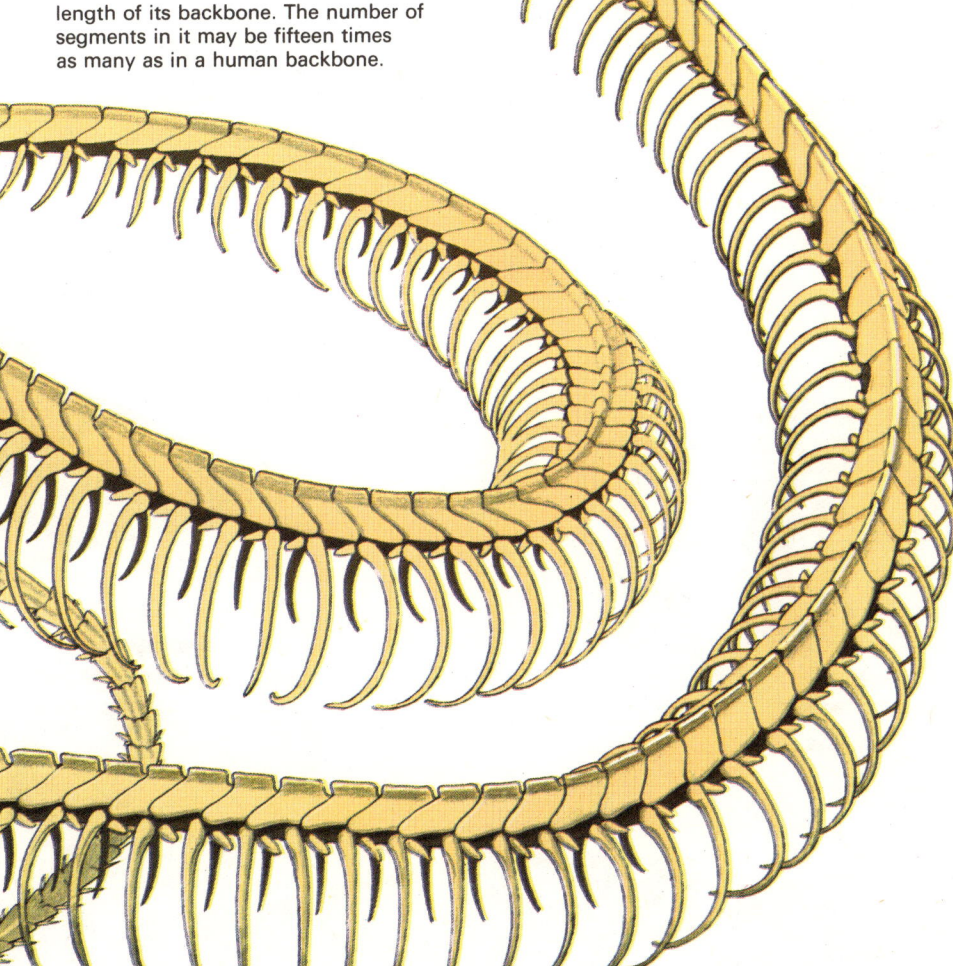

The skeleton of a snake shows the length of its backbone. The number of segments in it may be fifteen times as many as in a human backbone.

129

Fishes

Fishes are adapted for life under water. They are the oldest group of vertebrate animals and from them all other creatures with backbones, even man, have evolved. There are over 20,000 species and the variety within the class Pisces, to give them their zoological name, is perhaps greater than in any other vertebrate class.

They are able to live and breathe in water by means of gills, which are slits in the body through which they expel water after it has been taken in through the mouth. As the water passes over the gills the fish extracts the oxygen it needs and passes out carbon dioxide.

Fishes cannot live for long out of water although the length of time they can stay alive on dry land varies according to the capacity of the gills to retain moisture. Some air-breathing fishes can stay out of water for several hours, and even manage to 'walk' across land from one stretch of water to another by pushing themselves along on their pectoral fins, which are set into the shoulders and in some species give the appearance of limbs.

The general shape of fishes is torpedo-like but there is an immense variety of form and colour. Most of them swim by moving the rear part of their bodies from side to side, displacing water first on one side and then on the other. The ray employs a different method of propulsion: it uses broad fore-fins rather like wings and by muscular contraction moves water from front to back.

Freedom in Water

There are fishes that travel in vast shoals and others that lead a solitary life; some who inhabit the very depths of the oceans, and others best-suited to life near the surface of water; some are savage flesh-eaters and others simply absorb the microscopic organisms called plankton which drift invisibly through the water; some are swift and some are slow. But all are ideally suited to their environment. The freedom of fish to move in water can be compared with the ability of the bird to soar and fly through the air.

In most species of fish the body is protected by a covering of scales, which are attached to the skin by one edge and overlap each other. Some fishes, such as lampreys, do not have scales. In others, for example the freshwater eels, the scales are so tiny that the fish appears to be naked. Scale patterns are used to distinguish between different species, and the age of a fish can be told from its scales.

Reproduction is generally by means of eggs, vast numbers of which are eaten as food by fishes and other animals. If the death-rate before birth was not so high the sea could well be packed solid with fishes. Many types of fish lay millions of eggs at a time, but fortunately there is a great wastage of life. Eggs are not only eaten but they are left by the parents to the mercies of wind and tide, although some, such as the salmon and the stickleback, actually prepare nests for their offspring.

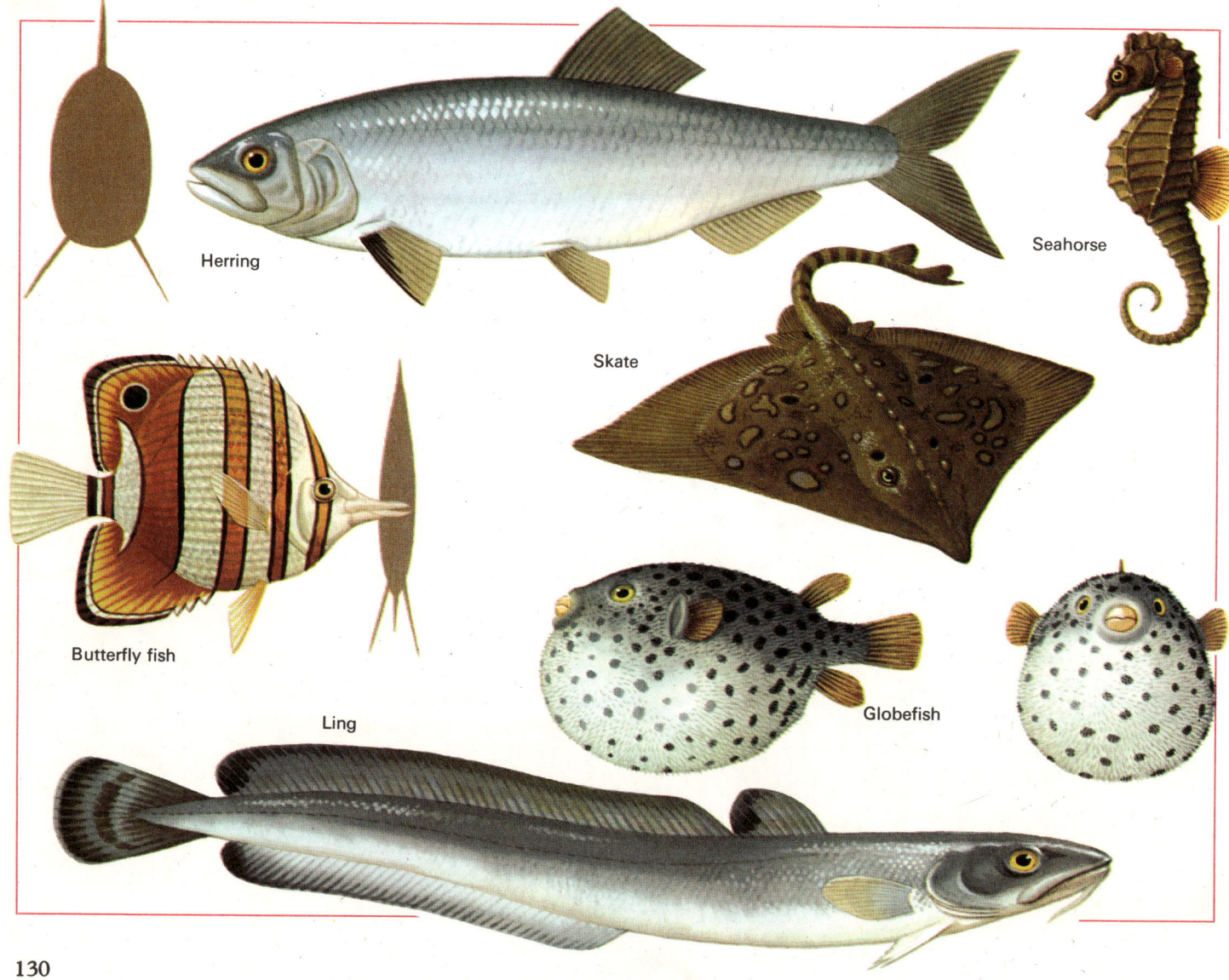

The manta ray can leap out of the water using its large wing-like pectoral fins.

Sharks and Rays

These fishes and their allies belong to one of the most primitive groups of vertebrates. They are called cartilaginous fishes, because their skeletons are made of gristle, or cartilage, and not of bone. They are jawed fish and each jaw has a row of teeth which are either sharply pointed and separate, or blunt and crowded together. In some species new teeth continue to grow throughout life to replace old ones that have fallen out.

All species prey on other sea creatures, although some of the largest live only on plankton and tiny molluscs. Sharks live mainly near the surface of the sea whereas rays are generally bottom-dwellers.

Sharks

Sharks have cigar-shaped bodies and are excellent swimmers, although less manoeuvrable than bony fishes because of their great weight. They have an acute sense of smell which they use when hunting, and some species can be dangerous to man. Among the fiercest sharks are the four-metre (twelve-foot) long whaler shark, which gets its name from its practice of following whaling ships to feed on dead whales. Other meat-eaters are the great white shark, the blue shark and the scavenging tiger shark. The biggest sharks of all, the whale shark and the basking shark, are both about six to nine metres (twenty to thirty feet) in length but are harmless plankton eaters.

Rays and Skates

Living mainly on the sea bottom, rays and skates have flattened bodies, roughly disc-shaped, often with long tails. The biggest rays are the huge mantas, or devil rays, which can measure as much as six metres (twenty feet) across their 'wings'. Unlike its fellow rays the manta lives near the surface of the water and sometimes actually leaps above it.

There are some rays which are capable of giving electric shocks and others, like the sting ray, which have poisonous barbed spines on their whip-like tails. One of the strangest looking rays is the sawfish, which has an extended upper jaw in the shape of a large flat sword-blade.

Chimaeras

Known as rabbit fishes, rat fishes, and even as elephant fishes, the chimaeras are very primitive relatives of the shark. They have a number of unusual features such as the bony hook which the male carries on its forehead, called a clasper, and the fact that they have nostrils through which they take water when breathing, only opening their mouths to feed.

Jawless fishes

The only survivors of an ancient race of jawless fishes are the hagfishes and the lampreys. They belong to a class which some scientists consider is quite different from other fishes, although they are fish-like creatures. Unlike other vertebrates they have only a single nostril and do not have a hinged lower jaw. There is also an absence of limbs and ribs. There are no teeth although some forms have horny structures in the mouth. Hagfishes are practically blind and live on the bottom of the sea, where they feed on the flesh of dead fishes. The lamprey, which can grow to nearly a metre (three feet) in length, has a powerful leech-like sucker on the front of its head in the middle of which is a mouth. With this it fastens on to the body of a living fish and rasps off the flesh on which it feeds. Lampreys migrate for hundreds of kilometres in order to mate and spawn up rivers.

The sight of a fin above water does not always indicate the presence of a shark, such as the porbeagle seen in the large picture below. Other fishes which display fins are shown in the smaller drawings. These are, from left to right, the dolphin, the swordfish and the ray.

Bony Fishes

The great majority of fishes existing in the world today fall into this class. They are distinguished from the cartilaginous fishes by the bony nature of their skeletons. The structure of the skeleton is important as a guide to the classification of the different kinds of fishes.

The sturgeon and its allies form a sub-class of bony fishes separate from all others. They are slow-moving, often heavy fish, some living in the open sea and going up river to spawn, and others spending all their lives in rivers. They are characterised by numbers of bony plates on their sides and a long bony snout with which they root about in the mud of river beds looking for food.

The typical sturgeons are confined to northern waters of temperate regions, where they are among the largest of freshwater fishes. Some specimens have been known over six metres (twenty feet) in length but the average size is much smaller. The sturgeon used to be important economically, particularly in Europe, before its numbers dropped. Its flesh was regarded as a delicacy, its eggs provided caviare, the lining of its swim bladder was used for making glue, and a grained fish leather was made from its skin. In Britain it has been a 'royal' fish since the reign of Edward II (1307–27), by whose act it was proclaimed that all sturgeon caught off the coasts of the kingdom should belong to the sovereign.

It is said of sturgeon that in winter they go into some form of hibernation. Stories from some localities tell of them burying their noses in the mud with bodies and tails standing straight upright like a series of posts.

Other members of this group include paddlefishes, birchirs and reedfishes.

Herring shoals can stretch for several kilometres. The fish are usually caught in drift nets, which are like huge curtains hung from buoys floating on the surface of the water.

Common sturgeon

Herrings

The herring is the most important food fish in the world. It is eaten fresh, salted or potted and, smoked and slit apart, it becomes that popular dish the kipper. It lives in the temperate seas of the northern hemisphere, particularly in the North Atlantic. Millions of them swim together in vast shoals near the surface of the water. For generations a complete industry has existed around their capture and marketing, particularly in Great Britain, France and the Scandinavian countries.

The herring has a strong claim to be the most numerous backboned animal in existence and thousands of millions of them are caught every year. Also popular and abundant as food fishes are sprats, whitebait (which are in fact the young of herrings and sprats), pilchards (and their young, sardines) and anchovies. The sardine has only feeble bones and is usually eaten whole. The largest shoals of them are found around the island of Sardinia, hence their name.

This skeleton of a perch illustrates the structure of a typical bony fish.

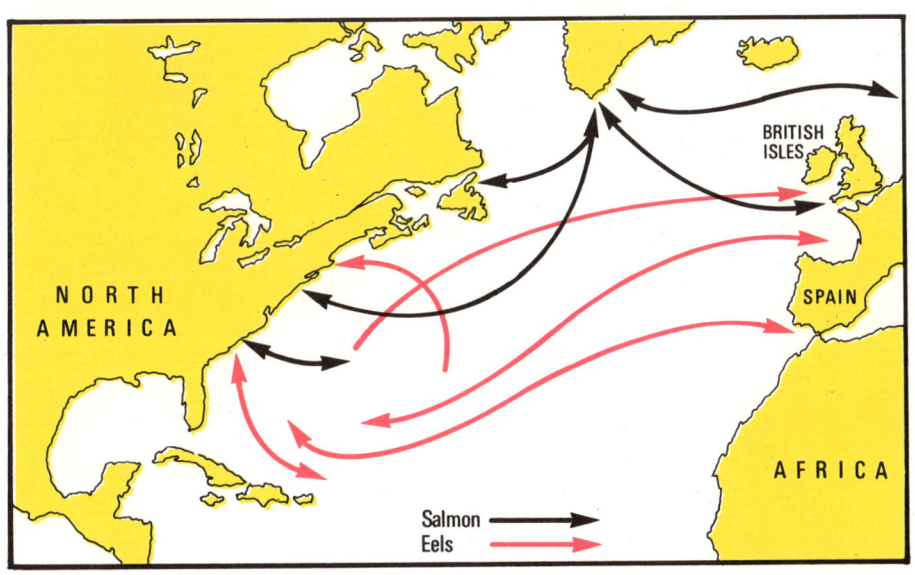

The common eel is widely distributed in fresh waters throughout the world.

Eels

The typical adult eel is long and snake-like in appearance. The majority of species live in the sea but the members of one family, the Anguillidae, spend their adult lives in rivers. The most familiar example is the common European eel, which is widely distributed all over the continent.

The eel's extraordinary life-history follows a regular pattern. It grows slowly and lives in the fresh water of rivers for an average of eight to ten years, although the males stay longer than the females. Each autumn a great number of eels decide to leave the rivers to breed.

During their journey into the Atlantic Ocean they do not eat, having stored up large food reserves

The map illustrates the general direction of the routes taken by salmon and eels on their migratory journeys across the Atlantic Ocean. The eel moves from rivers to the sea to spawn and the salmon does the same thing in reverse.

in their bodies. After several months the eels arrive at an area in the Atlantic near the Sargasso Sea and here they spawn and afterwards die, for no adult eels are known to have returned to their river homes. The young larvae then develop in the depths of the oceans and begin their long, slow trek back to the rivers. This takes them about three years, during which time they are tiny transparent beings. When they arrive in coastal waters off Europe they have grown to about 70 millimetres (three inches) in length and as they make for the rivers they gradually assume a cylindrical shape,

become elvers, or young eels and gain colour.

On their way back to the rivers the young eels will meet and overcome all kinds of obstacles, climb up waterfalls and even wriggle across a damp field to reach a new stretch of water. At their freshwater homes they repeat the cycle of events carried out by their parents by staying for about ten years before setting off themselves to seek the spawning grounds and an end to life.

There are many other eels which belong to the same group as the freshwater eels, among them the conger, which lives and spawns in deep sea waters, and the fierce and ugly moray.

The Salmon Family

Salmon are cold-water fishes, living in northern waters or rivers. Fully grown, they may be up to one and a half metres (four to five feet) long with an average top weight of 18 kilograms (40 pounds). But even larger specimens have been taken: a fish of 31 kilograms (70 pounds) has been recorded from the River Tay in Scotland. The most important game fish, salmon and trout, give wonderful sport to the angler: not only this, they are excellent to eat.

Although most fishes do not travel far from their original homes, some spend their lives almost constantly on the move, even though this movement is confined to a small area. Other species migrate from one place to another over long distances. The eel migrates from river to sea to spawn; the salmon does the same thing, only in reverse, leaving its home in the sea to spawn in rivers.

Salmon show extraordinary strength in overcoming obstacles such as river falls, up which they leap during their migrations.

133

The pike waits for its victim.

This migratory urge is very strong and the salmon travels up to 3,200 kilometres (2,000 miles) to and from the Atlantic seas and the river of its birth. It begins life in shallow, fast-moving rivers and here it remains for a number of years. At this stage of its life it is called a parr. Just before it leaves the river to set off for the open sea it acquires a deposit on its skin which gives it a silvery sheen, and now the fish is known as a smolt.

It arrives in the Atlantic as an adult and lives there for from one to three years. Eventually, driven by the urge to spawn it sets off to find the river where it was born. In many cases, fishes do actually track down the exact stretch of water from which they came. Just how they do this is not known, although it is believed that a sense of smell guides them.

Records of the journeys of salmon are now being built up by means of tagging selected fish, rather in the way that bird movements are traced by means of ringed birds. The homing instinct of salmon is so strong that they will overcome all kinds of obstacles and they are capable of swimming against strong currents and of leaping up river falls.

Trout
There are various kinds of trout, some of which are migratory and others which spend their lives in freshwater lakes and rivers. The rainbow trout is a native of North America which has been introduced into European rivers. The grayling and the smelt are unusual in that their flesh gives off a pleasant scent. In the case of the grayling this has inspired its scientific name, *Thymallus*, a reference to the plant thyme, which its smell is said to resemble.

The Japanese Ayu, or sweetfish, a relative of the salmon family, is the object of a unique form of fishing. The Japanese train cormorants to go with them in their boats to catch the fish in their beaks. A bird is prevented from swallowing the fish by means of a metal ring placed around its neck.

Pike
The pike has a slender body and is flat-snouted with strong teeth which curve inwards to prevent any creature escaping from its grip. Some have been caught measuring over one metre (four feet) and weighing 35 kilograms (77 pounds). The pike has been called a freshwater shark, for it is a greedy predator on all kinds of animal life. It lies motionless at the bottom of weed-choked lakes and rivers, blending with its background so that it becomes almost invisible.

Apart from eating other fish it will take worms, frogs, waterbirds, voles —almost any animal unlucky enough to stray near its lair. It is known throughout northern parts of Europe, Asia and America. Most of the stories about the great age of certain individual fish are legendary, the longest life-span ever recorded being about fifteen years.

Carp and Catfishes
The most familiar freshwater fishes throughout the world are members of the carp family. In addition to the carp itself it includes the roach, rudd,

Seen below are: 1 chub, 2 gudgeon, 3 char, 4 rudd, 5 minnow, 6 roach, 7 dace, 8 barbel, 9 carp, 10 grayling. All are members of the carp family except the char and the grayling.

tench, gudgeon, minnow, bream, dace, chub and loach. All of them are fishes which are popular with the fisherman as they provide good sport, fighting for their lives and testing the skill of the angler. In general, they have toothless jaws, with rows of grinding teeth at the back of their mouths. Many are flesh-eaters but some feed on vegetation.

Goldfish belong to the carp family and their popularity as pets in home aquaria and garden ponds has led to the controlled breeding of a variety of forms, some weird, some beautiful. They came to the western world from China and Japan.

The family of catfishes is large and they are distinguished by pairs of barbels around their mouths which look rather like thick whiskers and so prompt their name. It is possible that like a cat's whiskers the barbels are used by the fish to help it move about and find food. The majority of catfishes live in the river estuaries of tropical countries.

Deep-sea Fishes

There is a mystery about the depths of the oceans and the creatures that

Deep-sea fishes seen above are: *Diretmus argenteus*, 2 eel larva, 3 *Sternoptyx diaphana*, 4 roosterfish, 5 lantern fish, 6 snipe eel, 7 *Opisthoproctus soleatus*, 8 angler fish, 9 prawn, 10 rat-tail, 11 tripod.

live there which no amount of scientific enquiry will ever entirely dispel. Even the animals we know, which live in dark water beyond the reach of the sun's light, are frightening enough in appearance. But what weird things may still lurk unknown and unseen in the abyss of the oceans? There have always been tales of giant squids and fabled sea-monsters like the kraken, which rise up out of the water to crush boats and destroy human life, and it is difficult to feel confident that such tales have no basis in fact. However, most known animals which live in the depths of the sea are quite small.

In the lower parts of the sea not only is there little or no light, but enormous pressures build up which animals can only counteract by equal pressures within their bodies. If one of these deep-sea dwellers came rapidly to the surface it would burst as the balance of pressures changed.

The microscopic deep-sea plankton lives on dead animals and plant material which drops to the sea bed. In its turn this plankton becomes the food of many deep-sea creatures. Others feed directly from the organic material of larger creatures which die and sink to the bottom.

Fishes have developed a variety of special features to fit them for life in deep water. One is the enlargement of the eyes to obtain maximum vision in almost total blackness. Another is the expanding stomach which many species have, allowing them to swallow prey much bigger than themselves and to digest it over a long period, so that one meal may last a long time. A natural development of this function is the huge gaping mouth which many species have to help them swallow these gigantic meals.

The Angler Fish

The deep-water angler fish, which has been caught over 3,048 metres (10,000 feet) down, is one of the strangest members of a curious company. It has enormous jaws with backward pointing teeth and a luminous bait on its nose. The female angler fish is a giant compared with

Flying fish are capable of skimming across the surface of water. This is due to the impetus of a leap from the water rather than actual flight.

the male. When the tiny male meets up with a female (not an easy job since it depends on a chance encounter in total darkness in a vast featureless underwater landscape) he attaches himself to the underside of her body with his mouth and literally becomes a part of his partner. He loses not only his identity but his ability to function independently.

The Cod Family

The order of fishes to which the cod belongs contains a number of species which are caught and eaten by man. Fortunately, they are an abundant group, well able to survive the attentions of large-scale commercial fishing. The most familiar fish, apart from the cod, are hakes, haddocks and whiting. They all prefer the cold Arctic waters and are at their most numerous in the North Atlantic near the Dogger Bank and off the coasts of Iceland and Newfoundland.

The cod itself is generally between 60 and 120 centimetres (two and four feet) in length and about five kilograms (twelve pounds) in weight, although some fish of monster size have been caught which tipped the scales at ninety kilograms (200 pounds). The hake is a particularly greedy fish with a great liking for pilchard. When caught in a pilchard net it has been known to eat itself to a standstill even as the fishermen were gathering the catch. The haddock can be distinguished readily from its cousins by the blackish patch on each side of the body above the pectoral fin.

As well as the familiar fishes in this group there are related types which are comparatively unknown although some, like the rat-tails, are among the most numerous of deep-water fishes.

The Stickleback

Sticklebacks take their name from the isolated spines on their backs, which vary in number, generally from three to nine. They are mainly freshwater fish although there is a sea-stickleback. This marine species has as many as fifteen spines and has the distinction of being one of the few 'annual' vertebrates, since it usually dies within a year of its birth. Sticklebacks are very aggressive fish and the males engage in constant

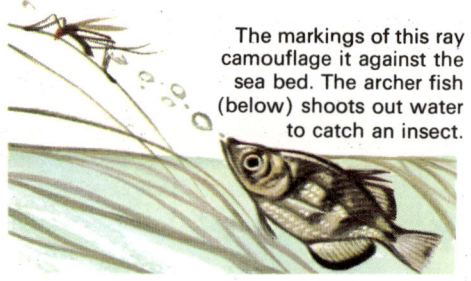

The markings of this ray camouflage it against the sea bed. The archer fish (below) shoots out water to catch an insect.

fights with each other, particularly at breeding time when favoured areas are being disputed. Two fish will dart at each other, attacking, retreating and feinting like a pair of wrestlers, until they grip one another in a stranglehold from which one fish will emerge the victor.

They have the interesting habit of nest-building, unusual in fishes. Some of these nests are made from weeds carefully bound together with a silk-like thread. In a single nest, eggs are laid by several females. The male stickleback also develops a breeding coloration in which parts of its body assume a reddish tinge.

The Perch Tribe

The vast order of perches and their allies includes most of the marine fishes. They breed in great quantities and number in their midst two which are very important to the fishing industry, the mackerel and the tunny.

The common perch is a handsome creature, its scales shading from greenish-brown to golden and white. It is a flesh-eater and exists largely on minnow, dace and other young fish, as well as worms and insects.

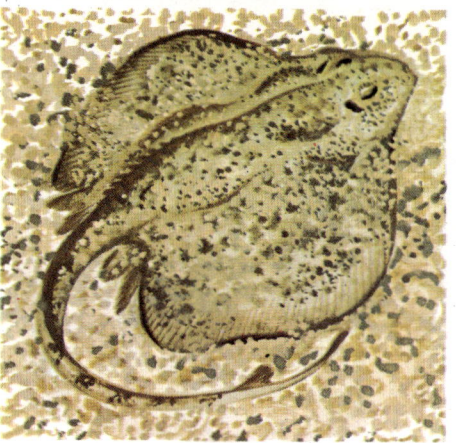

There are many other familiar species in the group, including bass, mullet and bream.

One of the oddities is the climbing perch which lives in Indian waters. Its pectoral fins are used as limbs and with them it drags itself across land for considerable distances. Whether it actually climbs trees is doubtful but certainly in wet weather it has been seen to clamber over

The coelacanth is a type of primitive fish which lived about 300 million years ago. Scientists believe it has not changed for the past 200 million years. Although it was thought to have been extinct for a very long time, a specimen was dragged up by a trawler fishing off the coast of East Africa in 1938. Other specimens of this living fossil have since been caught in tropical waters around India and Africa.

rain-soaked branches and other obstacles. It has a special organ which allows it to breathe for periods on land. Also related to the perch is the mudskipper, another fish which is well adapted to an existence out of water. It has very prominent, close-set eyes which can be protruded and retracted and a well-developed outer eyelid. As it lumbers across the ground, snapping at flies and raising itself on its pectoral fins as if they were elbows to peer around, it looks like an oversized newt.

Mackerel have specially beautiful colouring with bluish-green scales and a belly of iridescent silver. They congregate in shoals of immense size and have seasonal migrations when they leave the open sea and swim towards the shore to look for food. Mackerel are pelagic fishes (from the Greek word *pelagos* for the sea), that is, they live near the surface of the water and are caught in drift nets. The other great class of marine fish, to which cod belong, are called demersal (from the Latin word *demergere*, to sink) and they live on or near the sea bed and are usually caught by trawling.

Relatives of the mackerel are the tunny or tuna fish and the bonito, both valuable to man as a source of food. The body temperature of the tunny is higher than that of the water in which it lives, a feature unique in fishes. Its blood system is highly developed to act as a temperature regulator.

Colour in fishes is used for camouflage and display. Brightly coloured sea creatures such as these butterfly fishes usually live in tropical waters, often around a coral reef.

Flatfishes

A remarkable example of adaptation to a chosen environment is seen in the flatfish, the well-known plaice, soles, dabs and flounders. The typical flatfish is compressed sideways because of its habit of living on the bottom of the sea. When a young fish is hatched it is more or less the normal shape with an eye on each side of its head. As it grows it develops the flat look of the adult fish. The front part of the skull is gradually twisted and one eye begins to move across the top of the head to lie alongside the other so that both are on one side of the body. It is thought that this adaptation was a gradual process in which the fish assumed a shape that suited its way of life. When flatfish are lying on the sandy bottom of the sea they merge almost completely with their background, the spots on their bodies helping to camouflage them, and so hide them from their enemies.

137

Amphibians

The name amphibian comes from some Greek words which mean 'living in two places'. This is an apt description of the animals called the amphibians, as they divide their lives between water and land. Today they are all small animals, the largest being the giant salamander of the Far East, which grows to a length of about one and a half metres (five feet), but in the prehistoric past they included some which grew to three and a half metres (twelve feet) long.

Today there are about 2,000 different species of amphibians, mostly living in the warmer and damper regions of the world. They can be classified into three groups: first the caecilians or blindworms, a small tropical group of burrowing animals; second the newts and salamanders; and third, the frogs and toads.

The typical amphibian starts life in the water. The pattern of mating behaviour varies greatly between the different species, but the eggs which are produced are usually laid in large numbers. In frogs and toads they are fertilised externally, after they have left the female's body. In newts, although there is internal fertilisation, often there is no direct contact between the pair. Many of the tropical amphibians have developed methods of protecting the eggs. They do this by making a nest in which the eggs hatch, or by providing parental protection, or by laying shelled eggs, or by producing living young. But in general the spawn has only a gelatinous outer covering. This is protective to some extent, but it soon becomes dried up if there is no water. And it is no help against the many predators, including fish and birds, which can make short work of amphibians' eggs.

The toad sits motionless when it is about to feed. When an insect is within reach it darts out its tongue and in a flash its prey is caught.

Tadpoles and Adults

Each egg has only a small yolk, so that the embryo has little resources for development and is forced to hatch within a few days. The creature which emerges from the egg is very different from its parents. Not only is it tiny, but in shape it resembles a fish, with external gills and a long tail which is used for swimming. The tadpole, as the larval stage is called, has to change greatly as it grows. The external gills are soon lost and within a few weeks tiny hind limbs appear, followed by forelimbs. As it grows the tail diminishes in the frog group, until finally the little creature has changed completely to its adult form. An important internal change has also taken place in the digestive system, for tadpoles are plant-eaters, while adult amphibians are flesh-eaters and have a completely different type of gut.

The dangers of life are not over with metamorphosis, as the change from tadpole to adult is called, for many creatures–including mammals, birds, snakes and fishes–are always willing to make a meal of frogs or newts. Very few of the young amphibians survive to breed themselves. A peril greater than their natural enemies has recently beset them and this is the danger of chemical pollution. Amphibians have very small lungs and part of their breathing is through their soft, moist skin. This cannot prevent the entry into their bodies of many chemicals used today in agriculture, which are usually lethal to the animals. Amphibians of all kinds have decreased drastically in numbers wherever modern agricultural practices occur.

Lines of Defence

Helpless as they appear to be in the face of enemies, the amphibians have a number of lines of defence. The most important are the poison glands in the skin, the largest of which lie just behind the head and can be seen quite easily in toads and some salamanders. When stimulated they produce a whitish fluid, which is extremely irritating to the eyes, mouth and nose of any animal investigating the amphibian too closely. In some species in which these glands are well developed a pattern of warning colouration also occurs. The fire salamander of mainland Europe, for example, has dazzling yellow and black colours, a clear warning to predators not to attack. Any animal which is foolish enough to do so will have a very unpleasant experience, and will remember the general colour pattern and avoid similar looking animals in future.

Another defence, used by toads and frogs, is for the threatened animals to blow themselves up with air, often doubling their size in the process. This not only makes them look more fearful to the predator, but because the tissues are quite hard, like the surface of a fully inflated balloon, it may be much more difficult for a snake, say, to get a grip on a frog, which may eventually escape as a result.

European fire salamander

All amphibians feed on insects, snails, worms, grubs, or even young of their own kind. They are capable of surviving long periods without food, but may be extremely greedy when it becomes available. Frogs and toads are able to shoot the tongue out a surprisingly long distance to catch an insect or other small animal which may be several inches away. This is possible because the tongue is hinged in the front of the mouth with the tip folded back towards the throat so it can be flicked out at a moment's notice to catch the prey.

Secretive Animals

Although amphibians are widespread they frequently go unnoticed as they are small, secretive animals, keeping on the whole to moist places. In the temperate areas of the world they are forced to hibernate in the winter time, which takes them further from man's eyes. The only occasion when they make themselves obvious is during the breeding season, when large numbers of them travel to their traditional breeding ponds, sometimes congregating from an area of several square kilometres. Exactly what draws them is unknown, but it is thought that the algae in the water, which is the essential food for the tadpoles, may have a faint but very distinctive smell which attracts the animals. It is at this time of year that the frogs and toads become especially vocal, singing their trilling or croaking songs almost incessantly.

The ways in which animals develop often show similarities which are proof of close relationship, even when the adults are very unalike. The reverse is true and the different development patterns of frogs and newts show the marked difference between the two groups. The rate of growth in both cases is affected by temperature, but under ideal conditions a common frog should have completed its change, or metamorphosis, in about four months. Some newts take longer. In the diagram below the stages of development of the frog (above) and the newt (below) are seen.

The newts may change colour, the males developing a bright orange display dress and large crests which run along the back and tail. In the crested newt this is particularly noticeable, for it forms a jagged ridge, broken at the base of the tail, which increases the size of the animal considerably. In the palmate newt, the crest is smoother but continuous. In both species it is lost after the breeding season, and at other times of the year all that is visible is a low ridge running the length of the animal's back. The purpose of these changes of colour and shape is to attract the females, for the newts perform complicated dances before breeding.

Spotted salamander

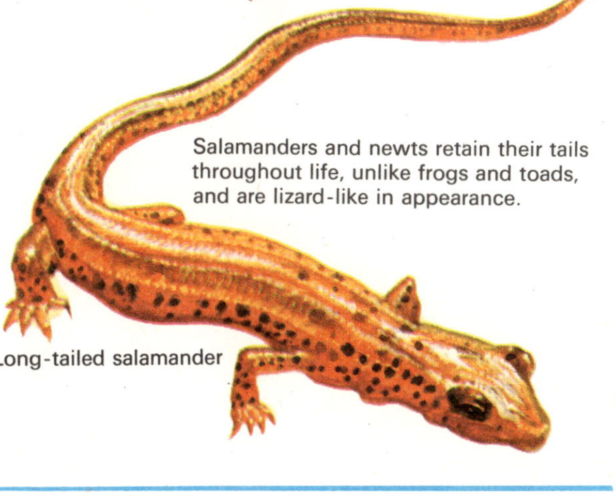

Salamanders and newts retain their tails throughout life, unlike frogs and toads, and are lizard-like in appearance.

Long-tailed salamander

Yellow-blotched salamander

Spotted tree frog

Dendrobates frog

Frogs and Toads

Frogs and toads are the most successful of the present day amphibians and are to be found in many environments throughout the world. They are quite unlike the newts in appearance, for they are all tail-less and all have hind legs very much longer than their forelimbs. Their usual method of movement is by hopping, although a few species can run. The distinctions between frogs and toads are internal and the terms are often used very loosely, but in general frogs have slenderer bodies and smoother skins, while toads have a more thickset appearance and drier, warty skins.

Common toad

Borneo flying frog

South American giant toad

In size they range from the giant goliath frog, which is about 300 millimetres (one foot) long, and can tackle prey as large as a rat, to tiny tree frogs only about 25 millimetres (one inch) long. Many of them are long-lived and there are records of pet toads having survived forty years in a garden. The poison glands of the skin are well developed in most toads, but the dendrobates frog is one of the most venomous of the group. An extract of the skins of these little animals is so poisonous that it was once used by certain South American Indians to tip their arrows for hunting or wars.

Climbing Frogs

Many frogs of the warmer parts have developed the ability to climb, and spend much time in the trees. Peron's tree frog, an Australian species, is in many ways typical. It is never found very far from water and has webbed fingers and toes, which help it as a swimmer. It has also developed large adhesive discs on each finger and these enable it to climb, so it may be found in trees and bushes from where its loud mating calls are often heard. Some climbing frogs have large webbed feet which are spread and used as parachutes when the animal jumps from one tree to another.

The Surinam Water Toad

Many kinds of frogs have developed ways of protecting their helpless young during the larval stage. The Surinam water toad has a complete system. The eggs, after laying and fertilisation, pass upwards towards the back of the female. The skin has become specially thickened during the breeding season and the eggs stick to this for a little while, before sinking into pits which form as a result of the chemical reaction between the egg and the skin. Before long the eggs are entirely hidden from the outside world as a lid forms over the top of the pit. In this position the young develop safely on their mother's back eventually hatching as complete toads.

Reptiles

Present day reptiles are the remnants of a group which was once dominant, containing some of the most bizarre and the biggest animals which have ever walked the earth. These cold-blooded scaly animals are now disliked by most people yet they are sometimes beautiful and often useful to man. But they are persecuted because of lack of knowledge of their nature and ways of life.

Reptiles are animals of the warm parts of the world. They are cold-blooded, which is to say that they have no control of their body temperature, and their energy is dependent on the temperature of their surroundings. If this is high the reptiles warm up and their bodily chemistry can proceed at a rate which ensures a rapid turnover of energy; if it is low the reptile becomes torpid and may be unable to move. Within this restriction, however, the reptiles occupy the world very fully. They are to be found in wet and dry tropical regions, as burrowers, tree-dwellers and water-dwellers. There are even some which lead a marine life and never come ashore, although they are air-breathing, like all other reptiles.

Egg Laying

The majority of reptiles lay eggs. These are fertilised internally, and are then laid on land, sometimes in a specially prepared nest but more usually in a protected place; under a fallen log or among leaves, for example. The eggs, which are very much like birds' eggs in construction, have an outer shell, which may be hard or parchment-like. Inside the egg the embryo develops using the food supply of the large yolk, buffered and protected by the albumen, or white, which is also used as it grows. Compared with birds' eggs, in which development of the chick is rapid, growth within the reptile egg is very slow. The egg of a Greek tortoise may take three months to hatch; a comparably sized bird's egg takes about three weeks. During this time, however, the embryo passes through its tadpole stages, and it hatches as a miniature, recognisable replica of its parents.

Although in a few cases the mother may remain near the eggs, once they have hatched her responsibilities cease and she takes no interest in the young, which are fully equipped to look after themselves. Some reptiles, especially those living in a somewhat unfavourable environment, retain the eggs inside the body of the female until they are ready to hatch. The young are then born alive, or within a very flimsy shell from which they escape immediately.

Eating and Movement

With their low turnover of energy, reptiles do not need to feed often. Many are flesh-eaters, but quite a large proportion eat plant food. Reptile teeth are all the same shape round the mouth, so biting and thorough chewing of the food does not occur as it does in mammals, and each mouthful is swallowed with very little mastication. Digestion is slow and many reptiles are capable of going several months between meals.

Reptiles often give the impression of moving very fast and indeed a lizard scuttling for shelter if danger threatens may be travelling quite quickly. On the whole, however, they are incapable of sustained activity, and when they run they throw their bodies into curves which may give a greater illusion of speed than is justified. This sinuous movement is because reptiles always use alternate limbs and cannot, however fast they wish to go, gallop, as mammals do. In legless reptiles such as snakes and slow-worms the sinuous movement is exaggerated and they appear to loop across the ground.

In the past many kinds of reptiles which were fairly fast moving became bipedal; that is they used their hind legs only, for their forelimbs were too small for weight bearing. A reptile which adopts this pose is the Australian frilled lizard. When frightened this animal rises on to its hind legs, and balancing its body with its tail, which curves up until it almost touches the head, it can run at a considerable speed for some distance. If it is finally cornered its last line of defence is to turn and stand, with its mouth defiantly open, and to spread a large fan of skin around its head. This makes it look bigger and fiercer than it really is and may deter a predator from pressing home an attack.

Methods of attack and defence used by reptiles vary—some snakes and a very few lizards are poisonous, but hardly any are aggressive and some which are venomous have warning colouration to give clear notice of the fact.

The frilled lizard frightens its enemies by expanding a frill round its neck.

Tortoises and Turtles

Although there are more than 200 different kinds of tortoises found throughout the warmer parts of the world, they are among the easiest of animals to recognise, for they all wear the most complete armour plating protection to be found anywhere among the land vertebrates. The naming of these animals is confused, however. In Britain, where there are no native members of the group, the term tortoises is generally used for land-dwellers, terrapins for freshwater-dwellers, and turtles for the marine species. In America, where many species occur, the word turtle is used very much more widely and terrapin has a much more restricted meaning.

The shell which all of these animals carry forms a box, made in two parts, an upper and a lower. Both are made of bony plates, overlaid by horny shields. The edges of the bone and horn plates overlap, so that the whole armour has a great deal of strength.

Growth Rings

Those species which live in the colder areas, such as the European pond tortoise, which is found in southern Europe, hibernate in the winter time and, because of this, they grow irregularly. This is reflected in the pattern of their horny plates, which show growth rings like trees, so that their age may be gauged by counting the rings. This is not an entirely reliable method of telling the age of a tortoise, for illness or injury which cause checks in growth look like age rings. When the animal ages, its growth slows up and it may not be easy to read the rings, which are very narrow, and wear may also make it more difficult. There is no doubt, though, that tortoises can live to a great age; one which was taken from the Seychelles to Mauritius in 1766 did not die until it was accidentally killed in 1918, at an age well over 150 years. Smaller species live for a much shorter time, but for longer than mammals of a comparable size.

The two halves of the shell are joined along the sides, but in many species the legs, head and tail can be pulled in under the protective covering.

Marine turtles come ashore each year to lay their eggs then return to the sea.

Box turtles have a hinge in the shell which folds up so that in time of danger the animal is completely shut in—a mechanism which defeats most predators. Land tortoises, such as the star tortoise, usually have a heavy high-domed shell; water tortoises usually have a lighter, flatter shell and often cannot withdraw their limbs into it. Land tortoises have a club-footed appearance; whereas in terrapins the toes are separate but connected with a web of skin. Marine turtles have limbs which form strong paddles for swimming.

Slow Movement

Although the shell is protective, it brings many drawbacks. Chief of these is the weight, which makes tortoises proverbial slowcoaches. Other difficulties are caused because the shell bones are fused with the ribs and the vertebrae; the body has become a rigid box; the strong muscles of the back are lost and movement is clumsy as well as slow. Tortoises cannot expand their chests when they breathe; instead air has to be forced into their lungs by a pumping action of the throat. Some freshwater species, although they are chiefly air-breathing, can also make use of oxygen dissolved in the water, which is absorbed through special membranes in their mouths and their vents.

Tortoises and turtles are entirely without teeth. Instead the jaws are covered with horny shields which are scissor-sharp and enable the animals to cut up their food. The land-livers are mainly vegetarian, but the terrapins and turtles which live in water are mostly flesh-eaters. Sometimes these search out the worms and shrimps on which they feed, but some of the larger forms, which eat fish and other active animals, are amazingly well camouflaged to resemble weed-covered logs, so they can snap up anything which approaches them unawares.

Most land and freshwater tortoises are small animals; the giants of the group are the marine turtles, the largest being about two and a half metres (eight feet) long and weighing close to 900 kilograms (2000 pounds). These are slow and clumsy on land, but swim effortlessly and elegantly when buoyed up by sea water. They still show their land heritage by the fact that the females must come ashore each year to lay their eggs. Having mated in the water they arrive at night on sandy beaches where they scoop out a nest above the tide line. In this they lay a hundred or more eggs, before filling the nest in and scattering sand about to disguise its position.

The route of the *Beagle* around the Galapagos Islands.

In 1835 the British ship the *Beagle* called at the Galapagos Islands in the Pacific, during a round-the-world survey. On board was a young naturalist called Charles Darwin. On the isolated volcanic Galapagos Islands he observed that there were many species of animal which, although obviously related to other forms on the mainland, were different in some vital respects. He saw that this was especially so with the giant tortoises which were recognisably different on separate islands. This set him thinking that the isolation had a bearing on their differences. This idea was elaborated into the theory of evolution through natural selection. The Galapagos tortoises are now almost extinct.

Return to the Sea

They then return to the sea, which they must reach before the break of day. Having no means of controlling their body-temperature, turtles die if exposed for long to the heat of the sun. Although the nest position itself is hidden, the turtle's tracks down the beach are not. The presence of a tail drag-mark indicates that eggs have been laid and egg hunters may come and find the nest, despite its disguise. Many eggs are taken by human and other predators, and this, combined with the hunting of the adults, has led to a great decline in turtle numbers.

The biggest land tortoises are always found on oceanic islands. Many animals which are swept by chance to these isolated places evolve into strange forms, unknown elsewhere, and this is the case with the tortoises. The tortoises of Aldabra, the Mascarene islands and Galapagos for example, have all grown to gigantic size in the absence of predators or competitors for food.

Marine turtles move in water with a grace that belies their clumsy appearance.

Lizards and Snakes

The Komodo dragon

Lizards and snakes are the most abundant of the reptiles. Within the warm parts of the world they have occupied almost every type of habitat and are found as tree dwellers, burrowers and desert animals, and living in swamps and rivers. Generally the distinction between them is clear, for most lizards have sprawling legs while snakes are totally limbless. However, there are many legless lizards, such as the slow-worm, and the external differences between these animals and some snakes may lie in details of their scale pattern.

The Ways of Lizards

Snakes and some lizards have forked tongues. Using them, the animals track their prey, tasting the trail as their tongues flicker out over the ground. The deep fork enables a wider area to be sampled than would be possible with a simpler shape. A lizard with a very extraordinary tongue is the chameleon. Living in trees, it feeds mainly on large insects, which it stalks cautiously to within several inches and then shoots out its long tongue to gather its prey on the end. The tongue is formed of elastic tissues, under compression when the mouth is closed.

The largest of all lizards is the Komodo dragon. This is related to the monitor lizards of the Old World, but living in isolation on its islands the Komodo has grown to a length of about three metres (ten feet). It is a powerful, slow moving, largely scavenging animal, far removed from the aerial monster of fables. The nearest that any lizard comes to flight is the gliding lizard, *Draco*, which has a web of skin along its sides. This is supported by extensions of the animal's ribs, which are hinged so that the membrane may be folded along the sides or held out stiffly as it leaps from one tree to another in a long, shallow glide.

Most lizards are small and often escape notice by their camouflage patterns or by their habit of hiding in crevices or under stones. Some are highly valued as destroyers of insects and the geckos, which are among the few noisy lizards, are welcome house animals in spite of this. These animals have feet on which a series of fine ridges of skin, like enlarged fingerprints, make each toe into a suction device so that they can run up walls and across ceilings in search of their prey.

The tails of lizards may serve many purposes. In some, such as the

The Tuatara
Reptiles, apart from snakes and lizards, may be regarded as living fossils, left over from a time when the earth was peopled with their kind. One reptile in particular is a relic from the past—the tuatara, a superficially lizard-like creature which is found only on islands off the coasts of New Zealand. Its skull bones show it to be related to a once widespread group, now extinct except for this one representative. It is a nocturnal, secretive animal, living in burrows. Recent researches have revealed that it is long-lived. The feature of a third eye on the top of its head, which may be light sensitive in young animals, is probably to do with a form of heat regulation, for they are more active at lower temperatures than most other reptiles.

monitors, they are long and whip-like and may be used in defence. In other species which live in desert areas the tail is short and stumpy and carries reserves of food, which enables the animal to survive long periods of drought without eating or drinking. In the chameleons the tail is prehensile and acts as an extra hand for a

Skeleton of a lizard

The chameleon captures food with its long tongue.

144

Snakes wind their way across the ground in a series of graceful curves but never in up and down loops. On a smooth surface a snake is helpless and cannot make any progress. Over areas of loose sand some desert snakes 'sidewind', moving two loops of their bodies simultaneously but keeping the rest clear.

can stretch so that they may gulp down creatures which may be bigger than themselves. The meal may take a long time and digestion even longer, for a small snack may last a snake for weeks or even months. Some snakes pursue their prey and catch and swallow it with no special adaptations. Others, such as the pythons and constrictors, throw a coil of their immensely strong bodies round the prey animal and suffocate it before they swallow it.

Poison Glands

A minority of snakes carry poison glands in their mouths. Although the poison is in many cases very powerful, few snakes are aggressive and most restrict its use to their prey alone, although if badly frightened they may use it in defence. Some snakes have very specialised food, some of the strangest being the egg-eating snakes. These slender inhabitants of the African bush swallow the eggs of ground-nesting birds and cut through the eggshell with a saw formed of the projecting tips of parts of the vertebrae in the throat. The shell is then ejected and the soft part of the egg swallowed. Between them, snakes feed on a wide variety of foods. Some feed on worms, some on other snakes, some on snails. Many are destroyers of rodent pests and as such should be valued.

The senses of snakes are limited and apart from their excellent senses of smell and taste they seem to be poorly endowed. Their eyesight is moderate, and they are totally deaf to air-borne sounds. Unlike lizards,

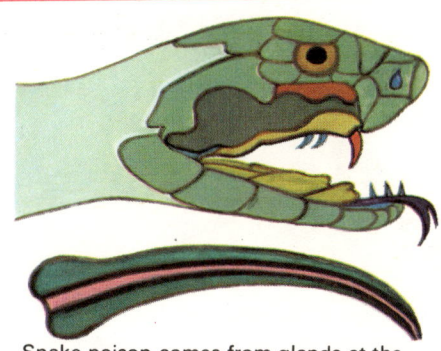

Snake poison comes from glands at the back of the upper jaw. It is then channelled down into the mouth. In some species, which are not normally considered very dangerous to man, the poison dribbles down teeth at the back of the palate. These back-fanged snakes have to take their prey right into their mouths before their poison can be effective. In snakes which have a more effective system, the venom is carried to the front of the mouth where it runs down enlarged fangs which ensure that the prey receives a dose of poison as it is bitten. In adders and rattlesnakes the poison fangs are hollow, like a hypodermic needle, so that the venom is injected with the bite. In these snakes the hollow teeth are so large that they have to be folded back when the jaw is closed.

which can hear well, snakes have no ears although they can detect vibrations coming from the ground through their jaw bones, so they can make their escape if a large and heavy animal approaches.

As they grow, snakes and lizards shed their skins. In lizards this is done piecemeal; in snakes the skin is peeled off complete, and the snake, which for a few days has been looking dull and behaving rather listlessly, becomes more active in its new, brightly coloured scales. The cast skin may sometimes be found, complete even to the eye covering, looking like the scaly ghost of its one-time owner.

more secure grip on the branches over which the lizard climbs. In the majority of lizards, however, the tail is extremely fragile. Across one of the vertebrae is a plane of weakness and if any stress is put on this, the tail breaks at that point. Any predator which grabs the tail is likely to find that it has just that, while the lizard escapes to grow another tail from the broken end.

Snakes probably evolved their legless shape as burrowing animals. Now only pythons have any trace of limbs at all, and these are in no way functional. Yet snakes survive in a wide range of environments and can often climb or swim well. All snakes are flesh-eaters, but since their teeth are simply sharp hooks in the mouth, they cannot bite pieces of their food or chew it, so they are forced to swallow their prey whole. Their jaws

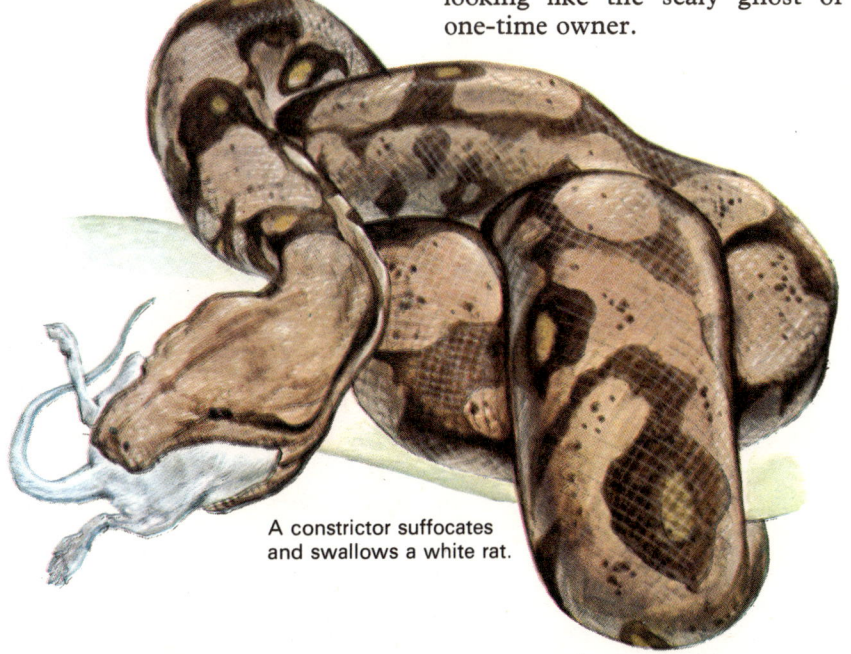

A constrictor suffocates and swallows a white rat.

Crocodiles

The largest of present day reptiles are to be found among the crocodiles. This seems fitting, for the twenty-five species are the sole survivors of a much larger group which in the distant past contained the dinosaurs. These were the largest reptiles ever to have lived and although no crocodile of today achieves their size, or ever has, there are records of animals up to seven metres (23 feet) long. Crocodiles are relentlessly hunted wherever they live and few really old animals which may approach maximum size now survive.

Water Animals

Crocodiles and their close relatives are rarely found far from water. The estuarine crocodile, which lives on the coasts of south-east Asia and north Australia, is often seen well out to sea, although it is not as totally marine as were some fossil forms. Today crocodiles are normally seen sprawled on sandbanks in a river or estuary, or on the edge of a lake. Their normal movement is the typical ungainly gait of the land reptile, with the body swinging into curves as they progress. If pressed, however, a crocodile can pick itself up on to its toes and run, holding the body well clear of the ground. It can travel in a straight line in this way and moves quite surprisingly fast, but the animal cannot maintain this position or speed for long and tires quickly. Once in the water, the crocodile is transformed into a creature of speed and power. Becoming streamlined by folding its limbs back against the body, it uses its heavy flattened tail as an oar to scull along, scarcely rippling the water as it goes.

The favourite haunts of the Nile crocodile are sandbanks alongside rivers where the currents are sluggish. They are ferocious animals and some live to a great age.

The crocodile's adaptation for its way of life may be seen in many features, but particularly in the head, in which the eyes and nostrils stand above the level of the rest of the face. This enables the animal to float, just submerged, but to be able to see and to continue breathing, while it stalks its prey unnoticed by potential meals or potential enemies. In most reptiles the nostrils open directly into the front of the mouth. In a crocodile the air is channelled, as it is in mammals, to a position in the back of the throat, leaving the mouth to be used for food alone. This enables it to catch and subdue prey under water, but to continue breathing, although the nostrils may be tightly closed if necessary.

Some large, old crocodiles may be a menace to man or his domestic stock, but their food for the greater part of their lives consists of insects, fish and rodents. In places where crocodiles have been exterminated, their prey animals have often increased to pest proportions. Crocodiles' teeth are sharp pegs unsuited to slicing or chewing food, which must, therefore, be swallowed whole. A big, old crocodile may tear limbs off a large victim by a twisting movement of its head. They certainly feed on the carrion bodies of drowned animals and having caught and killed

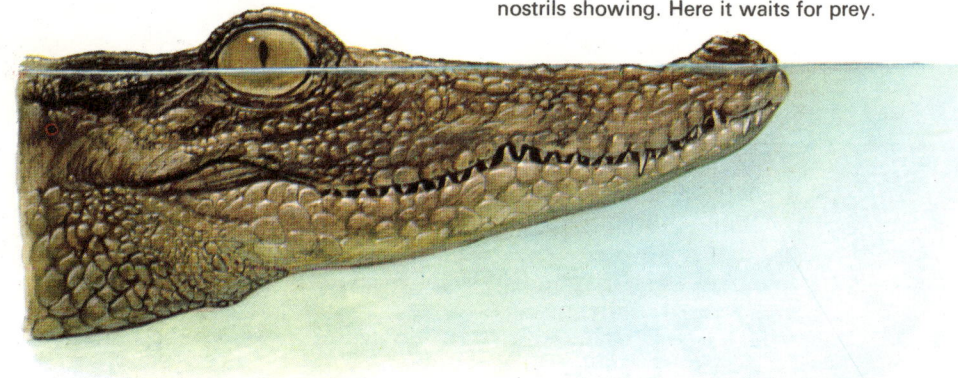

The crocodile is able to float near the surface of water with only its eyes and nostrils showing. Here it waits for prey.

a bullock or some such creature, may sometimes hide it in a place where it will rot to some extent so that it may more easily be torn apart.

Breeding Habits
The breeding season is the only time when crocodiles become at all noisy. The brawling males may be heard over long distances and both males and females develop musky scent glands, the secretion from which probably repels rivals and attracts mates. All crocodiles reproduce by eggs. These may be deposited in a hollow scooped in the sand of a river bank or laid in a nest of rotting vegetation, which releases heat to help them hatch. In some cases they are protected by their mother who remains in the area of the nest, driving away egg-stealing intruders such as rodents and small carnivores. She may even, as in the Mississippi alligator, hear cries of the hatching young and help them by opening up the nest pile and then escorting them to the water.

From then on the young creatures are on their own and the greatest enemies many of them have to fear are the larger members of their own kind. Snapping and active from the start, they grow rapidly in their early years in spite of the lack of parental care. Even when they have achieved adult size they continue to grow, although increasingly slowly. A big crocodile may be many years old although it is unlikely that in the wild it will reach the very great age claimed for captive specimens.

The differences between crocodiles and alligators are slight and the terms are often used wrongly. The easiest way to tell them apart is to look at the teeth. The fourth tooth from the mid-line in the lower jaw is much larger than the rest. In crocodiles this is easily visible when the mouth is shut, for there is a notch in the upper jaw to house it. In alligators the tooth fits into a pit in the upper jaw and so is invisible when the mouth is closed.

In some parts of the world crocodiles are protected and even farmed, mainly for the high quality leather produced from their skins, but generally they are feared and hated. Wherever possible they are destroyed and it seems likely that in many areas the crocodiles will follow the dinosaurs into extinction. In spite of this they are sometimes kept as aquarium animals, occasionally growing to an embarrassing size under such protected conditions.

Gavials and false gavials, although not closely related, appear similar because of their long slender snouts. These are fish traps, provided with a battery of narrow, interlocking teeth. These animals sweep their heads from side to side through schools of fish, which are their only food. The Mississippi alligator's nearest relative is the Chinese alligator. It is very unusual for two closely related animals to be found on opposite sides of the world with no connecting links, and no satisfactory explanation has been offered. Caimans are distantly related to crocodiles.

Birds

Birds, the last of the vertebrate classes to evolve, have certainly made up for lost time, for there are now nearly 9,000 bird species, compared to about only 3,200 kinds of mammals. Like the mammals, birds are active, warm-blooded animals, but their great specialisation is flight, which has enabled them to colonise many places unavailable to earthbound creatures.

Many of the modifications which have been made to achieve flight can be seen in the skeleton, which has the same basic elements as that of other land vertebrates. It is extremely lightly built, for like any other flying machine a bird cannot afford to carry unnecessary weight, so the limb bones are hollow, although they may be braced with internal struts for strength. The main part of the body is supported by a bony box, very strongly constructed, which carries the muscles for flight attached to the deep ridged breastbone. This box must also be strong to absorb the jar as a bird lands and to carry the hind limbs, which in most species are relatively small. They are however given extra length by the fact that birds stand on their toes—what we think of as a bird's knee is really its ankle.

The Organs of Flight

The forelimbs are normally much bigger, for these are the organs of flight. The bones can be compared to those of a human arm. The top bone of the forelimb is usually short and stout, and the outer and inner bones are well developed. The bones of the hand and fingers are to a large extent fused to make a strong base for the flight feathers, or primaries, which are attached to them. There is a separate 'thumb' bone to which a small bunch of feathers called the alula is fixed. This is raised and helps to control air flow over the wings at slow speeds and prevent stalling on take-off.

The skull is fairly big and contains a brain which, while not giving the bird much intellectual power, does allow large centres for sight, hearing, balance and co-ordination. The eyes of birds are large and they have very sharp vision, with a well developed sense of colour in most cases. Birds' ears are on the sides of their heads although not visible externally, and they hear very well. At the front of the skull is the beak, which is

Feathers perform several different functions. Chiefly, they are adapted to enable birds to fly and they form an insulating and streamlining cover to the body. Each feather consists of a single shaft, or quill, which grows from the skin; arising from the sides of this is a vane, or web, made of side struts called barbs. These are linked by minute hooks called barbules. Each feather is like a multiple zip fastener, for when the barbules become unlocked they can be fixed together again by the preening bird's beak. The body feathers, which may have a subsidiary feather or aftershaft growing from the base, lie in definite feather tracts, though the space between may be filled with down. The tail and wing feathers are arranged so that the bones of the hand carry the main flight feathers, or primaries, and the bones of the forearm bear secondaries, or lift, feathers.

sheathed in horny material and contains no teeth. The shape of the beak varies according to the food eaten. It may be like a fine forceps for picking up small insects, or a notched knife for tearing flesh or a heavy nutcracker for dealing with large seeds. Birds see or hear their food or prey, for, with one exception, they have no sense of smell and their sense of taste is very limited.

At the other end of the skeleton the tail bones are fused to form a ploughshare bone. However long a bird's tail may be the feathers all fan out from this.

Flying Machines

Birds obey many of the physical rules applying to flying machines in general. Flight is hard work, so they need large amounts of food to fuel themselves. Digestion is quick and very complete; it is not possible by looking at a bird's droppings to tell what food has been eaten, as may be done with many mammals. Flying machines and birds need a great deal of oxygen and birds' lungs work on a system which gives them a constant stream of air rather than being inflated and deflated as is the case with mammals. Insulated by their feathers, they need to prevent themselves from overheating. They do this by means of air sacs which receive the air as it is first breathed in and pass it on to the lungs after it has been used in the cooling system. The heartbeat of birds is rapid and their temperature high compared to that of most mammals. Their high turnover of energy makes them physically the most efficient of the vertebrates.

Flightless Birds

Among the many roles which birds play, few conflict directly with mammals. Some birds, however, have developed as grazing animals. These are to be found mainly in tropical grassland areas throughout the world alongside mammalian competitors. These birds are large and heavyweight creatures, incapable of flight, but able to run very fast. Their wings are tiny—those of an ostrich, which may be two and a half metres (eight feet) tall and weigh 136 kilograms (300 pounds), are smaller in area than those of a goose. They have no need for flight muscles and there is no deeply ridged breastbone as in most birds. Instead, they have a flat plate of bone and for this reason are called the raft-breasted birds or ratites. Although so different in many ways from flying birds, details of their structure prove that they have descended from ancestors which were capable of flight.

The largest of the ratites are now extinct. Some species of moa from New Zealand reached a height of four metres (thirteen feet), and finds of giant bird bones on the island of Madagascar gave rise to legends in Arab mythology of the roc, or elephant bird.

The Ratites

Most present day ratites are sombre coloured birds, the exception being the male ostrich which has white wing and tail plumes contrasting with his black body feathers. Most have some degree of social behaviour during the breeding season, when several females may lay their eggs in the same nest, and where the males take a large part in incubation. The large eggs of ratites are sought by many predators, some of which have developed ingenious methods for breaking the thick shell. The chicks are active as soon as they leave the egg and many of them fall to flesh-eaters of various kinds.

The ostrich is the most familiar of the ratites, for it is often seen in zoos. Hunted for its plumes, it has decreased greatly in numbers, although it is farmed in some areas of South Africa. In the wild it is often found with herds of antelope and zebra, where it acts as a watchman, for it has far sharper eyesight than the mammals. In South America there are several species of rhea—wary, fast-running birds, which use their rudimentary wings for balance when turning at speed. These also have become much rarer than they were, through hunting and because their home range has been taken for cattle and sheep.

Australasian Birds

The national bird of Australia is the emu, yet another grazing ratite and again one that has been drastically reduced because it competes with introduced domestic mammals. In some areas the emu is now protected, but elsewhere there is still a bounty on its head and it is ruthlessly destroyed. In the tropical forests of North Australia and New Guinea the cassowary can be found. This large bird is among the best armed of the flightless species, for its inner toenail is a huge spike of horn with which it can protect itself.

In New Zealand lives the smallest and strangest of the ratites. This is the kiwi, which is a nocturnal, secretive creature with a long down-curved bill with which it probes out the worms and other invertebrates on which it feeds. It is unique in that it smells out its prey and is the only bird to have this ability.

The ratites are by no means the only birds which cannot fly. A number of species have lost the power to do so, although in general they have kept the features which are characteristic of flying birds. All have feathers, and all have the remnants of wings. Flightless birds are often found on islands, which are windy places, so that birds with a

The rhea is sometimes called the American ostrich. The plumage colour of the male and female birds is somewhat similar. In their native land they merge readily with the general colouring of the South American pampas so as to be almost invisible, even when they are in the middle distance.

strong tendency to fly are often swept away, but those with a tendency to flightlessness survive. Examples of the end product of this trend are the now extinct dodo and solitaire birds and such isolated rarities as the Gough Island rail, a secretive non-flying bird of a southern Atlantic island.

Intermediate stages between flight and flightlessness may be seen in two of the inhabitants of different types of environment. The bustards of the plains, for example, typify heavy-weight birds which run rather than fly whenever possible, although they still have functional wings. Birds living near water may also tend towards flightlessness and many of them have small wings which are used as much for swimming as for flying.

Penguins

Penguins are the best known flightless water birds. Their wings have become stiff, flattened paddles, which can no longer be folded in the normal way when the bird is at rest. Instead they hang like arms beside the body, which with the upright stance of penguins increases their likeness to small human figures. Penguins are found throughout the oceans of the southern hemisphere; the most northerly species nests on the Galapagos Islands, which sit astride the equator, but the better known species come from the Antarctic.

The harshness of their environment has caused the two largest species, the emperor and the king penguins, to have modified their breeding behaviour in most drastic ways. There is no material for nest building, so the egg is held on the feet of the male and covered with a protective flap of skin. It takes a long time for the eggs to hatch and both these birds have developed different ways of meeting the demands which this makes on them at nesting time. King penguins return to their breeding rookeries at a later time each year, for the period taken in caring for the chick, followed by the time for moulting and building up their resources again, is more than one year. Finally a year comes when they cannot complete the cycle of rearing a chick and the parents set off for the sea early, but are among the first of the breeding birds to return in the next season. With this staggered breeding pattern they may manage on average to rear two young in every three years.

Emperor Penguins

Emperor penguins prolong their breeding season by starting to nest at the beginning of the coldest of the dark winter months. So harsh is the weather that the birds have given up territorial behaviour and huddle together for communal warmth. The female returns to take her share of chick care just as the egg hatches and the male goes off to the sea to break his two months' fast. As the chick grows and becomes more demanding, the shelf ice melts and the parents have only a short journey to make to collect food for it.

Adélie penguins nest near the sea in places where the wind sweeps the snow away early. In such barren areas there is no nest material for them, so they raise their eggs above the level of any water on a little pile of stones. In this apparently comfortless condition their fluffy chicks are raised through the Antarctic summer months.

Emperor penguin

The origin of the name penguin is not known for certain. Possibly it comes from the term 'pin-wing', short for pinioned, meaning 'cut-wing', a name given by sailors to a black and white flightless bird of the north Atlantic, the great auk. This bird was similar to the penguins in its appearance and way of life. When whalers and sealers first went to southern polar waters they thought the birds there were the same as the ones in the north. Like penguins, the great auks congregated in vast breeding rookeries and hundreds of thousands of them were killed in the eighteenth century. The species eventually became extinct in 1844.

Rock-hopper

Adélie penguin

From left to right, a red-throated grebe, a black-throated diver and a crested grebe.

Water Birds

Among freshwater birds there are no exact parallels to the extreme adaptations of the penguins. Grebes and divers are the most highly specialised for a life in fresh water. Both have their legs placed very far back on the body. This makes swimming more efficient, but they cannot stand upright like penguins and are helpless on land. The only time that divers come ashore is during the breeding period and their nests are within inches of the water; grebes make floating nests and never normally leave the water. Divers have webbed feet; grebes have each toe separately lobed with a stiff fin. Both dive and swim expertly under water and both can, in times of danger, expel the air from their feathers and sink from sight slowly and with no disturbance.

The great crested grebe is a handsome bird which was much in demand by the plumage trade in the early years of this century. Its numbers have been increased by protection and it is now a fairly common inhabitant of many stretches of inland water. In winter time the red-necked grebe might be mistaken for it, but this bird rarely moves from eastern Europe. The black-throated diver, like all the members of its group, is a northern bird. In winter when it loses its breeding plumage and migrates south it can be distinguished from its near relatives by the slender straight shape of its bill.

Tubenoses

An important group of seabirds is the tubenoses, so called because the bill is covered with horny plates and the nostrils lie in a tunnel which they form. Included among them are the petrels, shearwaters, fulmars and albatrosses. All have long narrow wings adapted to make use of the quirky air currents over the disturbed waters of the sea. Petrels are mostly small, dark-coloured birds, which look as though they are pattering over the surface of the waves.

Shearwaters and fulmars bank and glide. Albatrosses have a superb control of the air, scarcely moving their wings yet staying aloft and making progress under all sorts of conditions. None of these birds ever comes to land except during the breeding season. The shearwaters, which have their legs set very far back on their bodies and cannot stand upright, nest in burrows to which they return at night and where they are protected from enemies such as gulls.

The gannets, pelicans and cormorants belong to an order of birds linked by a number of structural and behavioural features. The most important of these is the fully webbed foot, in which the hind toe is turned forward and connected by a web of skin to the inmost of the forward pointing toes. They are used by the birds in swimming.

The longest winged of all birds are the albatrosses. The thirteen species of these giant tube-nosed birds are found in the southern oceans, apart from three Pacific species which cross the equator during migration after their breeding season. Mostly, they ride the winds effortlessly in the zone of the roaring forties, feeding on the abundant fish and plankton of that area and migrating huge distances yearly. Their breeding places are remote islands which are the only dry land that they ever encounter. They are slow-maturing and long-lived. According to some estimates, albatrosses reach ages of as much as seventy years.

The pelican dives towards water to catch its food.

Mute swans

Swans, Geese and Ducks

Swans, geese and ducks form one of the most successful and widespread groups of water birds and are found throughout the world in all sorts of freshwater habitats from small pools and ditches to large lakes or torrential streams. Many species have taken to a marine life and although they never occur as truly oceanic birds, they are found around coasts and in estuaries of all sorts. Features which they all share include their short legs and large webbed feet, long necks, and heads adorned with a big flattened bill. Easily recognised as members of their order, many species are familiar domestic or ornamental birds.

For part at least of their lives most of these birds are social species, forming in wintertime huge flocks, in which family groups may remain united. Swans will protect their territory fiercely when breeding; but geese and ducks often nest together. The young are ready to take to the water as soon as they hatch. At this time the adults moult, but unlike other birds in which the flight feathers are shed singly, they lose all the primaries at once, so they are unable to fly. This period of eclipse, when any distinctive breeding plumage is also lost, is one at which the birds normally keep to the water away from enemies as much as possible.

Swans are the largest and most clearly defined members of the group. All are large, with very long necks, which they dip into water when taking their mainly plant food. They are found throughout the world and most species are pure white in colour, although there is a black-necked swan from South America and a completely black swan from Australia. They are among the heaviest of flying birds and have difficulty in taking off, running across the water for a considerable distance before becoming airborne. Their strong, slow wing beats produce a loud whistling noise, quite unlike the flight sound of any other birds.

Types of Geese

Geese are more varied in size and appearance. The five species of grey geese, from one of which the main domestic species is descended, are to be found mostly in the Old World, while the white geese are chiefly New World in distribution. Black geese are found in both hemispheres and one species, the Canada goose is now becoming a common sight in Europe, where it has been imported as an

The dabbling ducks include the teal, which is the smallest among them, the mallard, the pintail, which is probably the most numerous duck in the world, and the shoveler, with its curiously shaped bill. The diving ducks include the tufted duck and the pochard. Eiders are sea ducks, feeding on sea urchins and crustaceans, while scoters, harlequins, goldeneyes and goosanders belong to a rather variable group which are all good divers. The ruddy duck and the white-headed duck are expert swimmers on inland waters. There are also shelducks and perching ducks.

ornamental bird, but continues to thrive when it escapes from domestication. When geese migrate from their sub-arctic breeding grounds, their wings make less noise in flight than those of swans. Many, especially those that migrate at night, call to each other in flight and can be heard over quite long distances. Like swans, geese are plant feeders, grazing on waterside pastures or stubble fields.

Duck Species

Ducks are the most numerous and varied of the group. Some, such as the shelduck are goose-like in size and appearance; others, such as the teals, are tiny with shorter necks than any geese. They tend to be more brightly coloured than swans or geese, and have a bright bar, the speculum, in the wing. Dabbling ducks, which are probably the best known species, are widespread surface swimmers, up-ending for their plant food. These birds are capable of springing directly from the water into flight.

Diving ducks, a group which again include many common species, are capable of swimming under water in their search for food, but they cannot take off without pattering across the water for some distance. Eiders are marine ducks, best known for the habit of the female of preening out her down feathers to line her nest. Other diving ducks also feed on sea urchins and molluscs, but the mergansers and their relatives have become specialised fish-eaters, with narrow, saw-edged bills for holding their slippery prey. The stiff-tailed ducks are also very good swimmers, but are found mainly in freshwater areas. These birds probably use their long, stiff tail feathers as underwater rudders.

One of the most important gods of ancient Egypt was Thoth, the god of intelligence and wisdom, and scribe to other gods. He is always represented as having the head of an ibis, and it may well be that the questing, alert look of the sacred ibis searching for food was the inspiration for this image.

Flamingos

Strangest of all, however, are the perching ducks, a group which includes many rather large birds, often referred to as geese. These birds, in spite of their webbed feet, are forest species and often perch and nest in trees. A number of species of ducks from several of the sub-groups have been domesticated, but the untamed kinds form a considerable wildfowl resource and many efforts have been made to conserve them.

Herons and Flamingos

The heron-like birds are another worldwide group of waterfowl, usually large in size, with long legs, long necks and long bills. Their food varies from one species to another. Herons and bitterns catch fishes and other small vertebrates in their long beaks. Larger invertebrates are the major food of the ibises and small water organisms are eaten by the spoonbills. A heron often stands motionless in shallow water until, perhaps, its long legs are mistaken for the stems of water plants by an unwary fish. The stillness of the heron is deceptive, for in a flash the fish is caught in its long beak, and quickly swallowed.

Some tropical species of heron stalk quietly through the water with their wings spread to cast a shadow, so that the bird can see more easily into the water. The heron's equipment for fish feeding includes powder down—a special structure of some of the feathers, which breaks down to make a substance like French chalk—and a comb-like structure on one of the toes. These two adaptations enable the bird to clean its plumage of the slime which might otherwise damage it.

Storks are large relatives of the herons. They are usually less aquatic in their way of life and in Europe the white stork, which often builds its bulky nests on chimney tops, is regarded as a symbol of good luck.

Flamingos are among the strangest looking of birds, yet their extremely long legs and necks and curiously heavy-billed heads all have a purpose in their way of life. They feed on the microscopic life suspended in the usually brackish or salty water near which they live. They wade into the

153

Cranes in flight

African crowned crane

shallows and twist their necks so that the deeply ridged upper part of the bill is upside down in the water. Water currents are forced through the partly open beak by the tongue, which acts as a piston, and the minute animal life is strained out by close-set horny flaps attached to the roof of the mouth. This mechanism must be very efficient, for the salt or alkaline water of the feeding places of the birds would be poisonous if taken in large quantities. The bright pink colour of the flamingos depends to some extent on the type of food which they eat. In captivity they may become paler unless special additives are included in their diet.

Cranes

Bearing a superficial likeness to the herons and storks, although not in fact closely related to them are the cranes. These large birds, with their long necks and heads, generally live in marshy areas, feeding on a wide variety of insects and small invertebrates. In flight they may be distinguished from similar birds by their outstretched necks, which are not carried tucked into the shoulders as in herons and storks. Some kinds of cranes migrate long distances between their breeding and wintering grounds. The whooping crane, one of the world's rarest birds, breeds in Alaska and migrates to the southern United States. Although many species of crane are recorded as flying at great height while on migration, they are easy prey for hunters and several species have been brought to the edge of extinction.

Cranes have spectacular courtship displays in which a number of birds dance and bow, flying up a few feet into the air, as if jerked on invisible strings. Cranes normally mate for life, usually rearing two young each year in nests which may be little more than a scrape in the open ground. Although not brightly coloured, apart from bright red skin round the face in some species, cranes have figured largely in oriental art. The crowned crane, with its attractive tuft of feathers on top of its head, is the national bird of Uganda, where it is valued, among other things, for the numbers of harmful insects and small vertebrates which it destroys.

Related to the cranes, and far less spectacular in size and behaviour although more numerous in species, are the rails and the crakes. These smallish, secretive birds, usually camouflaged in delicate shades of brown, hide in hedgerows or reed beds and may be very difficult to see. Some of the more obvious members of the group have taken to an aquatic life. In temperate latitudes flocks of moorhens and coots may be a common sight. The coots have lobed feet like the grebes; moorhens have only long, thin unwebbed toes. As they swim, their heads bob forward with each stroke, making it look as if life in water is a great effort for them.

The Waders

A large number of water birds, usually lumped together as waders, may be divided into the sandpipers and the plovers. The sandpipers are in general northern species. They are essentially birds of seashore and estuary where they make a living from the small worms and crustaceans

Herring gull

Great black-backed gull

below the surface of the mud. Their large feet support them over the softest of surfaces, their long legs enable them to wade into shallow water and their long necks and bills enable them to probe for their food.

The plovers, which in general have a more southerly distribution, and in many cases are found in more inland sites than the sandpipers, have usually a more compact form, and shorter beaks. Most waders migrate great distances between their breeding places, which are chiefly in areas of high moor and tundra, to the unfrozen estuaries and mudflats where they spend the winter. Great flocks migrate down the coastal flyways, feeding, resting and preening in suitably remote and undisturbed spots. One of the most amazing sights for the winter birdwatcher is to see a flock of perhaps 10,000 small waders take off and wheel through the air with military precision, every bird keeping station in relation to its nearest neighbours and the whole flock moving as one.

Waders nest on the ground, usually laying four pointed eggs which fit snugly with the narrow end inwards into the slight hollow where they are laid. The eggs are normally very well camouflaged and difficult to see, as is the incubating bird, for most waders' plumage is in shades of brown and grey which blend perfectly with their moorland home. A few species are black and white but these are mostly beach-nesters, so the abrupt patches of colour break up their outline and disguise them among the pebbles. The young are quickly independent of their parents and although in the first hours they look as if their outsize legs lead a life of their own unconnected to the rest of the body, they are soon running and feeding.

Gulls, Terns and Skuas

Gulls to many people are the most obvious birds of the sea. Strangely, though, they are creatures of the beach and inshore waters, and most of them never venture over the open oceans. Indeed, some gulls breed on inland marshes or lakes and never see the sea. A few kinds are becoming town birds: the black-headed gull, for instance, vies with the pigeons for food in many European cities, although it is far from being as confiding as the true land birds. The only oceanic gull in Europe is the kittiwake, a migratory bird which comes to the coasts of the north Atlantic to nest on sheer cliffs beyond the reach of predators.

Also highly oceanic are the terns. These long-winged, fork-tailed birds are sometimes called sea swallows, but their delicate appearance is misleading, for they can weather storms at sea and the longest-distance migrant of all birds is found among them. Nesting in noisy colonies on the edge of the beach, terns are among the most vulnerable of sea birds to disturbance.

The skuas are another group related to the gulls. These are among the pirates of the seas, for they rarely hunt for themselves but prefer to rob other birds of their catch. These large, brown, long-tailed birds seem to know when another bird is carrying fish in its crop—perhaps from its way of flight. They harry the hunter until in desperation, and perhaps to lighten itself for escape from the aggressor, the unfortunate bird drops its prey. Before the fish has hit the water it is scooped out of the air by the skua, which in spite of its size is very agile in flight. The appearance of a skua often seems to terrify other sea birds, especially terns.

Auks, which are short-winged, dark-coloured sea birds, are also related to the gulls. They spend almost the whole of their life at sea swimming and diving for their food. They are a further demonstration of the adaptability of this great group to a variety of marine environments.

The king vulture, which comes from Mexico, has a naked head with brilliantly coloured beak and neck and a warted appearance. It is one of the New World vultures, or condors, which differ in many respects from Old World vultures.

Parakeets are members of the parrot family and live in America. They have colourful plumage and a beak typical of the group. Below is another tropical bird, the anhinga, also from America, and a member of the gull family, a black skimmer.

155

Birds of Prey

Many kinds of birds feed on flesh, but two groups—the birds of prey and the owls—have become highly specialised in a hunting way of life, and feed mainly on the higher vertebrates. Both are usually brown-coloured birds, found on all the continents except Antarctica. Both kill their prey with their strong, sharp talons and pluck and tear the flesh with their narrow, hooked beaks. These birds normally swallow huge chunks of food and regurgitate pellets of indigestible matter.

However, there are many differences as well, for the two groups are not closely related. The similarities reflect a similar way of life. They can exist in the same area together since they are active at different times, the birds of prey during daylight hours and the owls at night. Owls' plumage, even the primary feathers, is soft, to reduce the noise of their wing-beats. Although their eyesight is excellent and adapted to make the best use of poor light, they also have a highly developed sense of hearing. Under experimental conditions it was discovered that a barn owl could catch its prey in total darkness, using its ears to judge the distance perfectly.

Types of Nest

Owls usually nest in holes, laying white eggs, which may be numerous when food is plentiful. Birds of prey normally make a nest of sticks, grass and mosses and lay a small clutch of brown blotched eggs. Both types of bird begin incubation with the laying of the first egg so that the young birds hatch on different days. The first chicks are bigger and stronger than the later members of the brood.

Owls, as a group, tend to be alike, but the birds of prey vary greatly in many respects. The smallest is the Philippine falconet, which is only about 6 centimetres (6 inches) long and eats insects; the largest is the Andean condor, with a wing-span of nearly three metres (ten feet), which feeds mainly on carrion. Some birds of prey are fast fliers; others soar or hover when looking for their food.

Standing apart from the group as a whole is the secretary bird of Africa. It gets its name from the long, drooping head-feathers which look like quill pens stuck behind the ears of a Dickensian clerk or secretary. It is a strong-legged bird which walks with long, stately strides. It feeds on large insects, reptiles, rodents and ground nesting birds. To kill its prey it kicks with its powerful feet. Because of its value as a destroyer of pests, it is protected over much of its range.

Vultures

Vultures are found in the warmer parts of both the Old and New Worlds. In spite of many similarities in appearance, the various species are very distantly related and have developed separately for a very long time. Vultures are all large birds, with huge, oblong wings, finger-like at the tips to control air flow during soaring flight. In spite of their size, vultures have relatively weak beaks and their talons are straight and unsuited for killing or rending. But their food is entirely carrion, often taken, as in the case of the Egyptian vulture, in a very rotten state. They use thermal air currents to soar to great heights, where they survey the ground for possible food. Any bird flying down at the sight of food will be seen by birds patrolling adjacent beats and they will follow. The result is that any dead animal is quickly surrounded by vultures which may have come to the feast from several miles away. They perform a valuable service, along with other scavengers, in removing carcasses which would otherwise rot and become a health hazard.

The rest of the birds of prey are active hunters, but their methods vary considerably. The eagles, which are powerful soaring birds, live mainly in open country and mountains,

Egyptian vulture

Falconry, the art of catching game with birds of prey, was first practised in the Far East before 1000 B.C. Introduced into Europe in the ninth century it was, until the invention of guns for shooting birds, the chief sport of the aristocracy. Almost all sorts of birds of prey have been used, from eagles to male sparrowhawks. The birds to be used for falconry must be taken from the nest shortly before they are able to fly. Taming the falcon is a job requiring skill and dedication and since the bird needs to be flown fairly frequently, should only be attempted by someone with plenty of time to give to it. The trained bird wears a hood which covers its eyes and prevents it from becoming frightened by strange sights and sounds, but can be removed very quickly if it is to be flown. At all times the hawk carries small bells on its legs. These enable the falconer to hear where the bird is if it hides in dense trees while being flown, and to keep an ear on its welfare while the bird is confined in its cage, which is called a mew.

Birds of prey attack in two ways. The kestrel, on the left, hovers over its prey before descending feet first. The falcon, on the right, "stoops" or dives head first at its prey. Both catch the prey in their talons.

mainly rabbits, mountain hares, grouse and very occasionally a sickly lamb. The buzzards, which are also soaring birds and are related to the true hawks, are a good deal smaller than eagles. They have much weaker beaks and feet and only tackle smaller prey. The fish eagles are large birds of prey which haunt lakes and rivers and the edge of the sea for their prey. The osprey is also a fish-eater, diving into the water to capture its prey with its talons. Kites, generally recognisable by their forked tails are often scavengers. Indeed in some parts of the world they are the most obvious birds of prey.

The true hawks are broad-winged, long-tailed birds, adapted to life in woodlands where they stalk and pounce on their prey, which consists mainly of small birds, although mammals and reptiles are also taken. The most spectacular of the birds of prey are the falcons. These vary from tiny species no bigger than a thrush to the gyrfalcon, which is 55 centimetres (22 inches) long. All falcons have long, pointed wings, and are capable of tremendous speed when stooping on their prey. They hunt mainly other birds, which they strike

Golden eagle swooping on its prey

down in flight, normally breaking the back with a blow of their half-closed talons, catching their victim before it flutters to the ground.

Because of their gracefully controlled flight and their apparent courage, the birds of prey have always appealed to man. But man has always feared for his flocks and his stock in their presence and so has tended to destroy the birds whenever possible. This destruction reached its zenith in Britain at the end of the last century, when one species of bird of prey, the osprey, was completely wiped out and several others were reduced to a very low level. Now, when few people wish them harm, the flesh-eating birds are under a greater threat than ever before. Throughout the world they are being destroyed by the remains of chemical pest-killers in their food; the build-up in their tissues means that they cannot reproduce and eventually they die.

although the largest of all, the harpy eagle of South America and the monkey-eating eagle of the Philippines are both forest-dwellers. Their large size often makes their movements look slow, but the speed of their attack as they stoop on their prey is as fast as any movement in the bird world.

They feed on a wide variety of animals; the golden eagle hunts

Game Birds

Chickens are the most familiar birds even if seen only when they have reached the poulterer's slab. But they are representatives of a large, world-wide group—the game birds—most of which share a good many of the domestic fowl's characteristics. They are almost all ground-living birds of medium size, with rather short, stout bills, curving down at the tip, suited to feeding on a wide variety of vegetable food. They have strong legs and can run well, and will often run rather than fly when they are alarmed.

Most species will not fly far, but their short, strongly curved wings make them capable of near vertical take-off and of agile movement through trees. In most cases the males are much more brightly coloured than the females and tend to mate with more than one partner. The dull-coloured females care for the nest and the young all resemble them until they are sexually mature, when the young males develop their bright plumage.

Male (right) and female pheasant

Primitive Species

The mound builders are usually thought of as being the most primitive of the game birds. These birds, which are found in Australasia, are the only birds in which there is no true incubation. Instead, the eggs are kept warm in a mound of sand and vegetation scratched up by the male, who tends it carefully throughout most of the year. Capable of flight almost as soon as they hatch, the young are not cared for by their parents.

Another curious member of the order is the hoatzin, which lives in tropical forests of north-east South America, where it nests in small trees overhanging streams. Should a chick fall from its nest, it will usually find its way back, for it can swim quite well and grab a low hanging branch, using well developed fingers on its wings—a feature shared by no other bird—to clamber up.

Other South American birds related to the chickens are the curassows and the guans, which are medium-sized birds, usually black or green, which feed on leaves, fruit, seeds and insects, much like the pheasants of the Old World.

Members of the group in the northern hemisphere include the grouse family. The largest of these is the capercaillie, a turkey-sized bird of coniferous forests. At one time a native of Scotland it became extinct there, but has been re-introduced. The black cock is another northern grouse. This bird, in common with all of its close relatives, mates with more than one partner. In the early spring all the males from one large area congregate on a communal display ground, where each cock takes up a territory. Here he displays, bowing, calling and fluttering in competition with other males to attract the waiting hens.

The Prairie Chicken

In America, the prairie chicken and sage grouse perform similar dances, to the accompaniment of booming noises made with the aid of inflatable air sacs on either side of the throat. Despite their name, wild turkeys are also American birds, now much rarer in the wild than formerly. Guinea fowls come from Africa, south of the Sahara. Both of these birds have been domesticated, and the turkey in particular has been changed by selective breeding. This has led to an increase in size and, in many forms, to a change from the bronze colours of the wild birds to the white feathers of domestic varieties.

By far the largest, most varied and most beautiful part of the group is that containing the pheasants and the

The peacock displays his plumage

true fowl. Many of these birds have been introduced by man to all corners of the earth, as domesticated birds, as game birds, or simply as living ornaments. Most have settled into their new environment so well that we may not now be certain of where their original home was.

The smallest birds of the whole order are the quails. In spite of this they are the only close relatives of the chickens to be migratory. In Europe and Asia these little birds used to be trapped at every stage on their journey and are now very rare. However, other species, especially in the New World, are flourishing.

Pheasants

In contrast to the usually well camouflaged quails and partridges, the male pheasants include some of the gaudiest of all birds with tails in which the longest feather, in some species, may measure more than a metre and a half (five feet). The females, who care for the nest and the young, are usually dressed in more subdued colours. Even the common pheasant, known as a game bird over much of the world, is a beautiful sight, with burnished copper and bronze body feathers, the bright red of his eye wattle contrasting with the greens and blues of head and neck.

Perhaps the most beautiful bird in the world among the larger species is the Lady Amherst pheasant, which is often kept as a decorative bird. Other species of pheasant, coming from upland areas of China and south-east Asia are hardly less beautiful, but in many cases have become very rare. Although they are extremely secretive and wary they all make succulent eating and have been hunted almost to extinction. Now efforts are being made to save some of them, for most will breed in captivity. In some cases birds from captive populations have been released in their old homelands.

Peafowl

The peafowl are of Indian origin, although there is also a recently discovered African species. These are among the best known decorative birds, reputed to have been used for this purpose as early as the time of Solomon. As with all members of the pheasant group, the male displays his gaudy plumage to the apparently indifferent female. In the peacock the huge-eyed tail is in fact made up of the upper tail coverts, while the true tail feathers are dull coloured stiff supports to the magnificent train. In spite of their long association with man, the peafowl are not truly domesticated. Although white and pied forms are bred, not one of the drastic changes in shape or size which usually indicate strongly selective breeding has occurred.

Domestic Fowl

This is far from being the case with the chickens, which are domesticated strains of one of the species of the Indian jungle fowl. They were probably first domesticated during the Bronze Age, and since then many varieties have been developed over the whole world. They form an important food source, both for meat and eggs. Like many of their relatives, if the eggs are removed the hen will continue laying, in some cases through most of the year.

An early practice, now illegal throughout most of Europe, was cock fighting. In this 'sport' the aggressive males were set against each other, armed with metal spurs with which they could inflict fatal damage to their opponents—something which never happens in nature. Chickens were used for sacrifice and divination in the ancient world. Right up to the present day they have been used for ornamental purposes.

Although the modern industrial world is fed by battery chickens, bred to mature early and to lay abundantly, there are still many varieties kept for their beauty, including what must be one of the strangest of birds—the Japanese fowl, whose central tail feathers are never shed, but continue to grow throughout the bird's life, reaching a length of six metres (twenty feet) or more in that time.

Tropical Birds

Grouped under this popular heading are nine orders of birds which include some of the most colourful and unusual species. The term 'tropical' has no exact meaning as used here. It is merely a convenient banner under which to list those birds, like parrots, which have come to represent for the people of northern Europe all the exotic qualities of tropical lands.

Parrots

No group of birds contains more colourful creatures than the parrots and their allies. Their names alone have a fascinating sound—parakeets, macaws, cockatoos, budgerigars. They come in all sizes, from the tiny pygmy parrots of New Guinea to the big spectacular macaws which live in the Amazon forests. A distinguishing feature is the shape of their beaks, short and strongly hooked with the upper part hanging far over the lower. Nearly all of them use this hooked beak to help them climb.

Parrots have always been popular pets, because they behave at times almost like humans, holding food in their feet as if they were hands and 'talking' to their owners. This ability to 'speak' is purely imitative and can only be learned in captivity. The greatest talker of them all is the African grey parrot, which has been taught to imitate the sound of the human voice since the days of ancient Greece and Rome.

The cockatoos are large, crested birds with beautiful plumage, and the parakeets include the most popular of all caged birds, the budgerigar.

Swifts

Among the most interesting things about the swift family are the nests some of them make, partly or wholly, from saliva. This is a stringy fluid, rather like a thick solution of gum which forms in the mouth of the bird and when exposed to the air rapidly dries and hardens.

Many animals make use of saliva as a means of binding together materials during building operations but the edible swift of eastern Asia and the Pacific islands is unique in providing man with birds' nest soup, regarded as a great delicacy, particularly in China. This is made from the nests themselves, the most favoured ones being white-coloured and built entirely of saliva, which are gathered from the caves where the bird lives.

Another extraordinary nest is made by one of the scissor-tailed swifts of Central America. This is a great hanging tube over half a metre (two feet) long and 150 millimetres (six inches) across, with an opening at the lower end for the birds to pass in and out.

Apart from nest-building the swifts' greatest distinction is their flying skill. No other bird can rival the swift of eastern Asia for speed and agility. It lives entirely on insects taken in flight, which it swoops down on and catches at speeds of over 160 kilometres (100 miles) per hour.

Allied to the swifts but distinctive because of their smallness and brilliant, multi-coloured plumage are the humming birds. They feed from the nectar of flowers, which they gather while hovering in the air. The incredibly fast beat of their wings as they hover produces the humming sound which gives them their name. The wings move so quickly that they seem to be almost invisible. There are over 300 species, mostly in South and Central America.

Trogons

If a choice had to be made of the typical tropical bird it might well be the male quetzal, one of the trogons, with its bright metallic colours and remarkably long tail plumes.

All trogons are striking, multi-hued birds and their distribution through three continents (South America, Africa and Asia) has proved something of a puzzle to scientists, for the trogon is a home-loving bird and hardly ever leaves its immediate area. Although the various species probably come from a common stock no one can be sure where they originated. The discovery of fossil remains of a trogon-type bird in rock strata dating back some thirty million years suggests that the present-day birds may be survivors of a very ancient group. All species live almost entirely on fruits and berries.

The quetzal gave its name to Quetzalcoatl, the chief god of the Toltecs. Its feathers, plucked from living birds, were used by the Aztecs and Mayas to make ceremonial helmets.

Kingfishers

It is one of the unexpected results of scientific classification to discover that the exquisite, darting kingfisher is placed in the same group of birds

Amazon parrot

Gold and blue macaw

as the great hornbill of south-east Asia, which can be over one and a half metres (five feet) long. Yet both have a particular body structure which relates them to each other.

Typical of the many species of kingfisher which are found in every part of the world is the common kingfisher, which decorates the shores of rivers and lakes in northern Europe, Asia and North Africa. It belongs to the group of fishing kingfishers which live on small fishes taken from the water. This tiny bird skims over the water to take its place on an overhanging bough of a tree. Here it will wait motionless until it marks out its prey. Then it darts like a flash into the water to take a fish in its long pointed bill.

Common in Australia is the kookaburra, or laughing jackass, which belongs to the kingfisher family and gets its name from its weird cry.

The hornbill uses its great beak partly as a defence weapon but chiefly to serve as a trowel for plastering up the holes in trees in which the female nests. These holes are found high up in the trunks of straight trees. When the female is safely settled inside, the male plasters up the opening with mud, leaving a tiny hole in the centre through which its mate can be fed.

Pigeons

There are pigeons all over the world and many of them are very decorative, such as the gay blue-crowned pigeon from New Guinea. More familiar in the Old World is the rock dove and in North America the mourning dove.

Fancy domestic pigeons and the homing pigeons kept for racing are probably descended from the rock dove, so too are the flocks of semi-tame pigeons which live in and around buildings in European cities in such great numbers that they create something of a nuisance. Rock doves and their descendants are very sociable birds, living in large flocks, eating, sleeping and moving about in unison.

Another group in the family are the fruit pigeons, so called because they

The kookaburra, or laughing jackass, of Australia belongs to a family of forest kingfishers. Its nickname comes from its weird cries, like a chorus of wild human laughter.

Common kingfisher

in the Old World. The common cuckoo spreads its cry over most parts of Europe and Asia and its name has found its way into many languages in words that imitate its call. The other very familiar thing about the cuckoo is the fact that it has the habit of laying its eggs in other birds' nests.

But the common cuckoo of Eurasia is only one of over a hundred cuckoo species which range from the emerald cuckoo of Africa to the stout-legged roadrunner which lives on the ground in the deserts of America. It is a very fast runner, feeds on snakes and lizards, but makes only a feeble effort at flying.

The dodo is an extinct bird, very heavily built and quite unable to fly. It belonged to a small family of birds confined to the islands of Mauritius, Réunion and Rodriguez in the Indian Ocean. It had a large, hooked beak, short stubby legs and rudimentary wings. Clumsy and defenceless, the dodo was an easy prey to the sailors who landed on the islands in the seventeenth century. Those birds which were not destroyed by human hand were attacked by other animals introduced by man to the islands. The appearance of the dodo is known today from contemporary drawings, from relics of stuffed specimens and from remains of skeletons dug up on the islands.

feed mainly on fruits and berries, especially wild nutmegs which they swallow whole.

There is no real technical difference between the use of the names pigeon and dove, although the larger birds are usually called pigeons and the smaller ones doves. Carrier or homing pigeons are not a separate breed but are the result of cross-breeding, controlled by man in his efforts to obtain a highly developed sense of direction and homing instinct.

Cuckoos

The call of the male cuckoo in springtime as it sings to its mate is possibly the best-known bird sound

Woodpeckers

Members of the woodpecker family spend their lives in trees, and wherever there is a forest the woodpecker will thrive. They have distinctive bills, straight and pointed for digging into the bark of trees. They also have very long tongues which can be thrust out a great distance to grub out from holes and crevices the hidden insect life on which they feed.

Perching Birds

Although many birds belonging to a number of orders are capable of perching, the members of one group, which includes over half of all known birds, are referred to as the perching birds. They are the common birds of garden and woodland, for they are all land-living and found throughout the world, except for Antarctica. They always have four strong, unwebbed toes, with the hind toe always well developed. Most perching birds have tuneful voices and song is an important part of their life, being used for territorial definition and—as call notes—for communication. Mimicry of other sounds occurs as part of some songs. The lyre bird, for example, will include snatches of all sorts of sounds in its song and it is well known that in many species the song has to be learned and may be modified in the process.

Perching birds vary in size from the raven, which is about 66 centimetres (26 inches) long to some of the tiny wrens and kinglets, which are about 8 centimetres (3 inches) long. Their colours vary from dull browns and blacks to vividly blotched patterns on some of the finches. Their food includes insects of all sorts, taken by bills well suited for the job—fine forceps for the smaller insects and coarser pincers for the bigger kinds. Some feed on buds, leaves or seeds. Those which feed on smaller types of food have short, stubby beaks and those which eat larger and tougher fruits have strong, conical beaks. The hawfinch, which can crack cherry and olive stones with ease, has such a beak.

All perching birds produce young which are naked, blind and helpless at birth and are tended for a period of at least two weeks in a well-constructed nest. Most nests are

Young cuckoo being fed by a female whitethroat

built in trees, well away from the ground, some in thickety branches like that of the blackbird and some hanging from a twig like the goldcrests. Blackbirds incorporate a foundation of mud into their nests; swallows and their relatives make mud the major material of the nest. In common with other perching birds, the swallow's nursery is furnished with a warm lining of hair, feathers, grass or moss. Some breed singly in a strongly defended territory, like robins. Others, like rooks, are social nesters, which may burden a single tree with twenty of their big, stick-based nests. African weaver birds band together in hundreds,

their finely woven nests looking like strange fruits hanging abundantly from the branches of their chosen trees.

Egg-laying

That such highly evolved animals as birds should have retained the old-fashioned, reptilian method of reproduction by laying eggs may at first seem surprising. But the system as adapted by the birds, is in fact ideal, for it enables the female to produce a large brood without overburdening herself. The eggs in most species are laid daily and incubation does not start until the clutch is complete. Initial cooling does not harm the embryo; cooling after development has started is quickly fatal. Eggs vary in shape from nearly round to long and oval, although most are more strongly pointed at one end than the other. Colours vary from white, which is usual in hole nesters, to blues and browns and eggs spotted in various shades, which

There is an astonishing variety of nests made by the different species of birds in which to raise their young. Nests seen here are: blackbird (left), goldcrest (below), swallow (right) and those in a rookery.

are the masterpieces of camouflage laid by ground nesters.

Perching birds are popular with most human beings because of their bright colours, their cheerful songs and their often comical display antics in the breeding season. In some parts of the world certain species have become pests of crops, but in general they are in more danger from man's wish to collect them to keep as pets, than from persecution because of any damage they may do. Some kinds of tropical finch are collected for sale all over the world, the duller coloured species having their colours heightened by being dyed bright pink or green. In some countries it is illegal

Birds' eggs belonging to 1 rook, 2 magpie, 3 jackdaw, 4 bullfinch, 5 yellowhammer, 6 chaffinch, 7 song thrush, 8 blackbird, 9 mistlethrush, 10 puffin, 11 guillemot, 12 partridge, 13 nightjar, 14 corncrake, 15 great tit, 16 nuthatch, 17 blue tit, 18 robin, 19 nightingale, 20 swallow.

to keep wild birds caged; but many people have the pleasure of birds' company by encouraging them in gardens and getting them to visit bird tables.

The provision of food, water and shelter will attract birds to a garden. The food can be in the form of berry-bearing plants, or a bird table furnished with nuts, fat, bread and other food enjoyed by garden birds. A bird table will be better patronised if it is placed near to some cover from which the birds can survey the situation and to which they can escape quickly if necessary. Water is a necessity both for drinking and for bathing, and cover can be provided in the form of thick bushes or hedges, supplemented by nest boxes in the breeding season.

Bird Tables

Even the commonest garden birds are attractive. In hard weather they will parade at a bird table and may be seen at close quarters. The thrushes include the small song thrush and its larger, greyer cousin, the mistle thrush. This bird is sometimes called the storm cock, for it starts to sing its fine territorial song in mid-winter and can often be heard, even in very rough weather, as it announces its early bid for nesting space. The blackbird, which is black in the male, with a bright yellow beak, but dark brown in the female, is a relative of the thrushes.

All of these birds may be seen tug-of-warring with worms on a lawn. The song thrush will catch snails and smash them open on a favourite anvil stone. Starlings are basically black birds, speckled with a 'milky way' of small spots, from which they get their name. The male has a fine green gloss to his feathers in springtime and it is then that he is most vocal, singing his curious, squeaky song, and giving imitations of other birds' sounds. Sparrows, which were common town birds until horses were replaced by motor transport, can still be seen in gardens. They squabble and dustbath and sunbathe, and through most of the summer build their untidy nests in any crevice into which they can squeeze. Finches include the greenfinch, in which the male is a handsome yellowish green, although his mate is less brightly coloured.

Male chaffinches are among the most colourful of garden birds, with rosy pink breasts and blue-grey heads, but again their mates are less attractive. Also very brightly coloured are bullfinches, which may invade suburban gardens. These are not always welcome, however, because of their habit of stripping ornamental shrubs or fruit trees of their buds, which does not endear them to most gardeners. Titmice are common bird table visitors. The tiny blue tit and its larger cousin the great tit are the

commonest visitors and give pleasure to many people with their acrobatic behaviour. Another acrobatic visitor to bird tables is the nuthatch. This bird has strong curved toes, which enable it to climb vertical and overhanging surfaces with ease.

The Robin
One of the most confiding birds of gardens is the robin who will quickly discover and exploit any food supply which is provided. It can become very tame, even to the extent of tapping on windows and demanding food when none is available outside. In some cases it will even enter houses. The robin is an enterprising and quick little bird, and with its bright appearance and cheerful song it has endeared itself to many people.

Common garden birds seen here are, from left to right, song thrush, starling, female and male chaffinch, male house sparrow (behind) great tit (top), nuthatch (centre), blue tit (below), male house sparrow and, from top to bottom, male blackbird, robin, male greenfinch and female house sparrow.

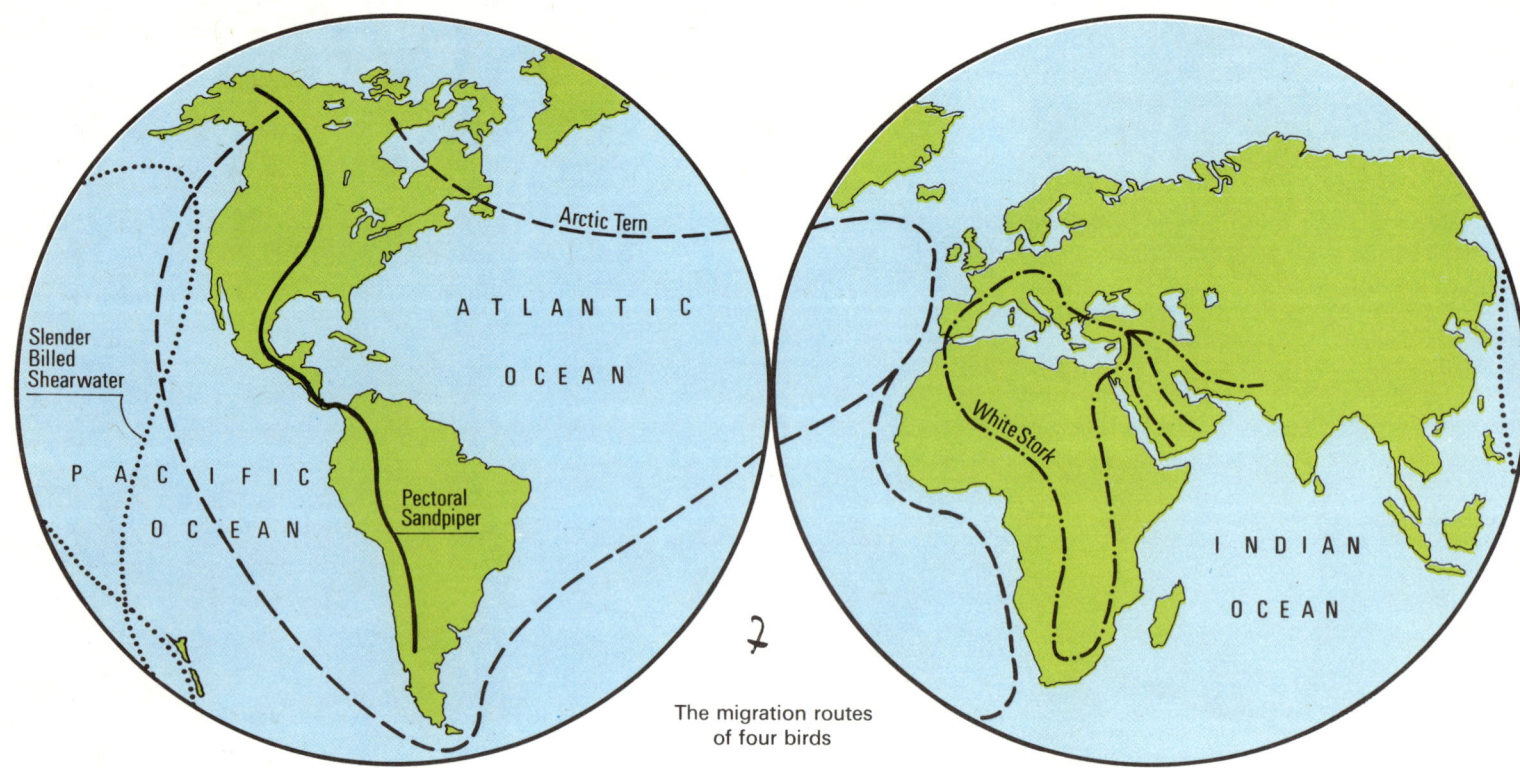

The migration routes of four birds

Bird Migration

One of the mysteries about birds, observed since Old Testament times but not explained until recently, is the fact that they are in many cases not permanent residents of any given area. At a certain time of year flocks will arrive, to disappear again a few months later. Only in modern times have the scale and scope of these migratory movements been realised. For many of the birds concerned are tiny and for long it was thought impossible that they should make journeys which are often tens of thousands of kilometres, involving long sea crossings.

Many birds die on these journeys, especially the smaller ones, yet the advantages must outweigh the difficulties and dangers, for migration is the habit of many species. Some birds migrate in large flocks, some in family parties and some singly. In a few cases the distances are short and may merely involve movement in level rather than latitude.

Migration Routes

In general the routes chosen tend to follow sea coasts, valleys and other landmarks which make a pattern of traditional flyways. The knowledge of these is inborn in many species but experiments have shown that in some cases, at least, the birds are able to navigate, using the sun and stars, and are able to correct their position if they are artificially displaced. Migration is normally in a northerly direction in the early part of the year, with a return south in later months. The reason for this is probably that the huge land masses of the northern continents offer space for breeding and longer daylight hours in which to collect food for the brood than would be available in the tropics.

The longest-distance traveller among migrant birds is the Arctic tern, which breeds in coastal and offshore areas of the northern hemisphere, but spends the winter months in the Antarctic, making a round trip of about 35,000 kilometres (22,000 miles) each year. Some other sea birds also make immense journeys. The slender-billed shearwater which nests on the coasts of South Australia, migrates across the Pacific Ocean to the west coast of America. Then, making a second more northerly ocean crossing, it completes the circle back to its nesting place by the next year.

Land birds may make journeys which are scarcely less great. The pectoral sandpiper is an American bird, nesting in the far north of the continent and migrating south in the winter time, paralleling the movements made by European and Asiatic waders.

Not all the members of a population migrate in the same direction when the time comes to leave the breeding grounds. The white storks of Europe travel over two distinct routes, those from the more westerly parts taking a western coastal route, those from eastern Europe taking a line south-east to fly over the lands which border the eastern side of the Mediterranean.

Tracing Bird Movement

Our knowledge of migration comes in a variety of ways. Observation was the first and is still used, sometimes to note the arrival and departure times of the birds, sometimes to track them on their journeys. Birds may be trapped in a number of harmless ways and banded with lightweight numbered metal rings. Later, recoveries—in traps on other migration journeys or after death—show the distance the bird has travelled. Hundreds of thousands of birds are banded each year. The percentage of recoveries is small, but enough over the years to have built up a complex picture of the long-distance movements of birds.

Movements during migration are traced by attaching metal rings to a bird's leg or by marking them with a harmless dye.

Mammals

To the majority of people, mammals are the most familiar animals. They are to be found almost everywhere: from the edge of the Arctic ice sheets to the tropics; from the sea to the driest deserts; from the tops of trees to below the ground. They range in size from the blue whale, which may be over thirty metres (100 feet) long and weigh more than 120 tons, to the pygmy shrews which are less than 50 millimetres (two inches) long and weigh only about seven grammes (a quarter of an ounce). Mammals may feed on meat, on insects, or on many kinds of vegetation. Some, like pigs or man, will eat almost any kind of food. Between them, mammals use to the full the area in which they live.

Varieties of Mammals

What are the qualities which make an animal a mammal? Appearances are nothing to go by, for mammals may have long legs like antelopes, or no legs like sea cows. They may have long necks like giraffes, or very short ones like elephants. They may have shaggy coats like bears, or smooth skins like whales. They may be a variety of colours, spotted, striped or blotched. Yet all are backboned animals, breathing air and warm-blooded. Most important of all, in most cases the young are born at a relatively advanced stage and they are always cared for and fed on milk by their mothers. No other kinds of creatures give this sort of protection and feeding to their young and it accounts, in large part, for the success of the mammals.

Mammals are physically efficient animals. Their constant temperature (which is what is meant by the term 'warm-blooded') means that the chemical activity of the cells of their bodies can proceed at a steady rate, regardless of outside conditions. Because of this they are able to be continuously active, even in cold weather, and can live in cool parts of the world. Their turnover of energy is rapid and mammals begin the digestion of their food as soon as it is taken into the mouth. Sliced or chewed with teeth specialised for the purpose and with saliva and other digestive juices added, food is quickly converted into the energy needed for life. Breathing is rapid and regular in mammals. Stale blood, with its load of body waste products, which is pumped from the heart to the lungs, is kept well separated from the blood which is returned, freshly mixed with oxygen, to be pumped round the body.

Well-developed Senses

Mammals are intelligent animals, with large and complex brains and well developed senses. The head of the baboon, for example, shows the enlarged brain case. The eyes, nose and ears are all on the head and although many animals have poor eyesight and are unable to distinguish colours, most have excellent hearing and sense of smell. The large whiskers round the snout are part of the delicate and highly developed sense of touch.

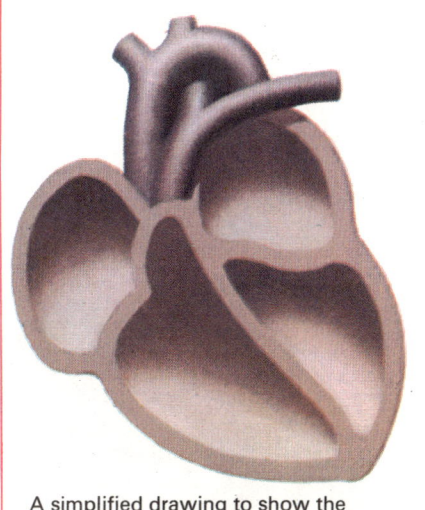

A simplified drawing to show the four-chambered heart of mammals which separates blood returning to the lungs from blood about to be pumped around the body.

All mammals share a number of features. All are vertebrates; all are air-breathing and warm-blooded; all have fur or hair; and all suckle their young on milk. Mammals are active animals with skeletons which support their bodies precisely. All of them have a definite size. Their limb bones grow at the ends, which have loose sections while the animal is young, but which fuse and prevent further growth when it becomes adult. Mammal lower jaws are composed of two bones fused together which carry the teeth for cutting (incisors), tearing (canines) and chewing (molars). Mammals have special blood cells which make them more efficient carriers of oxygen. Finally, all have large and complex brains and are generally intelligent.

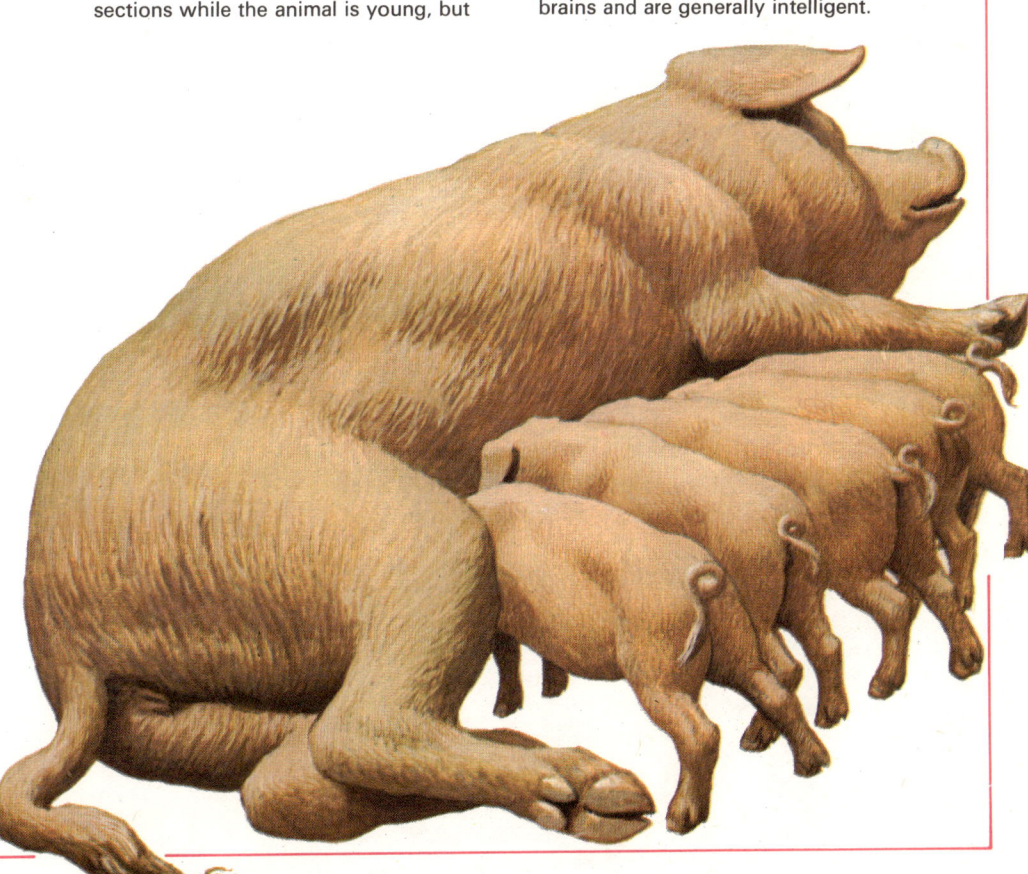

Primitive Mammals

The first mammals evolved from reptile ancestors about 200 million years ago. We do not know exactly what they were like, for their fossilised remains which are small and fragile are rarely found. There are however two creatures, the platypus from Australia and the spiny anteater found in Australia and New Guinea, which give us some clues. For both lay eggs, like reptiles do, although both suckle their young, like mammals. Both of these animals lead extremely specialised lives and their physical structure gives us no exact information on their ancient ancestors.

Marsupials

In Australia, South America and parts of North America, other primitive mammals live. These are called marsupials, a name that comes from the Latin word for a pouch. In the marsupials the young grow for a short time in their mothers' bodies. They are very tiny and under-developed at birth—the biggest measures only 25 millimetres (one inch) long and the smaller species of marsupials produce babies which are only about the size of a grain of rice. The little creature is strong enough for one thing, which is to push its way through its mother's fur and find the pouch on her underside where the milk glands are situated. The tiny animal clamps its jaws on to a nipple and remains feeding in safety and warmth in the pouch until it has grown big and strong enough to venture out on its own, a process that may take several months. Even then, it will return to take shelter when danger threatens.

At one time marsupial animals lived in many parts of the world, but they were mostly destroyed by more efficient and cleverer animals called placental mammals, when these evolved. Few placentals reached South America and none reached Australia so in these two areas the marsupials continued to flourish.

The best known of the marsupials are the kangaroos, which are the native grazing animals of Australia.

The koala is a tree-dweller and feeds on the leaves of eucalyptus trees.

There are many other kinds of pouched mammals, fitted for different ways of life. The koala, which looks so much like a bear, is a tree-living marsupial, feeding on certain species of Australian eucalyptus. Others, such as the almost extinct thylacine, which looks like a striped dog, feed on flesh. The opossums feed on small animals and the phalangers mainly on insects. Other marsupials look like mice, or moles or monkeys, but in all cases they are pouched mammals, survivors of the prehistoric past.

Kangaroos are timid animals, living in groups called droves. Each drove usually has a particular district and feeding ground which it frequents.

The platypus is a puzzle creature. In spite of its duck-like bill it has the furry body of a typical mammal, but it cannot control its body temperature as well as most mammals and, like a reptile, may become torpid on a cold day. Strangest of all, a female platypus lays eggs. She digs a burrow in a stream bank, where she makes a nest, blocking off the main tunnel for safety. In the nest she lays her eggs which are tiny compared with the size of the adult. After being kept warm for a fortnight the eggs hatch and the tiny babies, naked and blind, nuzzle at their mother's belly and cause milk to flow, which they lap up.

The European hedgehog's food is very varied. It will eat all kinds of insects, worms, slugs, rats, mice—even snakes and lizards. It also has a special liking for birds' eggs. Here, a hedgehog is shown attacking a viper which it will kill by a series of bites.

Insect-eaters

The vast majority of mammals in the world today belong to a group called the placentals. In them, there is a special organ, the placenta, through which the unborn young are nourished and this enables them to grow to a large size before birth. They are mostly intelligent, adaptable animals and are to be found throughout the world.

The most primitive among the placentals are the insectivores. These are all small, long-snouted animals, with sharp pointed teeth for holding and slicing insects and other small prey. The fur is usually velvety although there may be spines mingled with it. There are claws on all the toes and many of the insectivores are good burrowers. The eyes and ears are often small, but the sense of touch is well developed and most insectivores have big sensory whiskers round the snout. The star-nosed mole has gone even further in this respect and has fleshy feelers on the end of its nose.

Shrews

The insectivores are physically variable and are found in many different places, almost throughout the world. Some are becoming increasingly rare, but on the whole insectivores are well able to survive in the modern world. Shrews are among the commonest of the insectivores. They are tiny, restless creatures, living anywhere that abundant prey may be found, for they need to eat their own weight daily in grubs, snails and the like to fuel their constant activity. Their tiny, shrill voices, often mistaken for insect squeaks, may be heard in the countryside at almost any time of the day or night. They sleep only briefly, for to go without food for four hours can be fatal.

The Hedgehog

The hedgehog is probably the most familiar insectivore in the Old World. Protected by its spines, which it can erect by rolling up into a ball, it shows no fear of any natural enemies. Like the shrews, the hedgehogs' need for food is constant, and they will tackle almost any small animal that they meet. Slugs, worms, insects and

Hedgehogs are able to roll themselves into a compact ball for protection.

Digging is the mole's way of life. For this it uses the broad front feet, with which it first loosens the earth. Then, gripping the tunnel walls with its claws, it shoves its head and shoulders into the earth and pushes, so packing the soil firm. Sometimes the mole has to push extra soil up to the surface where it forms molehills, but when the earth is fairly loose, the mole can 'swim' below the surface. Seen above are a common mole and below it a star-nosed mole.

the eggs and even the young of ground-nesting birds fall prey to them. They are said to attack and kill adders, which exhaust themselves striking at the hedgehog's spines and cannot drive their poison home.

When food becomes scarce in the winter time, hedgehogs hibernate. They are among the mammals which have learned to live in harmony with man and many are to be found in gardens, tamed by householders who put out milk to encourage them. Hedgehogs do not, however, make good pets. Their spiny coats make grooming difficult, so they carry a zoological garden of parasites on their backs, a feature which most people find unattractive.

Moles are the expert burrowers of the insectivore world. They satisfy their enormous appetites by digging tunnels in which they catch grubs and worms to store in their nests.

Shrews produce litters of blind and toothless young which, in order to move about, form chains by holding tails.

Rodents seen below are 1 harvest mouse, 2 guinea pig, 3 brown rat, 4 prairie dog, 5 beaver, 6 lemming, 7 house mouse, 8 capybara, 9 red squirrel, 10 coypu, 11 porcupine.

The skull of a typical rodent

Rodents

Of all the mammals, by far the largest number of kinds are included among the gnawing mammals, or rodents. These creatures have found a way to live in every environment except the sea and are to be found as runners, burrowers, climbers, gliders or swimmers throughout the world, except in Australia. Most rodents are small, the giant among them being the capybara, which is the size of a half-grown pig. In spite of variations in appearance, all rodents have many things in common. Some of these may be seen in the skull, which is long and low, with a relatively small brain case. The area for the attachment of chewing muscles is, however, great and there are pulley-like muscles running from the skull to the lower jaw which enable them to feed on very tough plant food.

The teeth are always clearly divided into the incisors in the front of the mouth and, separated by a long gap, the molars at the back. There are only two incisors in either jaw, but they are extremely powerful tools, with roots which run back into the skull. The ends of the roots are open, which means that the tooth may receive nutriment and grow throughout the life of the animal. As it chews, the teeth work against each other and get worn down, but the open roots ensure that growth keeps pace with wear, so the rodents always have serviceable nibbling teeth. Rodent incisors have a very thick layer of enamel on one side only and the cutting edge is of this very hard material, ground by wear to razor sharpness.

Enemies of Rodents

Rodents are mainly small and defenceless animals. They are the main food of many kinds of flesh-eaters, including snakes, birds of prey and mammals. That they manage to survive is due in many cases to their huge capacity for reproduction. Many of the smaller rodents may live for only one year, but in that time may produce forty or more offspring. Most of the young do not survive their early months, but normally enough do so to preserve the species. In a few kinds of rodents, however, it sometimes happens that larger than average numbers of young manage to survive the season of their birth. The following summer they

become part of the breeding population and overall numbers rise accordingly, with more young again surviving. If this trend continues without being broken by exceptionally hard winters, or some other reason, numbers will build up to 'plague' proportions in a very few years.

In lemmings this seems to happen quite regularly, and the animals, under the huge pressure of their population explosion, try to migrate to new, less crowded areas. Large numbers of them move across the land, swimming rivers and lakes and sometimes even attempting to swim the sea. Some may find new quarters but most die. In the original areas of the plague the remaining population breeds at a reduced rate, due apparently to internal changes in their bodies because of the stress of constant competition.

A few kinds of rodents breed slowly. Beavers, for example, produce only one litter each spring and the young remain with their parents for two years. Beavers are long-lived animals, often surviving for twenty years.

Three Main Groups

Because of differences in their anatomies, rodents are often divided into three main groups, those of the squirrels, mice and porcupines. The squirrel group are mainly climbers, with long claws with which they can hold on to trees, and good eyesight which enables them to see accurately the distances they may have to jump from branch to branch. In some cases this ability is made easier by a flap of skin between the fore and hind legs—these are the flying squirrels. Some members of the group have taken to living in the ground, using their claws to excavate extensive tunnels.

The marmots of the Old World and the prairie dogs of the New World are ground-living squirrels. The beaver is a relative of the squirrel, although it is a swimmer and cuts trees down with its sharp teeth, rather than climbing them. The twigs and bark are used for food and the heavy wood is built into a dam, with which beavers block streams. In the dam, which is made of wood and stones and mud, the beavers build their lodge—a secure house and larder, protected by the water.

The second group of rodents includes mice, voles and hamsters. The majority of these animals do man no harm. Some, like the tiny harvest mouse, are rare, due to changes in farming methods. Others, such as the golden hamster, are scarcely known in the wild, although they are familiar pets. A few, which are particularly adaptable, have become major pests. The chief of these is the brown rat, which costs mankind a great deal of money every year through damage to property, destruction of food and spread of diseases. The house mouse, although smaller, is also a pest, yet both of these species are often used in laboratory experiments which may help man. White and fancy coloured varieties of both are sometimes kept as pets.

The porcupine, the capybara, the guinea pig, the coypu and a number of South American rodents belong to the third sub-group. Protected by their spines the porcupines have few enemies other than man. The capybara and the coypu take refuge in the water, and the guinea pigs are shy animals living in dense cover, although they may become tame in captivity.

Rabbits and Hares
These familiar creatures are also gnawing animals, but they are not rodents, and are not closely related to them. They have four teeth in the upper jaw, rather than two, and these are covered with equally thick enamel all over. As a result, they cannot gnaw as well as rodents can, which is probably why there are few sorts of them. Hare-like animals are usually creatures of open country. They have long hind legs and are able to run fast over long distances to escape their enemies. Usually they are solitary, but in springtime, which is the main mating period, the jack hares become the proverbial mad March hares, leaping and cavorting about. The leverets are born in the open, for the temperate country hares do not burrow. They are fully furred at birth with their eyes open and are taken by their mothers to different hiding places.

Rabbit

Rabbits are generally smaller animals, usually living where the country has denser vegetation. The European rabbit normally burrows below ground for protection, quite large numbers of animals inhabiting the same warren. The young are born blind and helpless and remain below ground for three weeks before they emerge.

Hare

The giant anteater lives in forests in South and Central America. It moves about at night and is rarely seen by man. It feeds on ants and termites.

Toothless Mammals

Insects are generally food for small animals only, but among the mammals three groups, which include some quite large creatures, have evolved as specialised insect-eaters. These are the aardvark of Africa, the pangolins of the tropical Old World and the edentates of South and Central America. All of these animals are toothless or nearly so, and they feed chiefly on termites and ants.

The aardvark is a pig-sized creature with huge claws on its feet with which it can tear open termite heaps. It laps up the exposed insects with its 450-millimetre (eighteen-inch) long tongue. It shelters in burrows which it digs; these may be large enough for a man to creep into and are often a danger to horses or vehicles on the plains.

The pangolins look like animated fir cones, protected as they are by overlapping horny scales. Some small species live in the trees, but the giant pangolin, which is one and a half metres (five feet) long, lives entirely on the ground. They have a different digestive system from the aardvark and can deal with hard-bodied ants as well as the soft-bodied termites. Like the aardvark, they have large claws and a long tongue on which the insects are quickly caught.

In South America the edentates include the sloths, which are tree

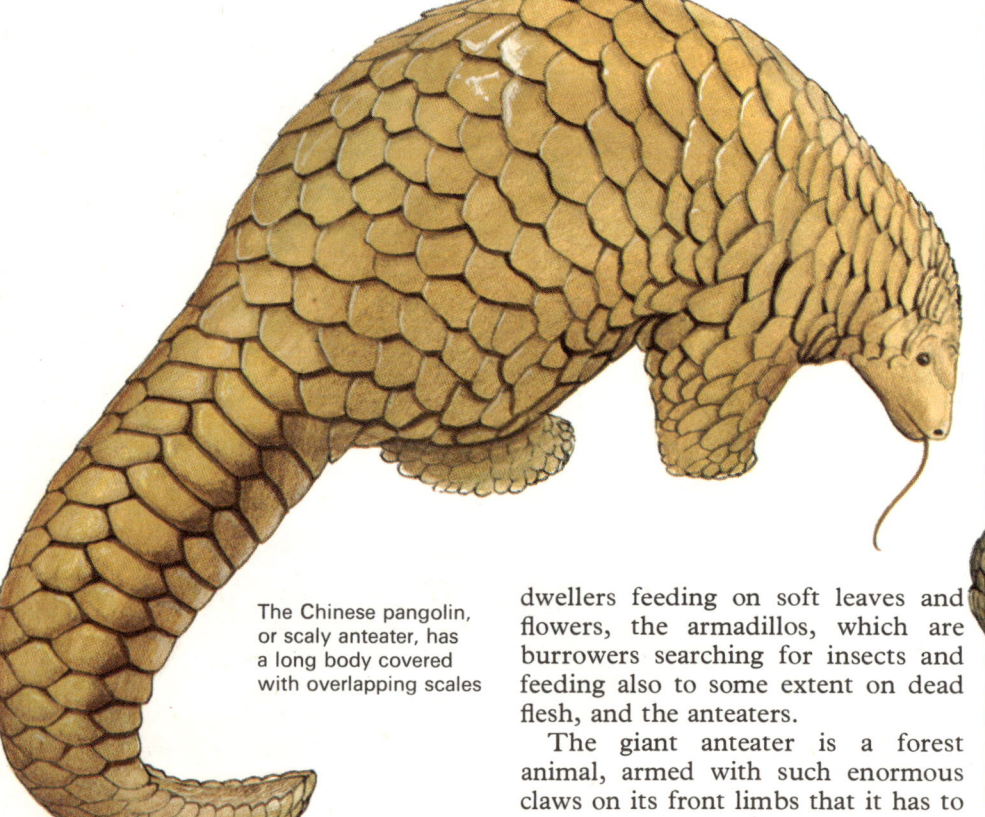

The Chinese pangolin, or scaly anteater, has a long body covered with overlapping scales

dwellers feeding on soft leaves and flowers, the armadillos, which are burrowers searching for insects and feeding also to some extent on dead flesh, and the anteaters.

The giant anteater is a forest animal, armed with such enormous claws on its front limbs that it has to walk on the sides of its feet. These claws are, however, ideal for breaking open ant and termite nests and the insects are then caught on the long sticky tongue. The giant anteater is curiously coloured with contrasting bands of black and white on its grey body. These markings help to disguise it, especially at rest, when it curls up, draping the large shaggy tail over the body. All of the toothless animals are inoffensive creatures but they are declining in numbers everywhere.

Protection
Animals are protected against their enemies in many ways. They may be able to run fast, they may have effective camouflage or they may, in some cases, carry protective weapons of armour. Among the mammals, armour is found only in the toothless insect-eating species. It consists of either bone or horn, formed in the skin and making a hard outer covering. Some, like the pangolins and the three-banded armadillo from South America can roll up into a tight ball when frightened and so present an enemy with a tough exterior which must be dealt with before an effective attack may be made. Armadillos which have a covering of bony plates cannot in most cases roll up, but defend themselves against attack by burrowing rapidly into the earth.

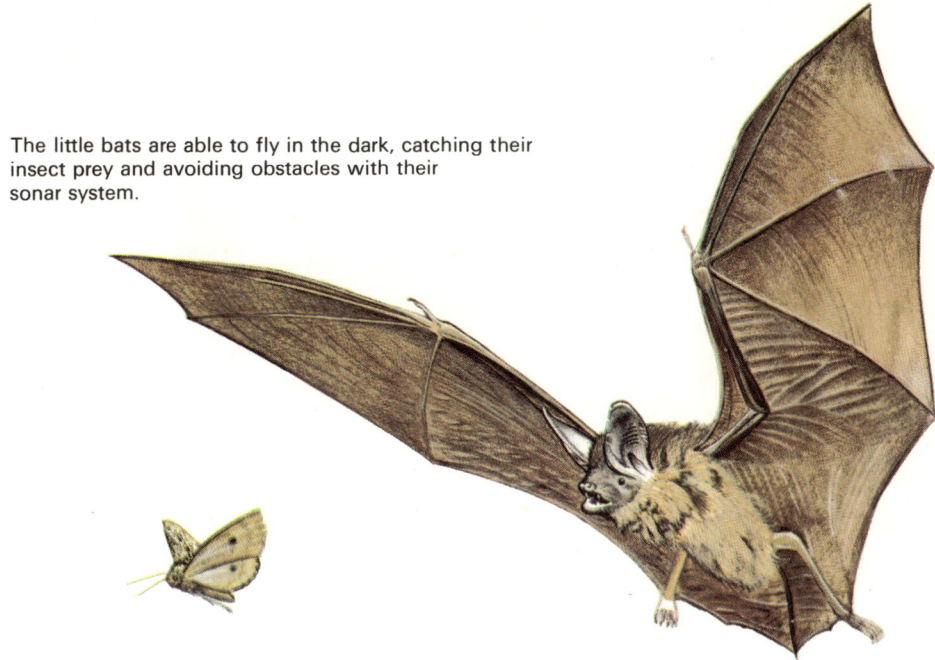

The little bats are able to fly in the dark, catching their insect prey and avoiding obstacles with their sonar system.

'Seeing in the dark'
The bat's sonar is based on ultrasonic squeaks, above the level of human hearing and ranging up to 100,000 cycles per second. Each squeak lasts about one five-hundredth of a second and in normal flight the bat produces about fifty per second. Any obstruction, whether moving or stationary, causes a reflection of sound as an echo which is detected by the bat's delicate ears. The time lag between the emission of the squeak and the reception of the echo informs the animal of the distance of the obstacle. It has been shown that bats approaching an obstacle increase their rate of squeak. They can detect tiny objects in their path such as the small insects which are their prey.

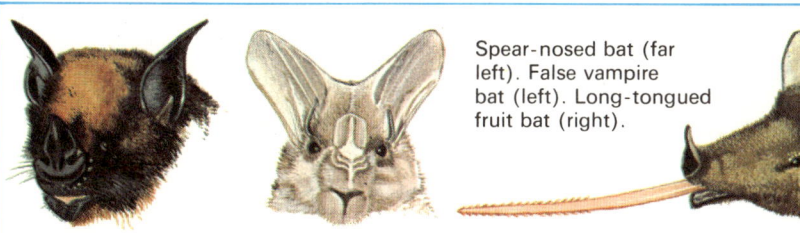

Spear-nosed bat (far left). False vampire bat (left). Long-tongued fruit bat (right).

The faces of insect-eating bats (above left) appear both evil and comic, but the shape of the mouth, nose and ears is important to the animal in the way it transmits and receives the sonar signals which help it to find its way about in the dark.

Flying Mammals

Mammals are usually thought of as ground-living creatures, but nearly a quarter of all known mammal species are bats, and are capable of true flight. In developing this way of life they do not come into conflict with the birds, which fly mainly by day, for bats are strictly night-flying creatures.

How Bats Fly

The modifications of the body for flight are quite different from those found in birds. This can be seen in the skeleton which is very lightly built, but strong, especially in the region of the shoulders and chest. The wings are supported by the forelimbs and strengthened by the very much elongated finger bones which run through them. The thumb is free and may be used by the bat to manipulate food and when moving about the walls of its roost. The wing membrane, which is made of soft skin and involves no feathers, is stretched from the shoulder to the ankle and sometimes continues to include the tail.

Bat's legs are swivelled at the hip joint so that the knee bends in the opposite direction from that of other mammals, but this helps to tension the trailing edge of the wing. Flight varies from the erratic fluttering of some of the tiny bats to the sustained flight of the larger species, some of which are capable of long migrations. Flight requires the output of a great deal of energy, and bats save this energy by becoming more or less inactive when they are not flying.

Bats are classified into two great groups, the big bats, which are all found in the tropical Old World and are fruit-eaters, and the little bats, found throughout the world. The little bats are flesh-eaters, most species feeding on night-flying insects, but some feed on fish or, in the case of vampires, on blood. Most bats are entirely harmless to man and the fear which they inspire is probably caused by their dark colour, their silent night flight and their curious faces.

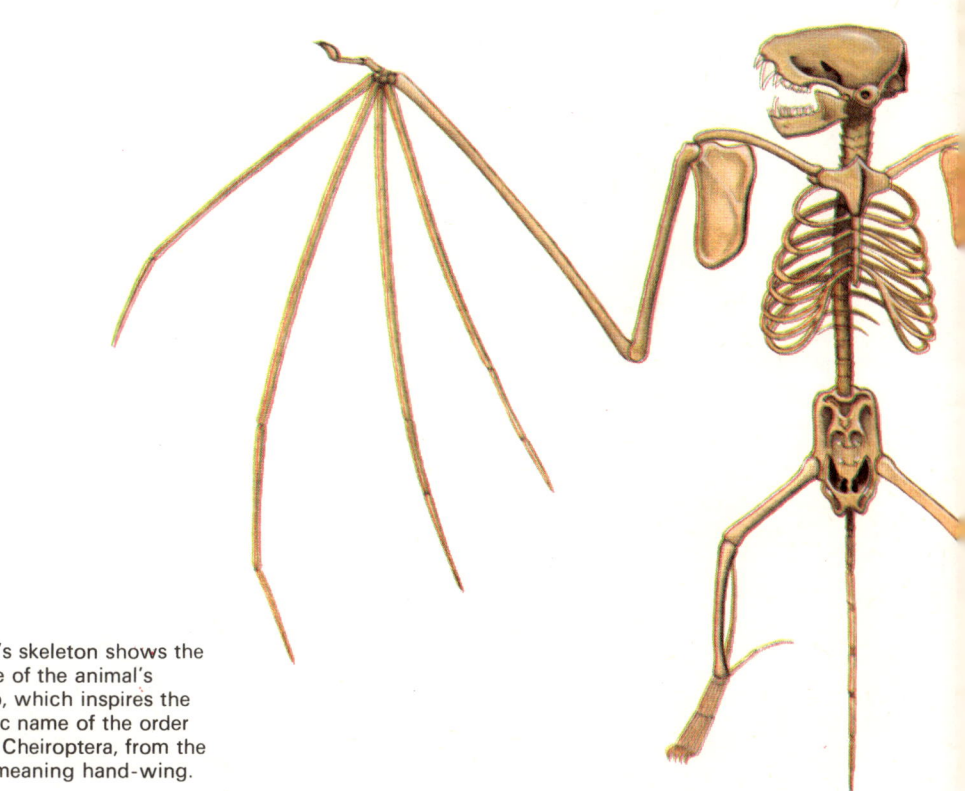

The bat's skeleton shows the vast size of the animal's forelimb, which inspires the scientific name of the order of bats, Cheiroptera, from the Greek, meaning hand-wing.

Bottle-nosed dolphins

Marine Mammals

With a group of animals as successful as the mammals, it is not surprising that some of them should have taken to the sea for their way of life. Three separate orders, the whales, the sea cows and the seals, are now totally aquatic and so highly adapted for this life that most cannot survive on land. In the case of the seals, they never depart far from the water where they are most at home.

Demands of the Sea

The sea makes many demands on its inhabitants and mammals adapted to live in it demonstrate these in their structure. Compared with air, water is very dense and successful locomotion demands that the animal should be streamlined. All marine mammals are sleek, curved creatures, presenting little obstacle to the smooth flow of water over their bodies. The sea is cold, so all marine mammals are protected by a thick deposit of fat under the skin. It is also a protection against many enemies and a support to weight, so most marine mammals are large and heavily built.

However well adapted to the sea marine mammals appear to be, they have all descended from land-living ancestors and they retain many features characteristic of land animals. The skeleton of the flipper of a whale, for instance, is exactly comparable to a human arm and hand and very different in structure from the fin of a fish. All marine mammals produce living young and suckle them, showing parental care typical of their land-living relatives. Also, marine mammals have to come to the surface to breathe. Although they can hold their breath much longer than land mammals, their lungs are similar and they cannot extract oxygen from the water as fishes can.

The whales are the most completely aquatic of the mammals. Although a few inhabit rivers, most are creatures of the open oceans. They are perfectly designed for life in the water, swimming by means of a horizontal tail fluke, or lobe. Their hind legs are reduced to a small remnant of internal bone and their forelimbs modified to form balancing flippers. They have no external ears and no fur to diminish their streamlining—the only hair present on their bodies being a small moustache found in some species.

There are two great groups of whales: the toothed whales and the baleen whales. The first group contains all of the small species and a few large ones, such as the sperm whale. They usually have a large number of pointed teeth, suitable for catching the fishes and squids which are their food. In some cases the teeth have become reduced in number, as for example in the narwhal, in which the female has no teeth at all and the male has only one tooth, a long, twisted incisor growing straight forward out of the mouth.

Baleen Whales

The baleen whales are all large. They include the blue whale, which may be over thirty metres (100 feet) long and weigh more than 120 tons. It is the biggest animal ever to have lived on earth. All baleen whales are toothless, but they have instead a series of triangular plates of material, a substance like fingernails, hanging from the roof of the mouth. These are the baleen plates, which on their inner edges are broken into a fine, hair-like fringe, although they are quite smooth on the outer, cheek side.

Baleen whales spend much of their lives in sub-polar regions where the rich nutrients in the water allow the growth of many marine plants and small animals. These in turn nourish shrimp-like creatures called krill which are the food of the largest whales. The baleen whale swims slowly through the huge schools of krill, taking water containing the shrimps

Underwater sounds
Whales are mostly sociable animals and schools of them may be heard conversing with clicking and squeaking noises quite audible to human ears. They also make sounds far above the level of human hearing, emitted as high-pitched bursts of sound, coming from the blowhole. These are used for echo-location of prey and obstacles in the water. Although there is no external ear, whales have exceedingly acute hearing and can detect subtle differences in the quality of the echoes.

The male narwhal has an enormous spirally twisted tusk, probably used in mating fights.

into its immense mouth. The water is expelled, usually by a rolling movement, but the krill get trapped in the fringed baleen and from here they are swallowed.

Some whales are said to be able to hold their breath for over two hours. Although their brains, which are large and active, must have oxygen, their bodies can run short for a while. This is called building up an oxygen debt, but this must be repaid when the animal comes up to breathe and it accounts for the fact that many whales pant noisily when breathing. When they are living in polar seas the air above the water is cold and causes condensation of the water vapour in their breath. This is the major part of the characteristic spout, or blow, of the whale. In toothed whales it forms a single cloud; in the baleen species a double spout, formed from the two separate nostrils of the blowhole, or nose. Whales also often blow out a fatty material which lines the air passages, and this may be seen as a thin cloud, even in warm-water areas. They do not blow out fountains of water. A whale with water in its lungs would drown, as surely as would any other mammal.

At the top of the page are sperm whales seen coming to the surface to 'blow'. The mighty blue whale is the greatest animal ever to have lived. In comparison, it dwarfs the largest modern mammal, the elephant.

Mermaid legends
Legends of sea maidens, singing enchanting songs, combing their golden tresses or cradling their young in their arms, are widespread. The source of these stories is to be found in the sea cows, a group of aquatic mammals of tropical waters, quite unrelated to land cows. Few animals could be less like the romantic image of the mermaid, for these heavyweight, placid creatures have a fish-like form with expanded tail flukes, forelimbs transformed into flippers and hairless bodies, although the face has heavy bristles. The young have a fairly long suckling period and while being fed are supported in their mother's flippers. A short-sighted sailor might, in a poor light, suppose that one of these creatures was akin to the women that he had not seen for a long while, but a closer look would bring disillusion. In order to feed, sea cows must be near to land, for their diet consists of coastal seaweeds.

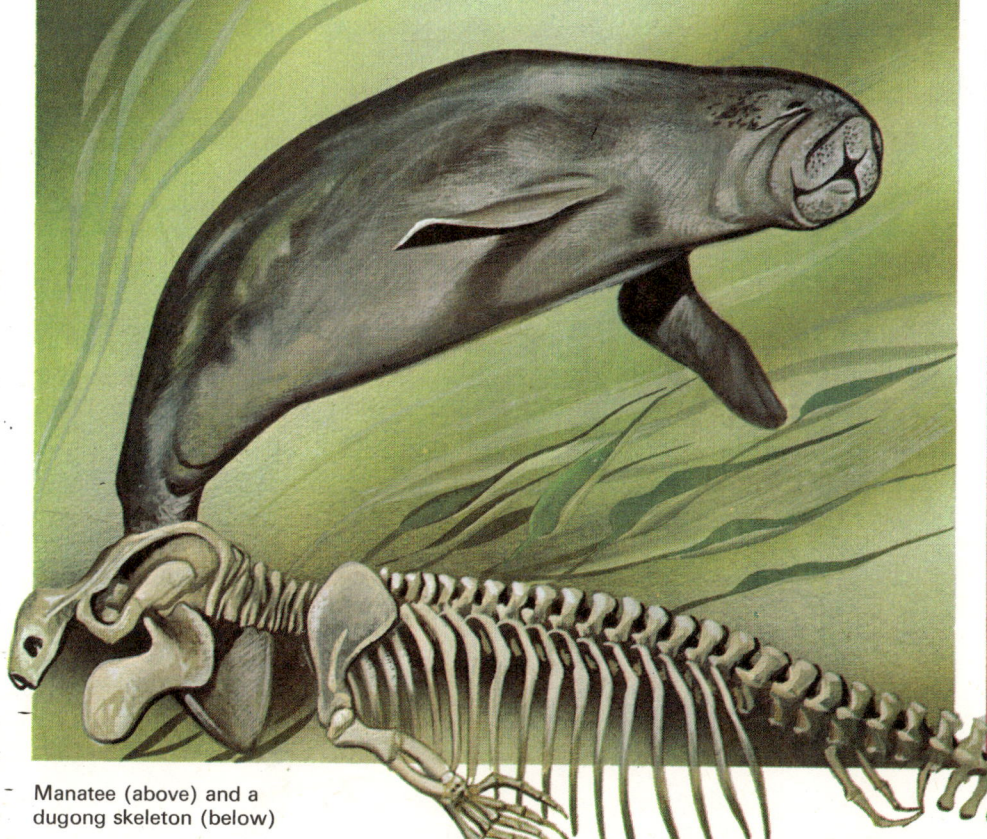

Manatee (above) and a dugong skeleton (below)

Elephant seal

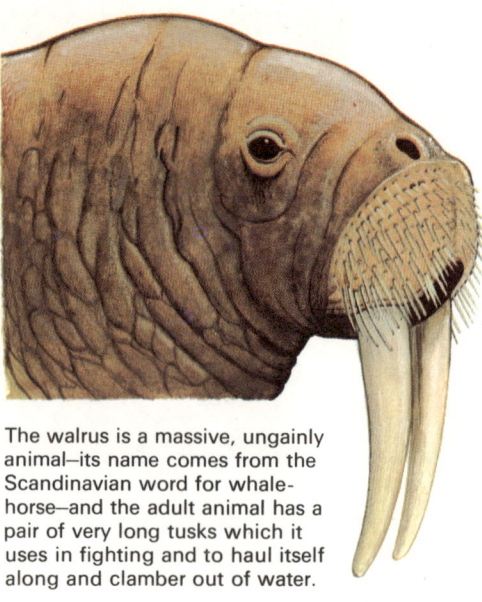

The walrus is a massive, ungainly animal—its name comes from the Scandinavian word for whale-horse—and the adult animal has a pair of very long tusks which it uses in fighting and to haul itself along and clamber out of water.

Seals are divided into two families, the true or earless seals (below) and the eared seals. The latter, such as the fur seal above, have obvious external ears and hind limbs.

The crab-eating seal (above) is the common seal of Antarctic waters. Its coat fades during the year to become a creamy white.

The dark grey, ringed seal lives in the extreme north, mostly in Arctic waters.

Seals

Seals are the third order of aquatic mammals. They are sometimes thought to be closely related to land carnivores but modern research shows that they have a separate ancestry, so they are placed in a special order, called the Pinnepedia.

In seals all four limbs are present, but they are transformed into paddles. In the true seals the hind limbs are twisted backwards and are used in a side-to-side motion in swimming. This is like the action of a fish's tail and the animals swim in a graceful, sinuous way. On land, however, they are helpless and have to hitch themselves along, using their front flippers and a humping, caterpillar-like movement of the body.

The other two groups, the eared seals and the walrus, swim using their large fore-flippers and steer with the hind. They can turn their hind feet under the body and can move on land with a clumsy, galloping gait. All seals have dense hair covering their bodies. In some species this is especially fine and rich and forms a heavy cape over the shoulders. As well as fur, seals have a heavy layer of blubber underneath the skin, which in the case of the elephant seal may be several inches thick.

In spite of their adaptations to water, the seals have to return to land

In Arctic regions seals remain in the area of pack and shelf ice, but since they have to breathe air they keep open holes in the ice. In the Antarctic, Weddell's seal gnaws through the ice as it forms. It is probable that tooth wear eventually prevents some of these seals from keeping their breathing holes open, so many of the older animals drown.

to reproduce. In some polar species they do this on ice floes, but generally they congregate in rookeries on remote rocky shores and islands. The males come ashore first to stake out their breeding territories. There is often a great deal of fighting, which looks and sounds terrifying, the bulls rearing up and roaring, sparring and slashing with their large canine teeth. Injuries are often severe, but fatalities are rare. The male elephant seal, which weighs over two tons, is made more fearsome by his huge inflated snout, which acts as a sounding box for his roars.

In some cases females are allowed to pass into the territory of any male they choose. In others, the females are herded into the harems of the biggest males and not allowed to leave. When the pups are born the mothers are permitted to return to the sea to feed, for they must keep up their reserves so they can provide their young with plenty of fat-rich milk. Soon after this they mate again and although in some cases they stay ashore, feeding their cubs for nearly three months, in others they return to the sea in about three weeks.

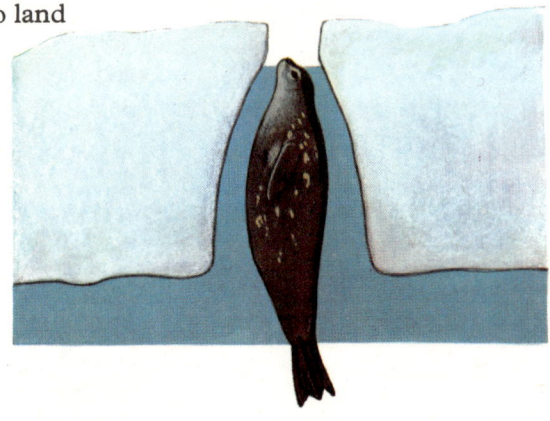

Hoofed Mammals

In some plant-eating animals which have no defence from their enemies but their speed and endurance when they run away, the toenails have developed into sheathing hooves. These protect the feet and enable them to travel without damage for long distances over hard ground. Two great groups of hoofed animals exist, those with an odd number of toes and those which have two or four toes to each of their feet. The odd-toed hoofed mammals include all of the horse-like animals, the tapirs and the rhinoceroses.

Wild Horses

The horse-like species are creatures of the plains. They live in herds and are extremely wary, their keen senses of smell and hearing and magnificent eyesight informing them of any danger. Each leg narrows to a single hard hoof and every step that they take is of maximum length, for they are, in effect, running on the tips of their toes. A single young one is born at a time and is capable of keeping up with the herd shortly after birth. Grass is their chief food and to combat the wear of such a harsh diet, the teeth are open-rooted and go on growing throughout the animals' lives.

The true wild horses of eastern Asia are now extremely rare, although in late prehistoric times they were probably the commonest open-country creatures from western Europe across the plains of Asia. It is from these animals that the domestic breeds of horse have been derived. The 'half asses' of western Asia and the true asses of North Africa are also nearly extinct. The zebras of Africa are the only abundant surviving members of the group. These are adapted to tropical grasslands, where they may still be seen in some numbers.

Tapirs are forest-living animals, which have three toes on their hind feet, but four, including one very small one, on the front feet. They are found in Malaya and in central and tropical South America. They are shy, solitary animals, taking refuge in water if they are chased by any enemies.

Rhinoceroses

The rhinoceroses are the heavy-weight members of the group. In distant prehistoric times there were many kinds of rhinoceros; now there are only five, of which three are in serious danger of extinction. All are large, grey, heavy-skinned animals, distinguished by one or sometimes

Zebras were known as horse-tigers by the ancient Romans, who used them in circuses. The various breeds have their own distinctive striped patterns.

The development of the one-toed leg of horses is one of the best known of all fossil stories. The earliest horse-like animal had four toes on its front feet and three on the back. Gradually the outer toes fused into one.

Malayan tapir

Despite its name, the white rhino is really a dusty grey.

177

two horns on the end of the nose. These are not true horn but are made of compressed hair. Most rhinoceroses are forest or bush animals, with pointed upper lips which aid them in browsing leaves from trees. The African white rhino (white being a corruption of the Afrikaans word for wide and having no reference to the colour of the animal) is a grazer and feeds on grasses in fairly open country.

The even-toed hoofed animals are a much more flourishing group than the odd-toed, and the vast majority of medium to large-sized, plant-eating mammals belong to it. Although many of them are now rare few are so close to extinction as the wild horses or the rhinos.

Even-toed animals have also gone up on to the tips of their toes but the weight is borne by the third and fourth toe of each foot. Each toe carries a large nail, giving the typical cloven-hoofed appearance of the group. In many cases the fifth and second toes are also present, but they rarely take any of the animal's weight. The difference in weight-bearing toes is reflected in completely different systems of balance in the two groups of hoofed animals. This shows in many features of their life; an easy one to observe is the way in which the animals rise from a lying position. A horse gets up fore feet first; a cow hind feet first. When they graze, many even-toed animals stoop down to the herbage, putting their weight on the 'wrists' of their front legs, something never seen in the odd-toed.

Pigs and Hippos

Pigs are the least specialised members of the order. They are medium-sized animals found throughout the forested regions of the world except Australasia. Hippos, which now survive only in Africa, are also structurally primitive but highly adapted to life in lakes or slow-flowing rivers.

Camels

Camels, which are found in Africa and Asia, are closely related to the llamas and vicuñas of South America. These are all animals of arid areas with two toes on their tough, padded feet, and thick protective fur which insulates them against great heat and the cold of desert nights. The camel has the ability to survive long periods without food or water. This led to their being of great value as a means of transport in desert regions. In Africa the one-humped camel, or dromedary, is found. This animal is totally domesticated and no wild ancestors are known. In Asia the two-humped Bactrian camel occurs. Recently, wild relatives of this domestic species have been found, but they are extremely rare.

When nothing else is available camels can feed on dry thorn scrub, digesting what they eat very completely by means of their complex three-chambered stomach. When water is scarce, they are capable of much greater endurance without it than any other mammals, but when it becomes available again they make up the lack very rapidly. A camel may drink more than 130 litres (thirty gallons) at one time under such circumstances.

All the rest of the even-toed animals share a number of characteristics not found in pigs, hippos or camels. The most obvious is the development on the heads of most of the males and some females, of bony outgrowths—antlers in deer and horns in sheep, cattle and antelopes. They all have a more complex digestive system, gathering their food very rapidly and then retiring to some safe spot for digestion. During this, they return the food to the mouth from the first, or storage, compartment of a four-chambered stomach to chew the cud.

Deer

The deer are the major even-toed group of the temperate world. Although there are some tropical species the majority are animals of deciduous and coniferous woodlands and the most northerly species, the reindeer (caribou of North America), migrates into the tundra for the summer months. They are mostly herd animals, with, in some cases, shifting groups of males and females at different times of the year.

The antlers of deer, present in the males only, except in the reindeer where the females have small growths,

The okapi is a rare Congo animal, discovered by Europeans in 1900.

When it drinks, the giraffe must spread its legs wide apart so that its head can reach the water.

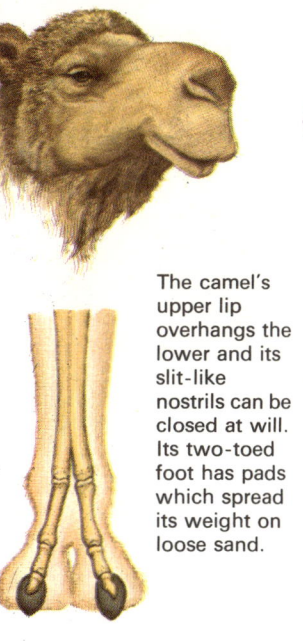

The camel's upper lip overhangs the lower and its slit-like nostrils can be closed at will. Its two-toed foot has pads which spread its weight on loose sand.

are bony outgrowths from permanent knobs on the skull, called the pedicles. In the young deer the antlers are small and simple but they are shed and regrown annually, and as the animal ages they become bigger and more complex. This is a considerable strain on the system. Deer which are poorly fed usually grow small antlers, and among red deer an abnormal male without antlers is usually a bigger and heavier beast than the stags which have them.

It is likely that antlers evolved as a device for spreading scent during the mating season, or rut. Now this has become a secondary purpose and the main use is in the battles waged by the males for mates. Fighting stags lock antlers and push at each other. When one feels that he can no longer compete, a sideways movement allows him to disengage and run away. In spite of the noise of deer battles, fatalities are rare, for the winner remains with the harem for which he has been fighting and the loser will not return.

Giraffes

Giraffes are tropical relatives of the deer. On their curiously shaped heads are bony outgrowths which are in effect pedicles, very occasionally

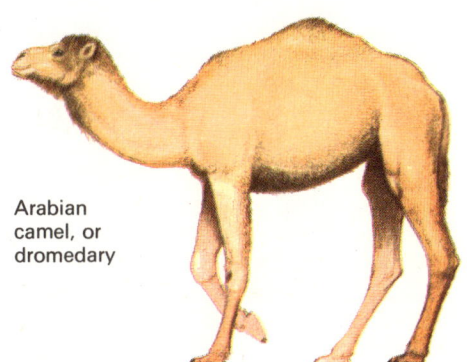

Arabian camel, or dromedary

The Bactrian camel has a double hump. With its shorter legs and bulkier build it is better suited to the rocky, hilly country of Central Asia than to the sandy deserts of Arabia.

The distinctive feature of the deer family is the branched growth on the skull called antlers, but not all deer possess them. Antlers grow from bony knobs in the skull and are shed each year when they are developed to their fullest extent.

carrying small antlers. Some prehistoric giraffes had huge antlers, but these creatures are now quite extinct. When they fight, giraffes swing their heads against each other. The force of the blows must be considerable, for the bone is heavy and thickens during the animal's life; an old male giraffe may have a head weighing eleven kilograms (twenty-four pounds), but in spite of this, little damage seems to be done. Their long legs and necks, which have the same number of joints as other mammals, enable them to reach the upper foliage of the trees of the savannah country where they live. Their tongues are also extraordinarily long and can pluck tiny leaves from among the thorns carried by many trees.

Drinking is for a giraffe a most difficult matter. It must either spread its legs or bend its wrist joints so that its head may reach the water. There are other problems too in having such a long neck, one of them being the control of blood to and from the brain. Giraffes have special valves in the blood vessels of their necks to keep the flow steady whether the head is up or down. Many variations on the colour camouflage patterns of the giraffe have been described, but there is only one species found (in suitable areas) throughout most of Africa.

The cattle, sheep, goats and antelopes are all horned animals. They are found in suitable country throughout the world, except Australia, and have colonised many types of habitat, including plains, swamps, forests and mountains. They usually produce only one young at a time, and it is active soon after birth. All northern domestic cattle are descended from the aurochs, an animal common in Europe in prehistoric times, but extinct since the seventeenth century.

The water buffalo is another cow-like horned animal widely domesticated in the Far East, but the cape buffalo of Africa is one of the most feared of game animals. It is said to be aggressive and dangerous, especially if frightened or wounded. The yak is a mountain animal of Central Asia, capable of surviving in barren uplands but not able to thrive in lush lowland areas. In domestication it may be crossed with cattle, but the pure form is used for milk, meat, hides and transport in the upper heights of the Himalayas.

In Europe, man's long occupation of the steppes has removed all large wild animals, but when white men first went to North America they found one large mammal dominant on the prairies. This was the American bison, often called the buffalo. It is estimated that the herds of bison numbered over 60 million animals in the days before the white man. Moving over the prairies, they were central to the fertility of the plains and the key figure in the economy of plants, other animals and man, for the Plains Indians had developed a way of life totally dependent on them. Partly in order to clear the land for agriculture and partly to subdue the Indians, a great campaign of destruction of the bison went on during the nineteenth century. Whole herds were destroyed; in many cases the carcasses and skins remained unused.

Sheep and Goats
Sheep and goats are also animals of arid upland areas. The sheep, which have huge curved horns, are hairy and do not have the thick fleeces of advanced domestic breeds. They are sure-footed creatures capable of taking to the highest slopes when danger threatens. The bighorn sheep of North America, which is the only sheep in the New World, is found at high levels in the northern Rockies.

Goats have horns which may be very large, but they are scimitar shaped and do not spiral. In some of the species of ibex they may measure more than one and a half metres (five feet) long. They have been prized

trophies for hunters, a fact which has contributed to their decline throughout their range. They are stocky looking animals, yet they have incredible agility and can find footholds on almost sheer rock faces.

Antelopes
The antelopes are the largest and most varied group of the even-toed mammals. They are all found in the Old World, chiefly in Africa where they range in size from the tiny pygmy antelopes of dense scrubland in East Africa to the eland, which stands up to 1·8 metres (six feet) at the shoulder. Almost all are good runners and some can make spectacular leaps as well. This is one of the features which has made them difficult to domesticate, for they are capable of jumping out of almost any enclosure. Most of the antelopes are herd animals, sometimes congregating in vast numbers, especially when on migration. Although they have been much reduced in recent years, some species are still widespread and numerous. The horns of antelopes are extremely varied in shape, ranging from the tiny straight points of the dik-diks to the knurled scimitars of the giant sable antelope, which may measure well over one and a half metres (five feet) in length. In some cases, such as the kudu, they form an open, corkscrew-like spiral, in others the curve is lyre-shaped while the oryx species generally have long straight horns.

In the past, antelopes were regarded as game animals to be hunted, or destroyed and replaced with domestic species if the land was to be farmed. Now in many places attempts are being made to tame them for the milk and meat which they could give. They are immune to many of the diseases which can kill off introduced farm animals and some species may be the future domestic animals of the tropics. An Asiatic antelope, the saiga, has, by careful conservation, been brought from the brink of extinction to large numbers again, and controlled cropping is now practised.

Antelopes have evolved a great variety of horns. The species seen here are (left to right) gnu, nilgai, kudu, sable antelope, oryx, hartebeeste and eland.

Elephants

Elephants are the largest land animals of the present day. Living in herds in the tropics of Africa and Asia, they are the remnants of a worldwide group which at one time colonised every continent except Australia and Antarctica, and occupied all types of environment including the tundra. Elephants are unmistakable; apart from their large size no other animal has tusks or trunk as they do. Its trunk is the elephant's lifeline. Through it he breathes and tests the air for alien scents; with it he collects food, ranging from berries which can be plucked individually with the sensitive finger-like tip, to whole trees which may be broken down. The trunk is used for drinking and for picking up dry earth with which the elephant dusts its body, probably as a protection against flies. The tusks are open-rooted incisor teeth which grow throughout the life of the animal; they tend to be larger in males than in females. The largest recorded was over $3\frac{1}{2}$ metres (twelve feet) in length and weighed over 90 kilograms (200 pounds). They are used as levers when trees are to be broken or uprooted for food; for boring for water, or digging up earth which will be eaten because it contains necessary minerals, and in defence.

Plant-eaters

Elephants are herbivores, eating a wide range of plants. They grind their food with large teeth placed far back in the mouth. These eventually wear out, but others grow in their place. In the course of an elephant's life it has twenty-six teeth—two tusks and twenty-four grinding teeth. For all of its life an elephant is, in effect, teething and when its last molars wear out the animal can no longer feed efficiently, so its lifespan is to a large extent determined by its teeth. Elephants need to eat a great deal and spend much of every day feeding. They may travel long distances looking for food and water, which they must also have in large quantities. Although an adult elephant has no enemies other than man, lions or tigers might attack the young and elephants are always alert to this possibility, their senses of hearing and smell in particular warning them of any danger.

The principal differences between the African elephant (above) and the Asiatic, or Indian, elephant (below) are the greater bulk and bigger ears of the African species and the high, domed forehead of the Asiatic.

Family group of African elephants

181

Carnivores

The carnivores form an extremely varied group of animals, unified by their adaptations for feeding on flesh. They range in size from tiny weasels to giant bears; the pattern of their coats may be spotted, striped or in plain colours; they may have long tails or no tails, but the fact that they are hunters gives them a number of features in common. Many of these can be seen in the skull, which always has a fairly large brain case, for carnivores are intelligent animals and must be able to outwit their prey. The eyes are large and usually point well forwards, which gives them a fair degree of three-dimensional vision, necessary for pouncing on and catching prey.

In most carnivores there are six small nipping teeth across the front of the jaw. These are followed by the canine teeth, which are long and pointed. They are used for slashing and in some cases for gripping so that the teeth in the back of the mouth can work to better advantage. Behind the canines, the pre-molar and molar teeth are generally narrow and give a cutting edge. In most carnivores one cheek tooth is greatly enlarged for slicing action. The jaw-hinge of carnivores is a very tight one, allowing no sideways movement as in ourselves or in most of the plant eaters: instead the jaws work like scissors and the typical meat eater cuts its food into pieces just small enough to swallow, and bolts it down.

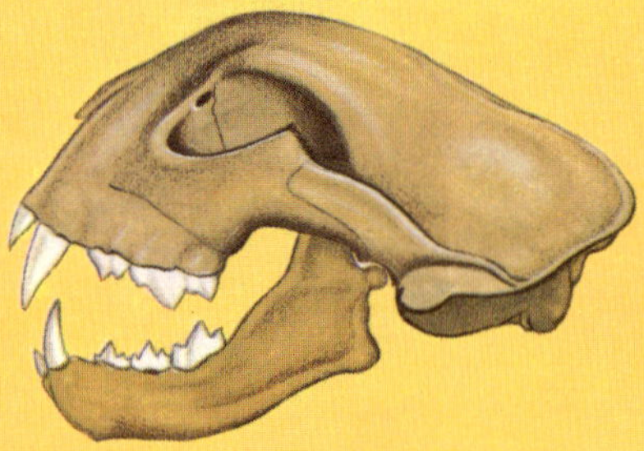

The carnivores may be classified into two main groups of animals: those related to the dogs and those nearer to the cats. The dogs, bears, pandas and weasels are related, while the cats, hyenas and civets form the other group. Each of these groups has, over a long period of time, followed particular lines of development.

Over short distances the cheetah (top) can probably run faster than any other mammal. The snarling tiger (right) reveals the enlarged canine teeth typical of carnivores, seen also in the skull above.

Male lion

The Cat Group

The cat group, which contains the 'big cats' such as tigers, lions and leopards, also includes many small creatures such as the ocelot, the Scottish wildcat and the domestic cat, which is probably of Egyptian origin. Cats all hunt their prey by stalking, followed by a brief sprint. The bored domestic cat hunting sparrows and the lion or cheetah after antelopes use the same technique. The cheetah, which is said to be the speediest of all mammals, is reputed to touch 110 kilometres (70 miles) per hour, but it never keeps up this speed for long. If it cannot catch its prey within a sprint of 180 metres (200 yards) it gives up and later tries to stalk closer before giving its presence away with a speedy dash. For this type of hunting, cats need, and have, good eyesight and excellent hearing, but their sense of smell is not so good as that of the dogs.

Members of the cat family often kill using their feet, which are armed with large, usually retractile claws. They are mostly solitary animals, but an exception is to be found in the lion, which is social, living in groups or prides of up to twenty animals. Lions, or more usually lionesses, may hunt communally and so are able to bring down larger and more dangerous prey than could be killed by a single animal. Lions are now found only in Africa and a very few in India. In the historic past the areas of the Middle East which are now mainly desert were sufficiently fertile to support many animals and the lions that preyed on them, but these conditions no longer exist.

The Weasel Family
Central to the weasel family, which is found mainly in the northern temperate parts of the world, are the weasels themselves and stoats. They are small animals with long bodies and short legs and an undulating way of moving. The female weasel is a tiny creature. Both she and her mate are able to enter mouseholes to catch their main food. Stoats are slightly larger and hunt bigger prey, especially rabbits. Often a stoat will mesmerise a rabbit by leaping and gambolling, but will come closer until it is near enough to catch it. Both stoats and weasels sometimes keep their young with them until they are nearly adult, and this gives rise to stories of packs of these animals hunting together.

With the exception of foxes, dogs are highly social animals, with a family and pack structure of considerable complexity. The domestic dog, which is almost certainly descended from wolf ancestors, shows this to some extent, but in most cases grown-up dogs have behaviour patterns more suited to wolf cubs than to adult animals. This can be seen in many features, but an obvious one is the noisiness of dogs compared to wolves. Wolf cubs yap, but the adults, apart from the howling parties which sometimes precede a hunt, are relatively silent animals. Domestic dogs tend to be noisy at all times, a feature which could easily lead to disaster for a wild animal.

All carnivores, whether solitary or social, have a prolonged childhood. During this period they may be reared solely by their mother, as with bears or tigers; by both parents, as with foxes; or as members of a pack in which aunts and uncles play a large part in their upbringing, as with wolves. During this time they are taught the main things that they should know—how to make a kill and how to defend themselves, for example. In spite of this, all carnivores

Hyenas
Hyenas are scavengers, living on the plains of Africa. They have powerful jaws with teeth strong enough to crack the leg bones of antelopes, which is often all that a lion will leave of its kill. If there are no pickings from the remains of meals of the bigger predators, hyenas will hunt for themselves, often catching zebra. The civets and their relatives are short-legged hunters of the tropics. They feed on a wide variety of food, including in many instances snakes and rodents, so they are often welcome in the region of homesteads.

The Dog Family
The members of the dog family, which includes wolves, jackals, coyotes and foxes, are all long-distance runners, tiring their prey and pulling it down after a chase which may have covered several miles. All of the dogs are medium to small-sized animals; even a large wolf may be only one quarter the weight of a lion. They all tend to have long legs, a good sense of hearing and a very good sense of smell, which they may need to use when hunting.

eat a certain amount of plant material. In some, such as bears or badgers, it is a very high proportion of their total food; in others, such as cats or weasels, it is a small proportion only. But meat by itself is not an adequate diet and some plant food is always taken.

Bears

Most carnivores are not large animals. There is usually an abundance of plant food to keep big herbivores (plant eaters) going, but the quantities of meat required for a large flesh eater may well not be available. The only really large carnivores are the bears and these animals have taken to a more varied diet, as can be seen by their flat-topped teeth, with none of the meat-slicing ability of the other members of the order, although they will often eat flesh in preference to other things.

Bears are found chiefly in the northern hemisphere and can be considered as belonging to three main groups: the brown bears, the black bears and the polar bear. The brown bears are to be found in North America, Europe and Asia and although they may vary considerably in size they are not significantly different from each other. The black bears are more varied. They include the American black bears and a number of Asiatic species, including the sloth bear of India. The polar bear is an Arctic species, spending much of its time hunting seals on the northern pack ice, often floating far out to sea as the floes break up.

One of the rarest mammals is the giant panda which lives in China and Tibet.

Polar bear

Brown bear

Bears are distinguished from all other carnivores by the nature of their teeth. Their molars are adapted for grinding, and the crowns are almost flat. They are best seen in a typical bear skull, demonstrating the vegetarian nature of the bear's diet.

Bears feed hugely during the summer and autumn months, when they become very fat. They then den up for the winter in a warm safe place, and snooze through until next spring, but they do not truly hibernate. It is at this time that bear cubs are born. Relative to the size of their mothers, they are the smallest young of any of the placental mammals. A female grizzly, weighing over 220 kilograms (500 pounds), will give birth to cubs weighing a few ounces each. They remain with her in the den, suckling, but making relatively small demands on her until the end of the winter, by which time they are able to come out and begin to feed themselves, although they will probably remain with their mother for three years in all.

The Giant Panda

The giant panda looks bear-like, but this is because, as with the bears, it is a carnivore which has taken to a diet consisting largely of plants. It is one of the rarest of mammals, being found only in the bamboo thicket zone of high mountains in south-west China. The red panda, which is smaller, has a wider distribution through the south-eastern Himalayas. It feeds on fruit, small animals and birds' eggs. Both of these animals are related to a group of American creatures. They include the raccoon, which can climb trees but feeds in streams on freshwater crabs or shells; the coatimundi, which is a forest animal feeding on vegetation and small animals including insects; and the kinkajou, which feeds entirely on soft fruit. This strange creature looks more like a monkey than anything else, but it is structurally a carnivore.

Red panda

Primates

This name has been given to a group of animals whose members at first sight appear to have little in common. They include some animals which are little different from the insectivores, as well as lemurs, monkeys, apes and man. Many of the features which are used to distinguish them are found also in other animals, but not in the combination in which they occur in the primates. These features include an enlarged brain case and complex brain; forward-looking eyes contained in bony orbits in the skull, hands and feet on which there are five digits, and nails rather than claws on at least some of the fingers and toes.

Tree Shrews and Lemurs

The tree shrews are the most primitive of the primates. As their name suggests, they are insectivore-like in many ways, but their brain structure is similar to that of some of the lemurs, and their hands and feet show some development towards a grasping ability, in spite of having claws rather than nails on each toe. Squirrel-like in appearance they have a degree of activity and curiosity which accords with primates rather than any other group.

The lemurs are more advanced in their primate characteristics. They are all rather small nocturnal animals, with a coat of thick fur and a long bushy tail. Their eyes point fairly well forwards, but in most cases they have a distinct snout, which means rather poor three-dimensional sight. They are found only in the Old World, especially in Madagascar where it seems that isolated populations of lemurs developed along specialised lines for a long period of time. Some of these animals are agile forest dwellers; others, such as the mouse lemurs, are small animals of drier areas.

The Aye-aye

The aye-aye is a strange creature adapted to feeding on grubs in dead wood. It has chisel-like teeth in the front of its mouth for tearing the wood open and a long thin finger for hooking out any grubs that may be there. In Africa the lemurs are represented by the bush babies and the potto and in India by the lorises. These animals are small, slender, tail-less creatures, moving through the branches of their forest home with great deliberation and slowness. They hold very firmly on to branches with hands and feet in which the index finger and second toes have become much reduced. Once they have decided to grasp anything firmly they are very difficult to dislodge.

The man-like primates include the monkeys, apes and man. There is sufficient obvious similarity between

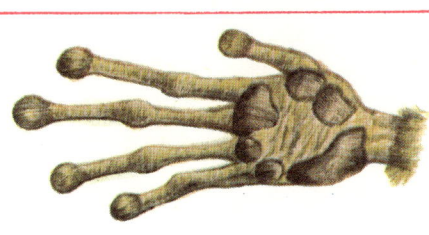

The tarsier is an animal from a once abundant group of early primates now surviving in south-east Asia. It shows the development of characteristics which in the past led to the higher members of this group. The tarsier is awake at night and very active, leaping from twig to twig in the forest, grasping and hanging on with hands and feet. The hands of the tarsier set the scene for later primate hands. All five digits are well grown, the thumb is separate from the rest of the fingers and opposable, so that objects can be grasped and held firmly and, if need be, examined. Each finger has a nail and beneath it a fleshy pad, which adds to the sensitivity of the finger tip. The skin of the pad is deeply creased and forms a friction area which enables the animal to gain a grip, even on extremely smooth surfaces.

The tarsier (above) and the slender loris (left) are primitive members of the primate group to which man himself belongs.

these three for the relationship to be clear, but man is not the descendant of any of the living species of ape or monkey. A common ancestor with the apes must be looked for among fossils which date back 30 million years; for an ancestor shared with monkeys we would have to go back nearer 50 million years.

New World Monkeys

Monkeys are essentially tree-living creatures of tropical forests. A few species, such as the baboons, spend a great deal of time on the ground and some, such as the langurs of the Himalayas and the monkeys of Japan, can survive in cold climates, but these are exceptions to the general rule. The monkeys of South America are thought to be more primitive because of such features as their dense fur and their long tails, which are never reduced in length. They have a larger number of teeth than the Old World monkeys. Many species carry claws rather than nails on at least some of their fingers and toes.

Some of the South American monkeys have prehensile tails, which means they can be used to grasp things. Monkeys support their whole weight on this extra 'limb' as they swing through the trees. Most of them are social, living in family groups and travelling through the treetops. Howler monkeys make themselves obvious by their howling concerts, in which the sound may carry for several miles through the forest. The capuchin monkeys, so called because of the cowl-like arrangement of hair on the top of their heads, are the commonest of South American forms and used to be popular pets. Marmosets are also kept as pets, but these smallest of monkeys are very delicate and seldom survive long in cold parts of the world.

Old World Monkeys

The monkeys of the Old World are generally regarded as being more closely related to apes and man. They have the same number of teeth as their bigger relatives, they are less hairy than the South American forms and may have short tails, which are never prehensile. A number of species are thumbless, for the hand is used as a hook with which to hang on to branches, but where the thumb is present the hands can be used to hold and handle things as we can ourselves.

Among the common Old World monkeys are the macaques, including the rhesus monkeys of India, well known as laboratory and zoo animals. Related to them are the barbary ape of North Africa and Gibraltar and the crab-eating macaque which lives in mangrove swamps and feeds mainly on crustaceans. Also related are some small forest-dwelling African monkeys, such as the mona and the diana monkeys. Baboons are found on the ground in non-forested areas in Africa. These are extremely social animals, living in large, mobile communities. Their snout is more dog-like than in other monkeys and they are armed with large canine teeth which will be used against any attacker.

Among the monkeys with small thumbs are the beautiful colobus monkeys of Africa, and the langurs of south-east Asia, some of which are high-altitude animals. It has been suggested that the footprints of one of these may account for stories of the 'abominable snowman' of the Himalayan Mountains.

A comparison of the hands and feet of man and his primate relatives shows that man uses his hind limbs exclusively for locomotion, while most other primates use their forelimbs as well. A comparison of the hands of a tree shrew, a South American monkey and man (top to bottom) show a progression in size and flexibility.

The walking posture of monkeys, apes and man show a progressive development towards upright locomotion on two legs. Monkeys, such as baboons, which spend a good deal of their time on the ground, walk on all fours, placing the hands palms down at each stride. When walking the great apes may be capable of a few paces upright but soon drop on to their front limbs. The knuckles and backs of the fingers are used for this but never the flat of the hands. In man, a fully upright pose on two legs has been evolved.

Gibbons are very agile and move rapidly through the forests, swinging from branch to branch.

Gorilla

Apes

The true apes are all larger animals with no visible tail, and with the exception of the gibbon a rather thin coat of hair. They are all forest-dwellers, swinging through the trees by their arms, which are very long and strong. Their legs by comparison are small and weak. The hands of apes have become specialised hooks for hanging on to branches; their feet, however, have retained much flexibility and they can hold and examine objects with their big toes to a much greater extent than they can with their thumbs.

The several species of gibbon are all found in south-east Asia. They are the smallest and lightest in weight of the apes and are the most highly acrobatic, swinging and leaping at very great speed through the treetops. They are capable of running upright on the ground or along a big branch, holding their arms out to balance themselves. They are noisy, sociable animals, with few natural enemies in their forest home.

The orang-utan, which comes from Sumatra and Borneo, is by contrast a slow-moving heavyweight animal, keeping to the trees as much as possible, for it cannot move easily on the ground. Its food is mainly fruit and some invertebrates.

Chimps and Gorillas

Chimpanzees and gorillas are both African species. The gorilla is the largest of the apes and may weigh as much as 220 kilograms (500 pounds). Chimpanzees are much smaller, and more agile. Both travel through the forests in family parties, active during the daytime and sleeping at night in nests made in the trees of woven branches. On the ground both normally have to support themselves on their knuckles, although chimpanzees may run a few paces on their hind legs alone.

Man's close relationship with them cannot be denied, for he shares with them many bodily similarities, including the same blood group system and the fact that both can catch the same diseases. Man's treatment of his nearest relatives has been far from good, and all of the great apes are declining in numbers as a result of the destruction of their habitat. Many animals have been captured as specimens for zoos or laboratories. Conservationists hope that a complete ban may be imposed on taking these animals from their forests or we shall destroy for ever creatures that we are still far from understanding and which almost certainly have much to teach us about ourselves.

Orang-utan

New World, or American, monkeys have a flat-faced look, with nostrils well separated. The Old World, or African and Asiatic, kinds have a nose in which the nostrils are close together, suggesting the prominent noses typical of human beings.

Index

Aardvark, 172
acorns, 50
adder, **145**, **169**
Aepyornis, 86
agave, 64
Age of Fishes, 76
agriculture, 8, 9, 43–6, 54–5, 56–7, 66–7; machinery, 46, **46**
albatross, 151, **151**
alder, 38
algae, 10, 11, **16**, 18, 22. See also seaweed
alizarin, 64
alligators, 147, **147**
Allosaurus, 79
almond, 50
alpine regions, 41
Amanita, **19**
amber, 73
amino-acids, 10
ammonites, 72, 75, 80, 113
amoeba, 88, **88**, 110
amphibians, 11, 76, **91**, 129, 138–40; prehistoric, 71, 76, 77, 78
anchovy, 132
anemone, **29**
angiosperms, 11, **15**, 16, 25, 27
angler fish, 135–6, **135**
Anguillidae, 133
anhinga, **155**
animals: behaviour, 93–8; characteristics, 33, 88–9; classification, 90–2; difference from plants, 13; domestic, **18**, 99–103; evolution, 68–87; experiment with, 106–7, **106**, **107**; in space, 107, **107**; kingdom of, **91**; pets, 100, **103**, 115, **115**, **122**, **123**; primitive, 109, 110
annelids, **91**, **108**, 109, **110**
Anning, Mary, 80
anteater, giant, 172, **172**; scaly, 172; spiny, see echidna
antelopes, 97, **104**, 180, **180**
anther, 28, **36**
antibiotics, 18, 62
antlers, 178–9, **179**
ants, 119–21, **120**
apes, 122, 185–6, 187, **187**
aphids, 123
apothecaries, 60–1
apple, 50, **50**
arachnids, 11, **108**, **108**, 125–7, **126**, **127**
Archaeopteryx, 71, **82**, 83
archer fish, 130
Arctic tern, 96, 166
argali, 100
Aristolochia, **39**
armadillos, 172, **172**
armeria, **49**
armoured animals, 75, 82, 142–3, 172
Arsinoitherium, 85, **85**
arthropods, **91**, 115–25, **115–25**; prehistoric, 77
ash tree, 31, 41, **58**, 60
Asia Minor, 62
asses, 177
auks, **150**, 155
Aulious, **114**
aurochs, 99–100, 180
Australopithecus, 87
aye-aye, 185

Baboon, 167, **167**, 186, **186**
bacteria, 11, 17, 33, 62
badger, 184
baleen whales, 124, 174–5, **175**
Baluchitherium, 85
bamboo, 30–1
banana, 30, 31, 50, **50**
banded brush beetle, **123**
Banks, Sir Joseph, 43
baobab tree, **40**
barbel, **134**, 135
barley, 44, **44**, 45
basil, **52**
bass, 136
bats, 107, 123, 173, **173**
Beagle, **143**
beaks, 148, 162
beans, **33**, 51
bears, 184, **184**
beaver, **170**, 171
bêche-de-mer, 114
beech, 34, 41, **58**, 66
bees, **96**, 97, 119–20, **120**
beet, 51
beetles, 121–2, **67**, **123**
belemnites, 72, 75, 80, 113
belladonna, **61**
berries, 50
biological control (of pests), 118–19
birch, 34; silver, **31**
birchir, 132
bird of paradise flower, **39**
birds, 11, 71, 83, 86, **91**, 94, 96–8, 103, 107, 148–66; eggs, 163, **163**; flight, 107; flightless, 149–50; game, 158–9; mating instinct, 94; migration, 96, 166; nestlings, **96**, 98; nests, 160, 162–3, **163**; of prey, **155**, 156–7; perching, 162–5, **165**; pets, **103**; prehistoric, 71, 83, 86; song, 162; tropical, **155**, 160–2; water, 151–5
birds' nest soup, 160
bird tables, 164–5
bison, 105, **100**, **180**; European, 105; Stone Age, 100

bittern, 98, 153
bivalves, 112, **114**
blackbird, 163, 164, **165**; egg, **163**; nest 163
black cock, 158
black skimmer, **155**
blindworms, 138
blockboard, **60**
bluebell, 32, 41
blue tit, 98, 164–5, **165**; egg, **163**
Boletus, **19**
bonito, 137
botany, 65–7
Bovista, **19**
brachiopods, 72, 75
Brachiosaurus, 78
bracts, 27
brain, 128
Brazilian weevil, **123**
breadfruit, **43**
bream, 135, 136
broccoli, 51
Brontosaurus, 78, 79, 83
Bronze Age, 101
Brown, 'Capability', 47–8
bryophytes, 11, **14**, 16, 22–3
bubonic plague, 122
buddleia, 117
budgerigar, **103**, 160, **161**
buds, 27, **27**, 49
buffaloes, 180
Buffon, Georges de, 10
bugs, 122–3
bulbs, **33**, 49
bulfinch, 164; egg, **163**
bulrush, 37
bush babies, 185
bustards, 150
buttercup, 14, **29**
butterflies, 117–18, **117**, **118**; caterpillars, **118**; eggs, **118**; migration, 96, 118
butterfly fish, **130**, 137
butterwort, 38, **38**
button shell (*Umbonium giganteum*), 114
buzzard, 157

Cabbage, 51, **51**
cactus, **29**, 41
caiman, **147**
Calcarea, **91**
California poppy, 49
Calotaenia celsia moth, **119**
calyx, 27
cambium, 29, 31
Cambrian period, 11, 70, 73–4, 124
cameleopard, **90**
camels, 178, **179**
camouflage, insects, 115, **115**, 117
Canada, 56, 73
canary, **103**, 107
capercaillie, 158
capitulum, 32
capsicums, 53
capybara, 170, **170**, 171
caraway, 53
carbon dioxide, 36, **37**
Carboniferous period, **8**, 11, 76–7, **76**
caribou, 178
carp, 134–5, **134**
carpels, 24, 27
cassowary, 149
castor oil, 62
catfish, 134–5
catkins, 32
cats, **95**, 102, **103**, 182, **182**, 184; sabre-toothed, **84**, 85, 86
cattle, 99–100, **102**, 180
cauliflower, 51
caviare, 132
cedar 60
cedar of Lebanon, **26**
cells, 8, 12, 36–7, 39; nucleus, 12, 39; wall, 39
cellulose, 37
centaur, 101
centipedes, 108, 127, **127**
cephalopods, 74, 75, 112–13, **112**
cereals, 44–5, **44**, **45**
chaffinch, 98, 164, **165**; egg, **163**
chalk, 82
chameleon, 144–5, **144**
char, **134**
Charles, *Viscount* Townshend, 46
cheetah, 182, **182**
chemosynthesis, 17
cherry, 50
chervil, **52**
chestnut, 66
chimaeras, 131
chimpanzee, 88, 187, **187**
China, 56, **60**, 61, 62, 64
chipboard, **60**
chitin, 123–4
chitons (placophora), 112, 114
chives, **52**
Chlamydomonas, 22
chlorophyll, 21, 36, **37**
chloroplasts, 36
Chondrichthyes, **91**
chordates, **91**, 129
chromoplasts, 36
chub, **134**, 135
cicada, **122**, 123
ciliates, 110
Ciliophora, **91**
cinchona bark, **61**
civets, 183
Clavaria, **19**
clematis, **49**
clover, 46
cloves, 53

club mosses, 11, **23**, 24–5, 77
club root, 67
coal, 12, 23, 63, 76–7; -tar, 64
coatimundi, 184
coca leaves, **61**
cochineal, 122
cockatoos, 160, **161**
cockle, 112, 114, **114**
cockroaches, 115
cocoa, 51, **53**
coconut, 32, 38, 50, **50**, 56, 118–19
coconut crab, 124
cod, 136, 137
coelacanth, 70–1, 75–6, **136**
coelenterates, **91**, **108**, 111, **111**
coffee plant, 43, 51
Columbus, Christopher, 56
commensalism, 124
common morrel, **19**
common polybody, **23**
common wentletrap, **114**
Compositae, 31, 32
condors, **155**, 156
cones, 24, 25–6, **25**, **26**, 27
conifers, 24–6, **24**, **25**, **26**, 41
constrictor, 145, **145**
Cook, *Captain* James, 43
coots, 154
copepods, 74
copra, 56
corals, 111, **111**, 114
cormorant, 134, 151
corn, 43
corn borer moth, 67
corolla, 27
Corsican pine, **26**
cortex (stem), 29
corymb, 32
cotton, 56, 63, **63**, 64; gin, **63**
cotyledon, 28, **33**
coyote, 183
coypu, **170**, 171
crabs, 123–4, **124**, 126
crakes, 154
crane fly, 121
cranes, 154, **154**
cranesbill, **36**
crayfish, 124
Cretaceous period, 11, 80–3, 84, 86
Crick, Francis, 12
crickets, 115–16
crocodiles, 79, 104, 146–7, **146**
crocus, 28, 49
Cro-magnon man, 87, **87**, 99
crop-rotation, 46, **46**
cross-pollination, 28
crowngall disease, 62
crustaceans, 11, **108**, **108**, 123–5, **124**, **125**
cuckoos, 162, **162**
cucumber, **50**
currasow, 158
currants, 54
cuttlefish, 80, 113
cycads, 12, 24–6, **24**, 78
Cycas, 26
Cyclops (freshwater crustacean), 125
cyme, 32
cytoplasm, 36

Dab, 137
dace, **134**, 135
daffodil, 30, 48
dahlia, 31
daisy, 16, **16**, **29**, 31
dandelion, 16, **28**, 32, **36**, 57
Daphnia (water flea), 125
Darwin, Charles, 68, 71, 92, 118, **143**
Darwin, Erasmus, 10
dates, 50
deadly nightshade, 14, 43, 62
decapods, 124
deer, 96, 101, 178–9, **179**; prehistoric, 86
delphinium, 30
Demospongia, **91**
desert, 40, 46
Devonian period, 11, **74**, 75, **76**
diatoms, 10, 22, 110
dicotyledons, **27**, 28–30, **28**, 31
digitalin, 62
dill, 53
dinosaurs, 12, 73, 78–83, 84
Dioscorides (Greek physician), 61
Diplodocus, 78, **78**
Diprotodon, 85
Diretmus argenteus, **135**
displacement activity, 95
divers, 151, **151**
DNA, 12, **12**, 37, 39
dodder, 42
dodo, 150, **162**
dogs, **18**, 95, 96, 98, 99, **101**, 102, 107, **107**, 183
dolphin, 107, **131**, 174
doves, 161–2. See also pigeons
dragonflies, 116–17, **116**; prehistoric, 77, **77**
drugs, 61–2. See also medicine
drupes, 50
ducks, 152, **152**, 153
duckweed, 32
dugong, **175**
dust bowls, 45
dyes, 64

Eagles, 156–7, **157**
Ebers, papyrus, the, 61
echidna, 85, 168
echinoderms, 11, **91**, **108**, 113, 114
ecology, 40–2, 104–5
Edal, 100

edentates, 172
eels, 96–7, **130**, 133, **133**, 135
eggs, 71; amphibian, 138; bird, 163, **163**; dinosaur, 83; fish, 130; reptile, 78, 141
Egypt, **43**, 56, 61, 62, 64
eland, 180, **180**
elderberry, 32
elephants, **84**, **104**, 181, **181**; prehistoric, **84**, 85
elm, **31**, 60
emu, 149, **149**
endosperm, 26, 28
endospores, 17
enzymes, 17, 18, 37
Eocene period, 84
Eohippus, 70
epidermis: leaf, 34–5; stem, 29
epiphytes, 40
eigeron, **49**
Eryops, 71, 78
ethology, 93
eucalyptus, **58**, 60
eurypterid, 74
Eusthenopteron, 71
evolution, 8, 10–12, 68–87; animals, 68–87, **186**; plants, 10–12

Falcons, **156**, 157
feathers, **148**
fennel, **52**, 53
ferns, 11, 22–3, **22**, **23**
fibres, 63–4. See also cotton, flax, hemp, jute, rayon, sisal
field horsetail, **23**
filament, **36**
filipendula, **48**
finches, 162, 163, 164, **165**
fir, **24**, **25**, 26, 60
fish, 11, 75, 129, 130–7; bony, 132–7; lobe-finned, 71, 75–6; ray-finned, 75; breeding, **94**; cartilaginous, 75, 131, **131**; deep-sea, 135–6, **135**; flying, **136**; migration, 96, 133, **133**, 134; pets, **103**; prehistoric, 71, **75**, 78, 80; swim bladder, 107
flagellates, 13, 110
flamingoes, 153–4, **153**
flatfish, **136**, 137
flax, 43, 56, 63, **64**
fleas, **121**, 122
Fleming, *Sir* Alexander, 62
flounder, **136**, 137
flowers, 27–9, 31–2, 39
flukes, 109
fly agaric, **19**
food chains, 8, 105, 110
food crops, 44–51
foraminifers, 73, 110
forest: coniferous, 40–1; deciduous, 40; floor, 18, 40, **40**; timber, 58–60; tropical, 40
fossils, 69, **70**, 72–4, 126; living fossil, 125
fowl, 159
fox, 183
foxglove, 43, **61**, 62
Franklin, Benjamin, 38
fritillaria, **29**
froghopper, 123
frogs, 76, 79, 90, 138, 139, **139**, 140, **140**; flying, 140, **140**
fruit, 50–1
fuchsia, **49**
fulmar, 151
fungi, 10, 11, 17, 18–19, 33, 34, 62

Gaillardia, **49**
gametes, 22, 24, 26, 66
gannet, 151
gardens, 47–9, **47**, **48**, **49**, 104; botanical, 65; herb, 61–2; medical, 65
garlic, 32, 43, 53
gasteropods, 68, 112, 114, **114**
gavial, 147
geckos, 144
geese, 96, 97–8, 101, 105, **106**, 152–3
Gerard, John, 61
germination, **33**, 65
gibbons, 187, **187**
gill-books, 126
gill-slits, 128, 130
ginger, 53
gingivitis, 110
ginkgo, **24**, 26, 78
giraffes, **104**, 178, 179
globefish, **130**
glow-worm, 122
gnu, **104**, 180
goatgrass, 37
goats, 99, 100, 180
goldcrest, nest, 163, **163**
goldeneye, 152
golden rod, 48
goldfish, 75, **103**, 135
Goodyear, Charles, 57
goosander, 152
goosegrass, **36**
gorilla, 186, 187, **187**
grain weevil, 67
grapefruit, 50
grapes, 54–5, **54**
grapevine, 54–5, **55**
graptolites, 74, 75
grasses, 30, 41, 43, 44, 64; flowers, 31–2; roots, 30
grasshoppers, 115–16
grayling, 134, **134**
Great Barrier Reef, 111, **111**
grebes, 151, **151**
greenfly, 123, 125
greyhound, 102

188

ground elder, **49**
grouse, 158
growth, 13, 39
guan, 158
gudgeon, **134**, 135
guillemot, egg, **163**
guinea fowl, 158
guinea pig, **170**, 171
gulls, 155, **155**
gymnosperms, 11, **15**, 16, 25. *See also* spermatophytes
gypsophila, **48**
gyrfalcon, 157

Habitat, 104–5
haddock, 136
hagfish, 75, **131**
hake, 136
Halosphaera, 13
hamsters, **103**, 171
Hancock, Thomas, 57
hands, **185**, **186**
Hanging Gardens of Babylon, 47
hardwoods, 60
hare, **171**
hartebeeste, **180**
harvest mouse, **170**, 171
Hawaii, 92
hawks, 157
hawthorn, 15
hazelnuts, 50, **50**
heart, **167**
hedgehog, 98, 169, **169**
hemerocallis, **48**
hemp, 63, **64**
Herball (Gerard), 61
herbs, 47, 52–3, 61–2, **62**
herons, 153
herring, 75, **130**, 132, **132**
Hesperornis, 83
Hevea brasiliensis, 56–7, **57**
Hexactinellida, **91**
hibiscus, **39**
hippopotamus, 87, **94**, 178
hoatzin, 158
hogweed, 32
holly, 41
homo deluvii testis, 72
homo sapiens, see man
honeycreepers, **92**
honeysuckle, 14
Hooke, Robert, 12
hoopoe, **161**
Hoplia coerulea beetle, **123**
hormones, 65, 94, 95
hornbill, 161, **161**
horse chestnut, **31**
horsefly, **121**
horses, 101, **101**, 102–3, **102**, 177; evolution, 70, 177; wild, **71**, 101
horsetails, **8**, 10, 11, 23, **23**, 77
hosta, **48**
housefly, 121
housemouse, **170**, 171
humming birds, 96, 160, **161**
hunting, **99**, 101–2, **101**, 104–5
hyaenodonts, 85
hybrids: animal, 90; plant, 14, 43, 48, 66
hyena, 183
hyphae, 18

Ibex, 180
ibis, 153
Ice Ages, 86–7
ichneumon (wasp), 119
Ichthyornis, 83
ichthyosaurs, **70**, 80
Ichthyostega, **71**, **75**
Iguanodon, 81
India, 56, 62, 64
Indian jungle fowl, 101
India-rubber, 56. *See also* rubber
indigo, **63**, 64
Indonesia, 53
inflorescence, 32
inkcap, **37**
insecticides, 67, **67**
insectivores, **13**, 169
insects, 11, 77, 108, **108**, 115–23, **115–23**; caterpillar (larva), 108, 117, **117**, 118, 120, 122; cocoon (pupa), 108, 118; eggs and egg-laying, 108, 116, **118**, 119, 120, 122; nymph, 116–17
instinct, 93–8
internode, 30
invertebrates, 89, 108–28; fossil, 74, **74**, 77; *see also under names of individual classes and species*
Iran, 62
iris, **29**

Jackal, 99, 183
jackdaw, 96; egg, **163**
Japan, 61, 64
Japanese fowl, 159
Jardin des Plantes (Paris), 65
jellyfish, **68**, 73, 74, **110**, 111
juniper, **32**
Jurassic period, 11, 12, 73, 78–80, 83
jute, 63, **64**

Kalahari bushman, 99
kale, 51
kangaroo, 85, 107, 168, **168**
kelp, 20
Kent, William, 47
kernel, 50
kestrel, **156**
Kew Gardens, 57, 65
kingfishers, 160–1, **161**, **162**

kinglet, 162
kinkajou, 184
kipper, 132
kites, 157
kittiwake, 155
kiwi, 149, **149**
kniphofia, **49**
koala, 168, **168**
Komodo dragon, 144, **144**
kookaburra, 161, **162**
kraken, **70**
krill, 124–5, 174–5
kudu, 180, **180**

Ladybird, **68**
lady's mantle, 14
Laika (space dog), **107**
Lamarck, J. B. de, 10, **71**
lamprey, 75, **130**, **131**
langur, 186
lantern fish, **135**
larch, 24, **26**, 60
Latimeria, **71**
lavender, **52**
lavendula, **49**
Lavoisier, Antoine, 37
Law of Priority, 92
laxatives, 62
leaf insects, 115, **115**
leaves, 29, 34–5; arrangement, 39; crops, 51
Leeuwenhoek, Anton, 106
lemming, **68**, **170**, 171
lemon, 50
lemurs, **70**, 95, 185
le Nôtre, André, 47
leopard, **182**
lettuce, 31
Levuana iridescens, 118–19
lice, 122
lichens, 18–19, **19**, 22, 68
life: origin, 8, 17; tree of, 10–12
liger, 90
lignin, 24, 34, 39
lily, **29**, 30
lime, **36**, 50
limpet, **114**
linen, 63
ling, **130**
Linnaea borealis (twinflower), 92
Linnaeus, Carolus, 10, 15–16, **16**, 65, 90, 92
linseed, 56, 63
lion, 87, 89, 104, 182, **182**
liverworts, 22–3
lizards, 141, **141**, 144–5, **144**
llama, 178
loach, 135
lobe-finned fishes, 71, 75–6
lobster, 123–4, **124**
locust, **67**, 115–16
lodicule, 31
lonicera, **48**
Lorenz, Dr Konrad, 97–8, **106**
lorises, 185, **185**
lumberjacks, 59
lung-books, 126
lung-fish, 75–6
lupinus, **48**
Luttrell Psalter, **46**
lycopods, 10
lyre bird, 162

Macaques, 186
macaws, 160, **160**
Macintosh, Charles, 57
mackerel, 136, 137
Macrocystis, 20
madder, 43, **63**, 64
magnolia, 31
magpie egg, **163**
maize, **44**, 45
malaria, 106, 110
Malaya, 43
mallard, **152**
mammals, 11, 71, 72, 73, 84–7, 88, **91**, 129, 167–84; carnivorous, 182–4; early, 71, 84–7; flying, 173; hoofed, 177–80; insectivorous, 169, 172; marine, 174–6; prehistoric, 73; primitive 168; rodents, 170–1, **170**; toothless, 172
mammoth, 72, **84**, 86–7
man, 8–9, 44, **71**, **86**, 87, 90, 95, 99–103, 122, 185–6, **186**, **187**; prehistoric, 44, 71, **86**, 87, 99; relationship with animals, 99–103
manatee, **175**
mangel, 51
mangrove, 34, **35**
Mantell, *Dr*, 81
mantichore, **90**
maple, 60
margarine, 56
marjoram, **52**
marmoset, 186
marmot, 171
marsh, salt, 46
marsupials, 85, 168
Mastigophora, **91**
Maxwell, Gavin, 100
mayfly, **116**
meal worm, 122
meat, synthetic, 51
medicine, 18, 43, 47, 56, 60, 61–2, 65, 103, 106–7
medullar rays, 30
medusa, 111
megaspores, 24–5
Megazostrodon, **71**, 84
melanism, 68
membrane (plants), 37
Mendelism, 66

Mendel, Johann, 66, **66**
mergansers, **152**, 153
mermaids, **175**
metamorphosis, 138, **139**
Metazoa, **91**
Mexico, 56
mice, **95**, **170**, 171
micropyle, 26
microscope, 8, 9, **12**, **17**, 46, 106
microspores, 24–5
Middle East, 99, 100
migration: birds, 96, 166; butterflies, 96, 118; eels, 96; fish, 96, 133–4, **133**; moths, 118; whales, 96
Mijbil, 100
millet, **44**
millipedes, 108, **108**
mimosa, **34**, 39
minnow, **134**, 135
mint, 53
mistle thrush, 164; egg, **163**
mites, **127**
moas, 86, 149
mock apple, **36**
moles, 169, **169**
molluscs, 11, 75, **91**, 108, **108**, 112–13, **112**, **113**, **114**
Mongolia, 101
monkey-eating eagle, 157
monkey puzzle tree, **26**
monkeys, 96, **96**, 98, 107, 122, 185–6, **187**
monocotyledons, 27–9, **27**, **28**, 30, 31
monotremes, 85
moorhens, 154
moray eel, 133
morphine, 62
Mosasaurus, 80
mosses, 22–3, **23**
mother-of-pearl, **113**, 114
moths, 117–19, **118**, **119**; antennae, 98
mouflon, 101
mound-building birds, 158
mosquito, 106, 110, 121
Mucor, 18
mudskipper, 137
mullet, 136
mushrooms, 18–19, **18**, 19
mussel, 112, 113, **114**
mustangs, 103
mustard, 43
mycelium, 18–19

Nacre, *see* mother-of-pearl
narcissus, **28**
narwhal, 174, **174**
nature reserves, 104–5
nautilus paper, 113; pearly, 113
Neanderthal man, **86**, 87, **87**, 99
nectar, 27
nectaries, 27
nematodes, **91**, 109
Neolithic Age, 99, 100
Nereocystis, 20
nervous system, 128
nests, birds, 156, 160, 162–3, **163**; fishes, 130, 136
nettle, 49, 64
Newfoundland dog, 102
New Stone Age, *see* Neolithic
newts, 76, **138**, 139, **139**
nightingale, egg, **163**
nightjar, egg, **163**
Nile, River, 45
nilgai, **180**
nits, 122
Nobel Prize, 12
Noctiluca, 110
node, 30
Norway spruce, 24
nucellus, 26
nucleic acids, 12
nucleus, 20
nuthatch, 165, **165**; egg, **163**
nuts, 39, 50
nux-vomica, seeds, 61
nylon, 63

Oak, **31**, 32, 34, 41, 58, **58**. *See also* acorns
oakum, 63–4
oarweed, 20
oats, **44**
ocelot, 182
octopus, 75, **107**, 112, **112**, 113
oil, vegetable, 56, 62
okapi, 178
old man's beard, **36**
oleine, 56. *See also* oil, vegetable
olive, 50, 56
Opisthoproctus soleatus, **135**
opium poppy, (*Papaver somniferum*), 62
opossums, 168
orange, 50
orang-utan, 187, **187**
orchids, 39, 40
Ordovician period, 11, **74**, 75
oreopithecus, **86**
Ornithischia, 83
oryx, 180, **180**
osprey, 157
Osteichthyes, **91**
ostracoderms, 75
ostrich, 149, **149**
otter, **100**, 183
ovary (plant), 27, **27**, 28, **36**
ovule, 26, 27, **27**, 28, **36**
Owen, *Sir* Richard, 82
owls, 156; eagle **93**
oxygen, 36, **37**, 38
oyster, 112, **113**; mother-of-pearl, 113, **113**; pearl, 113, **113**

Paddlefish, 132
Pakistan, 64
palaeontology (fossil study), 72–3
palm trees, 27, 30, 31, 38, 41, 50–1; oil, 56
pandas, 184, **184**
Pandorina, 22
pangolins, 172, **172**
panicle, 32
papermaking, **60**
parakeets, **155**, 160
parasites, 17, 18, 33, 40, **42**, 66–7, **67**, 109, 110, 119–20, 122, **127**
Parazoa, **91**
parr, 134
parrots, 160, **160**
parsley, 43, **52**, 53; fool's, 14
parsnip, 51
partridge, egg, **163**
Pasteur, Louis, 46
Pavlov, Ivan, 95
Peafowl, **158**, 159
peanut, 56, **56**
pear, 39, 50
peas, 50, 66
peat, 12, 74
pecking order, 96
pelagic fish, 137
pelican, 151, **151**
penguins, 150, **150**
penicillin, 18, 62
pepper, 53
peppered moth, 68
perch, 136–7; skeleton, **132**
Père David's deer, 105
perennial plants, 31, 48
pericarp, *see* carpels
Peripatus, 125
periwinkle, 112, **114**
Perkins, William, 64
Permian period, 11, 77, 78
Peron's tree frog, 140
pesticides, 67, 104
petals, 27, **27**, **36.**
petrel, 151, **151**
petrified forest, 73
pets, *see* animals, pets
phalangers, 168
pharmacopoeiae, 61
phasmids, 115, **115**
pheasants, **158**, 159
Phiomia, 85
phloem, 29
photosynthesis, 10, 13, 36, **37**
Physic Garden, 62
piddock, 112–13
pigeons, 96, **97**, 98, 161–2, **161**, 171
pigs, 99, 101, **167**, 178
pike, 134, 134
pilchard, 132
pineapple, **50**
pines, 24, 26, 30, 31, **32**, 58, 60
pintail, **152**
pistil, 28, **36**
pitcher plants, **38**, 39
pith, 30
placental mammals, 85, 86, 168, 169
placoderms, 75, **76**, 78
plaice, 137
plankton, 8, 33, 40, 108, **109**, 135
plants, behaviour, **13**, 18–19, 20–1, 22–3, **22**, 33; carnivorous, **13**, 38–9, **38**; cells, 10, 17, 18, 33, 36–8; classification, 14–16, **14–15**, 65, 90; colour and shape, 39; difference from animals, 10, 13; diseases of 66–7, **67**; ecology, 40–2, **40**; evolution, 10–12, 17, 19, 23–4; food, **21**, 44–51; fossil, 14, 72–3, **72**, 76–7, 79, 82, 86; genetics, 66; medicinal, 14, **61**; pests, 66–7, **67**, 116–17, 118–19, 123; poisonous, 18–19, 61–2, **62**; primitive, 17–19, 22–3, 24–6; propagation, 16, 17, 19, 20, 22–3, 24–6, 27; seed, 24–6. *See also* fungi; seaweeds; trees; *and under names of individual species*
Platyhelminthes, **91**, 109
platypus, duck-billed, 71, 85, 168, **168**
Pleistocene period, 86
plesiosaurs, 80, **81**
plovers, 154–5
plum, 50
plywood, **60**
pochard, **152**, 153
pointer, 102
poisonous animals, 106, 126, **126**, 127, **127**, 131, 138, 140, 141, **145**
polar bear, 184, **184**
pollen, 26–7; fossil, 74; tube, 28
pollination, 26–8, 38, 39; artificial, 66, **66**
pollution, 67, 68, 104, 124, 138
pomes, 50
pond skater, 123
ponies, 101, **102**
poplar, **31**, 32
poppy, **37**, **61**
population explosion, 68, 171
porcupine, **170**, 171
potato, 43, 46, 51; blight, **67**
potto, 185
prairie chicken, 158
prairie dog, **170**, 171
prawn, **135**
praying mantis, 115, **115**
Pre-Cambrian period, 73
Priestley, Joseph, **38**
primates, 85, 185–7
primrose, **27**
privet, 32
prospecting, 74
proteins, 10, 36
Proterozoic period, 11

prothalus, 23, 25
Protoceratops, 83
protoplasm, 8, 36
protozoans, 11, **91, 108, 109**, 110, **110**
Przewalsky's horse, **71**
psilopsids, 11
Pteranodon, 80
pteridophytes, **14**, 16, 23, **23**
pterosaurs (pterodactylis), 80–1, **81**
puffball, 18
puffin egg, **163**
python, 145

Quail, 159
Quaternary period, 11
quetzal, 160
quickbeam, 14

Rabbit, **103,** 171
rabbit fish, *see* chimaeras
raccoon, 184
raceme, 32
Rafflesia, **42**
rails, 150, 154
rainbow trout, 134
raisins, 54
Rajah Brooke's birdwing butterfly, **98**
ramie, 64
Ranunculus repens, **14**
rat, **106, 170**, 171
ratites, 149, **149**
rat-tail fish, **135**, 136
rattlesnake, **145**
raven, 162
ray-finned fishes, 75
Ray, John, 28
rayon, 63
rays, 75, 80, 128, **130,** 131, **131**
razor shell, **114**
red deer, 179
reedfish, 132
reflex action, 93
reindeer, 87, 97, 178
reindeer moss, **19, 40**
reptiles, 11, **91,** 129, 141–7; prehistoric, 71, 78–83, **80, 81, 82**
retriever, 102
rhea, 149, **149**
rhinoceros, 177–8, **177**; prehistoric, 73, 85, 86–7
rhizoids, 22
rhizomes, 23, **33**
Rhynchocephalia, 78
rice, **44,** 45, **45**
roach, 134, **134**
roadrunner, 162
robin, 98, 163, 165, **165**; egg, **163**
roc, 86, 149
rock, 72–6; igneous, 72; metamorphic, 72; sedimentary, 72;
rodents, 170–71, **170**
rook, 163; egg, **163**; nest, **163**
roosterfish, **135**
root crops, 51
roots, 28–9, 33–4, **33, 35**
rope, 63
Rosaceae, 50
rose, **27, 29,** 48
rosemary, **52**
rosewood, **58**
rotifers, 110
roundworms, *see* nematodes
rubber, 43, 56–7, **57**
rudd, 134, **134**
rye, **43**

Sabre-toothed cats, **84**, 85, 86
sacking, 64
safflower, 56
saffron, 53
saiga, 180
sailcloth, 63
salads, 51
salamanders, 76, 138, **138, 139**; fossil, 72; prehistoric, 77; spotted, **139**
salmon, 75, 96, 130, 133–4, **133**
sandhoppers, 125
sandpipers, 154–5, 166
sapele, **58**
saprophytes, 17, 18–19, 40
Sarcodina, 91
sardine, 132
Sargassum, 20
Saurischia, 82–3
savannah, 40
savory, **52**
sawfish, 131
sawflies, 119
sawmills, 59
scab disease, **67**
scales (fish), 130
scallops, **113**, 114
Scandinavia, **59**
Scelidosaurus, 79
Scolosaurus, 82
scorpions, **126**, 127
scoter, **152**
Scotland, 100, **102**
screw pines, 30, 31
sea anemones, **13, 94,** 111, **111,** 124
sea cows, **175**
sea cucumber, **113**, 114
sea horse, **97, 130**
sea lilies, 114
seals, 176, **176**
sea shells, **113**, 114, **114**
sea-stickleback, 136
sea urchins, **113**, 114
seaweed, 10, 20–1, **20, 21,** 33
secretary bird, 156

seed, 26, 28, 32, 33, **33, 36**–**7,** 38, **50,** 65, **65**; farm, **65**
selection, 68. *See also* evolution
senna pods, 62
sepals, 27, **27, 36**
Sequoia, **25,** 26, **58**
serpent stone, **90**
setter, 102
Seymouria, 71
sharks, 75, 78, 80, 128, 131, **131**
shearwater, 151, 166
sheep, 97, 99, 100, 180
shelduck, 153
shellac, 123
Shen Nung, *Emperor of China*, 61
ship-worm, *see* teredo
shire horse, **102**
shoveler, **152**
shrews, 84, 167, 169, **169**. *See also* tree shrews
shrimps, 123–4, **125**
sickle-wort, 14
Silurian period, 11, **74**, 75
sisal, 64, **64**
skates (fish), 75, **130,** 131
skeletons, 70, 84, 86, 89, 129, 132, 144, 148, 173, 175; bat, **173**; birds, 148; dugong, **175**; elephant, **84**; ichthyosaur, **70**; lizard, **144**; perch, 132; primate, **86**; snake, **129**
skuas, 155
skulls, 148, 170, 184; bear, **184**; bird, 148; rodent, **170**
sloths, 172
slow-worms, 141, 144
slugs, 112
smallpox, 106
smelt, 134
Smith, William, 73
smolt, 134
snails, 68, 112, 113, 114, **114**
snakes, 141, 144, 145, **145**; skeleton, **129**
soap, 56
Soay sheep, 100
social insects, 120–1. *See also* ants; bees; termites; *and* wasps
softwoods, 60
sole, 137
solitaire bird, 150
song thrush, 164, 165; egg, **163**
Sorghum, 45
sorus, 23
South Africa, 56
South-east Asia, 56–7
soya bean, 51, 56
spaniel, 102
sparrow, 164, **165**
specialisation, 68, 102
sperm, *see* gametes
spermatophytes, 16, 25–39
spices, 52–3
spiders, **67,** 108, **108,** 126–7, **126**; webs, 126, 127
spinal cord, 128
Spirogyra, 22
sponges, 11, 110–11; fossil, 72
spoonbill, 153
sporangium, 18, **37**
spores, 18–19, 22–3, 24–5, **37,** 38
sporozoans, **91,** 110
spotted salamander, **139**
sprat, 132
sprouts, 51
spruce trees, **24, 58**
Sputnik 2, **107**
squid, 75, 112, **112,** 113
squirrels, **170,** 171; flying, 171
stamens, 27, **27**
starfish, **108, 113,** 114
starling, 164, **165**
stater, **44**
steam plough, **46**
stearine, 56. *See also* oil, vegetable
Stegosaurus, 79, 83
stems, 27, **27, 28,** 29–30, 34
Sternoptyx diaphana, **135**
Sthenurus, 85
stick insects, 115, **115**
stickleback, 75, 94, **95,** 130, 136
stigma, 27, **27, 36**
stinging nettle, **49**
sting ray, 131
stoat, **183**
stomata, 35
Stone Age, 99, **100**
storks, 153, 166
strawberry, **50,** 65
streptomycin, 62
sturgeon, 132, **132**
style, **27, 36**
sugar, 36, **37**; beet, 51; cane, 45, **45**
sunflower, 31, 56, **56**
sunlight, 33
survival instinct, 97
swallow, egg, **163**; nest, 163, **163**
swallowtail butterfly, 118
swans, 152, **152**
swede, 51
sweetfish, 134
sweet pea, 66
swifts, 160, **161**
swordfish, **131**
sycamore, **36**
Sylvaticus, Mattheus, 65
symbiosis, 17, 19
Systema Naturae (Linnaeus), 99

Tadpoles, 76, 138
tapeworms, 109
tapir, 177, **177**
tarantula, 126

tarpan, 101
tar pits, 86
tarsier, **185**
tarsioid, 85
tea, **53**
teal, **152,** 153
teeth, carnivore, 182, **184**; elephant, 181; mammal, **167**; reptile, 78; rodents, 170
tench, 134
teredo, 113
Terramycin, 62
terrapins, 142, 143
territorial behaviour, 94, 95
Tertiary period, 11, 77
tetanus, 106
thallophytes, **14**, 16, 18–21, 22
thallus, 22, 25
thecodonts, 78
Theophrastus, 61
thistle, **16,** 31
Thoth, **153**
thrushes, 98, 164, **165**; egg, **163**
thylacine, 168
thyme, **52**
ticks, **127**
tiger, 182, **182**
tigridia, 29
timber, 58–60, **58, 59, 60**
titmice, 164–5, **165**; egg, **163**
tit, great, 164–5, **165**; egg, **163**
toads, 76, 90, 138, **138, 139,** 140, **140**
toadstools, 18–19, **18, 19**
tomato, **50**; leaf mould, **67**
tortoises, 78, 141, 142–3, **142, 143**
Trachodon, 81
traveller's tree, 40
tree frogs, 140, **140**
tree of life, 10–12
trees, 30–1, **30,** 34; dwarf, **32**; prehistoric, **8,** 10, 12, 77
tree shrews, 185, **186**
Triassic period, 11, 78, 84
Triceratops, 82, 83, **83**
trilobites, 72, 74, 75, 124
tripod fish, **135**
trogons, 160, **161**
tropisms, 39
trout, 133, 134
true moss, **23**
truffles, **18**
tsetse fly, 110, 121
tuatara, 71, 78, **144**
tubers, 23
tulip, **27**
Tull, Jethro, 46
tumbleweed, **41**
tundra, 41
tunny (tuna), 136, 137
turban shell, **114**
Turkey, 56, 100
turkey, wild, 100, 158
turnip, 46, 51
turtles, 78, 142–3, **142, 143**; prehistoric, **82**
tusk shells (Scaphopoda), 114
typhoid, 106
Tyrannosaurus, 82, 83, **83**

Umbel, 32
unicorn, **90**
United States, 56, 64, 96
univalves, 112, **114**
Upper Carboniferous period, **77**
urial, 100
Usher, James, **46**

Vaccination, 106
vacuoles, 36
vascular bundles, 29, 30, 34
vegetables, 51
veneers, 59–60
Venus's fly trap, **13,** 39
vertebral column, 128
vertebrates, 89, 90, 128–9; fossil, 75–87; *See also* animals; birds; *and* fish
vicuña, 178
viper, *see* adder
virgin birth, 125
voles, 171
vulcanisation, 57
vultures, **155,** 156, **156**

Waders, 154–5
Wallace, Alfred Russel, 68
wall paintings (and cave paintings), **43**, 47, **100,** 103
walnut, 50, **58**
walrus, 176, **176**
wasps, 119–20, **120**
water boatman, 123
water bugs, 123
water fleas, 74
water horsetail, **23**
water toad, **140**
Watson, James, 12
weasel, **183**, 184
weaver birds, 163
Weddell's seal, **176**
weeds, 48, **49**
West Africa, 56
West Indies, 43
Weymouth pine, **26**
whales, 88, 97, 167, 174–5, **174–5**; baleen, 124, **174–5, 175**; blue, **175**
wheat, **29**, 34, 44, **44,** 45, **45**
whelk, 112, **114**
whitebait, 132
whitethroat, **162**
whiting, 136

Whitney, Eli, 63
Wickham, *Sir* Henry, 57
wildcat, 101
willow, 30, 32, 60
wine, 43, 54–5, **55**
wings, 107, 148
wistaria, **48**
woad, 43, 64
wolf, 96, 99, 183, **183**
Wolffia, 32
wolfhound, 102
wombats, 85
wood, 30, 34, 58–60, **58, 59, 60,** 63
woodlice, 125
woodpeckers, 162
woodwasps, 119
wood worm, *see* beetles
woolly rhinoceros, 86–7
worms, 108, 109, **110**
wren, 162

Xerophytes, 40
xylem, 29

Yak, 180
yarrow, 32
yeasts, 19, 38
yellowhammer, egg, **163**
Yugoslavia, 56

Zebra, 104, 177, **177**
zebra volute, **114**
zooplankton, *see* plankton
zoos, 104, **105**. *See also* nature reserves
zoospore, 13, 20